G000075509

Searching for a Universal Ethic

Searching for a Universal Ethic

Multidisciplinary, Ecumenical, and Interfaith Responses to the Catholic Natural Law Tradition

Edited by

John Berkman and William C. Mattison III

WILLIAM B. EERDMANS PUBLISHING COMPANY
GRAND RAPIDS, MICHIGAN / CAMBRIDGE, U.K.

Wm. B. Eerdmans Publishing Co.

2140 Oak Industrial Drive N.E., Grand Rapids, Michigan 49505 /

P.O. Box 163, Cambridge CB3 9PU U.K.

www.eerdmans.com

Library of Congress Cataloging-in-Publication Data

Searching for a universal ethic: multidisciplinary, ecumenical, and interfaith responses to the
Catholic natural law tradition / edited by John Berkman and William C. Mattison III.
  pages cm
  Includes bibliographical references and index.
  ISBN 978-0-8028-6844-2 (pbk.: alk. paper)
  1. Natural law. 2. Natural law — Religious aspects — Catholic Church.
  I. Mattison, William C., III, 1971- editor. II. Berkman, John, 1964- editor.

K428.I57 2014
340´112 — dc23

          2014026852

The editors and publisher gratefully acknowledge permission to reprint the International Theological
Commission document *In Search of a Universal Ethic: A New Look at the Natural Law,* © 2009
Libreria Editrice Vaticana.

FOR

JOSEPH BOYLE

JOHN FINNIS

STANLEY HAUERWAS

JAMES F. KEENAN, S.J.

OLIVER O'DONOVAN

SERVAIS PINCKAERS, O.P.

JEAN PORTER

Contents

Acknowledgments

We would like to thank the numerous people who helped make this project possible. We are grateful to our editors at Eerdmans who have been most supportive of this book project from the start, especially Jon Pott. The Catholic University of America provided support through grants and research assistantships. This funding enabled us to benefit from the diligent work of two doctoral student research assistants, Matthew Martin and Siobhan Riley Benitez, both of whom greatly enriched this project.

Needless to say, this volume would have been impossible without the commitment of our essay authors who, like us, saw in the International Theological Commission's 2009 *In Search of a Universal Ethic: A New Look at the Natural Law* a valuable conversation starting point on natural law, both within the Catholic tradition and with interlocutors outside that tradition. Not knowing it would take three years for the official English translation to be released by the Vatican, they generously completed their essays at our request just months after we extended our invitations to them. The quality of their work made this book possible. We are particularly grateful for the contributions of Fr. Serge-Thomas Bonino, O.P., and Fr. Anthony Kelly, C.S.s.R., two members of the sub-committee of the International Theological Commission who composed *In Search of a Universal Ethic.*

Most especially, we'd like to thank those to whom this book is dedicated, our teachers of the natural law. Aquinas claims that the gratitude owed benefactors ought to exceed what has been received. In this case that is not possible since our teachers' impact on our lives and work extends far beyond any token of thanks we can offer. In particular, each of the teachers named on the dedication page was influential on one or both of us with regard to the natural law.

John Berkman was introduced to natural law ethics through tutorials with John Finnis and Oliver O'Donovan during undergraduate years at Keble College, Oxford. Joe Boyle provided an extraordinary historical introduction to the new natural law theory through a reading course at the University of Toronto. During John's doctoral studies at Duke University, Stanley Hauerwas — no fan of modern natural law theories — ultimately provided John with a richer and more theological way to think about the significance of natural law for moral theology. While John was researching the history of moral theology at the University of Fribourg, Servais Pinckaers proved an invaluable guide for understanding Aquinas's thought on natural law in its broader context.

Bill Mattison was introduced to moral theology and to the thought of Aquinas by Jim Keenan during Master's work at (what was then) Weston Jesuit School of Theology. During Bill's doctoral studies, Jean Porter and Servais Pinckaers offered invaluable complementary formation on natural law and in moral theology in general, Jean Porter as his advisor at the University of Notre Dame and Fr. Pinckaers as his mentor for a year of dissertation research in Fribourg, Switzerland.

And thus with gratitude and great affection, we dedicate this volume to our teachers: Joseph Boyle, John Finnis, Stanley Hauerwas, Jim Keenan, Oliver O'Donovan, Fr. Pinckaers, and Jean Porter.

Introduction

John Berkman and William C. Mattison III

"Are there objective moral values which can unite human beings and bring them peace and happiness?"[1] People seem to assume there are indeed such values when they recoil against genocide, rape, child abuse, slavery and human trafficking, senseless destruction of the environment, involuntary "medical" testing, corruption, and terrorism. This recoil is generally perceived to be not merely some learned or innate moral sentiment, but an indicator that some actions are truly wrong — wrong not merely because of the emotional responses they arouse; wrong not merely on the basis of a consensual agreement between people or societies; but truly wrong, meaning in violation of some standard for human action that is applicable to and (at least in principle) accessible to all human persons. Even if there is great difficulty specifying norms about wrong human actions, and even if the norms have needed revision, there is a common conviction that certain moral norms exist. This fundamental conviction that there is some sort of standard against which human actions can be evaluated, and that it is accessible and applicable to all, is the essence of the view that there is a universal ethic.

Belief in a universal ethic is widespread, but it can take many forms. Some formulate a universal ethic based on consensus on norms, or procedural guidelines to generate such consensus. Others articulate a universal ethic that begins with some (implicit or explicit) understanding of the capacities and perfections of human persons (of "human nature"), though varieties of this approach

---

1. These are the opening words of *In Search of a Universal Ethic: A New Look at the Natural Law,* henceforth referenced by parenthetical numbers in the text.

1

emphasize different aspects of persons (e.g., rationality, sentience, emotions, and/or inclinations). Any approach that articulates features of the human person individually and communally so as to determine norms that are accessible to and apply to all can be called a natural law approach.[2] "Natural law" as a tradition of moral, political, legal, and theological thought is most famously associated with Catholic Christianity. However, there are also many other traditions of natural law thought, found, for example, in Protestant and Orthodox Christianity, Judaism, Islam, and ancient Greek (especially Stoic) thought.

In 2009, with the publication of *In Search of a Universal Ethic: A New Look at Natural Law,* the International Theological Commission (ITC) of the Catholic Church offered a contribution both to a dialogue seeking a more adequate understanding of a universal ethic and to Catholicism's own tradition of reflection on natural law. It is worth noting that *In Search of a Universal Ethic* is not a new look at a universal ethic, but rather a new look at natural law. In the document we see an attempt by the ITC to situate the natural law ethical tradition within the search for a universal ethic. This raises two questions. First, what contribution does the ITC document offer to the "search" for a universal ethic? Second, what is "new" about its approach to natural law?

First, *In Search of a Universal Ethic* contributes to a more adequate "search" for a universal ethic by pointing to deficiencies in some alternative contemporary efforts to theorize a universal ethic. Without explicitly naming individual theorists, the document claims that some influential contemporary formulations of a universal ethic originate solely in *procedural* or "formal" guidelines for reaching consensus about norms (6-8). In neglecting any teleological account of individual and communal human flourishing, these minimalistic accounts may help identify a "least common denominator" ethical consensus, but they inevitably fail to address many of our deepest aspirations as human persons, aspirations that arise at least in part out of our very nature as human beings (2).[3] Thus, along with drawing on its tradition of natural law

2. For instance, "[the Catholic Church] calls natural law the foundation of a universal ethic which we seek to draw from the observation of and reflection on our common human nature" (113).

3. In addition to its concerns about the fact that purely procedural methods of searching for a universal ethic fail to seek substantive "agreement regarding the goods and values that represent the most profound aspirations" (2) of human beings, *In Search of a Universal Ethic* also emphasizes that while "dialogue and debate are always necessary for obtaining an achievable agreement on the concrete application of moral norms in any given situation . . . *they should not relegate moral conscience to the margins. A true debate does not replace personal moral convictions, but it presupposes and enriches them*" (8; emphasis added).

thought to present an account of a universal ethic, *In Search of a Universal Ethic* engages in an inductive search for convergences with a variety of "wisdom traditions" as a key source for understanding the authentic and universal aspirations of human persons in all their richness and diversity.

Second, *In Search of a Universal Ethic*'s approach is a "new look" at natural law in part because it forthrightly acknowledges inadequacies in past articulations of a natural law ethics in the Catholic tradition. In the past the natural law has been invoked at times by Catholic Church theologians or leaders to either implore passive resignation to physical laws of nature, or to justify moral viewpoints that were not in fact truly applicable to all human persons, but were rather moral viewpoints overly determined by a particular historical and cultural context (10). The ITC document therefore aims to present a universal ethic rooted in the natural law ethical tradition marked by "a more profound understanding of the relationships between the moral subject, nature and God"; a "better consideration of the historicity that affects the concrete applications of the natural law"; and a better grasp of the "personal and existential dimension of the moral life" (10). In summary, if a "look" at natural law is warranted in part by the lack of depth of influential alternative approaches to a universal ethic, a "new" look is warranted by the all too often impersonal and ahistorical presentations of Christian teaching on natural law in the past.[4]

This volume joins *In Search of a Universal Ethic* in seeking a deeper understanding of both "universal ethic" and "natural law," and of the relationship between them. As already noted, the ITC document explicitly refers to a "universal ethic" as a type of ethical guidance accessible to and applicable to all, and refers to a "natural law" ethical approach as one kind of a universal ethic, a kind that depends on some aspect of a "common human nature." *In Search of a Universal Ethic*'s understanding of the universal ethic–natural law ethic relationship as a genus-species relationship is clearly correct and important, and we have emphasized it above.

However, we also see in *In Search of a Universal Ethic* another way of understanding the universal ethic–natural law ethic relationship, a way we

---

4. Even if the document offers something "new," the search for a universal ethic is of course already happening. The document expresses admiration for the wisdom, generosity, and at times heroism of those men and women who "wish to live by the light of the ultimate truth and the absolute good," who contribute in their own way "to the promotion of peace, a more just political order, the sense of common responsibility, an equitable distribution of riches, as well as respect for the environment, for the dignity of the human person and his fundamental rights" (2). It acknowledges that "contemporary" (and presumably historical) "attempts to define a universal ethic are not lacking" (5).

consider true to the spirit of the document even if not in its letter. In addition to the genus-species relationship, universal ethics and natural law can represent alternative *paths*. On the one hand, the universal ethic path is a search for a "common moral patrimony" (6, 11, 12, 17) or moral "convergences" (11) through a comparative analysis of different "wisdom traditions."[5] The universal ethics path asks: What ethical values can we discern across cultures, time periods, and traditions as evidence for (and part of the content of) a universal ethic? Though no one enters dialogue absent her own historical particularity (including cultural and/or religious commitments), the emphasis here is on finding moral commonality across traditions. On the other hand, the natural law path is when a particular wisdom tradition — drawing on the riches of but not presupposing its distinctive cultural and/or theological commitments — seeks out of its own intellectual and moral capital to articulate the existence and the content of a universal ethic.

Although *In Search of a Universal Ethic* never speaks of a universal ethic path or a natural law path, it exemplifies these paths in its first chapter, on convergences and common moral patrimony, and in its fifth chapter, on Jesus Christ as fulfillment of the natural law. As editors of *Searching for a Universal Ethic: Multidisciplinary, Ecumenical, and Interfaith Responses to the Catholic Natural Law Tradition,* we find that thinking of universal ethic and natural law *paths* is a helpful way of categorizing the essays collected herein. Some of this volume's essays take the universal ethics path and look at *In Search of a Universal Ethic* in relation to another tradition or traditions. Other essays take the natural law path, critically evaluating the document's effort to revitalize the Catholic natural law tradition.

The emphasis on these two paths runs through the following three sections of this introduction: first, a brief overview of the subject matter is offered; second, *In Search of a Universal Ethic* is introduced (its genesis and content); third, a brief overview of the essays in this volume is offered. The introduction concludes with some questions on these essays as pedagogical aids to using this book.

---

5. "Wisdom traditions, which are often of a religious nature, convey an experience that identifies what favors and what hinders the full blossoming of personal life and the smooth running of social life. They constitute a type of 'cultural capital' available in the search for a common wisdom necessary for responding to contemporary ethical challenges" (12).

Situating Natural Law and a Universal Ethic

Before introducing *In Search of a Universal Ethic* and the essays contained in this volume, it may be helpful, especially for those new to this topic, (1) to offer a succinct description of natural law (something that is not offered in the document or in the essays on it in this volume); and (2) to contextualize this volume's discussions of natural law by presenting several criticisms of a natural law ethics and the ethical alternatives offered by such critics. These two tasks will be taken in reverse order, with the criticisms offered first so they may be kept in mind in the brief overview of a natural law ethic that follows.

Universal Ethics as Opposed to Natural Law

The mid-twentieth century saw the widespread criticism (and rejection) of a natural law ethic from a number of different directions. Some of these critics offered an alternative path to a universal ethic, while others altogether eschewed efforts to articulate any kind of a universal ethic. This section introduces a few influential criticisms of a natural law ethic. In each case a criticism of natural law is offered and the resulting attempt to articulate a universal ethic in a manner not susceptible to that critique is described. In each case mention is made of how the document explicitly or implicitly responds to this critique in its vision of natural law.

Perhaps the most well-known criticism of a natural law ethic in the twentieth century (although its roots date back to the Enlightenment) was associated with Anglo-American analytic philosophy (most famously G. E. Moore).[6] It was a criticism of any kind of ethic rooted in facts about human nature, arguing that no claims about human morality (claims about what "ought" to be done) could logically be derived from claims of human nature (facts about what "is"). While this problematic (typically referred to as the naturalistic fallacy, or the is-ought problem) only gained widespread credibility for a short period of time, and while a variety of critiques of that fallacy have marginalized that specific problem in contemporary theology and philosophy, the reluctance to appeal to a robust account of human nature when searching for a universal ethic remains widespread. After all,

---

6. See paragraph 73. For more on the Enlightenment as a project, and its culmination in the emotivism of G. E. Moore, see Alasdair C. MacIntyre, *After Virtue: A Study in Moral Theology,* 2nd ed. (Notre Dame, Ind.: University of Notre Dame Press, 1984).

it can seem that the more robust an account one offers, the less universal it must be.

One attempt to articulate a universal ethic with this concern in mind is a universal ethics path toward general moral agreement that prescinds from any attempts to articulate a vision of human nature as a basis for the agreement. For example, the 1948 Nuremburg Declaration took one particular universal ethics path to articulating universal agreement on certain moral standards without articulating the moral basis for them. Similarly, in the past generation some U.S.-government-sponsored ethical works have sought to draw on a moral tradition known as "casuistry," again looking to find moral agreement in conclusions to problems without any underlying agreement regarding how such conclusions were reached. In an analogous way, also emerging in the twentieth century was a variety of consequentialism known as preference utilitarianism. Preference utilitarianism seeks to account for all human preferences, whether or not any particular preference seem reasonable or ordered to any reasonably authentic human good. The ethical approaches in these three examples, while seeking universality in agreement or in a method of moral decision-making, have eschewed connecting that ethic to any explicit substantive view of the human person. *In Search of a Universal Ethic* echoes one common criticism of such efforts, calling them "impoverished" in their norms due to the eschewal of attention to the human person. The document's extensive attention to human nature is also an implicit endorsement of a second common critique of this approach, namely, that even when a vision of the human person is explicitly denied, it is always implicitly present.

Another alternative universal ethic that arose in the latter part of the twentieth century was an ethic derived from work in the field of sociobiology. Strictly speaking, sociobiology as a science is not capable of producing an ethic. The task of sociobiology is to give an account of human social behavior in relation to evolution, for example, to make evolutionary sense of the fact the humans are not typically psychological egoists acting only in their self-interest but rather (like many other animal species) often naturally aid each other. Sociobiology tends to emphasize the behavioral universals that underlie ethnic, cultural, and religious differences. However, its main theoretical problematic — how social concern (or "altruism") could arise — has led many of its theoretical expositors and popularizing proponents to speak about human motivation (which officially sociobiology is never supposed to be investigating). Thus although sociobiological terms like "selfishness" and "altruism" are in their technical sociobiological usage supposedly "value" or "motive" free, pop sociobiology and the sociobiological ethics derived from it inevitably speak of how humans act for their own survival or for the spread of their genes in the communal gene pool. When this occurs, like a dialogical ethic or preference utilitarianism, sociobiological ethics can be similarly reductive. First, they can presume that the basis for human choices is reduced to a combination of the survival and reproductive instincts. Second, they can be articulated in a manner that precludes the relevance of any metaphysical or otherwise non-sociobiological claims. Of course, when evolutionary or sociobiological ethics are not reductive in these senses, they can offer great contributions from the evolutionary sciences as to the nature of the human person.[7]

A final criticism of natural law voiced powerfully in the twentieth century (also with earlier roots) came from voices within religious traditions such as Protestant Christianity and Islam. This criticism questioned the significance and/or accessibility of a universal ethic in contradistinction to an ethic drawn from divine revelation or other non-universally accepted sources of wisdom and guidance. For example, a variety of strains of Protestantism, including ethical viewpoints influenced by the great twentieth-century theologian Karl Barth, raised serious theological objections to any kind of universal or natural law ethic. Their concern was that any such ethic seems to circumscribe God's sovereignty and/or render theological beliefs superfluous to ethics. Similarly, mainstream Sunni Islam is an ethic of religious obedience to divine commands, and there is widespread suspicion of any attempt to give significant authority to an ethic founded on any other basis, including an apprehension of human nature. *In Search of a Universal Ethic*'s extensive arguments for the compatibility of a natural law ethic and revealed theological claims is a clear indication both of how seriously it takes this criticism and how vehemently it disagrees with it.

Natural Law: The Christian Tradition's Take on a Universal Ethic

The Christian tradition has long debated the character, scope, and accessibility of a universal ethic through the term "natural law." This part of the introduction offers a succinct overview of natural law. *In Search of a Universal Ethic*

---

7. Both the document and the essays in this volume engage this criticism of natural law most minimally. The document's articulation of a richer vision of human flourishing than survival or reproduction, along with its insistence on the continuity between natural law claims and broader metaphysic claims, serve as reminders that evolutionary ethics shorn of these assumptions can provide valuable contributions to the new look at natural law articulated in the document.

addresses the fundamental features of the Christian tradition on natural law in its opening words on the search for a universal ethic. As noted above, the document begins by asking, "Are there objective moral values which can unite human beings and bring them peace and happiness?" (1).[8] In this opening question there are three elements that provide a helpful overview of Christian teaching on natural law. The three elements can be taken as descriptions of how the natural law is "natural."

First, the natural law "can unite human beings." That is to say, the natural law is *accessible to all persons*.[9] Or to put the matter in the negative, knowledge of the natural law cannot be in principle dependent on beliefs inherently specific to any particular moral tradition, or on any divine revelation. Of course, any natural law reflection will occur by historically situated and tradition-embedded persons, and thus moral guidance by the natural law is sure to be situated and reaffirmed in such traditions and revelation. That said, knowledge of the natural law's guidance for human action is not limited to any particular tradition or revelation. It is in principle knowable by human persons capable of understanding the world around them (including themselves) and acting in accordance with that understanding. Therefore it is natural since all human persons are "built" (by nature) to apprehend reality and act accordingly. The natural law is accessible to all, and thus "capable of uniting human beings."

Second, the natural law "brings human beings peace and happiness" (1).[10] While the first point above emphasizes the ability of humans to actually know the natural law, this second element directs us to the goal or *telos* of the natural law, namely, to *lead to peace and fulfillment* for all human persons. This is another sense in which it is "natural." People may be said to live naturally when they are functioning or operating well according to the capacities of and possibilities for human nature. Thus the natural law guides people in how to live well. This of course raises the question of what constitutes "living well," or happiness, for human persons. Inquiry into the meaning of human happiness, or "flourishing," is as old as philosophical and theo-

---

8. For other passages that offer a concise depiction of natural law, see paragraphs 9, 11, 113, and 116.

9. See, for example, paragraph 94: "The biblical revelation invites humanity to consider that the order of creation is a universal order in which all of humanity participates, and that this order is accessible to reason."

10. See, for example, paragraph 41: "The moral good corresponds to the profound desire of the human person who — like every being — tends spontaneously, naturally, towards realizing himself fully, towards that which allows him to attain the perfection proper to him, namely, happiness."

logical thought. So stating that the natural law is about happiness is a starting point, not an adequate conclusion. In addition, the point made here about peace as well as happiness is a reminder that humans are fundamentally social beings, and thus the reference to "peace" more obviously refers to the harmonious relations between people and peoples that must be included in any depiction of human happiness. Nevertheless, it is crucial to understand natural law in the context of the goal, namely, happiness or human flourishing, toward which that law leads. The natural law procures "peace and happiness."

Third, the natural law is not only capable of uniting people and procuring peace and happiness, as we noted above, but it also procures it "for them," that is, procures happiness for human persons. Here we get to perhaps the most fundamental claim of a universal ethic, as it is understood in the natural law tradition. It is *applicable to all persons as human persons.*[11] The natural law for birds is different from the natural law for human persons.[12] This is why the natural law is rightly regarded as universal among human beings, and in some sense unchanging. Though human persons are importantly different through time and cultures, they are nonetheless all human persons. This means the guidance of natural law applies to them all. There are some features of persons and thus norms of behavior that apply to all persons in every time or place. Of course, since persons live in different circumstances and act with regard to contingent matters, certain particular ways of living in accordance with one's nature as a human person may not apply to all persons everywhere. But this does not mean there are no natural law rules that are universally applicable, or that in such particular circumstances people are not living in accordance with the natural law. Hence the natural law is "natural" in the sense of applicable to creatures who share a human nature.

Note how closely related the above three points are. In each sense the

---

11. "In this way, certain behaviours are recognized as expressing an exemplary excellence in the manner of living and of realizing one's humanity. They define the main lines of a properly moral ideal of a virtuous life 'according to nature,' that is to say, in conformity with the profound nature of the human subject" (61).

12. Though when discussing natural law *In Search of a Universal Ethic* is typically referring to *human* natural law, the natural law applies to any living creatures that can be said to live according to the law of its nature. Obviously how the natural law operates differs based on the type of nature a creature possesses. So, for instance, the human ability to use reason to understand the world and act accordingly in freedom makes any discussion of the natural law for human persons particularly interesting and challenging.

natural law's contribution to a universal ethic is based on human *nature*. First, the natural law is accessible because of how we operate as human persons, namely, as persons who are capable of understanding our environment and choosing to act in accordance with that understanding. Second, the happiness toward which the natural law leads is true *human* happiness, a flourishing apt for the embodied, sexual, social, and rational creatures that we as human beings are. Third, the natural law is applicable to all persons who possess a human nature. It enjoins activities that are constitutive of true human fulfillment and flourishing, and prohibits activities that are antithetical to those goals. Natural law is an approach to ethical guidance that roots its universality (in terms of its accessibility, orientation toward happiness, and applicability) in explicit or implicit claims about the very nature of the human person.

Much more can and will be said of the Christian tradition on natural law. For instance, though the natural law is accessible and applicable to all persons, this feature of it does not of course guarantee that all will recognize, let alone live according to, the natural law. It should be clear that though the natural law is in principle universally accessible and applicable, and indeed directs people to peace and happiness, the natural law is not necessarily obvious or uncontested. If our inquiry into the natural law begins as a search for detailed moral guidance that is immediately compelling to and thus accepted by all rational persons, then we are sure to be disappointed. As will be seen below, any account of natural law as universally accessible and applicable must offer a convincing (or at least plausible) account of why people at times choose to not live according to, or even know, the natural law. This and many other points central to an understanding of the natural law are taken up in *In Search of a Universal Ethic* and the essays that constitute this book.

Genesis and Content of the Document *In Search of a Universal Ethic: A New Look at the Natural Law*

This introduction does not provide an evaluation of the document. It instead provides background on how it came to be written, and gives a brief summary of its structure and content. Once again the complementary emphases on universal ethics and natural law are evident in both the origin and content of the document.

Genesis of In Search of a Universal Ethic: A New Look at the Natural Law and *This Volume of Essays*

In Search of a Universal Ethic was written by the International Theological Commission (ITC) of the Catholic Church, a body of thirty scholars appointed to five-year terms to give advice to the Congregation for the Doctrine of the Faith (CDF), which is the foremost doctrinal committee of the Catholic Church, on issues of theological importance.[13] Why did the ITC write this document? In 2004, shortly after a new group of scholars had been appointed, Pope John Paul II addressed the commission, noting that the "natural moral law" would be one of the topics examined by them. The pope observed:

> The Church has always been convinced that with the light of reason God has endowed man with the ability to attain knowledge of the fundamental truths about his life and destiny, and indeed about the norms of right conduct. For dialogue with all people of good will and for coexistence in the most varied forms founded on a common ethical basis, this possibility must be brought to the attention of our contemporaries. The Christian revelation does not make this research pointless; on the contrary, it spurs us to carry it out with the light of Christ, in whom all things hold together (cf. Col 1:17).[14]

These words would guide the drafting of the document, and thus we can see that from the very beginning the twin themes of a "common ethical basis" among peoples as well as how the Christian revelation spurs Christians "on to carry out [the search for fundamental moral truths about human life and destiny] with the light of Christ."

The members of the ITC are appointed to advise the CDF, and the leader of the CDF is the *ex officio* leader of the ITC. In 2004 the leader (prefect) of the CDF was Joseph Cardinal Ratzinger. Once Ratzinger became Pope Benedict XVI in April 2005, he continued to oversee the ITC's project on universal ethics and natural law, personally addressing the ITC in both December 2005 and October 2007. In the latter address, he reiterated Pope John Paul II's ob-

13. The actual development and composition of the document was carried out by a ten-member subcommission of the ITC. We are fortunate enough to have two subcommittee members, Serge-Thomas Bonino, O.P. (chair of the subcommittee), and Anthony J. Kelly, C.Ss.R., as contributors to this volume.

14. Address of Pope John Paul II to members of the International Theological Commission, October 7, 2004, accessed May 21, 2013, at http://www.vatican.va/holy_father/john_paul_ii/speeches/2004/october/documents/hf_jp-ii_spe_20041007_commissione-teologica_en.html.

servation that the natural law both contains "the foundations of a universal ethic" and is "illuminated and developed to the full in the light of Christian revelation and the fulfillment of man in the mystery of Christ."[15]

The bulk of Pope Benedict XVI's comments in the 2007 address were focused on the importance of the natural law as a resource for "dialogue with all people of good will and more generally, with civil and secular society." In that address he was particularly concerned with the erosion of the *recognition* of the natural moral law, and with that a trend in contemporary Western culture toward ethical relativism. He claimed this would have serious political consequences since in the absence of any grasp of "the roots of the human being and his ethical behavior," "the democratic order itself would be challenged."

> Natural law thus becomes the true guarantee offered to each one in order that he may live in freedom, have his dignity respected and be protected from all ideological manipulation and every kind of arbitrary use or abuse by the stronger.[16]

Echoing a consistent theme of his papacy, evident especially in his 2009 encyclical *Caritas in veritate*, Pope Benedict XVI emphasizes here the inextricable connection between the natural law — a topic easily regarded as one of individual morality — and the social order. He claims that the democratic social order, far from being threatened by a robust notion of the natural moral law, actually requires it.

As the ITC developed *In Search of a Universal Ethic* over five years starting in 2004, there was parallel work being done on the natural law in other academic settings at the request of the Vatican. For example, in the same week as Pope John Paul II's 2004 address to the ITC, Ratzinger wrote to three U.S. Catholic universities requesting that they do academic symposia on the possibility of a universal ethic. Ratzinger wrote, "The Catholic Church has become increasingly concerned by the contemporary difficulty in finding a common denominator among the moral principles held by all people, which are based on the constitution of the human person and which function as the funda-

---

15. Address of His Holiness Benedict XVI to members of the International Theological Commission, October 5, 2007, accessed May 21, 2013, at http://www.vatican.va/holy_father/benedict_xvi/speeches/2007/october/documents/hf_ben-xvi_spe_20071005_cti_en.html.

16. In his October 5, 2007, address, Pope Benedict XVI claims "symposiums or study days were held or are being organized by various university centres and associations in order to find constructive pointers and convergences for an effective deepening of the doctrine on natural law."

mental criteria for laws affecting the rights and duties of all." He went on to say, "The recognition of such moral truths has also constituted a starting point for the Church's dialogue with the world."[17] In these words Ratzinger shows his concern not only for the pursuit of a universal ethic, but also for an elaboration of the natural moral law as part of the Catholic Church's proper self-understanding.[18]

The clear importance of *In Search of a Universal Ethic*, published in 2009,[19] led the editors of this volume to organize a session at the January 2010 meeting of the Society of Christian Ethics. The Ethics and Catholic Theology Interest Group invited Stanley Hauerwas, M. Cathleen Kaveny, and Michael Sherwin, O.P., to comment on the document. The lively discussion they prompted made two things clear. First, the document was a high-quality contribution to scholarship on universal ethics, one that was less susceptible to common criticisms of the Catholic tradition's natural law approach to universal ethics, criticisms that historically came both from outside *and* within the Christian tradition. Second, this fruitful exchange, as well as numerous positive comments from the large audience at the session, prompted the editors to conclude that further academic reflection on *In Search of a Universal Ethic* would prove rewarding. So in the time it took the Vatican to prepare the official English translation of the text, the editors commissioned more than twenty essays to critically comment on some aspect of the document. Once the official English translation was released in early 2013, this volume was sent to the publisher. The editors hope through this anthology to promote continued dialogue and substantive

17. For an account of this letter and initiatives it engendered, see William Wagner, "In Gratitude for What We Have Been Given: A Common Morality for 'the Global Age'?" *Journal of Law, Philosophy and Culture* 3, no. 1 (2009): 7-53. For this exact quote (which is misquoted in the previously mentioned essay), see J. Budziszewski, "Natural Law as Fact, Theory and Sign of Contradiction," in *Natural Moral Law in Contemporary Society*, ed. Holger Zaborowski (Washington, D.C.: Catholic University of America Press, 2010), 76-98, at 76.

18. One example of how a university responded is the Catholic University of America conference, *A Common Morality for a Global Age: In Gratitude for What We Have Been Given.* For published papers of this conference, see *Journal of Law, Philosophy, and Culture* 3, no. 1 (Spring 2009). The University of Notre Dame's response to this letter included the book *Intractable Disputes about Natural Law: Alasdair MacIntyre and His Critics* (Notre Dame, Ind.: University of Notre Dame Press, 2009).

19. The document was published in 2009 in French and Italian. A German translation was issued in 2011, and the official English translation appeared on the Vatican homepage in early 2013. However, by early 2009 Joseph Bolin produced an unofficial translation of *In Search of a Universal Ethic*, which was of great assistance to the editors and to many of the contributors to this volume. We are deeply grateful to him for his work.

reflection between and among both Christian communities and a diverse religious and scholarly community on universal ethics and the natural law approach to it.

Content and Organization of the Document

In Search of a Universal Ethic contains an introduction, five chapters, and a conclusion. The introduction explains the importance of the search for a universal ethic, and reviews some recent (post–World War II) formulations of a universal ethic, as well as the practical abandonment of a universal ethic "in certain sectors of contemporary culture" (7). Noting the weaknesses of inductive ("minimalistic") and dialogical approaches ("cannot produce new substantial contents" [8] and hence parasitic on other moral traditions), it hospitably "invite[s] all those pondering the ultimate foundations of ethics . . . to consider the resources that a renewed presentation of the doctrine of the natural law contains" (9). And this is the document's task — to present a new look at a natural law ethic as a contribution to the search for a universal ethic, and "to invite the experts and proponents of the great religious, sapiential and philosophical traditions of humanity to undertake an analogous work . . . in order to reach a common recognition of universal moral norms based on a rational approach to reality" (116).

The first chapter offers an overview of "convergences" in various religious and philosophical traditions. It identifies resonances of the Golden Rule ("And what you hate, do not do to anyone" [Tob. 4:15, cited at 12]) in various world religions (Hinduism, Buddhism, Taoism, African religions, and Islam), in Greco-Roman sources (Plato, Aristotle, Stoicism), and in Jewish and Christian scripture and tradition. These are all posited as evidence of, rather than an explanation for, a *de facto* "common moral patrimony" (11), and that one can "see in this consensus a manifestation of that which . . . is the human in the human being, namely 'human nature'" (36).

The chapter also identifies three intellectual movements that eventually undermined the almost universal recognition of a universal ethic: the voluntarist philosophy of the late medieval period that rooted law solely in the will and authority of the lawgiver and divested from law its intrinsic intelligibility (30); a "secularization" of natural law, where revelation or other sapiential traditions are ruled out as sources of knowledge of human nature, natural law being based solely "on the light of reason common to all people" (31); and a modern rationalism that transforms natural law into a kind of deductive moral code, one that regulates almost all human behavior (33). Therefore, despite the evidence from many sapiential traditions for a common moral patrimony, intellectual, political, and cultural developments in the West served to impede recognition of that common moral patrimony.

Having given evidence for a universal moral patrimony in its first chapter, the second chapter of *In Search of a Universal Ethic* describes the experiential process whereby an individual human person — from birth on — comes to grasp fundamental moral values, that is, comes to participate in the common moral patrimony. All human persons, born into and raised in a web of human relationships, are inculcated into various activities as worthwhile things to pursue, as examples to follow, and toward a vision of the ends and goals of life that are worthy of her or him as a human being. The fundamental realization that some kinds of activities are truly worthy of one as a human being and will lead to one's true happiness and fulfillment, and that other kinds of activities will frustrate one's pursuit of fulfillment, is what St. Thomas Aquinas calls the first principle of practical reason, that is, that "the good is to be done and pursued and evil is to be avoided."[20] *In Search of a Universal Ethic* considers the universal ability of a human person to evaluate whether a particular kind of activity can be integrated into "the authentic realization of the person" (42) to be of momentous importance, for that ability to morally evaluate one's actions is the basis for real dialogue with persons of other cultural or religious convictions.

The document's third chapter begins with the acknowledgment that although a moral patrimony (chapter 1) and the experiential appropriation of moral convictions (chapter 2) are indeed universal, the philosophical and metaphysical explanations for such commonality are not uncontested. Indeed, it recognizes that such "foundations" are not necessary to either know or act in accordance with the natural law. Nonetheless, it takes up the task of exploring just such foundations by offering reflection on how nature can be understood in a non-static sense; how inclinations that orient a person toward happiness can be compatible with human freedom; and how divine and human agency can be understood in an analogous noncompetitive sense such that one does not diminish the other. Though far from uncontested, such claims are nonetheless accessible to all. More important, this chapter guards against the unquestioned assumption of certain positions on these philosophical and metaphysical questions, positions that undermine an accurate conception of natural law.

Recognizing that the human person is an inherently social animal, the fourth chapter of *In Search of a Universal Ethic* examines the common good

20. St. Thomas Aquinas, *Summa Theologiae* (New York: Benziger, 1948), I-II 94,2.

and the role of natural law (or natural right) in the political order. Particularly relevant to the search for a universal ethic, it notes that though the political order is historically situated and thus ever changing, the natural law nonetheless serves as a measure to uphold the kind of relationships within a society and between peoples that are truly just. The chapter also offers a clear distinction between the political and the religious (or "ultimate") spheres, in order to indicate why it is that political authorities are not morally permitted to impose religious or otherwise ultimate claims on the people they govern and serve.

In the fifth and final chapter, *In Search of a Universal Ethic* focuses on how a natural law ethic (as understood by Christians) is to be related to Christian theological commitments, even while intelligible and applicable to all persons. Here the document offers an account of how a natural law ethic, despite having its own integrity (i.e., that it is an ethic in principle accessible without grace, and an ethic that is neither foreign to nor destroyed by grace) nonetheless only reaches its ultimate fulfillment in the context of the Christian tradition's understanding of the new law of grace. Most specifically, *In Search of a Universal Ethic* claims that it is in Jesus Christ that a natural law ethic finds its true fulfillment.

While this introduction is not the place to give extensive analysis of the document (that is a task taken up by the essayists in this volume), a few brief observations are perhaps in order. While much of *In Search of a Universal Ethic* will be familiar to those schooled in the Christian natural law tradition, there are some noteworthy developments. For instance, Christian natural law thinking in the modern period post-Kant has not typically supported its universality by appeal to what it shares in common with a variety of other wisdom traditions. In addition, the document is unusually candid in acknowledging the historical situatedness of a natural law ethic, duly admitting past Christian errors in labeling as natural law what were actually "positions . . . conditioned by the historical and cultural context" (10). Furthermore, the amount of attention given to environmental issues, as opposed to the more common "conjugal" issues, is noteworthy. These developments, along with the novel ways that perennial topics have been treated, make this document indeed a "new look" at the natural law.

Second, as editors we believe the above summary reveals that the two "paths" of a universal ethic and a natural law ethic are evident throughout the document. At the individual and political levels, and across time periods and cultures, the document takes "convergences" among "wisdom traditions" as one of its important emphases. Though present throughout the document, this is particularly evident in chapter 1. Yet no less does the document rely on the Christian tradition in articulating a new look at natural law, even situating its affirmation of universal ethical guidance within its claims about fulfillment in Christ. This emphasis is also present throughout the document, but is most clearly evident in chapter 5.

Essays Engaging the Document

Hopefully this brief overview of the origin and structure of the document has revealed the complementary emphases of *dialogue across traditions (universal ethic)* and *reflection on broadly applicable ethical guidance within the Christian tradition (natural law).* Unsurprisingly, the collection of essays in this volume can be organized according to these dual emphases, with a few opening essays attending to the overall context of the document. The first three essays in this collection contextualize the document. We are fortunate enough to have essays from two of the ten members of the ITC subcommittee that authored the document. Serge-Thomas Bonino, O.P., contextualizes the document within recent papal statements. He then carefully outlines the different audiences of the document, as well as explains what is "new" about natural law in a document subtitled "a new look." Anthony J. Kelly, C.Ss.R., explains a bit more about the process for generating the document, as well as the main questions that were on the authors' minds as they prepared it. Both of these essays, given their authors and their quality, are invaluable for an understanding of the document. We also add a third essay to this opening cluster on context. Russell Hittinger was not involved with the writing of the document. But his essay does a phenomenal job of identifying its overall purposes, and how these goals are best understood in the content of the past century or so of official Catholic teaching on natural law. Though in some ways his essay could fit in either of the two ensuing sections, it is placed in the opening cluster on context due to its splendid job in situating the document.

The second group of essays is grouped together under the heading "In Search of a Universal Ethic" (the main title of the document). They hold in common a starting point of dialogue between different traditions addressing the topic of a universal ethic. Of course, since each contributor has been asked to write an essay in response to the document, each author has as a starting point a dialogue between that document's presentation of natural law and some other tradition's approach to a universal ethic. This is warranted given the document's concerted effort to engage varying traditions and approaches to the question of a universal ethic. But that endeavor raises obvious questions. Would representatives of those different traditions agree on claims about a universal ethic offered in the *In Search of a Universal Ethic*? Are those different religions, traditions, or schools of thought portrayed accurately? Are all the necessary interlocutors actually engaged by the document? All of the essays in this group address these types of questions.

Certain essays in this section focus on how *In Search of a Universal Ethic* engages (or fails to engage) some prominent religious tradition or school of thought. For instance, we are most fortunate to have represented in this volume some (though not all) of the various religious traditions addressed in the document. In his essay, Anver M. Emon commends the document's attempt to engage Islam, laments its reference to the Mu'tazilites as selective and divisive, and tries to provide a broader account of debates over natural law within Islam. David Novak writes as a Jewish proponent of natural law who is sympathetic to the project of the document, and from this perspective examines the exact audience of the document, the adequacy of its metaphysical assumptions, and especially whether its account of the Jewish people is supersessionist.

Certain other authors similarly examine the adequacy of the document's dialogue across traditions, yet focus on schools of thought rather than religious traditions. Jean Porter explores whether the document accurately portrays positivism, and suggests what a more robust engagement with that approach to law might yield. Tracey Rowland examines whether the document fails to address a most important contemporary interlocutor — namely, secularists — and is thereby impeded from establishing the sort of common moral basis to which it aspires. Fergus Kerr, O.P., examines the document's portrayal of analytic philosophy (and the work of Hume and Moore in particular) in order to find out if that tradition is as antithetical to natural law thinking as the document suggests. Michael S. Northcott looks at the document in the context of current environmental crisis and its intellectual roots in late medieval nominalism in order to determine what resources there are in the document's account of natural law for a "global civilization" that is more "ecologically benign." Finally, David Burrell, C.S.C., appeals to recent linguistic philosophy for guidance on fundamental characteristics of human language and rhetoric that may illuminate important forms of moral agreement.

The third section of essays is grouped under the ITS document's subtitle, "A New Look at the Natural Law." What distinguishes the second group of essays is the starting point of dialogue between traditions or schools of thought. It would of course be inaccurate to say that the authors in this third group of essays are uninterested or uninvolved in dialogue. But in each of the essays included in this section, the primary concern is less the adequacy of the document's assessment of or contribution to dialogue across traditions, but rather the adequacy of the document's articulation of the natural law in light of the Christian tradition of thought on natural law.

Some of the essays in this group address the document's account of natural law in relation to central Christian theological claims, and do so in some sort of Protestant context.[21] Jennifer A. Herdt asks how successful the document is in responding to concerns about natural law raised by Protestants, relying particularly on the work of John Calvin. Similarly, David Cloutier examines the adequacy of the document's portrayal of natural law in light of long-standing Protestant critiques, critiques he presents through the work of Stanley Hauerwas. The Protestant Gilbert Meilaender's essay is not focused on Protestant critiques of natural law, but he evidences such a perspective when he assesses how adequately the document develops its closing section on the natural law's fulfillment in Christ. He also assesses the relative level of treatment given to theoretical justifications of natural law on the one hand and the role of virtue in natural law on the other hand.

Other essays in this group examine the general portrait of natural law in light of recent developments in Catholic moral thought. M. Cathleen Kaveny relies on recent scholarship on the interpretation of Vatican II to claim that the document at hand, like Vatican II, represents a shift in "style" in how it examines natural law, a shift Kaveny endorses. Lisa Sowle Cahill examines how the document's recognition of the importance of historicity in the derivation of natural law norms represents an important advance in Catholic thinking on natural law, and she evaluates whether that advance goes far enough. Joseph Capizzi examines the document's understanding of the relationship between the common good and the state, arguing that the document de-emphasizes the role of the state with regard to the highest reaches of the political common good.

Another group of essays in this section examines the document's portrayal of natural law in relation to questions central to Thomistic thought on natural law. Steven A. Long addresses the perennial Thomistic debate over the relationship between speculative and practical reason, arguing that the document correctly emphasizes the priority of speculative reason. He also lauds the doc-

---

21. In a sense these three essays could be placed in the previous section, since they examine the document's Catholic vision of natural law in relation to Protestantism. Thus there is clearly a sense of "dialogue with other traditions" in these three essays. Yet they are placed in this group since the document, though Catholic, purports to offer a "Christian" account of natural law. Furthermore, each of these three essays scrutinizes the adequacy of the document's portrayal of natural law in relation to central Christian theological commitments.

ument's endorsement of Thomistic vision of the relationship between human and divine causality, which he claims the document rightly understands to be noncompetitive. Martin Rhonheimer uses the document's depiction of natural law to emphasize the status of natural law as most properly a "work of reason," thereby distinguishing its formal definition from both its material content and metaphysical justification. Given his insistence that the document affirms the priority of practical reason, his essay is fruitfully read in conjunction with Long's. William C. Mattison III's essay examines how the document employs new language in its treatment of the perennial topic of natural inclinations, and in doing so he speculates on the reasons for that shift and the adequacy of the new terminology.

Finally, two essays of this group address how the document presents natural law in relation to certain central theological commitments of Christianity. Livio Melina explains how natural law, understood most fruitfully through analogy with language and as explanatory of the human experience of embodiedness, finds true fulfillment in Jesus Christ. His essay can be understood as a further reflection on chapter 5 of the document. Robert P. George and Sherif Girgis press the document's claim that "revelation assumes the requirements of the natural law" (34) and explore "what *theoretical* contribution does revelation make to our *understanding* of the moral law." They seek to substantiate the document's stalwart Catholic claim that there is harmony between faith and reason.

In sum, this volume offers an entry point into some of the best thinking on the monumentally important questions of the possibility of a universal ethic and the character of the natural law. It is hoped that this volume will be of service both to students seeking to discover the natural law tradition as a locus of thinking on universal ethics, and to practitioners who can see how this recent document and reactions to it are continuing that tradition.

Pedagogical Guidance in Using This Volume

In the above overviews of the document's genesis and structure as well as this volume's organization, a case has been made that there are complementary emphases on dialogue across traditions and reflection on universal ethical guidance from within a tradition. This provides one lens through which the reader can explore this volume. But there are other questions or "lenses" through which to explore the material in this volume. Of course there are far too many questions concerning a universal ethic and the natural law to even attempt any comprehensive list in this introduction. And many questions are rather technical given the long history of reflection on them. Yet rather than simply neglect those questions here, a non-exhaustive list is offered below of important topics addressed in this volume, topics that are treated in the document and more than one essay in this collection. They are simply "flagged" here, with both the names of the authors whose essays address them (either explicitly or implicitly), and the paragraphs in the document that address them. This section is intended as a pedagogical aid to readers, teachers, and students in using this book.

1. What are some different ways of understanding a "universal ethic"? Is "natural law" just another term for "universal ethic"? If not, how does it differ? (ITC §§1-21, 36-47) (Berkman and Mattison, Cloutier, Hittinger, Kelly, Kerr, Meilaender, Novak)

2. Which (if not all) accounts of a universal ethic are grounded in human nature? Are those accounts of human nature the same? If so, what is the key element(s) of human nature that grounds a universal ethic? If they vary, what different aspects of human nature do they emphasize? (ITC §§48-52, 61, 64-70, 78-82) (Burrell, Cahill, George and Girgis, Kelly, Kerr, Meilaender, Melina, Rowland)

3. Does belief in a universal ethic require particular philosophical/metaphysical commitments? What is the relationship between practical natural law norms and metaphysical justifications for those norms? Does the rejection of a universal ethic require particular philosophical/metaphysical commitments (e.g., nominalism? naturalism? moral relativism? positivism?)? (ITC §§7-11, 26-33, 60-82) (Burrell, Cloutier, Emon, George and Gergis, Hittinger, Kaveny, Kelly, Kerr, Long, Melina, Meilaender, Novak, Porter, Rhonheimer, Rowland)

4. Does a universal ethic require a timeless human nature or reason, or can it incorporate developments in history and culture or even changes in human nature (e.g., trans-humanism)? (ITC §§38-47, 52-59, 64-82) (Emon, Herdt, Hittinger, Northcott, Rowland, Berkman and Mattison)

5. What is the importance of the UN *Universal Declaration of Human Rights* for thinking about a universal ethic? Are "rights" essential (or even necessary) for a universal ethic? (ITC §§5-6, 28, 35, 51, 92, 115) (Cahill, Capizzi, Meilaender, Rowland)

6. Is a universal ethic necessary for, or helpful in, avoiding totalitarianism? (ITC §§5, 35, 81, 97-98) (Bonino, Capizzi, George and Girgis, Northcott, Novak)

7. How should a universal ethic influence politics or law? (ITC §§83-100) (Capizzi, Cloutier, Emon, Kaveny, Novak, Porter)

8. Can anyone understand the natural law? Are the virtuous (or highly intelligent) more likely to understand it? Are those who are morally corrupt unable to know it? Or do all people (as sinners) have equal difficulty understanding it? (ITC §§39-47, 53-63) (Cloutier, Herdt, Meilaender, Bonino)

9. Advocates of natural law differ on the importance of the (pre-rational) natural inclinations versus the importance of rationality. How do natural law advocates understand "natural inclinations" and why do they think they are important? Do the natural inclinations promote or detract from human freedom? (ITC §§29, 45-52, 63, 74, 79, 86) (Bonino, George and Gergis, Herdt, Mattison, Rhonheimer)

10. How can the natural law simultaneously be said to oblige, and yet be internal to us and directed toward our happiness? In other words, how are freedom and natural law related? (ITC §§43, 66-68, 71-72, 77) (Bonino, Hittinger, Mattison, Rhonheimer)

11. Is the natural law fundamentally about general principles of good and evil, or does it include specific moral principles? (ITC §§39-54) (Cahill, George and Gergis, Herdt, Hittinger, Novak, Porter, Rhonheimer)

12. What is the relationship between the natural law and different wisdom traditions or religious traditions? Does it in some way depend on religious convictions of some sort? (ITC §§12-27, 31-35, 42) (Bonino, Burrell, Emon, George and Gergis, Herdt, Melina, Rowland, Berkman and Mattison)

13. For Christians, what is the relationship between the natural moral law and discipleship to Jesus Christ? (ITC §§3, 9, 24-27, 67, 101-12) (Cloutier, George and Gergis, Herdt, Kaveny, Kelly, Meilaender, Melina, Novak)

14. How should we understand the relationship between God's eternal (or divine) law and the human ability to understand that (i.e., natural) law? Does this understanding influence the way we see nation-states that seek to impose a religious law? (ITC §§21, 26-27, 42, 63, 91-100) (Bonino, Burrell, Capizzi, Emon, Kaveny, Long, Mattison, Porter, Rhonheimer, Berkman and Mattison)

15. What can one learn about how to understand the natural law from studying its history, especially debates over nominalism and physicalism? (ITC §§18-35, 71-82) (Emon, Herdt, Hittinger, Kerr, Long, Mattison, Northcott, Porter, Kerr)

16. Does a universal ethic have anything to say about sexual morality? Which of the following could one argue is problematic in relation to a universal

ethic or the natural law: adultery, anal sex, bestiality, bigamy, contraception, extramarital intercourse, homosexuality, oral sex, polygamy or poly-
andry, sadism, sexual assault, sexual relations between an adult and a child
(e.g., marriage to a minor)? (ITC §§79-80) (Cahill, Cloutier, Hittinger,
Novak)

17. What is the importance of a universal ethic in relation to flowering global
concern for ecological justice? (ITC §§81-82) (Kelly, Northcott)

18. What is the relationship between practical and speculative intellect as
regards the natural law? (ITC §§39, 43, 47, 53, 57-59, 90) (Long, Rhonheimer, Mattison)

In Search of a Universal Ethic:

A New Look at the Natural Law

INTERNATIONAL THEOLOGICAL COMMISSION

INTRODUCTION

1. Are there objective moral values which can unite human beings and bring them peace and happiness? What are they? How are they discerned? How can they be put into action in the lives of persons and communities? These perennial questions concerning good and evil are today more urgent than ever, insofar as people have become more aware of forming one single world community. The great problems that arise for human beings today have an international, worldwide dimension, inasmuch as advances in communications technology have given rise to closer interaction among individuals, societies and cultures. A local event can have an almost immediate worldwide repercussion. The consciousness of global solidarity is thus emerging, which finds its ultimate foundation in the unity of the human race. This finds expression in the sense of planetary responsibility. Thus, the question of ecological balance, of the protection of the environment, resources and climate, has become a pressing preoccupation faced by all humanity, and whose solution extends

* PRELIMINARY NOTE. The topic "In Search of a Universal Ethic: A New Look at the Natural Law" was submitted to the study of the International Theological Commission. To undertake this study a Subcommittee was formed, composed of Archbishop Roland Minnerath, the Reverend Professors P Serge-Thomas Bonino OP (Chairman of the Subcommittee), Geraldo Luis Borges Hackmann, Pierre Gaudette, Tony Kelly CSSR, Jean Liesen, John Michael McDermott SJ; Professors Dr Johannes Reiter and Dr Barbara Hallensleben, with the collaboration of Archbishop Luis Ladaria SJ, Secretary General, and with the contributions of other members. The general discussion took place on the occasion of the plenary sessions of the International Theological Commission, which took place in Rome in October 2006 and 2007 and in December 2008. The document was approved unanimously by the Commission and was then submitted to its president, Cardinal William J Levada, who has given his approval for publication.

far beyond national boundaries. Likewise, threats of terrorism, organized crime and new forms of violence and oppression that weigh upon societies have a global dimension. The accelerated developments of biotechnologies, which sometimes threaten the very identity of man (genetic manipulation, cloning…), urgently call for an ethical and political reflection of a universal breadth. In this context, the search for common ethical values experiences a revival of relevance.

2. By their wisdom, their generosity and sometimes their heroism, men and women give active witness to these common ethical values. Our admiration for such people is a sign of a spontaneous initial grasp of moral values. Academic and scientific reflection on the cultural, political, economic, moral and religious dimensions of our social existence nourishes this reflection on the common good of humanity. There are also artists who, by the manifestation of beauty, react against the loss of meaning and give renewed hope to men and women. Likewise, some politicians work with energy and creativity to put programs into place for the elimination of poverty and the protection of fundamental freedoms. Very important also is the constant witness of the representatives of religions and spiritual traditions who wish to live by the light of the ultimate truth and the absolute good. All contribute, each in his own manner and in a reciprocal exchange, to the promotion of peace, a more just political order, the sense of common responsibility, an equitable distribution of riches, as well as respect for the environment, for the dignity of the human person and his fundamental rights. However, these efforts cannot succeed unless good intentions rest on a solid foundational agreement regarding the goods and values that represent the most profound aspirations of man, both as an individual and as member of a community. Only the recognition and promotion of these ethical values can contribute to the construction of a more human world.

3. The search for this common ethical language concerns everyone. For Christians, it is mysteriously in harmony with the work of the Word of God, "the true light that enlightens every man" (Jn 1:9), and with the work of the Holy Spirit who knows how to germinate in hearts "love, joy, peace, patience, kindness, goodness, faithfulness, gentleness, self-control" (Gal 5:22-23). The community of Christians, which shares "the joys and hopes, the griefs and the anxieties of the men of this age" and "therefore experiences itself really and intimately in solidarity with mankind and its history,"[1] cannot in any way hide

---

1. Vatican Council II, Pastoral constitution *Gaudium et spes*, preface, n. 1.

from this common responsibility. Enlightened by the Gospel, engaged in a patient and respectful dialogue with all persons of good will, Christians participate in the common endeavour to promote human values: "Whatever is true, whatever is honorable, whatever is just, whatever is pure, whatever is lovely, whatever is gracious, if there is any excellence, if there is anything worthy of praise, think about these things" (Phil 4:8). They know that Jesus Christ, "our peace" (Eph 2:14), who has reconciled all human beings to God by his cross, is the principle of the most profound unity towards whom the human race is called to converge.

4. The search for a common ethical language is inseparable from an experience of conversion, by which persons and communities turn away from the forces that seek to imprison them in indifference or cause them to raise walls against the other and against the stranger. The heart of stone — cold, inert and indifferent to the lot of one's neighbor and of the human race — must be transformed, under the action of the Spirit, into a heart of flesh,[2] sensitive to wisdom that calls us to compassion, to the desire for peace and hope for all. This conversion is the condition for true dialogue.

5. Contemporary attempts to define a universal ethic are not lacking. Shortly after the Second World War, the community of nations, seeing the consequences of the close collusion that totalitarianism had maintained with pure juridical positivism, defined in the *Universal Declaration of Human Rights* (1948) some inalienable rights of the human person. These rights transcend the positive law of states and must serve them both as a reference and a norm. These rights are not simply bestowed by a lawmaker: they are declared, which is to say, their objective existence, prior to any decision of the lawmaker, is made manifest. They flow, in fact, from the "recognition of the inherent dignity . . . of all members of the human family" (Preamble).

The *Universal Declaration of Human Rights* constitutes one of the most beautiful successes of modern history. It "remains one of the highest expressions of human conscience in our times,"[3] and it offers a solid basis for promoting a more just world. Nevertheless, the results have not always been as high as

---

2. Cf Ezek. 36:26.

3. John Paul II, *Address of October 5, 1995, to the General Assembly of the United Nations for the celebration of the 50th anniversary of its founding (Insegnamenti di Giovanni Paolo II* 18,2 [1995], p. 732).

the hopes. Certain countries have contested the universality of these rights, judged to be too Western, prompting a search for a more comprehensive formulation. Moreover, a certain propensity towards multiplying human rights more according to the disordered desires of the consumerist individual or the demands of interest groups, rather than the objective requirements of the common good of humanity, has — in no small way — contributed to their devaluation. Disconnected from the moral sense of values, which transcend particular interests, the multiplication of procedures and juridical regulations leads into a quagmire, which, when all is said and done, only serves the interests of the most powerful. Above all, a tendency comes to the fore to reinterpret human rights, separating them from the ethical and rational dimension that constitutes their foundation and their end, in favor of pure utilitarian legalism.[4]

6. In order to make explicit the ethical foundation of human rights, some have tried to elaborate a "global ethic" in the framework of a dialogue between cultures and religions. The "global ethic" refers to the collection of fundamental obligatory values which for centuries have formed the patrimony of human experience. It is found in all the great religious and philosophical traditions.[5]

---

4. Cf. Benedict XVI, *Address of April 18, 2008, before the General Assembly of the United Nations Organization in New York* (AAS 100 [2008], p. 335): "The merit of the *Universal Declaration* is that it has enabled different cultures, juridical expressions and institutional models to converge around a fundamental nucleus of values, and hence of rights. Today, though, efforts need to be redoubled in the face of pressure to reinterpret the foundations of the *Declaration* and to compromise its inner unity so as to facilitate a move away from the protection of human dignity towards the satisfaction of simple interests, often particular interests. . . . Experience shows that legality often prevails over justice when the insistence upon rights makes them appear as the exclusive result of legislative enactments or normative decisions taken by the various agencies of those in power. When presented purely in terms of legality, rights risk becoming weak propositions divorced from the ethical and rational dimension which is their foundation and their goal. The *Universal Declaration*, rather, has reinforced the conviction that respect for human rights is principally rooted in unchanging justice, on which the binding force of international proclamations is also based. This aspect is often overlooked when the attempt is made to deprive rights of their true function in the name of a narrowly utilitarian perspective."

5. In 1993, some representatives of the Parliament of the World's Religions published a *Declaration Toward a Global Ethic* which states that "there already exists among religions a consensus capable of founding a global ethic, a minimum consensus concerning binding values, irrevocable norms, and essential moral attitudes." This *Declaration* contains four principles. (1) "There is no new global order without a new global ethic." (2) "Every human being must be treated humanely." Taking human dignity into account is considered as an end in itself. This

This project, worthy of interest, is indicative of the current need for an ethic possessing universal and global validity. But does a purely inductive search, conducted on the parliamentary model, for an already existing minimal consensus, satisfy the requirements for basing law on what is absolute? Moreover, does not this minimal ethic lead to relativizing the strong ethical requirements of each of the religions or particular schools of wisdom?

7. For several decades, the question of the ethical foundations of law and politics has been set aside in certain sectors of contemporary culture. Under the pretext that every claim to possess an objective and universal truth would be the source of intolerance and violence, and that only relativism can safeguard the pluralism of values and democracy, a juridical positivism is espoused, which renounces any reference to an objective ontological criterion of what is just. In this perspective, the final horizon of law and the moral norm is the law in force, which is considered to be just by definition since it is the will of the legislator. But this opens the way to the arbitrary use of power, to the dictatorship of the numerical majority and to ideological manipulation, which harm the common good. "In today's ethics and philosophy of law, the postulates of juridical positivism are widespread. As a result, legislation often only becomes a compromise among different interests: one seeks to transform into law private interests or desires that are opposed to the duties flowing from social responsibility."[6] But juridical positivism is notoriously insufficient, for a legislator can only act legitimately within certain limits, which derive from the dignity of the human person, and in service to the development of what is authentically human. Now, the legislator cannot abandon the determination of what is human to extrinsic and superficial criteria, as would be the case, for example, if he were to legalize, on his own, everything that is possible in the realm of biotechnology. In brief, he must act in an ethically responsible manner. Politics cannot cut itself off from ethics nor can civil laws and the juridical order prescind from a higher moral law.

---

principle takes up the "golden rule" that is found in many religious traditions. (3) The *Declaration* enunciates four irrevocable moral directives: non-violence and respect for life; solidarity; tolerance and truth; equality between men and women. (4) Regarding the problems of humanity, a change of mentality is necessary, so that each one becomes aware of his urgent responsibility. It is a duty of the religions to cultivate this responsibility, to deepen it, and to hand it on to future generations.

6. Benedict XVI, *Address of February 12, 2007, to the International Congress on Natural Moral Law organized by the Pontifical Lateran University* (AAS 99 [2007], p. 244).

8. In this context in which reference to absolute objective values, universally recognized, has become problematic, some people, wishing nevertheless to give a rational basis to common ethical decisions, advocate "discourse ethics" in keeping with a "dialogical" understanding of morality. Discourse ethics consists in using, in the course of ethical debate, only norms to which all the concerned participants — renouncing "strategies" aimed at imposing their own views — can give their assent. In this way, one can determine if a rule of conduct and action, or a specific behaviour, is moral because, by bracketing off cultural and historical conditioning, the principle of discussion offers a guarantee of universality and rationality. Discourse ethics is above all interested in a method by which, thanks to debate, ethical principles and norms can be tested and become obligatory for all the participants. It is essentially a process for testing the value of proposed norms, but it cannot produce new substantial contents. Discourse ethics is, therefore, a purely formal ethic that does not concern fundamental moral orientations. It also runs the risk of limiting itself to the search for compromise. Certainly, dialogue and debate are always necessary for obtaining an achievable agreement on the concrete application of moral norms in any given situation, but they should not relegate moral conscience to the margins. A true debate does not replace personal moral convictions, but it presupposes and enriches them.

9. Aware of what is currently at stake in the question, we would like, in this document, to invite all those pondering the ultimate foundations of ethics and of the juridical and political order, to consider the resources that a renewed presentation of the doctrine of the natural law contains. This law, in substance, affirms that persons and human communities are capable, in the light of reason, of discerning the fundamental orientations of moral action in conformity with the very nature of the human subject and of expressing these orientations in a normative fashion in the form of precepts or commandments. These fundamental precepts, objective and universal, are called upon to establish and inspire the collection of moral, juridical and political determinations that govern the life of human beings and societies. They constitute a permanent critical instance of them and guarantee the dignity of the human person in the face of the fluctuations of ideologies. In the course of its history, in the elaboration of its own ethical tradition, the Christian community, guided by the Spirit of Jesus Christ and in critical dialogue with the wisdom traditions it has encountered, has assumed, purified and developed this teaching on the natural law as a fundamental ethical norm. But Christianity does not have the monopoly on the natural law. In fact, founded on reason, common to all human beings,

the natural law is the basis of collaboration among all persons of good will, whatever their religious convictions.

10. It is true that the term "natural law" is a source of numerous misunderstandings in our present cultural context. At times, it evokes only a resigned and completely passive submission to the physical laws of nature, while human beings seek instead — and rightly so — to master and to direct these elements for their own good. At times, when presented as an objective datum that would impose itself from the outside on personal conscience, independently of the work of reason and subjectivity, it is suspected of introducing a form of heteronomy intolerable for the dignity of the free human person. Sometimes also, in the course of history, Christian theology has too easily justified some anthropological positions on the basis of the natural law, which subsequently appeared as conditioned by the historical and cultural context. But a more profound understanding of the relationships between the moral subject, nature and God, as well as a better consideration of the historicity that affects the concrete applications of the natural law, help to overcome these misunderstandings. It is likewise important today to set out the traditional doctrine of the natural law in terms that better manifest the personal and existential dimension of the moral life. It is also necessary to insist more on the fact that the expression of the requirements of the natural law is inseparable from the effort of the total human community to transcend egotistical and partisan tendencies and develop a global approach of the "ecology of values" without which human life risks losing its integrity and its sense of responsibility for the good of all.

11. The idea of the natural law takes on numerous elements that are common to humanity's great wisdom traditions, both religious and philosophical. In chapter 1, therefore, our document begins by evoking "convergences." Without pretending to be exhaustive, it indicates that these great religious and philosophical wisdom traditions bear witness to a largely common moral patrimony that forms the basis of all dialogue on moral questions. Even more, these suggest, in one way or another, that this patrimony reveals a universal ethical message inherent in the nature of things, which everyone is capable of discerning. The document then calls to mind several essential milestones in the historical development of the idea of the natural law and mentions certain modern interpretations that are partially at the origin of the difficulties that our contemporaries have concerning this notion. In chapter 2 ("The perception of common moral values"), our document describes how, beginning with

the most basic data of moral experience, the human person immediately apprehends certain fundamental moral goods and formulates, as a result, the precepts of the natural law. These do not constitute a code entirely made of intangible prescriptions but a permanent and normative guiding principle in the service of the concrete moral life of the person. Chapter 3 ("The foundations of the natural law"), passing from common experience to theory, deepens the philosophical, metaphysical and religious foundations of the natural law. In order to respond to some contemporary objections, it specifies the role of nature in personal action and inquires into the possibility of nature constituting a moral norm. Chapter 4 ("Natural Law and the City") makes explicit the regulating role of natural law precepts in political life. The doctrine of the natural law already possesses coherence and validity on the philosophical level of reason, common to all human beings, but chapter 5 ("Jesus Christ, the fulfillment of the natural law") shows that it acquires its full meaning within the history of salvation: sent by the Father, Jesus Christ is, in fact, by his Spirit, the fullness of all law.

Chapter 1: Convergences

1.1. The wisdom traditions and religions of the world

12. In diverse cultures, people have progressively elaborated and developed traditions of wisdom in which they express and transmit their vision of the world as well as their thoughtful perception of the place that man holds in society and the cosmos. Before all conceptual theorizing, these wisdom traditions, which are often of a religious nature, convey an experience that identifies what favors and what hinders the full blossoming of personal life and the smooth running of social life. They constitute a type of "cultural capital" available in the search for a common wisdom necessary for responding to contemporary ethical challenges. According to the Christian faith, these traditions of wisdom, in spite of their limitations and sometimes even their errors, capture a reflection of the divine wisdom at work in the hearts of human beings. They call for attention and respect, and can have value as a *praeparatio evangelica*.

The form and extent of these traditions can vary considerably. Nevertheless, they testify to the existence of a patrimony of moral values common to all human beings, no matter how these values are justified within a particular worldview. For example, the "golden rule" ("And what you hate, do not do to anyone" [Tob 4:15]) is found in one form or another in the majority of wisdom traditions.[7]

---

7. Cf. St. Augustine, *De doctrina christiana*, III, xiv, 22 (*Corpus christianorum*, series latina, 32, p. 91): "The precept: 'what you do not want done to yourself, do not do to another' cannot in any way differ according to the diversity of peoples." ("'Quod tibi fieri non vis, alii ne feceris,'

Furthermore, these traditions generally agree in recognizing that the great ethical rules not only impose themselves on a specific human group, but also hold true for each individual and for all peoples. In fact, several traditions recognize that these universal moral behaviours are demanded by the very nature of man: they express the manner by which he is to enter, in a creative and harmonious way, into a cosmic or metaphysical order that transcends him and gives meaning to his life. This order is, in fact, filled with an immanent wisdom. It carries a moral message that human beings are capable of discerning.

13. In the Hindu traditions, the world — the cosmos as well as human societies — is regulated by an order or fundamental law (*dharma*), which one must respect in order not to cause serious imbalances. *Dharma* then defines the socio-religious obligations of man. In its specificity, the moral teaching of Hinduism is understood in the light of the fundamental doctrines of the *Upanishads:* belief in an indefinite cycle of transmigrations (*samsāra*), with the idea that good and bad actions committed during the present life (*karman*) have an influence on successive rebirths. These doctrines have important consequences for one's behaviour with respect to others: they entail a high degree of goodness and tolerance, a sense of disinterested action for the benefit of others, as well as the practice of non-violence (*ahimsā*). The principal current of Hinduism distinguishes between two bodies of texts: *śruti* ("that which is understood," namely, revelation) and *smrti* ("that which one remembers," namely, tradition). The ethical prescriptions are especially found in the *smrti,* most particularly in the *dharmaśātra* (of which the most important is the *mānava dharmaśātra* or laws of Manu, ca. 200-100 B.C.). Besides the basic principle according to which "the immemorial custom is the transcendent law approved by sacred scripture and the codes of the divine legislators (consequently, all men of the three principal classes, who respect the supreme spirit that is in them, must always conform themselves with diligence to the immemorial custom"),[8] one also finds an equivalent practice of the golden rule: "I will tell you what is the essence of the greatest good of the human being. The man who practices the religion (*dharma*) of do no harm to anyone without exception (*ahimsā*) acquires the

---

nullo modo posse ulla eorum gentili diversitate variari.") Cf. L. J. Philippidis, *Die "Goldene Rege" religionsgeschichtlich Untersucht* (Leipzig, 1929); A. Dihle, *Die Goldene Regel. Eine Einfuhrung in die Geschichte der antiken und fruhchristlichen Vulgarethik* (Gottingen, 1962); J. Wattles, *The Golden Rule* (New York: Oxford, 1996).

8. *Mānava dharmaśāthtra,* 1, 108 (G.C. Haughton, *Mānava Dharma śāstra* or *The Institutes of Manu, Comprising the Indian System of Duties, Religious and Civil,* ed. P. Percival, New Delhi, 1982(4), 14.

greatest good. This man is the master of the three passions: cupidity, anger and avarice, and renouncing them in relation to all that exists, acquires success. . . . This man who considers all creatures like 'himself' and treats them as his own 'self', laying down the punishing rod and dominating his anger completely, assures for himself the attainment of happiness. . . . One will not do to another what one considers harmful to oneself. This, in brief, is the rule of virtue. . . . In refusing and in giving, in abundance and in misery, in the agreeable and the disagreeable, one will judge all the consequences by considering one's own 'self'."[9] Several precepts of the Hindu tradition can be placed in parallel with the requirements of the Decalogue.[10]

14. One generally defines Buddhism by the four "noble truths" taught by the Buddha after his enlightenment: 1) reality is suffering and lack of satisfaction; 2) the origin of suffering is desire; 3) the cessation of suffering is possible (by the extinction of desire); 4) a way exists leading to the cessation of suffering. This way is the "noble eightfold path" which consists in the practice of discipline, concentration and wisdom. On the ethical level, the favorable actions can be summarized in the five precepts (*śila, sīla*): 1) do not injure living beings nor take away life; 2) do not take what is not given; 3) do not engage in immoral sexual conduct; 4) do not use false or lying words; 5) do not ingest intoxicating products that diminish mastery over oneself. The profound altruism of the Buddhist tradition, which is expressed in a resolute attitude of non-violence, amicable benevolence and compassion, thus agrees with the golden rule.

15. Chinese civilization is profoundly marked by the Taoism of Lǎozǐ or Lao-Tse (or Tzu) (6th century B.C.). According to Lao-Tse, the Way or Dào is the primordial principle, immanent within the entire universe. It is an indiscernible principle of permanent change under the action of two contrary and complementary poles, the *yīn* and the *yáng*. It is up to man to espouse this natural process of transformation, to let himself go in the flux of time by means of the attitude of non-action (*wú-wéi*). The search for harmony with nature, inseparably material and spiritual, is thus at the heart of the Taoist ethic. As for Confucius

9. *Mahābhārata, Anusasana parva*, 113, 3-9 (ed. Ishwar Chundra Sharma and O. N. Bimali; translation according to M. N. Dutt [Parimal Publications, Delhi], vol. IX, p. 469).

10. For example: "Let him say what is true, let him say what is pleasing, let him declare no disagreeable truth, and let him utter no lie to please someone; such is the eternal law" (*Mānava dharmaśāstra*, 4, 138, p. 101); "Let him always consider the action of striking a blow, reviling, and harming the good of one's neighbour, as the three most pernicious things in the string of vices produced by wrath" (*Mānava dharmaśāstra*, 7, 51, p. 156).

(551-479 B.C.), "Master Kong," he attempts, on the occasion of a period of profound crisis, to restore order by respect for rites, founded on filial piety that must be at the heart of all social life. Social relations, in fact, take family relations as their model. Harmony is obtained by an ethic of the happy mean, in which the ritualized relation (the *li*), which places man into the natural order, is the measure of all things. The ideal to be attained is *ren*, the perfect virtue of humanity, achieved by self-control and benevolence towards others. "'Reciprocity (*shù*)': is not this the key word? That which you would not wish done to you, do not do to others."[11] The practice of this rule expresses the way of heaven (*Tiān Dào*).

16. In the African traditions, the fundamental reality is life itself. It is the most precious good, and the ideal of man consists not only in living to old age sheltered from cares, but most of all in remaining, even after death, a vital power continually reinforced and vivified in and by his progeny. Life is, in fact, a dramatic experience. Man, the microcosm at the heart of the macrocosm, intensely lives the drama of the confrontation between life and death. The mission that falls to him of assuring the victory of life over death, orients and determines his ethical action. In a consistent and rational ethical horizon, man, therefore, must identify the allies of life, win them to his cause and thus assure his survival that is, at the same time, the victory of life. Such is the profound meaning of traditional African religions. The African ethic thus manifests itself as an anthropocentric and vital ethic: the acts deemed favorable to the opening up of life, to conserving, protecting and causing it to flourish or to increasing the vital potential of the community, are, because of this, considered good; every act presumed prejudicial to the life of individuals or the community is judged to be bad. Traditional African religions thus appear to be essentially anthropocentric, but attentive observation coupled with reflection shows that neither the place accorded to the living man nor the cult of the ancestors constitutes something closed. The traditional African religions attain their highest point in God, the source of life, the creator of all that exists.

17. Islam understands itself as the restoration of the original natural religion. It sees in Muhammad the last prophet sent by God to put human beings definitively back on the right path. But Muhammad has been preceded by others: "For there is no community in which an 'admonisher' has not appeared."[12] Islam, therefore, ascribes to itself a universal vocation and addresses itself to all

---

11. Confucius, *Analects* 15, 23.
12. *Koran,* sura 35, 24; cf. sura 13, 7.

human beings, who are considered as "naturally" Muslims. Islamic law, inseparably communitarian, moral and religious, is understood as a law directly
given by God. The Islamic ethic is, therefore, fundamentally a morality of obedience. To do good is to obey the commandments; to do evil is to disobey them.
Human reason intervenes to recognize the revealed character of the law and to
derive from it the concrete juridical implications. To be sure, in the 9th century,
the Mu'tazilite school proclaimed the idea that "good and evil are in things,"
which is to say, that certain behaviour is good or bad in itself, prior to the divine
law that commands or forbids it. The Mu'tazilites, therefore, judged that man
could by his reason know what is good and evil. According to them, man spontaneously knows that injustice or falsehood is bad and that it is obligatory to
return what has been entrusted to one, to keep harm away from oneself, to
show gratitude to one's benefactors, of whom God is the first. But the Ash'arites,
who dominate Sunni orthodoxy, have upheld an opposing theory. As partisans
of occasionalism, which does not recognize any consistency in nature, they
consider that the divine positive revelation of God alone defines good and evil,
right and wrong. Among the prescriptions of this divine positive law, many take
up again or repeat the great elements of the moral patrimony of humanity and
can be placed in relation to the Decalogue.[13]

---

13. *Koran*, sura 17, 22-38 (pp. 343-345): "Your Lord has decreed that you may adore none but
Him. He has prescribed kindness with respect to your father and mother. If one of them or even
both of them have attained old age near you, don't say to them: 'Fie'! do not push them away, but
address them with respectful words. Take them kindly under your wing and say: 'My Lord! Be
merciful towards them, as they were towards me at the time they raised me when I was an infant.'
Your Lord knows perfectly what is in you. If you are just, he then is the one who pardons those
who come back repentant to him. Give to your near of kin what is their due as well as to the poor
and the traveler, but do not be wasteful. The wasteful are brothers of demons, and the Devil is
very ungrateful towards his Lord. If, being in search of mercy that you hope from your Lord, you
are obliged to go away, speak a benevolent word to them. Do not hold your hand closed at your
neck, and neither extend it too generously; otherwise you would find yourself held in contempt
and miserable. Yes, your Lord gives his gifts generously or sparingly to whom he wishes. He
knows his servants quite well and he sees them perfectly. Do not kill your children for fear of
poverty. He will provide for their subsistence along with your own. To kill them would be an
enormous sin. Avoid fornication: it is an abomination! What a detestable path! Do not kill the
man whom God has forbidden you to kill, except for a just reason. [. . .] Do not touch the fortune
of the orphan until he has come of age, except for its better use. Fulfill your commitments, for
men will be interrogated on their commitments. Give a just measure when you measure; weigh
with the most exact balance. This is something good and the result is excellent. Do not follow
that of which you have no knowledge. There will surely be an accounting for all things: whatever
is heard, seen or in the heart. Do not walk the earth with insolence. You cannot rip the earth
apart or attain the height of mountains. What is evil in all this is detestable before the Lord."

1.2. The Greco-Roman sources of the natural law

18. The idea that there exists a norm of natural justice (the term "droit natural" translated as "norm of natural justice") prior to positive juridical determinations is already encountered in classical Greek culture with the exemplary figure of Antigone, the daughter of Oedipus. Her two brothers, Eteocles and Polyneices, confront each other to attain power and kill each other. Polyneices, the rebel, is condemned to remain unburied and burned on the pyre. But in order to fulfill the demands of piety towards her dead brother, Antigone appeals to "the unwritten and immutable laws" against the prohibition of burial pronounced by the king Creon.

> *Creon:* And so, you have dared to transgress my laws?
> *Antigone:* Yes, for it was not Zeus who proclaimed them,
>> Nor justice which abides with the gods below
>> Neither the one nor the other established these laws among men;
>> I do not consider your decrees so powerful
>> That you, mortal man, can disregard the unwritten and immutable
>>> laws of the gods.
>> They don't exist since today or yesterday but always;
>> No one knows when they appeared.
>> Out of fear of the wishes of a man
>> I ought not have risked being punished by the gods.[14]

19. Plato and Aristotle take up the distinction made by the Sophists between the laws that have their origin in a convention, that is, in a purely positive decision (*thesis*), and those that have force "by nature." The first are neither eternal nor are they in force everywhere and they do not oblige everyone. The second oblige everyone, always and everywhere.[15] Certain Sophists, like Callicles of Plato's *Gorgias,* had recourse to this distinction in order to challenge

---

14. Sophocles, *Antigone,* v. [scene ii] 449-460.

15. Cf. Aristotle, *Rhetoric,* I, XIII, 2 (1373 b 4-11): "Particular law is that which each group of men determines in relation to its members and these sorts of laws are divided into unwritten law and written law. Common law (*nomos koinos*) is that which is according to nature (*kata physin*). In fact there is, as everyone recognizes by a kind of divination, a just and an unjust, common to all by nature, even though there is no communication or mutual covenant among peoples. Thus, one sees the Antigone of Sophocles declare that it is just to bury Polyneices, whose burial was forbidden, affirming that this burial is just, as being in accord with nature." Cf. also *Nichomachean Ethics* V, ch. 10.

the legitimacy of the laws instituted by human cities. To these laws, they opposed their narrow and erroneous idea of nature, reduced to its physical component alone. Thus, in opposition to the political and juridical equality of the citizens of the city, they advocated what seemed to them the most evident of the "natural laws": the stronger must prevail over the weaker.[16]

20. There is nothing of this sort in Plato and Aristotle. They do not set the norm of natural justice in opposition to the positive laws of the city [πόλις]. They are convinced that the laws of the city are generally good and constitute the implementation, more or less successful, of a norm of natural justice which is in conformity with the nature of things. For Plato, the norm of natural justice is an ideal norm, a rule for both legislators and citizens, which permits the grounding and the evaluation of positive laws.[17] For Aristotle, this supreme norm of morality corresponds to the realization of the essential form of nature. What is natural is moral. The norm of natural justice is invariable; positive law changes according to peoples and different epochs. But the norm of natural justice is not situated beyond positive law. It is embodied in the positive law, which is the application of the general idea of justice to social life in its variety.

---

16. Cf. Plato, *Gorgias* (483c-484b) [Speech of Callicles]: "Nature herself shows that it is just for the best to have more than the weakest, and the most powerful than the most helpless. She shows in many circumstances, that it works out well this way, as much in other living beings as in all the cities and races of men, and that the just is thus determined, by the fact that the most powerful commands the weakest and possesses a greater share. For on what conception of justice did Xerxes base his campaign against Greece, or his father against the Scythians? And one could cite innumerable other examples. But, it seems to me that these men did what they did according to the nature of the just and by Zeus, according to the law of nature, and, thus, probably not according to what was instituted by us, shaping the best and strongest among us, taking them from their youngest age, as one would do with lions, bewitching them with our spells and incantations, we enslave them by repeating that each one is equal to the others, and that this is the beautiful and the just. But if a man were born, endowed with a sufficiently strong nature, then, getting rid of all hindrances with a jolt, reducing them to pieces and fleeing them, stomping on our writings, our spells, our incantations and our laws, all without exception against and raising himself above us, behold, the slave thus reveals himself as our master, and then the just according to nature shines forth in full light."

17. In the *Theaetetus* (172 a-b) Plato's Socrates displays the harmful political consequences of the relativistic thesis attributed to Protagoras according to which each man is the measure of truth: "'Therefore, in politics, also, beautiful and ugly, just and unjust, pious and impious, all that each city believes as such and declares legally such for itself, all of this, in truth, is such for each one. [. . .] In questions of just and unjust, of piety and impiety, one agrees to sustain rigorously that nothing of this is from nature and nothing possesses its essence exclusively; but simply what seems true to the group becomes true from the moment it seems such and for as long as it seems so."

21. In Stoicism, the natural law becomes the key concept of a universalist ethic. What is good and ought to be done is that which corresponds to nature, understood in both a physico-biological and rational sense. Every man, whatever the nation to which he belongs, must integrate himself as a part in the Whole of the universe. He must live according to his nature.[18] This imperative presupposes that an eternal law exists, a divine *Logos*, which is present both in the cosmos — which it infuses with rationality — as well as in human reason. Thus, for Cicero the law is "the supreme reason inserted in nature, which commands what must be done and forbids the contrary."[19] Nature and reason constitute the two sources of our knowledge of the fundamental ethical law, which is of divine origin.

1.3. The teaching of Sacred Scripture

22. The gift of the law on Sinai, of which the "Ten Words" constitute the centre, is an essential element of the religious experience of Israel. This law of the Covenant includes fundamental ethical precepts. They define the manner in which the chosen people must respond to God's choice by their holiness of life: "Say to all the congregation of the sons of Israel, you shall be holy; for I the Lord your God am holy" (Lev 19:2). But these ethical behaviours are also valid for other peoples, in that God demands an account from foreign nations that violate justice and what is right.[20] In fact, God had already sealed, in the person of Noah, a covenant with the totality of the human race, which implied, in particular, respect for life (Gen 9).[21] More fundamentally, creation itself appears as the act by which God structures the entire universe by giving it a

18. Cf., for example, Seneca, *De vita beata*, VIII, 1: "It is nature that one must take as one's guide; it is nature that reason observes, and what it consults. To live happily or according to nature is, therefore, the same." *("Natura enim duce utendum est: hanc ratio observat, hanc consulit. Idem ergo beate vivere et secundum naturam.")*

19. Cicero, *De legibus*, I, VI, 18: "Lex est ratio summa insita in natura quae iubet ea quae facienda sunt prohibetque contraria."

20. Cf. Amos 1-2.

21. Rabbinic Judaism refers to the seven moral imperatives that God gave to Noah for all men. They are enumerated in the Talmud (*Sanhedrin* 56): 1) You shall not commit idolatry; 2) You shall not kill; 3) You shall not steal; 4) You shall not commit adultery; 5) You shall not blaspheme; 6) You shall not eat the flesh of a living animal; 7) You shall establish tribunals of justice to enforce respect for the preceding six commandments. If the 613 *mitzvot* of the written Torah and their interpretation in the oral Torah only concern the Jews, the laws of Noah are addressed to all human beings.

law: "Let them [the stars] praise the name of the Lord! For he commanded and they were created. And he has established them for ever and ever; he set down a law which cannot pass away" (Ps 148:5-6). This obedience of creatures to the law of God is a model for human beings.

23. Alongside the texts associated with the history of salvation, with the major theological themes of election, promise, law and covenant, the Bible also contains a wisdom literature that does not directly treat the national history of Israel, but deals with the place of man in the world. It develops the conviction that there is a correct way, a "wise" way, of doing things and conducting one's life. Man must apply himself to the search for this wisdom and then make every effort to put it into practice. This wisdom is not so much found in history as in nature and everyday life.[22] In this literature, Wisdom is often presented as a divine perfection, sometimes hypostasized. In a striking way, she manifests herself in creation, of which she is "the fashioner" (Wis 7:22). The harmony that reigns among creatures bears witness to wisdom. In many ways, man is made a participant in this wisdom that comes from God. This participation is a gift from God that one must ask for in the prayer: "I prayed, and understanding was given to me; I called upon God, and the spirit of wisdom came to me" (Wis 7:7). This wisdom is again the fruit of obedience to the revealed law. In fact, the Torah is like the incarnation of Wisdom. "If you desire wisdom, keep the commandments, and the Lord will supply it for you. For the fear of the Lord is wisdom and instruction" (Sir 1:26-27). But wisdom is also the result of a wise observation of nature and human morals in order to discover their immanent intelligibility and their exemplary value.[23]

---

22. Wisdom literature is interested in history especially insofar as it shows forth certain constants in relation to the way that leads man towards God. The sages do not underestimate the lessons of history and their value as divine revelation (cf. Sir 44-51), but they have a vivid awareness that the connections among events depend on a coherence that is not itself an historical event. In order to comprehend this identity at the heart of mutability and to act in a responsible manner according to it, wisdom searches for principles and structural laws rather than precise historical perspectives. In so doing, wisdom literature concentrates on protology, namely, on creation at the beginning along with what it implies. In fact, protology attempts to describe the coherence that is found behind historical events. It is an *a priori* condition that permits the ordering of all possible historical events. Wisdom literature tries, therefore, to highlight the value of the conditions that make everyday life possible. History describes these elements in a successive manner; wisdom goes beyond history towards an a-temporal description of what constitutes reality at the time of creation, "in the beginning," when human beings were created in the image of God.

23. Cf. Prov 6:6-9: "Go to the ant, O sluggard; consider her ways, and be wise. Without

24. In the fullness of time, Jesus Christ preached the coming of the Kingdom as a manifestation of the merciful love of God made present among human beings through his own person and calling for conversion and the free response of love on their part. This preaching is not without consequences for ethics, for the way in which the world and human relations are to be structured. In his moral teaching, presented in a succinct form in the Sermon on the Mount, Jesus takes up the golden rule: "So, whatever you wish that men would do to you, do so to them; for this is the law and the prophets" (Mt 7:12).[24] This positive precept completes the negative formulation of the same rule in the Old Testament: "And what you hate, do not do to anyone" (Tob 4:15).[25]

25. At the beginning of the Letter to the Romans, the Apostle Paul, intending to show the universal need for the salvation brought by Christ, describes the religious and moral situation common to all of humanity. He affirms the possibility of a natural knowledge of God: "For what can be known about God is plain to them, because God has shown it to them. Ever since the creation of the world his invisible nature, namely, his eternal power and deity, has been clearly perceived in the things that have been made" (Rom 1:19-20).[26] But this knowledge has been perverted into idolatry. Placing Jews and pagans on the same level, Paul affirms the existence of an unwritten law inscribed in their hearts.[27] It permits everyone to discern good and evil by himself: "When Gen-

---

having any chief, officer or ruler, she prepares her food in summer, and gathers her sustenance in harvest. How long will you lie there, O sluggard? When will you arise from your sleep?"

24. Cf. also Lk 6:31: "And as you wish that men would do to you, do so to them."

25. Cf. St. Bonaventure, *Commentarius in Evangelium Lucae*, c. 6, n. 76 (*Opera omnia*, VII, ed. Quaraechi, p. 156): "In hoc mandato [Lk 6:31] est consummatio legis naturalis, cuius una pars negativa ponitur Tobiae quarto et implicatur hic: 'Quod ab alio oderis tibi fieri, vide ne tu aliquando alteri facias' "; (Pseudo-) Bonaventura, *Expositio in Psalterium*, Ps 57,2 (*Opera onmia*, IX, ed. Vivès, p. 227); "Duo sunt mandata naturalia: unum prohibitivum, unde hoc 'Quod tibi non vis fieri, alteri ne feceris'; aliud affirmativum, unde in Evangelio 'Omnia quaecumque vultis ut faciant vobis homines, eadem facite illis'. Primum de malis removendis, secundum de bonis adipiscendis."

26. Cf. Vatican Council I, Dogmatic Constitution *Dei Filius*, c. 2. Cf. also Acts 14:16-17: "In past generations he allowed all the nations to walk in their own ways; yet he did not leave himself without witness, for he did good and gave you from heaven rains and fruitful seasons, satisfying your hearts with food and gladness."

27. In Philo of Alexandria, one finds the idea according to which Abraham, without the written law, was already leading "by nature" a life in conformity with the law. Cf. Philo of Alexandria, *De Abrahamo*, § 275-276 (translation by C. D. Yonge, *The Works of Philo Judaeus*, vol. 2 [London: Bohn, 1854], p. 452): "Moses says: 'This man [Abraham] fulfilled the divine law and all the commandments of God' (Gen 26:5), not having been taught to do so by written

tiles who do not have the law do by nature what the law requires, they are a law unto themselves, even though they do not have the law. They show that what the law requires is written on their hearts, while their conscience also bears witness and their conflicting thoughts accuse or perhaps excuse them" (Rom 2:14-15). Nevertheless, knowledge of the law does not in itself suffice in order to lead a righteous life.[28] These texts of St. Paul have had a decisive influence on Christian reflection in regard to natural law.

1.4. The developments of the Christian tradition

26. For the Fathers of the Church, the *sequi naturam* and the *sequela Christi* are not in opposition to each other. On the contrary, the Fathers generally adopt the idea from Stoicism that nature and reason indicate what our moral duties are. To follow nature and reason is to follow the personal *Logos*, the Word of God. The doctrine of the natural law, in fact, supplies a basis for completing biblical morality. Moreover, it allows us to explain why the pagans, independently of biblical revelation, possess a positive moral conception. This is indicated to them by nature and corresponds to the teaching of revelation. "From God are the law of nature and the law of revelation which function as one."[29] The Fathers of the Church, however, do not purely and simply adopt the Stoic doctrine. They modify and develop it. On the one hand, the anthropology of biblical inspiration, which sees man as the *imago Dei* — the full truth of which is manifested in Christ — forbids reducing the human person to a simple element of the cosmos: called to communion with the living God, the person transcends the whole cosmos while integrating himself in it. On the other hand, the harmony of nature and reason no longer rests on an immanentist vision of a pantheistic cosmos but on the common reference to the transcendent wisdom of the Creator. To conduct oneself in conformity with reason amounts to following the orientations that Christ, as the divine *Logos*, has set down by virtue of the *logoi spermatikoi* in human reason. To act against reason is an offense against these orientations. Very significant is the definition of St. Augustine: "The eternal law is the divine reason or the will of God, or-

---

books, but in accordance with the unwritten law of his nature, being anxious to obey all healthful and salutary impulses."

28. Cf. Rom 7:22-23: "I delight in the law of God, in my inmost self, but I see in my members another law at war with the law of my mind and making me captive to the law of sin which dwells in my members."

29. Clement of Alexandria, *Stromata*, I, c. 29, 182, 1 (*Sources chrétiennes*, 30, p. 176).

dering the conservation of the natural order and forbidding its disruption."[30] More precisely, for St. Augustine, the norms of the righteous life and of justice are expressed in the Word of God, who then imprints them in the heart of man "as the seal of a ring passes to the wax, but without leaving the ring."[31] Moreover, for the Church Fathers the natural law is henceforth understood in the framework of the history of salvation, which leads to distinguishing different states of nature (original nature, fallen nature, restored nature) in which the natural law is realized in different ways. This Patristic doctrine of the natural law is transmitted to the Middle Ages, along with the closely related concept of the "law of nations (*ius gentium*)," according to which there exist, apart from Roman civil law (*ius civile*), universal principles of law, which regulate the relations among peoples and are obligatory for all.[32]

27. In the Middle Ages the doctrine of natural law attains a certain maturity and assumes a "classical" form that constitutes the background of all further discussion. It is characterized by four traits. In the first place, in conformity with the nature of scholastic thought that seeks to gather the truth wherever

---

30. St. Augustine, *Contra Faustum,* xxii, c. 27 (PL 42, col. 418): "Lex vero aeterna est, ratio divina vel voluntas Dei, ordinem naturalem conservari iubens, perturbari vetans." For example, St. Augustine condemns lying because it goes directly against the nature of language and its calling to be the sign of thought; cf. *Enchiridion,* VII, 22 (*Corpus christianorum,* series latina, 46, p. 62): "Speech has not been given to men mutually to deceive each other, but rather to bring their thoughts to the knowledge of others. To make use of speech to deceive and not for its normal end is, therefore, a sin." ("Et utique verba propterea sunt institua non per quae invicem se homines fallant sed per quae in alterius quisque notitiam cogitationes suas perferat. Verbis ergo uti ad fallaciam, non ad quod instituta sunt, peccatum est.")

31. St. Augustine, *De trinitate,* XIV, xv, 21 (*Corpus christianorum,* series latina, 50A, p. 451): "Where are these rules written? Where does the man, even an unjust one, recognize what is just? Where does he see that he must have what he himself does not have? Where are these written, except in the book of this light that one calls the Truth? It is there that every just law is written; from there it passes into the heart of the man who practices justice, not that it migrates into him but places its imprint there, as the seal of a ring passes into the wax without leaving the ring." ("Ubinam sunt istae regulae scriptae, ubi quid sit justum et iniustus agnoscit, ubi cernit habendum esse quod ipse non habet? Ubi ergo scriptae sunt, nisi in libro lucis illius quae veritas dicitur unde omnis lex iusta describitur et in cor hominis qui operatur iustitiam non migrando sed tamquam imprimendo transfertur, sicut imago ex anulo et in ceram transit et anulum non relinquit.")

32. Cf. Gaius, *Institutes,* 1. 1 (Second century A.D.) (ed. Julien Reinach, *Collection des universités de France* [Paris, 1950], p. 1): "Quod vero naturalis ratio inter onmes homines constituit, id apud onmes populos peraeque custoditur vocaturque ius gentium, quasi quo iure omnes gentes utuntur. Populus itaque romanus partim suo proprio, partim communi omnium hominum iure utitur."

it is found, it takes up prior reflections on natural law, pagan or Christian, and tries to propose a synthesis. Second, in conformity with the systematic nature of scholastic thought, it locates natural law in a general metaphysical and theological framework. Natural law is understood as the rational creature's participation in the eternal, divine law, thanks to which it enters in a free and conscious manner into the plans of Providence. It is not a closed and complete set of moral norms, but a source of constant guidance, present and operative in the different stages of the economy of salvation. Third, with the recognition of the consistency of nature, in part linked to the rediscovery of the thought of Aristotle, the scholastic doctrine of the natural law considers the ethical and political order as a rational order, a work of human intelligence. The scholastic notion of natural law defines an autonomous space for that order, distinct but not separated from the order of religious revelation.[33] Finally, in the eyes of scholastic theologians and jurists, natural law constitutes a point of reference and a criterion in the light of which they evaluate the legitimacy of positive laws and of particular customs.

1.5. Further developments

28. In certain aspects, the modern history of the idea of natural law represents a legitimate development of the teaching of medieval scholasticism in a more complex cultural context, marked in particular by a more vivid sense of moral subjectivity. Among these developments, we point out the works of the Spanish theologians of the 16th century, who, following the example of the Dominican Francis of Vitoria, had recourse to natural law to contest the imperialist ide-

---

33. St. Thomas Aquinas clearly distinguishes the natural political order founded on reason and the supernatural religious order founded on the grace of revelation. He opposes the medieval Muslim and Jewish philosophers who attributed an essentially political role to religious revelation. Cf. *Quaestiones disputatae de veritate*, q. 12, a. 3, ad 11: "The society of men insofar as it is ordered to the end which is eternal life can only be conserved by the justice of the faith, whose principle is prophecy. [. . .] But since this end is supernatural, both the justice ordered toward this end, and prophecy, which is its principle, will be supernatural. In truth, the justice by which human society is governed and ordered towards the good of the city, can be sufficiently achieved by means of the principles of the *ius naturale* implanted in men." ("Societas hominum secundum quod ordinatur ad finem vitae aeternae, non potest conservari nisi per iustitiam fidei, cuius principium est prophetia. [. . .] Sed cum hic finis sit supernaturalis, et iustitia ad hunc finem ordinata, et prophetia, quae est eius principium, erit supernaturalis. Iustitia vero per quam gubernatur societas humana in ordine ad bonum civile, sufficienter potest haberi per principia iuris naturalis homini indita.")

ology of some Christian states of Europe and to defend the rights of the non-Christian peoples of America. In fact, such rights are inherent in human nature and do not depend on one's concrete situation vis-à-vis the Christian faith. The idea of natural law also allowed the Spanish theologians to establish the foundations of an international law, i.e., of a universal norm that regulates the relations of peoples and states among themselves.

29. But in other aspects the idea of natural law in the modern age took on orientations and forms that contributed to making it difficult to accept today. During the last centuries of the Middle Ages, there developed in scholasticism a current of voluntarism, the cultural hegemony of which has profoundly modified the idea of natural law. Voluntarism proposes to highlight the transcendence of the free subject in relation to all conditioning. Against naturalism that tended to subject God to the laws of nature, it emphasizes, in a unilateral way, the absolute freedom of God, with the risk of compromising his wisdom and rendering his decisions arbitrary. In the same manner, against intellectualism, suspected of subjecting the human person to the order of the world, it exalts a freedom of indifference, understood as a pure capacity to choose contraries, which runs the risk of disconnecting the person from his natural inclinations and from the objective good.[34]

30. The consequences of voluntarism for the doctrine of natural law are numerous. Above all, while in St. Thomas Aquinas the law was understood as a work of reason and an expression of wisdom, voluntarism leads one to connect the law to will alone, and to a will detached from its intrinsic ordering to the good. Henceforth, all the force of the law resides only in the will of the lawmaker. The law is thus divested of its intrinsic intelligibility. In these conditions, morality is reduced to obedience to the commandments that manifest

34. Cf. Benedict XVI, *Discourse at Regensburg on the occasion of the meeting with the representatives of the world of science*, September 12, 2006 (AAS 98 [2006], p. 733): "In the late Middle Ages we find trends in theology which would sunder this synthesis between the Greek spirit and the Christian spirit. In contrast with the so-called intellectualism of Augustine and Thomas, there arose with Duns Scotus a voluntarism which, in its later developments, led to the claim that we can only know God's *voluntas ordinata*. Beyond this is the realm of God's freedom, in virtue of which he could have done the opposite of everything he has actually done. This gives rise to positions which [. . .] might even lead to the image of a capricious God, who is not even bound to truth and goodness. God's transcendence and otherness are so exalted that our reason, our sense of the true and good, are no longer an authentic mirror of God, whose deepest possibilities remain eternally unattainable and hidden behind his actual decisions."

the will of the lawmaker. Thomas Hobbes will end up holding the position that *auctoritas, non veritas, facit legem* (it is authority and not truth that makes law).[35] Modern man, loving autonomy, could only rebel against such a vision of the law. Then, with the pretext of preserving the absolute sovereignty of God over nature, voluntarism deprives it of all internal intelligibility. The thesis of the *potentia Dei absoluta,* according to which God could act independently of his wisdom and his goodness, relativizes all the existing intelligible structures and weakens the natural knowledge that man can have of them. Nature ceases to be a criterion for knowing the wise will of God: man can expect this knowledge only from a revelation.

31. In addition, several factors have led to the secularization of the notion of natural law. Among these, one can recall the increasing divide between faith and reason which characterizes the end of the Middle Ages or some aspects of the Reformation,[36] but above all the will to overcome the violent religious conflicts that bloodied Europe up until the dawn of modern times. Thus a desire arose to establish the political unity of human communities by putting religious confession in parentheses. Henceforth, the doctrine of natural law prescinds from all particular religious revelation, and therefore from all confessional theology. It claims to be founded solely on the light of reason common to all people and is presented as the ultimate norm in the secular field.

35. This phrase appears in the Latin version of Thomas Hobbes, *Leviathan* (see François Tricaud, *Léviathan* [Paris: Sirey, 1971], p. 295, note 81). The English text states: "The interpretation of the laws of nature in a commonwealth dependeth not on the books of moral philosophy. The authority of writers, without the authority of the commonwealth, maketh not their opinions law, be they never so true . . . it is by the sovereign power that it is law."

36. The attitude of the Reformers with respect to the natural law was not monolithic. Basing himself on St. Paul, John Calvin — more than Martin Luther — recognized the existence of the natural law as an ethical norm even if it is radically incapable of justifying man. "It is a common thing, that man is sufficiently instructed in the correct rule of living well by this natural law of which the Apostle speaks. [. . .] The end of the natural law is to render man inexcusable; this, therefore, allows us to define it properly: it is an awareness of the conscience by which it discerns sufficiently between good and evil in order to remove man from the cover of ignorance, so that he is reproached by his very own testimony" (*Institutes of the Christian Religion,* book II, ch. 2, 22). During the three centuries that follow the Reformation, the natural law served as a foundation for jurisprudence among Protestants. Only with the secularization of the natural law did Protestant theology, in the 19th century, distance itself from it. Only then does an opposition between Protestant and Catholic opinions on the natural law become apparent. In our own time, however, Protestant ethics seems to be showing renewed interest in this notion [of the natural law].

32. Further, modern rationalism posits the existence of an absolute and normative order of intelligible essences accessible to reason and accordingly relativizes the reference to God as the ultimate foundation of the natural law. Certainly, the necessary, eternal, and immutable order of essences needs to be actualized by the Creator, but it is believed that this order already possesses in itself its coherence and rationality. Reference to God therefore becomes optional. The natural law would be binding on all "even if there were no God (*etsi Deus non daretur*)."[37]

33. The modern rationalist model of natural law is characterized: 1) by the essentialist belief in an immutable and ahistorical human nature, of which reason can perfectly grasp the definition and essential properties; 2) by putting into parentheses the concrete situation of human persons in the history of salvation, marked by sin and grace, which however have a decisive influence on the knowledge and practice of the natural law; 3) by the idea that it is possible for reason to deduce *a priori* the precepts of the natural law, beginning from the definition of the essence of the human being; 4) by the maximal extension thus given to those deduced precepts, so that natural law appears as a code of premade laws regulating almost the entire range of behaviour. This tendency to extend the field of the determinations of natural law was at the origin of a grave crisis when, particularly with the rapid development of the human sciences, Western thought became more aware of the historicity of human institutions and of the cultural relativity of many ways of acting that at times had been justified by appeal to the evidence of natural law. The gap between an abstract maximalist theory and the complexity of the empirical data explains in part the disaffection for the very idea of natural law. In order that the notion of natural law can be of use in the elaboration of a universal ethic in a secularized and pluralistic society such as our own, it is therefore necessary to avoid presenting it in the rigid form that it assumed, particularly in modern rationalism.

1.6. The Magisterium of the Church and natural law

34. Before the 13th century, because the distinction between the natural and the supernatural order was not clearly elaborated, natural law was generally assimilated into Christian morals. Thus the decree of Gratian, which provides

---

37. This expression finds its origin in Hugo Grotius, *De jure belli et pacis,* Prolegomena: "Haec quidem quae iam diximus locum aliquem haberent, etsi daremus, quod sine summo scelere dari nequit, non esse Deum."

the fundamental canonical norm in the 12th century, begins thus: "Natural law is that which is contained in the law and in the Gospel." It then identifies the content of the natural law with the golden rule and explains that the divine laws correspond to nature.[38] The Fathers of the Church had recourse to natural law and to Sacred Scripture to provide a foundation for the moral behaviour of Christians, but the Magisterium of the Church, early on, had to make very few interventions to settle disputes on the content of the moral law.

When the Magisterium of the Church was led not only to resolve particular moral discussions, but also to justify its own position before a secularized world, it appealed more explicitly to the notion of natural law. It is in the 19th century, especially during the pontificate of Leo XIII, that recourse to natural law becomes more necessary in the acts of the Magisterium. The most explicit presentation is found in the Encyclical *Libertas praestantissimum* (1888). Leo XIII refers to natural law to identify the source of civil authority and to fix its limits. He vigorously recalls that one must obey God rather than men when the civil authorities command or recognize something contrary to divine law or to the natural law. He also looks to natural law to protect private property against socialism and to defend the right of workers to an adequate living wage. In this same line, John XXIII refers to natural law to provide a foundation for the rights and the duties of man (Encyclical *Pacem in terris* [1963]). With Pius XI (Encyclical *Casti connubii* [1930]) and Paul VI (Encyclical *Humanae vitae* [1968]), natural law is revealed as a decisive criterion for questions relating to conjugal morality. Certainly, natural law is a law accessible to human reason, common to believers and nonbelievers, and the Church does not have exclusive rights over it, but since revelation assumes the requirements of the natural law, the Magisterium of the Church has been established as the guarantor and interpreter of it.[39] The *Catechism of the Catholic Church* (1992) and the Encyclical *Veritatis splendor* (1993) assign a decisive place to the natural law in the exposition of Christian morals.[40]

35. Today the Catholic Church invokes the natural law in four principal contexts. In the first place, facing the spread of a culture that limits rationality to the pos-

---

38. Gratian, *Concordantia discordantium canonum,* pars 1, dist. 1 (PL 187, col. 29): "Humanum genus duobus regitur, naturali videlicet iure et moribus. Ius naturale est quod in lege et Evangelio continetur, quo quisque iubetur alii facere quod sibi vult fieri, et prohibetur alii inferre quod sibi nolit fieri. [. . .] Omnes leges aut divinae sunt aut humanae. Divinae natura, humanae moribus constant, ideoque hae discrepant, quoniam aliae aliis gentibus placent."

39. Cf. Paul VI, Encyclical *Humanae vitae,* n. 4 (AAS 60 [1968], p. 483).

40. Cf. *Catechism of the Catholic Church,* n. 1954-1960; John Paul II, Encyclical *Veritatis splendor,* n. 40-53.

itive sciences and abandons the moral life to relativism, it insists on the natural capacity of human beings to obtain by reason "the ethical message contained in being"[41] and to know in their main lines the fundamental norms of just action in conformity with their nature and their dignity. The natural law thus responds to the need to provide a basis in reason for the rights of man[42] and makes possible an intercultural and interreligious dialogue capable of fostering universal peace and of avoiding the "clash of civilizations." In the second place, in the presence of relativistic individualism, which judges that every individual is the source of his own values, and that society results from a mere contract agreed upon by individuals who choose to establish all the norms themselves, it recalls the non-conventional, but natural and objective character of the fundamental norms that regulate social and political life. In particular, the democratic form of government is intrinsically bound to stable ethical values, which have their source in the requirements of natural law and thus do not depend on the fluctuations of the consent of a numerical majority. In the third place, facing an aggressive secularism that wants to exclude believers from public debate, the Church points out that the interventions of Christians in public life on subjects that regard natural law (the defence of the rights of the oppressed, justice in international relations, the defence of life and of the family, religious freedom and freedom of education), are not in themselves of a confessional nature, but derive from the care which every citizen must have for the common good of society. In the fourth place, facing the threats of the abuse of power, and even of totalitarianism, which juridical positivism conceals and which certain ideologies propagate, the Church recalls that civil laws do not bind in conscience when they contradict natural law, and asks for the acknowledgment of the right to conscientious objection, as well as the duty of disobedience in the name of obedience to a higher law.[43] The reference to natural law, far from producing conformism, guarantees personal freedom and defends the marginalized and those oppressed by social structures which do not take the common good into account.

41. Benedict XVI, *Speech of February 12, 2007, to the International Congress on Natural Moral Law organized by the Pontifical Lateran University* (AAS 99 [2007], p. 243).

42. Cf. Benedict XVI, *Address of April 18, 2008, before the General Assembly of the United Nations:* "These rights [the rights of man] are based on the natural law inscribed on the heart of man and present in the different cultures and civilizations. To detach human rights from this context would mean restricting their range and yielding to a relativistic conception, according to which the meaning and interpretation of rights could vary and their universality could be denied in the name of different cultural, political, and social conceptions and even religious outlooks."

43. Cf. John Paul II, Encyclical *Evangelium vitae,* n. 73-74.

Chapter 2: The Perception of Common Moral Values

36. The examination of the great traditions of moral wisdom undertaken in the first chapter shows that certain kinds of human behaviour are recognized, in the majority of cultures, as expressing a certain excellence in the way in which a human being lives and realizes his own humanity: acts of courage, patience in the trials and difficulties of life, compassion for the weak, moderation in the use of material goods, a responsible attitude in relation to the environment, and dedication to the common good. Such ethical conduct defines the main lines of a properly moral ideal of a life "according to nature", that is, in conformity with the profound being of the human subject. On the other hand, some forms of behaviour are universally recognized as calling for condemnation: murder, theft, lying, wrath, greed, and avarice. These appear as attacks on the dignity of the human person and on the just requirements of life in society. One is justified to see in this consensus a manifestation of that which — beyond the diversity of cultures — is the human in the human being, namely "human nature." But at the same time, one must admit that such agreement on the moral quality of certain behaviour coexists with a great variety of explanatory theories. Whether we look at the fundamental doctrines of the Upanishads in Hinduism, or the four "noble truths" of Buddhism, or the Tao of Lao-Tse, or the "nature" of the Stoics, every school of wisdom or every philosophical system understands moral action within a general explanatory framework that comes to legitimize the distinction between what is good and what is evil. There is a diversity among these explanations, which makes both dialogue and the grounding of moral norms difficult.

37. Nevertheless, apart from any theoretical justifications of the concept of natural law, it is possible to illustrate the immediate data of the conscience of which it wants to give an account. The object of the present chapter is precisely to show how the common moral values that constitute natural law are grasped. It is only later that we will see how the concept of natural law rests on an explanatory framework which both undergirds and legitimizes moral values, in a way that can be shared by many. To do this, the presentation of the natural law by St. Thomas Aquinas appears particularly pertinent, since, among other things, it places the natural law within a morality that sustains the dignity of the human person and recognizes his capacity of discernment.[44]

2.1. The role of society and culture

38. The human person only progressively comes to moral experience and becomes capable of expressing to himself the precepts that should guide his action. The person attains this to the degree to which he is inserted in a network of human relationships from birth, beginning with the family, relationships which allow him, little by little, to become aware of himself and of reality around him. This is done in particular by the learning of a language — one's mother tongue — which teaches the person to name things and allows him to become a subject aware of himself. Oriented by the persons who surround him, permeated by the culture in which he is immersed, the person recognizes certain ways of behaving and of thinking as values to pursue, laws to observe, examples to imitate, visions of the world to accept. The social and cultural context thus exercises a decisive role in the education in moral values. There is, however, no contradiction between such conditioning and human freedom. Rather, it makes freedom possible, since it is through such conditioning that the person is able to come to moral experience, which will eventually allow him to review some of the "obvious facts" that he had interiorized in the course of his moral apprenticeship. Moreover, in the present context of globalization, societies and cultures themselves must inevitably practice sincere dialogue and exchange, based on the co-responsibility of all in regard to the common good of the planet: they must leave aside particular interests to attain the moral values that all are called to share.

44. Cf. John Paul II, Encyclical *Veritatis splendor*, n. 44: "The Church has often made reference to the Thomistic doctrine of natural law, including it in her own teaching on morality."

2.2. Moral experience: "one must do good"

39. Every human being who attains self-awareness and responsibility experiences an interior call to do good. He discovers that he is fundamentally a moral being, capable of perceiving and of expressing the call that, as we have seen, is found within all cultures: "One must do good and avoid evil." All the other precepts of the natural law are based on this precept.[45] This first precept is known naturally, immediately, by the practical reason, just as the principle of non-contradiction (the intellect cannot at the same time and under the same aspect both affirm and deny the same thing about something) which is at the base of all speculative reasoning, is grasped intuitively, naturally, by the theoretical reason, when the subject comprehends the sense of the terms employed. Traditionally, such knowledge of the first principle of the moral life is attributed to an innate intellectual disposition called *synderesis*.[46]

40. With this principle, we find ourselves immediately in the sphere of morality. The good that thus imposes itself on the person is in fact the moral good; it is behaviour that, going beyond the categories of what is useful, is in keeping with the authentic realization of this being — at the same time one and differentiated — who is the human person. Human activity cannot be reduced to a simple question of adaptation to the "ecosystem": to be human is to exist and to be placed within a broader framework that defines meaning, values and responsibilities. By searching for the moral good, the person contributes to the realization of his nature, beyond impulses of instinct or the search for a particular pleasure. This moral good testifies to itself and is understood from itself.[47]

---

45. St. Thomas Aquinas, *Summa theologiae*, I-II, q. 94, a. 2: "The first precept of the law is that the good is to be done and pursued and evil is to be avoided. And upon this precept all the other precepts of the law of nature are based: namely that all those things to be done or avoided pertain to the precepts of the law of nature, which practical reason naturally apprehends to be human goods." ("Hoc est [. . .] primum praeceptum legis, quod bonum est faciendum et prosequendum, et malum vitandum. Et super hoc fundantur omnia alia legis naturae, ut scilicet omnia illa facienda vel vitanda pertineant ad praecepta legis naturae, quae ratio practica naturaliter apprehendit esse bona humana.")

46. Cf. St. Thomas Aquinas, *Summa theologiae*, I, q. 79, a. 12; *Catechism of the Catholic Church*, n. 1780.

47. Cf. Romano Guardini, *Freedom, Grace, and Destiny: Three Chapters on the Interpretation of Existence* (translation by John Murray, S.J. [New York: Pantheon, 1961], p. 48): "Good action also signifies action that fructifies and enriches being. Good preserves life and completes it, but only when it is done for its own sake."

41. The moral good corresponds to the profound desire of the human person who — like every being — tends spontaneously, naturally, towards realizing himself fully, towards that which allows him to attain the perfection proper to him, namely, happiness. Unfortunately, the subject can always allow himself to be drawn by particular desires and to choose goods or to do deeds that go against the moral good which he perceives. A person can refuse to go beyond himself. It is the price of a freedom limited in itself and weakened by sin, a freedom that encounters only particular goods, none of which can fully satisfy the human heart. It pertains to the reason of the subject to examine if these particular goods can be integrated into the authentic realization of the person: if so, they will be judged morally good, and if not, morally bad.

42. This last claim is of capital importance. It is the basis of the possibility of dialogue with persons belonging to different cultural or religious horizons. It values the eminent dignity of every human person, in stressing his natural aptitude to know the moral good that he must accomplish. Like every creature, the human person is defined by a combination of dynamisms and finalities, prior to the free choices of the will. But, unlike beings that are not endowed with reason, the human person is capable of knowing and of interiorizing these finalities, and thus of appreciating, in accordance with them, that which is good or bad for him. Thus he recognizes the eternal law, i.e., the plan of God regarding creation, and participates in God's providence in a particularly excellent manner, guiding himself and guiding others.[48] This insistence on the dignity of the moral subject and on his relative autonomy is rooted in the

---

48. Cf. St. Thomas Aquinas, *Summa theologiae*, Ia-IIae, q. 91, a. 2: "But among all others, the rational creature is subject to divine providence in a more excellent way than all beings, insofar as it partakes of a share of providence, providing both for itself and for others. Thus it has a share of the Eternal Reason, whereby it has a natural inclination to its proper act and end. This participation of the eternal law in the rational creature is called natural law." ("Inter cetera autem rationalis creatura excellentiori quodam modo divinae providentiae subiacet, inquantum et ipsa fit providentiae particeps, sibi ipsi et aliis providens. Unde et in ipsa participatur ratio aeterna, per quam habet naturalem inclinationem ad debitum actum et finem. Et talis participatio legis aeternae in rationali creatura lex naturalis dicitur.") This text is cited in John Paul II, Encyclical *Veritatis splendor*, n. 43. Cf. also Vatican Council II, Declaration *Dignitatis humanae*, n. 3: "The highest norm of human life is the divine law — eternal, objective and universal — whereby God orders, directs and governs the entire universe and all the ways of the human community, by a plan conceived in wisdom and love. Man has been made by God to participate in this law, with the result that, under the gentle disposition of divine Providence, he can come to perceive ever increasingly the unchanging truth."

recognition of the autonomy of created realities and corresponds to a fundamental given of contemporary culture.[49]

43. The moral obligation that the subject recognizes does not come, therefore, from a law that would be exterior to him (pure heteronomy), but arises from within the subject himself. In fact, as indicated by the maxim we have cited — "One must do good and avoid evil" — the moral good that reason determines "imposes itself" on the subject. It "ought" to be accomplished. It takes on a character of obligation and of law. But the term "law" here does not refer to scientific laws that limit themselves to describing the factual constants of the physical or social world, nor to an imperative imposed arbitrarily on the moral subject from without. Law here designates an orientation of the practical reason which indicates to the moral subject what kind of action is in accord with the basic and necessary dynamism of his being that tends to its full realization. This law is normative in virtue of an internal requirement of the spirit. It springs from the heart itself of our being as a call to the realization and transcending of oneself. It is not therefore a matter of subjecting oneself to the law of another, but of accepting the law of one's own being.

2.3. The discovery of the precepts of the natural law: universality of the natural law

44. Once we posit the basic affirmation that introduces us to the moral order — "One must do good and avoid evil" — we see how the recognition of the fundamental laws that ought to govern human action take effect in the subject. Such recognition is not the fact of an abstract consideration of human nature, nor of the effort of conceptualization, which will afterwards be the distinctive characteristic of philosophical and theological theorizing. The perception of fundamental moral goods is immediate, vital, based on the connaturality of the spirit with values, and engages affectivity as much as intelligence, the heart as much as the mind. It is an acquisition often imperfect, still obscure and dim, but it has the profundity of immediacy. It deals with the data of the most simple and common experience, implicit in the concrete action of persons.

45. In his search for the moral good, the human person sets himself to listen to what he is, and takes note of the fundamental inclinations of his nature,

---

49. Vatican Council II, Pastoral Constitution *Gaudium et spes*, n. 36.

which are something quite different from the simple blind impulses of desire. Perceiving that the goods to which he tends by nature are necessary for his moral realization, he formulates for himself, under the form of practical commands, the moral duty of actualizing them in his own life. He expresses to himself a certain number of very general precepts that he shares with all other human beings and that constitute the content of that which we call natural law.

46. One traditionally distinguishes three great sets of natural dynamisms that are at work in the human person.[50] The first, which is in common with all substances, comprises essentially the inclination to preserve and to develop one's own existence. The second, which is in common with all living things, comprises the inclination to reproduce, in order to perpetuate the species. The third, which is proper to the human person as a rational being, comprises the inclination to know the truth about God and to live in society. From these inclinations, the first precepts of the natural law, known naturally, can be formulated. Such precepts remain very general, but they form the first substratum that is at the foundation of all further reflections on the good to be practiced and on the evil to be avoided.

47. To leave this generality and to make clear the concrete choices about what to do, it is necessary to have recourse to discursive reason, which will determine what are the concrete moral goods capable of fulfilling the person — and humanity — and will formulate more concrete precepts capable of guiding him in his action. In this new stage the knowledge of the moral good proceeds by way of reasoning. At its origin this reasoning remains very simple: a limited experience of life suffices, and it remains within the intellectual possibility of everyone. One speaks here of the "secondary precepts" of the natural law, discovered through the consideration (to varying degrees) of practical reason, in contrast to the general fundamental precepts that reason picks up spontaneously and which are called "primary precepts."[51]

2.4. The precepts of the natural law

48. We have identified in the human person a first inclination that he shares with all beings: the inclination to preserve and develop his own existence. In

---

50. Cf. St. Thomas Aquinas, *Summa theologiae*, Ia-IIae, q. 94, a. 2.
51. Cf. ibid., Ia-IIae, q. 94, a. 6.

living beings there is habitually a spontaneous reaction to an imminent danger of death: one flees it, one defends the integrity of one's own existence, one struggles to survive. Physical life appears naturally as the fundamental, essential, primordial good, from which comes the precept to protect one's own life. Within this category of the preservation of life are included the inclinations to everything that contributes, in a way proper to the human person, to the maintenance and quality of biological life: bodily integrity; the use of external goods necessary for the sustenance and the integrity of life, such as food, clothing, housing, work; the quality of the biological environment ... Taking his bearings from these inclinations, the human being formulates for himself goals to be realized that contribute to the harmonious and responsible development of his own being and which, as such, appear to him as moral goods, values to pursue, duties to accomplish and indeed as rights to assert. In fact, the duty to preserve one's own life has as its correlative the right to demand that which is necessary for one's preservation in a favourable environment.[52]

49. The second inclination, which is common to all living beings, concerns the survival of the species that is realized by procreation. Reproduction is included in the prolongation of the tendency to persevere in being. If the perpetuity of biological existence is impossible for the individual himself, it is possible for the species and, thus, in a certain measure, overcomes the limits inherent in every physical being. The good of the species appears in this way as one of the fundamental aspirations present in the person. We become particularly aware of it in our time, when certain issues such as global warming revive our sense of responsibility for the planet, as well as for the human species in particular. This openness to a certain common good of the species is already an assertion of certain aspirations proper to the human person. The dynamism towards procreation is intrinsically linked to the natural inclination that leads man to woman and woman to man, a universal datum recognized in all societies. It is the same for the inclination to care for one's children and to educate them. These inclinations imply that the permanence of the union of man and woman, indeed even their mutual fidelity, are already values to pursue, even if they can only fully flourish in the spiritual order of interpersonal communion.[53]

50. The third set of inclinations is specific to the human being as a spiritual being, endowed with reason, capable of knowing the truth, of entering into dialogue

---

52. Cf. *Universal Declaration of Human Rights*, articles 3, 5, 17, 22.
53. Cf. ibid., article 16.

with others and of forming relations of friendship. Therefore, this third level is particularly important. The inclination to live in society derives first of all from the fact that the human being has need of others to overcome his own intrinsic individual limits and to achieve maturity in the various spheres of his existence. But for his spiritual nature to fully flourish, a person has the need to form relations of generous friendship with his fellow human beings and to develop intense cooperation in the search for the truth. His integral good is so intimately linked to life in community that he enters into political society by virtue of a natural inclination and not by mere convention.[54] The relational character of the person also expresses itself by the tendency to live in communion with God or the absolute. It manifests itself in religious sentiment and in the desire to know God. Certainly, it can be denied by those who refuse to admit the existence of a personal God, but it remains implicitly present in the search for truth and meaning, experienced by every human being.

51. Corresponding to these tendencies that are specific to the human person, there is the need, recognized by reason, to realize concretely this life in relationship and to construct life in society on just foundations that correspond to the norm of natural justice. This entails the recognition of the equal dignity of every individual of the human species, beyond the differences of race and culture, and a great respect for humanity wherever it is found, including that of the smallest and in the most despised of its members. "Do not do to another that which you would not want done to you." Here we encounter the golden rule, which today is posited as the very principle of a morality of reciprocity. In the first chapter of this text, we were able to find the presence of this rule in the greater parts of the wisdom traditions, as well as in the Gospel itself. It is in referring to a negative formulation of the golden rule that St. Jerome manifested the universality of several moral precepts. "That is why the judgment of God is just, who writes in the heart of the human race: 'That which you do not want done to you, do not do to another.' Who does not know that homicide, adultery, theft and every kind of greed are evil, since one does not want them done to oneself? If a person did not know that these things were bad, he would never complain when they are inflicted on him."[55] To the golden rule are linked several commandments of the Decalogue, as are numerous Buddhist precepts, and, indeed, some Confucian rules, and also the greater

54. Cf. Aristotle, *Politics*, I, 2 (1253 a 2-3); Vatican Council II, Pastoral Constitution *Gaudium et spes*, n. 12, § 4.
55. St. Jerome, *Epistola* 121, 8 (PL 22, col. 1025).

part of the orientations of the great Charters that enumerate the rights of the person.

52. After this brief exposition of the moral principles that derive from reason's consideration of the fundamental inclinations of the human person, we find a set of precepts and values that, at least in their general formulation, can be considered as universal, since they apply to all humanity. They also take on the character of immutability to the extent that they derive from a human nature whose essential components remain the same throughout history. It can still happen that they are obscured or even erased from the human heart because of sin and because of cultural and historical conditioning, which can negatively affect the personal moral life: ideologies and insidious propaganda, generalized relativism, structures of sin.[56] We must therefore be modest and prudent when invoking the "obviousness" of natural law precepts. But this does not mean that we cannot recognize in these precepts the common foundation for a dialogue in search of a universal ethic. Those undertaking such a dialogue, however, must learn to distance themselves from their own particular interests, in order to be open to the needs of others, and to allow themselves to be summoned by the common moral values. In a pluralistic society, where it is difficult to agree on philosophical foundations, such a dialogue is absolutely necessary. The doctrine of natural law can make its contribution to such a dialogue.

2.5. The application of the common precepts: historicity of the natural law

53. It is impossible to remain at the level of generality, which is that of the first principles of the natural law. In fact, moral reflection must descend into the

---

56. Cf. St. Thomas Aquinas, *Summa theologiae,* Ia-IIae, q. 94, a. 6: "But as regards the other secondary precepts, the natural law can be destroyed from men's hearts, either on account of evil persuasions — just as also in speculative matters errors may arise concerning necessary conclusions — or on account of depraved customs and corrupt habits, as some men did not consider stealing a sin, or even the vices against nature, as the Apostle says in Rom 1:24." ("Quantum vero ad alia praecepta secundaria, potest lex naturalis deleri de cordibus hominum, vel propter malas persuasiones, eo modo quo etiam in speculativis errores contingunt circa conclusiones necessarias; vel etiam propter pravas consuetudines et habitus corruptos; sicut apud quosdam non reputabantur latrocinia peccata, vel etiam vitia contra naturam, ut etiam apostolus dicit, ad Rom 1.")

concreteness of action to throw its light on it. But the more it faces concrete and contingent situations, the more its conclusions are affected by a note of variability and uncertainty. It is not surprising, therefore, that the concrete application of the precepts of the natural law can take different forms in different cultures, or even in different epochs within a single culture. It is sufficient to recall the evolution of moral reflection on questions such as slavery, lending at interest, duelling or the death penalty. Sometimes such evolution leads to a better comprehension of moral requirements. Sometimes, in addition, the evolution of the political or economic situation leads to a re-evaluation of particular norms that had been established before. Morality, in fact, deals with contingent realities that evolve over time. Although he lived in the epoch of Christendom, a theologian such as St. Thomas Aquinas had a very clear perception of this. Practical reason, he wrote in the *Summa theologiae,* "deals with contingent realities, about which human actions are concerned. Therefore, although there is some necessity in the general principles, the more we descend to particular matters, the more we encounter indeterminacy.... In matters of action, truth or practical rectitude is not the same for all in its particular applications, but only in its general principles: and where there is the same rectitude in particular actions, it is not equally known to all.... And here, the more one descends to particulars the more the indeterminacy grows."[57]

54. This perspective gives an account of the historicity of natural law, whose concrete applications can vary over time. At the same time, it opens the door to the reflection of moralists, inviting them to dialogue and to discussion. This is all the more necessary because in morality pure deduction by syllogism is not adequate. The more the moralist confronts concrete situations, the more he must have recourse to the wisdom of experience, an experience that integrates the contributions of the other sciences and is nourished by contact with men and women engaged in the action. Only this wisdom of experience enables one to consider the multiplicity of circumstances and to arrive at a position on how to accomplish what is good *hic et nunc.* The moralist must also (and this is the difficulty of his work) have recourse to the combined resources

---

57. St. Thomas Aquinas, *Summa theologiae,* Ia-IIae, q. 94, a. 4: ("Ratio practica negotiatur circa contingentia, in quibus sunt operationes humanae, et ideo, etsi in communibus sit aliqua necessitas, quanto magis ad propria descenditur, tanto magis invenitur defectus. [...] In operativis autem non est eadem veritas vel rectitudo practica apud omnes quantum al propria, sed solum quantum ad communia, et apud illos apud quod est eadem rectitudo in propriis, non est aequaliter omnibus nota. [...] Et hoc tanto magis invenitur deficere, quanto magis ad particularia descenditur.")

of theology, of philosophy, as well as of the human, economic and biological sciences, in order to discern clearly the given facts of the situation and to identify correctly the concrete requirements of human dignity. At the same time, he must be particularly attentive to safeguard the fundamental givens expressed by the precepts of the natural law that remain valid despite cultural variations.

2.6. The moral dispositions of the person and his concrete action

55. To reach a just evaluation of the things to be done, the moral subject must be endowed with a certain number of interior dispositions that allow him both to be open to the demands of the natural law and, at the same time, informed about the givens of the concrete situation. In the context of pluralism, which is ours, one is more and more aware that one cannot elaborate a morality based on the natural law without including a reflection on the interior dispositions or virtues that render the moralist capable of elaborating an adequate norm of action. This is even more true for the subject personally engaged in action and who must formulate a judgment of conscience. It is, therefore, not surprising that one witnesses today a new blossoming of "virtue ethics" inspired by the Aristotelian tradition. Insisting in this way on the moral qualities required for adequate moral reflection, one comprehends the important role that the various cultures attribute to the figure of the wise man. He enjoys a particular capacity of discernment in the measure in which he possesses the interior moral dispositions that allow him to formulate an adequate ethical judgment. A discernment of this kind should characterize both the moralist, when he endeavours to concretize the precepts of the natural law, as well as every autonomous subject charged with making a judgment of conscience and with formulating the immediate and concrete norm for his action.

56. Morality cannot, therefore, be content with producing norms. It should also favour the formation of the subject so that, engaged in action, he may be capable of adapting the universal precepts of the natural law to the concrete conditions of existence in diverse cultural contexts. This capacity is ensured by the moral virtues, in particular by prudence that masters the particulars of a situation in order to direct concrete action. The prudent man must possess not only the knowledge of the universal but also knowledge of the particular. In order to indicate well the proper character of this virtue, St. Thomas Aquinas is not afraid to say: "If he should happen to have only one of the two kinds

of knowledge, it is preferable that it be knowledge of the particular realities that more closely affect the action."[58] With prudence it is a matter of: penetrating a contingency that always remains mysterious to reason; modelling itself on reality in as exact a manner as possible; assimilating the multiplicity of circumstances; and, taking as accurate an account as possible of a situation that is original and ineffable. Such an objective necessitates the numerous operations and abilities that prudence must put in place.

57. The subject, however, must not lose himself in the concrete and the particular, a fault for which "situation ethics" was criticized. He must discover the "right rule of acting" and establish an adequate norm of action. This right rule follows from preliminary principles. Here one thinks of the first principles of practical reason, but it also falls to the moral virtues to open and connaturalize both the will and the sensitive affectivity with regard to different human goods, and so to indicate to the prudent person the ends to be pursued in the midst of the flux of everyday events. It is only then that he will be able to formulate the concrete norm that applies and to imbue the given action with a ray of justice, of fortitude or of temperance. It would not be incorrect to speak here of the exercise of an "emotional intelligence"; the rational powers, without losing their specific character, are at work within the affective field, in such a way that the totality of the person is engaged in the moral action.

58. Prudence is indispensable to the moral subject because of the flexibility required to adapt universal moral principles to the diversity of situations. But

58. Cf St. Thomas Aquinas, *Sententia libri Ethicorum*, Lib. VI, 6 (ed. Leonine, t. XLVII, 353-354): "Prudence considers not only universals, a domain in which there is no action, but must also know singulars, since it is active, i.e., a principle of acting. Action, however, regards singulars. Hence some who do not have knowledge of universals are more active regarding some particular things than those who have universal knowledge because they have experience of particular realities. [. . .] Therefore since prudence is active reason, the prudent man must have each kind of knowledge, namely of universals and of particulars; or if he happens to have only one, it should rather be knowledge of particulars, which are closer to operation." ("Prudentia enim non considerat solum universalia, in quibus non est actio; sed oportet quod cognoscat singularia, eo quod est activa, idest principium agendi. Actio autem est circa singularia. Et inde est, quod quidam non habentes scientiam universalium sunt magis activi circa aliqua particularia, quam illi qui habent universalem scientiam, eo quod sunt in aliis particularibus experti. [. . .] Quia igitur prudentia est ratio activa, oportet quod prudens habeat utramque notitiam, scilicet et universalium et particularium; vel, si alteram solum contingat ipsum habere, magis debet habere hanc, scilicet notitiam particularium quae sunt propinquiora operationi.")

this flexibility does not authorize one to see prudence as a way of easy compromise with regard to moral values. On the contrary, it is through the decisions of prudence that the concrete requirements of moral truth are expressed for a subject. Prudence is a necessary element in the exercise of one's authentic moral obligation.

59. This is an approach which, within a pluralist society like our own, takes on an importance that cannot be underestimated without considerable harm. Indeed, it takes account of the fact that moral science cannot furnish an acting subject with a norm to be applied adequately and almost automatically to concrete situations; only the conscience of the subject, the judgment of his practical reason, can formulate the immediate norm of action. But at the same time, this approach does not abandon conscience to mere subjectivity: it aims at having the subject acquire the intellectual and affective dispositions which allow him to be open to moral truth, so that his judgment may be adequate. Natural law could not, therefore, be presented as an already established set of rules that impose themselves *a priori* on the moral subject; rather, it is a source of objective inspiration for the deeply personal process of making a decision.

Chapter 3: The Theoretical Foundations of the Natural Law

3.1. From experience to theory

60. The spontaneous grasp of fundamental ethical values, which are expressed in the precepts of the natural law, constitutes the point of departure of the process that then leads the moral subject to the judgment of conscience, in which he formulates the moral requirements that impose themselves on him in his concrete situation. It is the task of the theologian and of the philosopher to reflect on this experience of grasping the first principles of ethics, in order to test its value and base it on reason. The recognition of these philosophical or theological foundations does not, however, condition the spontaneous adherence to common values. In fact, the moral subject can put into practice the orientations of natural law without being capable — by reason of his particular intellectual formation — of explicitly discerning their ultimate theoretical foundations.

61. The philosophical justification of natural law presents two levels of coherence and depth. The idea of a natural law is justified first of all on the level of the reflective observation of the anthropological constants that characterize a successful humanization of the person and a harmonious social life. Thoughtful experience, conveyed by the wisdom traditions, by philosophies or by human sciences, allows us to determine some of the conditions required so that each one may best display his human capacities in his personal and communal life.[59]

59. For example, experimental psychology emphasizes the importance of the active presence of the parents of both sexes for the harmonious development of the child's personality,

In this way, certain behaviours are recognized as expressing an exemplary excellence in the manner of living and of realizing one's humanity. They define the main lines of a properly moral ideal of a virtuous life "according to nature," that is to say, in conformity with the profound nature of the human subject.[60]

62. Nevertheless, only the recognition of the metaphysical dimension of the real can give to natural law its full and complete philosophical justification. In fact metaphysics allows for understanding that the universe does not have in itself its own ultimate reason for being, and manifests the fundamental structure of the real: the distinction between God, subsistent being himself, and the other beings placed by him in existence. God is the Creator, the free and transcendent source of all other beings. From him, these beings receive, "with measure, number and weight" (Wis 11:20), existence according to a nature that defines them. Creatures are therefore the epiphany of a personal creative wisdom, of an originating Logos who expresses and manifests himself in them. "Every creature is a divine word, because it speaks of God," writes St. Bonaventure.[61]

63. The Creator is not only the principle of creatures but also the transcendent end towards which they tend by nature. Thus creatures are animated by a dynamism that carries them to fulfil themselves, each in its own way, in the union with God. This dynamism is transcendent, to the extent to which it proceeds from the eternal law, i.e., from the plan of divine providence that exists in the mind of the Creator.[62] But it is also immanent, because it is not

---

and the decisive role of paternal authority for the construction of the child's identity. Political history suggests that the participation of all in decisions that regard the totality of the community is generally a factor of social peace and political stability.

60. At this first level, the expression of the natural law sometimes abstracts from an explicit reference to God. Certainly the openness to transcendence is part of the virtuous behaviour that one rightly expects from a fully developed human being, but God is not yet necessarily recognized as the foundation and the source of the natural law, nor as the last end that mobilizes and arranges in a hierarchy the different kinds of virtuous behaviour. This lack of an explicit recognition of God as the ultimate moral norm seems to prevent the "empirical" approach to the natural law from being constituted as properly moral doctrine.

61. St. Bonaventure, *Commentarius in Ecclesiasten*, cap. 1 (*Opera omnia*, VI, ed. Quaracchi, 1893, p. 16): "Verbum divinum est omnis creatura, quia Deum loquitur."

62. Cf. St. Thomas Aquinas, *Summa theologiae*, Ia-IIae, q. 91, a. 1: "Law is nothing other than a certain dictate of practical reason in the leader who governs some perfect community. Now it is evident, supposing that the world is ruled by divine providence, [. . .] that the whole community of the universe is governed by the divine reason. Hence the very idea [. . .] of the governing of things in God the ruler of the universe, has the aspect of law. And since the divine reason's conception of things is not subject to time, but is eternal [. . .] therefore it is necessary

imposed on creatures from without, but is inscribed in their very nature. Purely material creatures realize spontaneously the law of their being, while spiritual creatures realize it in a personal manner. In fact, they interiorize the dynamisms that define them and freely orient them towards their own complete realization. They formulate them to themselves, as fundamental norms of their moral action — this is the natural law properly stated — and they strive to realize them freely. The natural law is therefore defined as a participation in the eternal law.[63] It is mediated, on the one hand, by the inclinations of nature, expressions of the creative wisdom, and, on the other hand, by the light of human reason which interprets them and is itself a created participation in the light of the divine intelligence. Ethics is thus presented as a "participated theonomy."[64]

3.2. Nature, person and freedom

64. The notion of nature is particularly complex and is not at all univocal. In philosophy, the Greek thought of *physis* enjoys a role as a matrix. In it, nature refers to the principle of the specific ontological identity of a subject, i.e., its essence which is defined by an ensemble of stable, intelligible characteristics. This essence takes the name of nature above all when it is envisaged as the internal principle of movement that orients the subject towards its fulfilment. Far from referring to a static given, the notion of nature signifies the real dynamic principle of the homogeneous development of the subject and of its specific activities. The notion of nature was formed at first to think about material and perceptible realities, but it is not limited to this "physical" domain and it applies analogically to spiritual realities.

65. The idea that beings possess a nature is convincing as an explanation of the immanent finality of beings and of the regularity that is perceived in their way

---

to call this kind of law eternal." ("Nihil est aliud lex quam quoddam dictamen practicae rationis in principe qui gubernat aliquam communitatem perfectam. Manifestum est autem, supposito quod mundus divina providentia regatur [. . .], quod tota communitas universi gubernatur ratione divina. Et ideo ipsa ratio gubernationis rerum in Deo sicut in principe universitatis existens, legis habet rationem. Et quia divina ratio nihil concipit ex tempore, sed habet aeternum conceptum [. . .]; inde est quod huiusmodi legem oportet dicere aeternam.")

63. Cf. ibid., Ia-IIae, q. 91, a. 2: "Unde patet quod lex naturalis nihil aliud est quam participatio legis aeternae in rationali creatura."

64. John Paul II, Encyclical *Veritatis splendor*, n. 41.

of acting and reacting.[65] To consider beings as natures, therefore, amounts to recognizing in them a proper consistency and affirming that they are relatively autonomous centres in the order of being and of acting, and not simply illusions or temporary constructions of the consciousness. These "natures" are, however, not closed ontological unities, locked in themselves and simply placed one alongside the other. They act upon each other, and have complex relations of causality among themselves. In the spiritual order, persons weave intersubjective relations. Natures therefore form a network, and in the last analysis, an order, i.e., a series unified by reference to a principle.[66]

66. With Christianity, the *physis* of the ancients is rethought and integrated into a broader and more profound vision of reality. On the one hand, the God of Christian revelation is not a simple component of the universe, an element of the great All of nature. On the contrary, he is the transcendent and free Creator of the universe. In fact the finite universe cannot be its own foundation, but points to the mystery of an infinite God, who out of pure love created it *ex nihilo* and remains free to intervene in the course of nature whenever he wills. On the other hand, the transcendent mystery of God is reflected in the mystery of the human person as an image of God. The human person is capable of knowledge and of love; he is endowed with freedom, capable of entering into communion with others and called by God to a destiny that transcends the finalities of physical nature. He fulfils himself in a free and gratuitous relationship of love with God that is realized in a history.

67. By its insistence on freedom as the condition of man's response to the initiative of God's love, Christianity has contributed in a decisive way towards giving the notion of person its rightful place in philosophical discourse, in a manner which has had a decisive influence on ethical teachings. Moreover,

65. Does not the theory of evolution, which tends to reduce species to a precarious and provisory equilibrium in the flux of becoming, put radically into question the very concept of nature? In fact, whatever its value on the level of empirical biological description, the notion of species responds to a permanent requirement of the philosophical explanation of living beings. Only recourse to a formal specificity, irreducible to the sum of the material properties, allows one to give an account of the intelligibility of the internal functioning of a living organism considered as a coherent whole.

66. The theological doctrine of original sin strongly underlines the real unity of human nature. This cannot be reduced to a simple abstraction, nor to a sum of individual realities. It indicates rather a totality that embraces all human beings who share the same destiny. The simple fact of being born (*nasci*) puts us in enduring relations of solidarity with all other human beings.

the theological exploration of the Christian mystery has led to a very significant deepening of the philosophical theme of the person. On the one hand, the notion of person serves to designate, in their distinction, the Father, the Son, and the Spirit, within the infinite mystery of the one divine nature. On the other hand, the person is the point in which, with respect to the distinction and distance between the two natures, divine and human, the ontological unity of the God-man, Jesus Christ, is established. In the Christian theological tradition, the person presents two complementary aspects. On the one hand, according to the definition of Boethius, taken up again by scholastic theology, the person is an "individual substance (subsistent) of a rational nature."[67] It refers to the uniqueness of an ontological subject who, being of a spiritual nature, enjoys a dignity and an autonomy that is manifested in self- consciousness and in free dominion over his actions. Furthermore, the person is manifested in his capacity to enter into relation: he displays his action in the order of intersubjectivity and of communion in love.

68. Person is not opposed to nature. On the contrary, nature and person are two notions that complement one another. On the one hand, every human person is a unique realization of human nature understood in a metaphysical sense. On the other hand, the human person, in the free choices by which he responds in the concrete of his "here and now" to his unique and transcendent vocation, assumes the orientations given by his nature. In fact, nature puts in place the conditions for the exercise of freedom and indicates an orientation for the choices that the person must make. Examining the intelligibility of his nature, the person thus discovers the ways of his own fulfilment.

3.3. Nature, man and God: from harmony to conflict

69. The concept of natural law presupposes the idea that nature is for man the bearer of an ethical message and is an implicit moral norm that human reason actualizes. The vision of the world within which the doctrine of natural law developed and still finds its meaning today, implies therefore the reasoned conviction that there exists a harmony among the three realities: God, man, and nature. In this perspective, the world is perceived as an intelligible whole,

---

67. Boethius, *Contra Eutychen et Nestorium*, c. 3 (PL 64, col. 1344): "Persona est rationalis naturae individua substantia." Cf. St. Bonaventure, *Commentaria in librum I Sententiarum*, d. 25, a. 1, q. 2; St. Thomas Aquinas, *Summa theologiae*, Ia, q. 29, a. 1.

unified by the common reference of the beings that compose it to a divine originating principle, to a *Logos*. Beyond the impersonal and immanent *Logos* discovered by stoicism and presupposed by the modern sciences of nature, Christianity affirms that there is a *Logos* who is personal, transcendent and creator. "It is not the elements of the universe, the laws of matter, which ultimately govern the world and mankind, but a personal God who governs the stars, that is, the universe; it is not the laws of matter and of evolution that have the final say, but reason, will, love — a Person."[68] The personal divine *Logos*, the Wisdom and Word of God, is not only the origin and transcendent, intelligible exemplar of the universe, but also the one who maintains it in a harmonious unity and leads it to its end.[69] By the dynamisms that the creator Word has inscribed in the innermost part of beings, he orients them to their full realization. This dynamic orientation is none other than the divine government that realizes within time the plan of divine providence, i.e., the eternal law.

70. Every creature, in its own manner, participates in the *Logos*. Man, since he is defined by reason or *logos,* participates in it in an eminent manner. In fact, by his reason, he is capable of freely interiorizing the divine intentions manifested in the nature of things. He formulates them for himself under the form of a moral law that inspires and orients his action. In this perspective, man is not "the other" in relation to nature. On the contrary, he maintains with the cosmos a bond of familiarity founded on a common participation in the divine *Logos.*

71. For various historical and cultural reasons, which are linked in particular to the evolution of ideas during the late Middle Ages, this vision of the world has lost its cultural supremacy. The nature of things ceased being law for modern man and is no longer a reference point for ethics. On the metaphysical level, the change from thinking about the univocity of being to thinking about the analogy of being, which was then followed by nominalism, have undermined the foundations of the doctrine of creation as a participation in the

---

68. Benedict XVI, Encyclical *Spe salvi,* n. 5.

69. Cf. also St. Athanasius of Alexandria, *Traité contre les paiens,* 42 (*Sources chrétiennes,* 18, p. 195): "As a musician who has just tuned his lyre, puts together by his art the low notes with the high notes, the middle notes with the others, in order to execute a single melody, so the Wisdom of God, the Word, holding the whole universe like a lyre, unites the beings of the air with those of the earth, the beings of heaven with those of the air; combines the whole with the parts; leads all by his command and his will; thus he produces, in beauty and harmony, a single world and a single order of the world."

Logos, a doctrine that gives an explanation of a certain unity between man and nature. The nominalist universe of William of Ockham is thus reduced to a juxtaposition of individual realities without depth, since every real universal, i.e., every principle of communion among beings, is denounced as a linguistic illusion. On the anthropological level, the development of voluntarism and the correlative exaltation of subjectivity, defined by the freedom of indifference with respect to every natural inclination, have created a gulf between the human subject and nature. From that point on, some people deemed that human freedom is essentially the power to count as nothing what man is by nature. The subject should therefore not attribute any meaning to that which he has not personally chosen and should decide for himself what it is to be a human being. Man, therefore, comes to understand himself more and more as a "denatured animal," an anti-natural being who affirms himself to the extent to which he opposes himself to nature. Culture, proper to man, is then defined not as a humanization or a transfiguration of nature by the spirit, but as a pure and simple negation of nature. The principal result of these developments has been the split of the real into three separate, indeed opposed spheres: nature, human subjectivity, and God.

72. With the eclipse of the metaphysics of being, which alone is able to give the foundation of reason to the differentiated unity of spirit and of material reality, and with the rise of voluntarism, the realm of spirit has been radically opposed to the realm of nature. Nature is no longer considered as an epiphany of the *Logos,* but as "the other" of the spirit. It is reduced to the sphere of corporality and of strict necessity, and of a corporality without depth, since the world of bodies is identified with extension, certainly regulated by intelligible mathematical laws, but stripped of every immanent teleology or finality. Cartesian physics, then Newtonian physics, have spread the image of an inert matter, which passively obeys the laws of universal determinism that the Divine Spirit imposes on it and which human reason can perfectly know and master.[70] Only man can infuse sense and design into this amorphous and meaningless mass that he manipulates for his own ends with technical skill. Nature ceases being a teacher of life and of wisdom, in order to become the place where the Promethean power of man is asserted. This vision seems to

---

70. The *physis* of the ancients, taking note of the existence of a certain non-being (matter), preserved the contingency of earthly realities and put up a resistance to the pretensions of human reason to impose on the totality of reality a purely rational deterministic order. Thus, it left open the possibility of an effective action of human freedom in the world.

place great value on human freedom, but, in fact, by opposing freedom and nature, it deprives human freedom of every objective norm for its exercise. It leads to the idea of an entirely arbitrary human creation of values, indeed to nihilism, pure and simple.

73. In this context, in which nature no longer contains any immanent teleological rationality and seems to have lost all affinity or kinship with the world of spirit, the passage from knowledge of the structures of being to moral duty which seems to derive from it becomes effectively impossible and falls under the criticism of "naturalistic fallacy" denounced by David Hume and then by George Edward Moore in his *Principia Ethica* (1903). The good is actually disconnected from being and from truth. Ethics is separated from metaphysics.

74. The evolution of the understanding of the relationship of man to nature also finds expression in the resurgence of a radical anthropological dualism that opposes spirit and body, since the body is in some way the "nature" in each of us.[71] This dualism is manifested in the refusal to recognize any human and ethical meaning in the natural inclinations that precede the choices of the individual reason. The body, judged a reality external to subjectivity, becomes a pure "having" or "possession," an object manipulated by technical skill according to the interests of the individual subjectivity.[72]

71. Cf. John Paul II, *Letter to Families*, n. 19: "The philosopher who enunciated the principle of 'Cogito, ergo sum,' 'I think, therefore I am,' also impressed on the modern concept of man its distinctive dualistic character. It is the distinctive feature of rationalism to draw a radical opposition in man between spirit and body, and between body and spirit. On the contrary, man is a person in the unity of his body and his spirit. The body can never be reduced to mere matter: it is a spiritualized body, just as man's spirit is so closely united to the body that he can be described as an embodied spirit."

72. The ideology of *gender*, which denies all anthropological or moral significance to the natural difference of the sexes, is inscribed in this dualistic perspective. Cf. Congregation for the Doctrine of the Faith, *Letter to the Bishops of the Catholic Church on the Collaboration of Men and Women in the Church and in the World*, n. 2: "In order to avoid the domination of one sex or the other, their differences tend to be denied, viewed as mere effects of historical and cultural conditioning. In this leveling, physical difference, termed sex, is minimized, while the purely cultural element, termed gender, is emphasized to the maximum and held to be primary. [. . .] While the immediate roots of this second tendency are found in the context of the question of woman, its deeper motivation must be sought in the attempt of the human person to be freed from one's biological conditioning. According to this anthropological perspective, human nature itself does not possess characteristics that impose themselves in an absolute manner: all persons can and ought to constitute themselves as they like, since they are free from every predetermination linked to their essential constitution."

75. Furthermore, on account of the emergence of a metaphysical conception in which human and divine action are in competition with each another — since they are conceived in a univocal fashion and placed, wrongly, on the same level — the legitimate affirmation of the autonomy of the human subject leads to the exclusion of God from the sphere of human subjectivity. Every reference to something normative coming from God or from nature as an expression of God's wisdom, that is to say, every "heteronomy," is perceived as a threat to the subject's autonomy. The notion of natural law thus appears as incompatible with the authentic dignity of the subject.

3.4. Ways towards a reconciliation

76. To give the notion of the natural law all its meaning and strength as the foundation of a universal ethic, a perspective of wisdom needs to be promoted, belonging properly to the metaphysical order, and capable of simultaneously including God, the cosmos and the human person, in order to reconcile them in the analogical unity of being, thanks to the idea of creation as participation.

77. It is above all essential to develop a non-competitive conception of the connection between divine causality and the free activity of the human subject. The human subject achieves fulfilment by inserting himself freely into the providential action of God and not by opposing himself to this action. It is his prerogative to discover with his reason the profound dynamisms that define his nature, and then to accept and direct these dynamisms freely to their fulfilment. In fact, human nature is defined by an entire ensemble of dynamisms, tendencies and internal orientations within which freedom arises. Freedom actually presupposes that the human will is "activated" by the natural desire for the good and for the last end. Free will is exercised then in the choice of the finite objects that allow the attainment of this end. As regards these goods, which exercise an attraction that does not determine the will, the person retains mastery of his choice by reason of an innate openness to the absolute Good. Freedom is therefore not an absolute creator of itself, but is rather an eminent property of every human subject.

78. A philosophy of nature, which takes note of the intelligible depth of the sensible world, and especially a metaphysics of creation, allow then for the surmounting of the dualistic and Gnostic temptation of abandoning nature to

moral insignificance. From this point of view, it is important to go beyond the reductionist perspective on nature which is inculcated by the dominant technical culture, in order to rediscover the moral message borne in nature, as a work of the *Logos*.

79. The rehabilitation of nature and of corporality in ethics, however, could not be the equivalent of any kind of "physicalism." In fact, some modern presentations of natural law have seriously failed to recognize the necessary integration of natural inclinations into the unity of the person. Neglecting to consider the unity of the human person, they absolutize the natural inclinations of the different "parts" of human nature, juxtaposing these inclinations without placing them in a hierarchy and omitting to integrate them into the unity of the overall, personal plan of the subject. As John Paul II explains, "natural inclinations take on moral relevance only insofar as they refer to the human person and to his authentic fulfilment."[73] Today, therefore, it is important to hold fast to two things simultaneously. On the one hand, the human subject is not a collection or juxtaposition of diverse and autonomous natural inclinations, but a substantial and personal whole, who has the vocation to respond to the love of God and to unify himself by accepting his orientation towards a last end that places in hierarchical order the partial goods manifested by the various natural tendencies. This unification of natural tendencies in accordance with the higher ends of the spirit, i.e., this humanization of the dynamisms inscribed in human nature, does not in any way represent a violence done to them. On the contrary, it is the fulfilment of a promise already inscribed in them.[74] For example, the high spiritual value that the gift of self in mutual spousal love represents is already inscribed in the very nature of the sexual body, which finds its ultimate reason for being in this spiritual fulfilment. On the other hand, in this organic whole, each part preserves a proper and irreducible meaning, which must be taken into account by reason in the elaboration of the overall mission of the human person. The doctrine of the natural moral law must, therefore, maintain at the same time both the central

73. John Paul II, Encyclical *Veritatis splendor,* n. 50.

74. The duty to humanize the nature in man is inseparable from the duty to humanize external nature. This morally justifies the immense effort of human beings to emancipate themselves from the constraints of physical nature to the degree to which these hinder the development of properly human values. The struggle against disease, the prevention of hostile natural phenomena, the improvement of living conditions are in themselves works that attest to the greatness of man called to fill the earth and to subdue it (cf. Gen 1:28). Cf. Pastoral Constitution *Gaudium et spes,* n. 57.

role of reason in the actualization of a properly human plan of life, and the consistency and the proper meaning of pre-rational natural dynamisms.[75]

80. The moral significance of the pre-rational natural dynamisms appears in full light in the teaching concerning sins against nature. Certainly, every sin is against nature insofar as it is opposed to right reason and hinders the authentic development of the human person. However, some behaviours are described in a special way as sins against nature to the extent that they contradict more directly the objective meaning of the natural dynamisms that the person must take up into the unity of his moral life.[76] So, deliberately chosen suicide goes against the natural inclination to preserve and make fruitful one's own existence. Thus some sexual practices are directly opposed to the reproductive finalities inscribed in the sexual body of man. By this very fact, they also contradict the interpersonal values that a responsible and fully human sexual life must promote.

81. The risk of absolutizing nature, reduced to its purely physical or biological component, and of neglecting its intrinsic vocation to be integrated into a spiritual project, is a threat in some radical tendencies of the ecological movement today. The irresponsible exploitation of nature by human agents who seek only economic profit and the dangers that this exploitation poses to the biosphere rightly cry out to consciences. However, *"deep ecology"* represents an excessive reaction. It extols a supposed equality of living species, to the point that it no longer recognizes any particular role for man, paradoxically undermining the responsibility of man for the biosphere of which he is a part. In a still more radical manner, some have come to consider man as a destructive virus that would supposedly strike a blow at the integrity of nature, and they refuse him any meaning and value in the biosphere. And so one arrives

75. Reacting to the danger of physicalism and rightly insisting on the decisive role of reason in the elaboration of the natural law, some contemporary theories of natural law neglect, indeed reject, the moral significance of the pre-rational natural dynamisms. The natural law would be called "natural" only in reference to reason, which would define the whole nature of man. To obey the natural law would therefore be reduced to acting in a rational manner, i.e., to applying to the totality of behaviours a univocal ideal of rationality generated by practical reason alone. This amounts to wrongly identifying the rationality of the natural law with the rationality of human reason alone, without taking into account the rationality immanent in nature.

76. Cf. St. Thomas Aquinas, *Summa theologiae*, IIa-IIae, q. 154, a. 11. The moral evaluation of sins against nature should take into account not only their objective gravity but also the subjective dispositions — often attenuating — of those who commit them.

at a new type of totalitarianism that excludes human existence in its specificity and condemns legitimate human progress.

82. There cannot be an adequate response to the complex questions of ecology except within the framework of a deeper understanding of the natural law, which places value on the connection between the human person, society, culture, and the equilibrium of the bio-physical sphere in which the human person is incarnate. An integral ecology must promote what is specifically human, all the while valuing the world of nature in its physical and biological integrity. In fact, even if man, as a moral being who searches for the ultimate truth and the ultimate good, transcends his own immediate environment, he does so by accepting the special mission of keeping watch over the natural world, living in harmony with it, and defending vital values without which neither human life nor the biosphere of this planet can be maintained.[77] This integral ecology summons every human being and every community to a new responsibility. It is inseparable from a global political orientation respectful of the requirements of the natural law.

77. Cf. Gen 2:15.

Chapter 4: Natural Law and the City [πόλις]

4.1. The person and the common good

83. Turning to the political order of society, we enter into the space regulated by norms or laws. In fact, such norms appear from the moment in which persons enter in relation. The passage from person to society sheds light on the essential distinction between natural law and the norm of natural justice.

84. The person is at the centre of the political and social order because he is an end and not a means. The person is a social being by nature, not by choice or in virtue of a pure contractual convention. In order to flourish as a person, he needs the structure of relations that he forms with other persons. He thus finds himself at the centre of a network formed by concentric circles: the family, the sphere of life and work, the neighbourhood community, the nation, and finally humanity.[78] The person draws from each of these circles the elements necessary for his own growth, and at the same time he contributes to their perfection.

85. By the fact that human beings have the vocation to live in society with others, they have in common an ensemble of goods to pursue and values to

---

78. Cf. Vatican Council II, Pastoral Constitution *Gaudium et spes*, n. 73-74. *The Catechism of the Catholic Church*, n. 1882, clarifies that "certain societies, such as the family and the civic community, correspond more immediately to the nature of man."

defend. This is what is called the "common good." If the person is an end in himself, the end of society is to promote, consolidate and develop its common good. The search for the common good allows the city to mobilize the energies of all its members. At a first level, the common good can be understood as the ensemble of conditions that allow a person to be a more human person.[79] While being articulated in its external aspects — the economy, security, social justice, education, access to employment, spiritual searching, and other things — the common good is always a human good.[80] At a second level, the common good is that which assigns an end to the political order and to the city itself. The good of all and of each one in particular, it expresses the communal dimension of the human good. Societies can be defined by the type of common good that they intend to promote. In fact, if it concerns the essential requirements of the common good of every society, the vision of the common good evolves with the societies themselves, according to conceptions of the person, justice, and the role of public power.

4.2. The natural law, measure of the political order

86. The organization of society in view of the common good of its members responds to the requirements of the social nature of the person. The natural law then appears as the normative horizon in which the political order is called to move. It defines the ensemble of values that appear as humanizing for a society. As soon as we are in the social and political sphere, values can no longer be of a private, ideological or confessional nature: they concern all citizens. They do not express a vague consensus among citizens, but instead are based on the requirements of their common humanity. So that society may correctly fulfil its own mission of serving the person, it must promote the realization of the person's natural inclinations. The person is therefore prior to society, and society is humanizing only if it responds to the expectations inscribed in the person insofar as he is a social being.

87. This natural order of society at the service of the person is indicated, according to the social doctrine of the Church, by four values that follow from the natural inclinations of the human being and which delineate the contours

---

79. Cf. John XXIII, Encyclical *Mater et magistra*, n. 65; Vatican Council II, Pastoral Constitution *Gaudium et spes*, n. 26 § 1; Declaration *Dignitatis humanae*, n. 6.
80. Cf. John XXIII, Encyclical *Pacem in terris*, n. 55.

of the common good that society must pursue, namely: freedom, truth, justice, and solidarity.[81] These four values correspond to the requirements of an ethical order in conformity with the natural law. If one of these is lacking, the city will tend towards anarchy or the rule of the strongest. Freedom is the first condition of a humanly acceptable political order. Without the liberty to follow one's conscience, express one's own opinions and pursue one's own plans, there is no human city, even if the pursuit of private goods must always be related to the promotion of the common good of the city. Without the search and respect for truth, there is not a society but a dictatorship of the strongest. Truth, which is not the property of anyone, is alone capable of bringing all human beings together in view of pursuing common objectives. If it is not truth that imposes itself, it is the most clever who imposes "his" truth. Without justice there is no society, but the reign of violence. Justice is the highest good that the city can procure. It means that what is just is always sought, and that the law is applied with attention to the particular case, since equity is the highest part of justice. Finally, it is necessary for society to be regulated by a kind of solidarity which assures mutual assistance and responsibility for others, as well as the use of society's goods in response to the needs of all.

4.3. From natural law to the norm of natural justice

88. Natural law (*lex naturalis*) becomes the norm of natural justice (*ius naturale*) when one considers the relations of justice among human beings: relations among physical and moral persons, relations between persons and the public authority, relations of everyone with the positive law. We pass from the anthropological category of the natural law to the juridical and political category of the organization of the city. The norm of natural justice is the inherent standard of the right interaction among members of society. It is the rule and immanent measure of interpersonal and social human relations.

89. This norm is not arbitrary: the requirements of justice, which flow from the natural law, are prior to the formulation and enactment of the norm. It is not the norm which determines what is just. Nor is politics arbitrary: the norms of justice do not result only from a contract established among men, but arise first from the very nature of the human being. The norm of natural

---

81. Cf. ibid., n. 37; Pontifical Council for Justice and Peace, *Compendium of the Social Doctrine of the Church*, n. 192-203.

justice anchors human law in the natural law. It is the horizon from which the human legislator must take his bearings when he issues rules in his mission to serve the common good. In this sense, it honours the natural law, inherent in the human person's humanity. By contrast, when the norm of natural justice is denied, it is the mere will of the legislator that is the basis of law. Then, the legislator is no longer the interpreter of what is just and good, but has arrogated to himself the prerogative of being the ultimate criterion of what is just.

90. The norm of natural justice is never a standard that is fixed once and for all. It results from an appreciation of the changing situations in which people live. It articulates the judgment of practical reason in its estimation of what is just. Such a norm, as the juridical expression of the natural law in the political order, thus appears as the measure of the just relations among the members of the community.

4.4. The norm of natural justice and positive law

91. Positive law must strive to carry out the norm of natural justice. It does this either by way of conclusions (natural justice forbids homicide, positive law prohibits abortion), or by way of determination (natural justice prescribes that the guilty be punished, positive penal law determines the punishments to be applied in each category of crime).[82] Inasmuch as they truly derive from the norm of natural justice and therefore from the eternal law, positive human laws are binding in conscience. In the opposite case, they are not binding. "If the law is not just, it is not even a law."[83] Positive laws can and even must

82. Cf. St. Thomas Aquinas, *Summa theologiae,* Ia-IIae, q. 95, a. 2.

83. St. Augustine, *De libero arbitrio,* I, V, 11 (*Corpus christianorum,* series latina, 29, p. 217): "In fact a law that is not just does not seem to me to be a law"; St. Thomas Aquinas, *Summa theologiae,* Ia-IIae, q. 93, a. 3, ad 2: "Human law has the nature of law insofar as it is in accord with right reason, and in this respect it is evident that it derives from the eternal law. But insofar as it departs from reason, it is called an unjust law, and does not have the nature of law, but rather of a certain violence" ("Lex humana intantum habet rationem legis, inquantum est secundum rationem rectam, et secundum hoc manifestum est quod a lege aeterna derivatur. Inquantum vero a ratione recedit, sic dicitur lex iniqua, et sic non habet rationem legis, sed magis violentiae cuiusdam"); Ia-IIae, q. 95, a. 2: "Consequently every law made by men has just so much of the nature of law to the extent that it is derived from the natural law. But if in some matter it deflects from the natural law, then it will not be law, but a perversion of law." ("Unde omnis lex humanitus posita intantum habet de ratione legis, inquantum a lege naturae derivatur. Si vero in aliquo a lege naturali discordet, iam non erit lex sed legis corruptio.")

change to remain faithful to their purpose. In fact, on the one hand, human reason makes progress little by little, becoming more aware of what is most suitable to the good of the community, and on the other hand, the historical conditions of the life of societies change (for better or for worse) and the laws must adapt to this.[84] Thus the legislator must determine what is just in concrete historical situations.[85]

92. The norms of natural justice are thus the measures of human relationships prior to the will of the legislator. They are given from the moment that human beings live in society. They express what is naturally just, prior to any legal formulation. The norms of natural justice are expressed in a particular way in the subjective rights of the human person, such as the right to respect for one's own life, the right to the integrity of one's person, the right to religious liberty, the right to freedom of thought, the right to start a family and to educate one's children according to one's convictions, the right to associate with others, the right to participate in the life of the community, etc. These rights, to which contemporary thought attributes great importance, do not have their source in the fluctuating desires of individuals, but rather in the very structure of human beings and their humanizing relations. The rights of the human person emerge therefore from the order of justice that must reign in relations among human beings. To acknowledge these natural rights of man means to acknowledge the objective order of human relations based on the natural law.

4.5. The political order is not the eschatological order

93. In the history of human societies, the political order has often been understood as the reflection of a transcendent and divine order. Thus the ancient cosmologies provided the foundation and justification for political theologies in which the sovereign ensured the link between the cosmos and the human

---

84. Cf St. Thomas Aquinas, *Summa theologiae*, Ia-IIae, q. 97, a. 1.

85. For Saint Augustine, the legislator, to do a good work, must consult the eternal law; cf. St. Augustine, *De vera religione*, XXXI, 58 (*Corpus christianorum*, series latina, 32, p. 225): "The legislator of temporal laws, if he is a good and wise man, consults that eternal law, about which it is given to no soul to judge, so that, according to its immutable rules, he may discern what should be commanded and what should be forbidden at a given time." In a secularized society, in which everyone does not recognize the mark of this eternal law, it is the search for, the safeguarding of, and the expression of the norm of natural justice by means of positive law that guarantee its legitimacy.

universe. It was a question of bringing the universe of men into the pre-established harmony of the world. With the appearance of biblical monotheism, the universe was understood as obedient to the laws which the Creator gave it. The order of the city is achieved when the laws of God are respected, laws which moreover are inscribed in the human heart. For a long time, forms of theocracy were able to prevail in societies organized according to principles and values drawn from their holy books. There was no distinction between the sphere of religious revelation and the sphere of the organization of the city. But the Bible desacralized human authority, even if centuries of theocratic osmosis — in Christian contexts as well — obscured the essential distinction between the political order and the religious order. In this regard, one must carefully distinguish the situation of the first covenant, in which the divine law given by God was also the law of the people of Israel, from that of the new covenant, which introduces the distinction and the relative autonomy of the religious and political orders.

94. The biblical revelation invites humanity to consider that the order of creation is a universal order in which all of humanity participates, and that this order is accessible to reason. When we speak of natural law, it is a question of this order willed by God and grasped by human reason. The Bible formulates the distinction between the order of creation and the order of grace, to which faith in Christ gives access. The order of the city is not this definitive or eschatological order. The domain of politics is not that of the heavenly city, a gratuitous gift of God. It concerns the imperfect and transitory order in which human beings live, all the while advancing towards their fulfilment in what lies beyond history. According to St. Augustine, the distinctive characteristic of the earthly city is to be mixed: the just and unjust, believers and unbelievers rub shoulders together.[86] They must temporarily live together according to the requirements of their nature and the capacity of their reason.

95. The state, therefore, cannot set itself up as the bearer of ultimate meaning. It cannot impose a global ideology, nor a religion (even secular), nor one way of thinking. In civil society religious organizations, philosophies and spiritualities take charge of the domain of ultimate meaning; they must contribute to the common good, strengthen the social bond and promote the universal values that are the foundation of the political order itself. The political order

---

86. Cf St. Augustine, *De civitate dei*, I, 35 (*Corpus christianorum*, series latina, 47, pp. 34-35).

is not called to transpose onto earth the kingdom of God that is to come. It can anticipate the kingdom by advances in the area of justice, solidarity, and peace. It cannot seek to establish it by force.

4.6. The political order is a temporal and rational order

96. If the political order is not the sphere of ultimate truth, it must, nevertheless, be open to the perpetual search for God, truth, and justice. The "legitimate and sound secularity of the state"[87] consists in the distinction between the supernatural order of theological faith and the political order. This latter order can never be confused with the order of grace to which all persons are called to freely adhere. It is, rather, linked to the universal human ethics inscribed in human nature. The city must thus procure for the people who compose it what is necessary for the full realization of their human life, which includes certain spiritual and religious values, as well as freedom for the citizens to make up their mind with respect to the Absolute and the highest goods. But the city, whose common good is temporal in nature, cannot procure strictly supernatural goods, which are of another order.

97. If God and all transcendence were to be excluded from the political horizon, only the power of man over man would remain. In fact, the political order has sometimes presented itself as the ultimate horizon of meaning for humanity. Totalitarian ideologies and regimes have demonstrated that such a political order, without a transcendent horizon, is not humanly acceptable. This transcendence is linked to what we call natural law.

98. The politico-religious osmosis of the past as well as the totalitarian experiences of the twentieth century have led to a healthy reaction in which the value of reason in politics is today once again valued, thus conferring a new relevance to the Aristotelian-Thomistic discourse on natural law. Politics, that is, the organization of the city and the elaboration of its collective projects, pertains to the natural order and must undertake a rational debate open to transcendence.

99. The natural law which is the basis of the social and political order does not demand the adherence of faith, but of reason. Certainly, reason itself is often

---

87. Cf. Pius XII, *Address given on March 23, 1958* (AAS 25 [1958], p. 220).

obscured by passions, by contradictory interests, and prejudices. But constant reference to natural law presses for a continual purification of reason. Only in this way does the political order avoid the trap of the arbitrary, of particular interests, organized lying, and manipulation of minds. The reference to natural law keeps the state from yielding to the temptation to absorb civil society and to subject human beings to an ideology. It also avoids the development of the paternalistic state that deprives persons and communities of every initiative and takes responsibility away from them. Natural law contains the idea of the state, based on law, structured according to the principle of subsidiarity, respecting persons and intermediate bodies, and regulating their interactions.[88]

100. The great political myths were only able to be unmasked with the introduction of the rule of rationality and the acknowledgment of the transcendence of the God of love, who forbids the worship of the earthly political order. The God of the Bible willed the order of creation so that all people, conforming themselves to the law inherent in creation, can freely search for this order, and having found it, may project onto the world the light of grace, which is its fulfilment.

88. Cf Pius XI, Encyclical *Quadragesimo anno,* n. 79-80.

Chapter 5: Jesus Christ, the Fulfilment of the Natural Law

101. Grace does not destroy nature but heals, strengthens, and leads it to its full realization. As a consequence, while the natural law is an expression of the reason common to all human beings and can be presented in a coherent and true manner on the philosophical level, it is not foreign to the order of grace. The demands of the natural law remain present and active in the various theological stages of salvation history through which humanity passes.

102. The plan of salvation initiated by the eternal Father is realized by the mission of the Son who gives humanity the new law, the law of the Gospel, which consists principally in the grace of the Holy Spirit acting in the hearts of believers to sanctify them. The new law aims above all to procure for human beings a participation in the Trinitarian communion of the divine persons, but at the same time takes up and realizes the natural law in an eminent manner. On the one hand, the new law recalls clearly the demands of the natural law that can be obscured by sin and by ignorance. On the other hand, by emancipating us from the law of sin, on account of which "I can will what is right, but I cannot do it" (Rom 7:18), the new law gives human beings the effective capacity to overcome their self-centredness in order to put fully into action the humanizing requirements of the natural law.

5.1. The incarnate *Logos,* the living Law

103. Thanks to the natural light of reason, which is a participation in the divine light, human beings are capable of scrutinizing the intelligible order of the universe so as to discover there the expression of the wisdom, beauty and goodness of the Creator. On the basis of this knowledge, they are to enter into this order by their moral action. Now, in virtue of a deeper perspective on God's plan, of which the creative act is the prelude, Scripture teaches believers that this world has been created in, by and for the *Logos,* the Word of God, the beloved Son of the Father, uncreated Wisdom, and that the world has life and subsistence in him. In fact the Son is "the image of the invisible God, the firstborn of all creation, for in him [*en auto*] all things were created, in heaven and on earth, visible and invisible. . . . All things were created through him [*di'auton*] and for him [*eis auton*]. He is before all things, and in him [*en auto*] all things hold together" (Col 1:15-17).[89] The *Logos* is therefore the key of creation. The human person, created in the image of God, bears in himself a very special imprint of this personal *Logos.* Consequently, he has the vocation to be conformed and assimilated to the Son, "the firstborn of many brethren" (Rom 8:29).

104. But by sin man has made bad use of his freedom and has turned away from the source of wisdom. By doing so, he has distorted the perception that he was able to have of the objective order of things, even on the natural level. Human beings, knowing that their works are bad, hate the light and elaborate false theories to justify their sins.[90] Thus the image of God in man is seriously obscured. Even if their nature still refers them to a fulfilment in God beyond themselves (the creature cannot pervert himself to this point of no longer perceiving the testimony that the Creator offers of himself in creation), men, in fact, are so gravely affected by sin that they do not recognize the profound meaning of the world and interpret it in terms of pleasure, money or power.

105. By his salvific incarnation, the *Logos,* assuming a human nature, restored the image of God and gave man back to himself. Thus Jesus Christ, the new Adam, brings the original plan of the Father for humanity to fulfilment and by this very fact reveals man to himself: "In reality, only in the mystery of the Incarnate Word does the mystery of man become clear. For Adam, the first

89. Cf. also Jn 1:3-4; 1 Cor 8:6; Heb 1:2-3.
90. Cf. Jn 3:19-20; Rom 1:24-25.

man, was a figure of him who was to come, namely, Christ the Lord. Christ, the new Adam, in the very revelation of the mystery of the Father and his love, fully reveals man to man himself and makes known to him the sublimity of his vocation. . . . 'The image of the invisible God' (Col 1:15), he is the perfect man, who has restored to the sons of Adam the divine likeness deformed from the first sin onward. Because the human nature in him was assumed, not destroyed, by that very fact it has also been raised up to a sublime dignity in us too."[91] In his person Jesus Christ, therefore, manifests an exemplary human life, fully conformed to the natural law. He is thus the ultimate criterion for correctly discerning the authentic natural desires of man, when these are not concealed by the distortions introduced by sin and disordered passions.

106. The Incarnation of the Son was prepared by the economy of the old law, a sign of God's love for his people Israel. For some of the Fathers of the Church, one of the reasons why God gave Moses a written law was to remind human beings of the requirements of the law naturally written in their hearts, but which sin had partially obscured and erased.[92] This law, which Judaism iden-

---

91. Vatican II, Pastoral constitution *Gaudium et spes*, n. 22; cf. St. Irenaeus of Lyon, *Contre les hérésies*, V, 16, 2 (*Sources chrétiennes*, 153, pp. 216-217: "In times past, one properly said that man had been made in the image of God, but this did not appear, for the Word was still invisible, he in whose image man had been made: it is moreover for this reason that the likeness was easily lost. But when the Word of God became flesh, he confirmed the one and the other: he made the image appear in all its truth, by becoming himself what was his image, and he re-established the likeness in a stable manner, by making man completely like the invisible Father by means of the Word, henceforth visible."

92. Cf. St. Augustine, *Enarrationes in Psalmos*, l, vii, 1 (*Corpus christianorum*, series latina, 39, p. 708): "By the hand of our Creator, the Truth, has written these words in our very hearts: 'Do not do to others what you would not want done to you.' Before the law was given no one was permitted to be ignorant of this principle, so that they could be judged to whom the law was not given. But in order to prevent men from complaining that they lacked something, it was written on the tablets what they were not reading in their hearts. It is not that they did not have something written; it is that they did not want to read it. One placed, therefore, before their eyes what they would be compelled to see in their conscience. As if moved by the voice of God from without, man was compelled to look inside himself." ("Quandoquidem manu formatoris nostri in ipsis cordibus nostris veritas scripsit: 'Quod tibi non vis fieri, ne facias alteri.' Hoc et antequam lex daretur nemo ignorare permissus est, ut esset unde iudicarentur et quibus lex non esset data. Sed ne sibi homines aliquid defuisse quaererentur, scriptum est et in tabulis quod in cordibus non legebant. Non enim scriptum non habebant, sed legere nolebant. Oppositum est oculis eorum quod in conscientia videre cogerentur; et quasi forinsecus admota voce Dei, ad interiora sua homo compulsus est.") Cf. St. Thomas Aquinas, *In III Sent.*, d. 37, q. 1, a. 1: "Necessarium fuit ea quae naturalis ratio dictat, quae dicuntur ad legem naturae pertinere, populo in praeceptum dari, et in scriptum redigi [. . .] quia per contrariam

tified with the pre-existing Wisdom that presides over the destinies of the universe,[93] thus placed within the reach of human beings marked by sin the concrete practice of true wisdom, which consists in the love of God and neighbour. It contained positive liturgical and juridical precepts, but also moral prescriptions, summarized in the Decalogue, which corresponded to the essential implications of the natural law. That is why the Christian tradition has seen in the Decalogue a privileged and always valid expression of the natural law.[94]

107. Jesus Christ did not "come to abolish but to fulfil" the law (Mt 5:17).[95] As is evident from the gospel texts, Jesus "taught as one who had authority, and not as the scribes" (Mk 1:22) and he did not hesitate to relativize, indeed to abrogate, certain particular and temporary dispositions of the law. But he also confirmed the essential content of them and, in his person, brought the practice of the law to its perfection, taking up by love the different types of precepts — moral, cultural and judicial — of the Mosaic law, which correspond to the three functions of prophet, priest, and king. St. Paul affirms that Christ is the end (*telos*) of the law (Rom 10:4). *Telos* has here a twofold sense. Christ is the "goal" of the law, in the sense in which the law is a pedagogical means with the calling to lead people to Christ. But also, for all those who by faith live in him from the Spirit of love, Christ "puts an end" to the positive obligations of the law added on to the requirements of the natural law.[96]

108. Jesus, in effect, has highlighted in different ways the ethical primacy of charity, which inseparably unites love of God and love of neighbour.[97] Charity

---

consuetudinem, qua multi in peccato praecipitabantur, jam apud multos ratio naturalis, in qua scripta erant, obtenebrata erat"; *Summa theologiae*, I-II, q. 98, a. 6.

93. Cf. Sir 24:23 (Vulgate: 24:32-33).

94. Cf. St. Thomas Aquinas, *Summa theologiae*, Ia-IIae, q. 100.

95. Byzantine liturgy of St. John Chrysostom expresses well the Christian conviction when it puts in the mouth of the priest who blesses the deacon in thanksgiving after the communion: "Christ our God, who are yourself the fulfilment of the Law and the Prophets, and have fulfilled the whole mission received from the Father, fill our hearts with joy and gladness, at all times, now and always, forever and ever. Amen."

96. Cf. Gal 3:24-26: "Thus the law served as a pedagogue leading us to Christ, so that we might obtain our justification by faith. But now that faith has come, we are no longer under a pedagogue; for in Christ Jesus you are all sons of God, through faith." On the theological notion of fulfilment, cf. Pontifical Biblical Commission, *The Jewish People and Their Sacred Scriptures in the Christian Bible*, especially n. 21.

97. Cf. Mt 22:37-40; Mk 12:29-31; Lk 10:27.

is the "new commandment" (Jn 13:34) that recapitulates the whole law and gives the key to its interpretation: "On these two commandments depend all the law and the prophets" (Mt 22:40). Charity also reveals the profound meaning of the golden rule. "And what you hate, do not do to anyone" (Tob 4:15) becomes with Christ the commandment to love without limit. The context in which Jesus cites the golden rule determines its comprehension in depth. It is found at the centre of a section that begins with the commandment: "Love your enemies, do good to those who hate you" and culminates in the exhortation "Be merciful, even as your Father is merciful."[98] Beyond a rule of commutative justice, the golden rule takes on the form of a challenge: it invites one to take the initiative in a love that is a gift of self. The parable of the Good Samaritan is characteristic of this Christian application of the golden rule: the centre of interest passes from care of self to care for the other.[99] The beatitudes and the Sermon on the Mount make explicit the manner in which one must live the commandment of love, in the spirit of gratuity and sense of the other, elements proper to the new perspective assumed by Christian love. Thus the practice of love overcomes every closure and every limitation. It acquires a universal dimension and a matchless strength, because it renders the person capable of doing what would be impossible without love.

109. But it is especially in the mystery of his holy passion that Jesus fulfils the law of love. There, as Love incarnate, he reveals in a fully human manner what love is and what it entails: to give one's life for those whom one loves.[100] "Having loved his own who were in the world, he loved them to the end" (Jn 13:1). Through loving obedience to the Father, and through the desire for the Father's glory which consists in the salvation of human beings, Jesus accepts the suffering and death of the Cross on behalf of sinners. The very person of Christ, *Logos* and Wisdom incarnate, thus became the living law, the supreme norm for all Christian ethics. The *sequela Christi*, the *imitatio Christi* are the concrete ways of carrying out the law in all its dimensions.

---

98. Cf. Lk 6:27-36.
99. Cf. Lk 10:25-37.
100. Cf. Jn 15:13.

5.2. The Holy Spirit and the new law of freedom

110. Jesus Christ is not only an ethical model to imitate, but by and in his paschal mystery, he is the Saviour who gives us the real possibility of putting the law of love into action. In fact, the paschal mystery culminates in the gift of the Holy Spirit, the Spirit of love common to the Father and the Son, who unites the disciples among themselves, to Christ and finally to the Father. By "pouring the love of God into our hearts" (Rom 5:5), the Holy Spirit becomes the interior principle and the supreme rule of the action of believers. It makes them accomplish spontaneously and with discernment all the requirements of love. "Walk by the Spirit, and do not gratify the desires of the flesh" (Gal 5:16). Thus the promise is fulfilled: "A new heart I will give you, and a new spirit I will put within you; and I will take out of your flesh the heart of stone and give you a heart of flesh. And I will put my spirit within you, and cause you to walk in my statutes and be careful to observe my ordinances" (Ezek 36:26-27).[101]

111. The grace of the Holy Spirit constitutes the principal element of the new law or law of the Gospel.[102] The preaching of the Church, the celebration of the sacraments, the measures taken by the Church to promote in her members the development of life in the Spirit are totally referred to the personal growth of every believer in the holiness of love. With the new law, which is an essentially interior law, "the perfect law, the law of liberty" (Jas 1:25), the desire for autonomy and freedom in the truth that is present in the human heart attains here below its most perfect realization. It is from the very core of the person inhabited by Christ and transformed by the Spirit, that his moral action springs forth.[103] But this freedom is entirely at the service of love: "For you were called

---

101. Cf. also Jer 31:33-34.

102. Cf. St. Thomas Aquinas, *Summa theologiae,* Ia-IIae, q. 106, a. 1: "That which is most prominent in the law of the New Testament, and in which its whole power consists, is the grace of the Holy Spirit, which is given through the faith in Christ. And therefore the new law is principally the grace of the Holy Spirit, which is given to the Christian faithful." ("Id autem quod est potissimum in lege novi testamenti, et in quo tota virtus eius consistit, est gratia Spiritus sancti, quae datur per fidem Christi. Et ideo principaliter lex nova est ipsa gratia Spiritus sancti, quae datur Christi fidelibus.")

103. Cf. ibid., Ia-IIae, q. 108, a. 1, ad 2: "Therefore since the grace of the Holy Spirit is like an interior habit infused into us, inclining us to act rightly, it makes us do freely the things becoming to grace, and avoid the things opposed to grace. Thus the new law is called the law of freedom in two ways. In one way, because it does not compel us to do or avoid certain things unless they are of themselves necessary for or opposed to salvation, which are commanded or forbidden by the law. Second, because it makes us fulfil precepts or prohibitions of this kind

to freedom, brethren; only do not use your freedom as an opportunity for the flesh, but through love be servants of one another" (Gal 5:13).

112. The new law of the Gospel includes, assumes and fulfils the requirements of the natural law. The orientations of the natural law are not therefore external normative demands with respect to the new law. They are a constitutive part of it, even if they are secondary and completely ordered to the principal element, which is the grace of Christ.[104] Therefore, it is in the light of reason enlightened henceforth by living faith that man best grasps the orientations of natural law, which indicate to him the way to the full development of his humanity. Thus, the natural law, on the one hand, has "a fundamental link with the new law of the Spirit of life in Christ Jesus, and on the other hand, offers a broad basis for dialogue with persons who come from another cultural orientation or formation in the search for the common good."[105]

---

freely, insofar as we fulfil them from the interior impulse of grace. And on account of these two things the new law is called the 'law of perfect freedom' in Jas 1:25." ("Quia igitur gratia Spiritus sancti est sicut habitus nobis infusus inclinans nos ad recte operandum, facit nos libere operari ea quae conveniunt gratiae, et vitare ea quae gratiae repugnant. Sic igitur lex nova dicitur lex libertatis dupliciter. Uno modo, quia non arctat nos ad facienda vel vitanda aliqua, nisi quae de se sunt vel necessaria vel repugnantia saluti, quae cadunt sub praecepto vel prohibitione legis. Secundo, quia huiusmodi etiam praecepta vel prohibitiones facit nos libere implere, inquantum ex interiori instinctu gratiae ea implemus. Et propter haec duo lex nova dicitur lex perfectae libertatis, Ja 1.")

104. St. Thomas Aquinas, *Quodlibeta,* IV, q. 8, a. 2: "The new law, which is the law of freedom, is constituted by the moral precepts of the natural law, by the articles of faith, and by the sacraments of grace." ("Lex nova, quae est lex libertatis, est contenta praeceptis moralibus naturalis legis, et articulis fidei, et sacramentis gratiae.")

105. John Paul II, *Address of January 18, 2002* (AAS 94 [2002], p. 334).

Conclusion

113. The Catholic Church, aware of the need for human beings to seek in common the rules for living together in justice and peace, desires to share with the religions, wisdoms and philosophies of our time the resources of the concept of natural law. We call natural law the foundation of a universal ethic which we seek to draw from the observation of and reflection on our common human nature. It is the moral law inscribed in the heart of human beings and of which humanity becomes ever more aware as it advances in history. This natural law is not at all static in its expression. It does not consist of a list of definitive and immutable precepts. It is a spring of inspiration always flowing forth for the search for an objective foundation for a universal ethic.

114. Our conviction of faith is that Christ reveals the fullness of what is human by realizing it in his person. But this revelation, specific as it may be, brings together and confirms elements already present in the rational thought of the wisdom traditions of humanity. The concept of natural law is first of all philosophical, and as such, it allows a dialog that, always respecting the religious convictions of each, appeals to what is universally human in every human being. An exchange on the level of reason is possible when it is a question of experiencing and expressing what is common to all persons endowed with reason, and of setting out the requirements of life in society.

115. The discovery of natural law responds to the quest of a humanity that from time immemorial always seeks to give itself rules for moral life and life in society. This life in society regards a whole spectrum of relations that reach

from the family unit to international relations, passing through economic life, civil society, and the political community. To be able to be recognized by all persons and in all cultures, the norms of behaviour in society should have their source in the human person himself, in his needs, in his inclinations. These norms, elaborated by reflection and upheld by law, can thus be interiorized by all. After the Second World War, the nations of the entire world were able to create a *Universal Declaration of Human Rights,* which implicitly suggests that the source of inalienable human rights is found in the dignity of every human person. The present contribution has no other aim than that of helping to reflect on this source of personal and collective morality.

116. In offering our own contribution to the search for a universal ethic and in proposing a rationally justifiable basis for it, we want to invite the experts and proponents of the great religious, sapiential and philosophical traditions of humanity to undertake an analogous work, beginning from their own sources, in order to reach a common recognition of universal moral norms based on a rational approach to reality. This work is necessary and urgent. Beyond the differences of our religious convictions and the diversity of our cultural presuppositions, we must be capable of expressing the fundamental values of our common humanity, in order to work together for understanding, mutual recognition and peaceful cooperation among all the members of the human family.

BACKGROUND AND CONTEXT

An Introduction to the Document *In Search of a Universal Ethic: A New Look at the Natural Law*

Serge-Thomas Bonino, O.P.

After a stay in purgatory, the natural law has made a noteworthy return in the past several years into magisterial discourse on ethical and political matters. In the 1968 encyclical *Humanae vitae,* Pope Paul VI invoked natural law to reject artificial methods of birth control, including the infamous "pill." This encyclical, as is well known, was poorly received at the time. At a time when man, by means of technical reason, was liberating himself from the natural constraints that had weighed him down for centuries, the invitation to respect the biological rhythms of the woman appeared to many as a provocation. Many opponents wanted to reduce the natural law to a form of physicalism, that is, to an ethic that would advocate humanity's submission to natural processes. Yet such physicalism on the one hand rested on an extremely narrow and impoverished view of nature restricted to the realm of the bodies, and on the other hand went against the modern view of the autonomy of the human person. The doctrine of natural law, understood (wrongly) as physicalism, thus passed through a sort of desert — which proved to be beneficial. For in order to respond to this charge of physicalism, theologians and philosophers have been led to deepen the notion of natural law. They have done so in two complementary directions.

Some wanted to overcome the impasses of a rationalistic, modern approach to natural law, founded on an ahistorical and *a priori* conception of human nature that had widely contaminated Catholic moral theology. They thus returned to the origins of the doctrine, especially as found in St. Thomas

Translated by William C. Mattison III

Aquinas. They worked to better place the doctrine of natural law within the whole framework of Thomistic thought. The Thomistic doctrine of natural law, as participation in the eternal law (i.e., in God's plans for the world), is inseparable from a metaphysics of creation. Moreover, it is part of a view of morality identified by attraction to happiness, the role of the virtues, the primacy of grace, and the like.

Others, following the example of Pope John Paul II, elaborated a personalist presentation of the doctrine of natural law. Rejecting the idea of the human subject's totally passive submission to an impersonal nature, they articulated in a more satisfactory manner the relationship between the person as the subject of moral autonomy and nature as an expression of divine thinking.

Thanks to these efforts, the 1992 *Catechism of the Catholic Church* and the 1993 encyclical *Veritatis splendor* have been able to once again afford a decisive place to natural law in their presentations of the foundations of Christian morality. Following his election in April 2005, Pope Benedict XVI clearly made the defense of and explication of natural law one of the major pillars of his teaching. For him, natural law was the flipside of his denunciation of ethical relativism, which he perceived as a radical threat to civilization. For ethical relativism undermines the bases of respect for human dignity. It also instills a conception of democracy that, neglecting the substantive ethical values presupposed by democracy, can encourage a dangerous drift toward a form of totalitarianism. Pope Benedict XVI warned, "If, due to a tragic obscuring of collective conscience, skepticism and relativism manage to erase the principal foundations of the natural moral law, the democratic order itself would be radically wounded at its foundations."[1] The Holy Father also made clear reference to the natural law while addressing representatives of British society in September 2010: "Where can the ethical foundation of political choices be found? The Catholic tradition maintains that the objective norms which direct right action are accessible to reason, even without the content of Revelation."[2] For the doctrine of natural law affirms, against ethical relativism, that

> persons and human communities are capable, in the light of reason, of discerning the fundamental orientations of moral action in conformity with the very nature of the human subject and of expressing these orientations in a normative fashion in the form of precepts or commandments. These

1. Pope Benedict XVI, address to the International Theological Commission, October 5, 2007.

2. Pope Benedict XVI, address to representatives of British society, Westminster, September 17, 2010.

fundamental precepts, objective and universal, are called upon to establish and inspire the collection of moral, juridical and political determinations that govern the life of human beings and societies. (*In Search of a Universal Ethic,* §9)

In this general context, it is understandable that the Catholic Church has sensed a need to deepen and refine its philosophical and theological understanding of natural law so as to propose it to all persons as an invaluable resource for avoiding the pitfalls of the "dictatorship of relativism." It is in this context that the seventh quinquennial of the ITC, inaugurated in February 2004 while Joseph Ratzinger was still president of it as prefect for the Congregation of the Doctrine of the Faith, was charged with drawing up a document on this question. This document, written in French, appeared in 2009 under the title *In Search of a Universal Ethic: A New Look at the Natural Law.*

Two root problems presented themselves straightaway to the members of the ten-member subcommission charged with writing the document. To whom is the document addressed? What "new" things can one hope to say about natural law?

The Audience of the Document

Determining the audience of the document not only dictates the style of communication but also and especially raises the difficult problem of the epistemological status of the doctrine of natural law. Today reference to natural law is contested on two opposite fronts. On the one hand, outside the Catholic Church many see in this doctrine merely a Catholic Trojan horse in ethical debate, a thinly veiled confessional teaching presented under the guise of universal discourse. Against this tendentious reading, it was necessary to show that a natural law ethic is authentically rational and that it can consequently serve as a basis of constructive dialogue between people of different beliefs. On the other hand, inside the Church many fear that reference to the natural law, that is to say to a "universal ethic," encourages the establishment of a "least common denominator ethic," which would end up in the secularization of Christian morality. Historically the modern rationalistic doctrine of natural law was indeed a formidable tool for emptying Christian morality of its specific content. To respond to this concern, it was necessary to show that the rational coherence of natural law discourse is not in contradiction to a specifically Christian theological approach. Natural law doctrine can be inserted without rupture into a properly theological discourse.

In short, to dissipate these fears and better grasp the epistemological status of teaching on natural law it was necessary to rely on an accurate conception of the relationship between nature and grace since the natural law is at the intersection of natural knowledge and revelation. By definition the natural law is accessible to reason, which is common to all men. In principle, in the abstract, knowledge of its requirements does not necessitate faith. But in fact, in the concrete, due to sin, which has wounded human nature and obscured knowledge of the natural law, grace — what is traditionally called *gratia sanans,* or healing grace — must come to the aid of nature to restore it to itself. Consequently, even if man can, apart from the Christian faith, attain a certain knowledge of the requirements of natural law, it is clear — as history has shown — that the concrete influence of revelation is often necessary in order that the natural law find its most complete expression.

Due to the natural law's presence at the border of nature and grace, the manner of presenting it can have two distinct accents. They are more or less harmoniously combined in the document of the ITC. There are certain people, placing the accent especially on the rational dimension of the natural law, who wish the document to be a sort of "message to the world," an invitation addressed to all men of goodwill whatever their particular beliefs, to become aware of the existence of a common ethical patrimony, capable of constituting a basis for intercultural ethical dialogue. The beginning of chapter 1 ("Convergences"), wholly inductive, is written in this perspective. Through the theme of the Golden Rule ("And what you hate, do not do to anyone"), it identifies the clear existence of a certain consensus on fundamental ethical values. Similarly, the conclusion of the document is an appeal for cooperation in the development of a universal ethic capable of framing the phenomenon of globalization.

This perspective also explains, at least in part, the placement of reference to Jesus Christ, who only explicitly appears in the final chapter (chapter 5: "Jesus Christ, the Fulfillment of the Natural Law"). In the spirit of *Gaudium et spes,* Jesus Christ appears as the ultimate response to questions about humanity. But this final chapter also attempts to demonstrate how the doctrine of natural law is not simply a philosophical cyst within Christian teaching, but rather has a place in a larger theological framework that is both Christological and Trinitarian. The reflections of Jean Porter on this point (as well as others) in her 2005 *Nature as Reason: A Thomistic Theory of Natural Law* have exercised a certain influence on the authors of the document.[3] To be avoided here

---

3. Jean Porter, *Nature as Reason: A Thomistic Theory of the Natural Law* (Grand Rapids: Eerdmans, 2004).

is a separatist approach to the relationship between the natural and supernatural orders, an approach that has been among the principal causes of the secularization of natural law and its cultural decline. "I am convinced," says Pope Benedict XVI, "that what is necessary is a more profound sense of the intrinsic relationship between the Gospel and the natural law."[4] In fact, far from being opposed, the gospel and the natural law imply one another: the gospel cannot be lived without honoring the requirements of natural law, and the natural law only finds its true measure while integrated within the New Law of Jesus Christ.

Without denying this dimension of invitation to dialogue directed to those outside the Church *(ad extra)*, others stressed the reflexive character of the document, meant to offer assistance to those (bishops, theologians, etc.) whose mission is to teach in the Church *(ad intra)* and who are regularly confronted by critiques of the natural law. Given that the concept of natural law is being challenged on the basis of philosophical presuppositions inherent in modern culture, it is fitting to examine the historical and conceptual reasons behind this challenge, so as to offer an appropriate response able to justify in a critical fashion the validity of natural law. Thus chapter 1 presents certain developments of the notion of natural law since the late Middle Ages as well as certain basic philosophical shifts that have rendered natural law incomprehensible for the majority of our contemporaries. But it is especially chapter 3 ("The Theoretical Foundations of Natural Law") that treats this issue. The ITC insists there, among other things, on situating natural law within a metaphysical framework, and more particularly, one linked to the doctrine of creation. As Pope John Paul II had already observed, the natural law is only revealed in all its relevance in light of a metaphysics of creation: "For many contemporary thinkers," he explains, "the concepts of 'nature' and 'natural law' appear to apply only to the physical and biological world, or, as a way of expressing the order of the cosmos, in scientific research and ecology. Unfortunately, in such a view, it becomes difficult to use natural law to mean human nature in a *metaphysical* sense and to use natural law for the *moral order.* What makes it more difficult to *see the depth of reality* is the fact that our culture has greatly restricted the concept of creation, a concept that refers to the entire cosmic reality, and that takes on a particular meaning in relation to man."[5] This "passage to the depths," that is to say the passage from phenomenon to being, is

---

4. Pope Benedict XVI, *Answers to Questions Posed by American Bishops* (April 16, 2008).
5. Pope John Paul II, address to the participants in the Eighth General Assembly of the Pontifical Academy on Life, February 27, 2002.

characteristic of a metaphysics such as that defined in the encyclical *Fides et ratio* (83), and it is essential for the one who wishes to show the "ontological foundations of the essential values of human life."[6] The ultimate justification of the doctrine of natural law is found in a metaphysics that embraces the totality of what is real in the analogical unity of being, which has its ultimate source in God. Only such a metaphysics enables us to get beyond the dialectical opposition between nature and spirit that undermines the basis of the very idea of natural law, and that finds expression today through a radical form of anthropological dualism where human subjectivity is defined above all by its opposition to nature.

What *New* Could Be Said about Natural Law?

What could one say that is "new" about natural law? The ITC took as its model the "scribe who became a disciple of the kingdom of heaven" who "is like the head of a household bringing from his storeroom both the new and the old" (Matt. 13:52). The "old" in this case is the doctrine of natural law, which has its roots in Greek and Roman thought but which has been taken up and renewed in Christian thought and has found its "canonical" form in the Thomistic synthesis. The "new" is also the doctrine of natural law, but "revisited." That is to say, the "new" is a doctrine of natural law brought up to date and developed, on the one hand in reference to new challenges and questions posed to ethical reflection by the contemporary context, and on the other hand in reference to the achievements of the contemporary renewal of moral theology. This updating is intended in particular to present a traditional doctrine of natural law that avoids some of the caricatures by which it has been held captive. Let us identify some aspects (among others) of this relative "novelty."

A consideration of the contemporary is evident, for example, in the document's attention to the theme of globalization, as well as to ecological questions. While it warns against the dangers of a certain radical ecology surrounding humanism, it also takes note of the positive changes in perspective prompted by ecological concerns. Ecological concerns have laudably directed attention to the planetary dimension of problems concerning respect for the environment, and by this very fact makes a pressing appeal for a universal ethical responsibility. Furthermore, it helps promote an attitude of listening,

6. Pope Benedict XVI, address to the International Theological Commission, December 1, 2005.

respect, and accommodation with regard to nature in place of a technical and dominating approach, evident in earlier mentalities. It is thus fully appropriate that the ethical requirements of the natural law are formulated in the terms of an "integral ecology" (82).

The interest in renewing moral theology during the past several decades is seen in this document in the relativization of the legalistic and casuistic perspective that had prevailed for so long. Catholic moral theology is presented today as normative reflection guiding the progressive development of the moral subject in the movement toward happiness. That is why chapter 2 ("The Perception of Common Moral Values") firmly takes a genetic approach in presenting the place of natural law in the moral life. Inspired partially by Jacques Maritain's reflections on how people grasp the principles of natural law, it starts from concrete moral experience, common to all men, to draw out from that experience little by little the content and implicit requirements of natural law. The chapter "describes how, beginning with the most basic data of moral experience, the human person immediately apprehends certain fundamental moral goods and formulates, as a result, the precepts of the natural law" (11). To do this, a person starts to attend to who he is, and by the work of his reason to draw out the moral requirements inherent to the dynamisms of his nature, a nature that is inseparably bodily and spiritual.

Often the universal first principles, which express these fundamental inclinations of human nature, remain at a highly generalized level even while actions always take place in concrete, contingent situations. It belongs thus to reason — reason that is in dialogue — to determine the more particular rules that will govern concrete choices to make. The margin of indeterminacy between the immutable first principles and their concrete application explains the inherent historicity of any ethic founded on natural law. It also explains the possibility of legitimate cultural diversity in the enactment of the precepts of natural law. Furthermore, the establishment of appropriate norms for acting requires certain moral dispositions in the subject. Thus the virtues, especially important to ethical perspectives inspired by Aristotle, play a defining role to the extent that they are the realization of the natural dynamisms of the person in search of his fulfillment.

The life of virtuous persons helps to identify the behavior corresponding to the natural law. Among the virtues, a prominent place belongs to prudence. As the possession of true practical wisdom, this complex virtue renders men capable of making good decisions in the concrete. The natural law is thus not at all a complete code of intangible rules that imposes itself from the outside on the human person. It is rather an interior, permanent, and normative principle of inspiration at the service of the personal and communal concrete moral life of a subject. It is a stable point of reference rendering possible the ethical dialogue that persons living in the context of a pluralist society must undertake. Actually, the progressive character of the subjective conscience's grasp of the requirements of the natural law explains the necessity of a dialogue where interlocutors, shaped as they are by their own cultural contexts, endeavor to reach ethical consensus, which is not simple compromise but which is rooted in objective moral truth.

Therefore, in the face of the new challenges of our time, it seems the natural law can return to the forefront of the scene as a credible project. Among these challenges the disconnect, becoming day after day more increasingly pronounced, between the political and social order on the one hand, and the ethical order on the other hand, is surely the most worrisome. It is as if the economic, social, political, and legal realms can, and even should, carry on without any reference to objective moral good or evil. But the stakes here are nothing short of the future of the human person. It is either one or the other; we must choose. Either we choose the current form of globalization — with its accompanying enormous upheavals in the lives of persons and of societies — which is a road to disaster, regulated more or less by a purely positivistic legal order that is incapable of withstanding for long arbitrary power, where "might makes right." Or we choose to take control of the process of globalization and apply ourselves to mastering it, guiding it toward properly human goals, all of which depends on a minimal ethical consensus expressing absolute values that are objective and universal, removed from fluctuations of opinion and manipulation by the powerful. Such consensus is precisely one that is based on the natural law.

Revisiting Natural Law: An Ongoing Challenge

Anthony J. Kelly, C.Ss.R.

Revisiting the hallowed natural law tradition in the present global context of moral responsibility, the International Theological Commission's (ITC) *In Search of a Universal Ethic: A New Look at the Natural Law* was necessarily a work in progress. As a member of the subcommittee that wrote this document, I raise the questions that follow in the hope of facilitating a critical reading of this text and contributing to the theoretical and practical development of its content. These questions were somewhere in the background of our discussions, even if not all could be treated, even in a cursory fashion. Needless to say, I am speaking only for myself, and gladly acknowledge that my fellow members of the subcommittee would have different approaches and suggestions in reviewing the document.[1] The way the ITC works is that its thirty members can opt for one of the particular projects suggested. Truth be told, because of the anticipated difficulty of this project, there was no rush to be part of this subcommittee! But with a little gentle persuasion, our working group finally took shape, chaired by Serge-Thomas Bonino, O.P., of Toulouse and the esteemed editor of the *Revue Thomiste* — who, from all our different languages, came up with the limpid French of the official version.

Admittedly, as far as the subcommittees of the ITC go, ours was heavily European with no Asian or African representatives, so we had to look beyond ourselves for assistance when it came to dealing with natural law or what re-

---

1. On the issue of communication, see Anthony J. Kelly, C.Ss.R., "The Global Significance of Natural Law: A Communications Problem?" *Studia Moralia* 47, no. 1 (January–June 2009): 141-68.

sembled it in non-European cultures. This is one area undoubtedly in which rereadings of the present document can fruitfully take place in many other cultural settings, especially in regard to the ethical inheritance of any number of indigenous cultures. But we did what we could, growing in enthusiasm with the task and finding the form of collaboration and communication adapted to the group made up of one American, one French Canadian, two Germans, one Spaniard, one Brazilian, one Netherlander, two French, and one Australian (the present writer).

But now on to some of the quandaries we faced. The first one facing the subcommittee turned on the kind of contribution we might be expected to make. On the one hand, a simple reissue of the natural law tradition would not add very much. On the other hand, the creativity of this tradition as it now finds expression in the social doctrine of the Church (see the *Compendium of the Social Doctrine of the Church*) itemizes most of the key issues. Then, in terms of an accessible expression of social if not global ethics was the book of our colleague, the archbishop of Dijon Monsignor Roland Minnerath, *Pour une ethique sociale universelle. La proposition Catholique* (Paris: Cerf, 2004). Minnerath, formerly a professor of history in Strasbourg, had been chaplain to the Catholic members of the European Parliament based in that city, and the book was written as a resource for them. It was a real question then: What more can be said without falling into an otiose repetition of what has already been so well presented? If we did not intend to "reinvent the wheel," it seemed desirable to concentrate on a number of critical issues, and to take the discussion of them to a new depth. *What, therefore, might the most provocative issues be, in fact?*

There is the question of language. If we intend to speak in a language that might help a global conversation on basic ethical responsibilities and common values, our language cannot be too theological or limited to the terms of a particular philosophy, culture, or language group. While there are rich resources in our Catholic natural law tradition, these need to be critically transposed in such a way as to meet the ethical concerns of other cultures. While faith provides the motivation, it does not supply the terms. While love reaches beyond the boundaries of the Church to embrace all human beings in their sufferings and hopes, it does not automatically speak a common language to name the values of justice, decency, freedom, community, cosmic harmony, and self-realization prized in different cultures.

In our discussion, therefore, there was a tension that was never quite resolved, between the theological and, broadly speaking, the philosophical. Some were of the view that a document such as this should not appeal to theological sources or perspectives, or presume that everyone for whom it was intended was religious, let alone Christian. Hence, there was only passing reference to the Parliament of World Religions since the proposed document was about natural law, not religious ethics, and its substance could not essentially depend on a parliamentary consensus of any kind. It was pointed out, however, that this particular document was primarily intended for Church leaders and, though appealing to the richness of the natural law tradition, would profit from a specifically theological or Christological orientation.

In this regard, it strikes me that St. Paul's Letter to the Philippians confronts exercises such as this, and the applications that might result, with a productive dialectic. In the third chapter of the letter, he confesses his absolute commitment to the crucified and risen Christ:

> I regard everything as loss because of the surpassing value of knowing Christ Jesus my Lord. For his sake I have suffered the loss of all things, and I regard them as rubbish, in order that I might gain Christ. (Phil. 3:8)

You would not expect after that the apostle would have much time for natural law approaches. On the other hand, a few verses later in his letter, he opens a window into the wide world of common values:

> Whatever is true, whatever is honorable, whatever is just, whatever is pure, whatever is pleasing, whatever is commendable, if there is any excellence and if there is anything worthy of praise, think about these things. (Phil. 4:8)

That Pauline exhortation might serve as a foundational text for the natural law tradition of moral reflection. *But how can these two Pauline statements be held together?*

Such is the dialectic, but dialogue in the global context possesses inherent difficulties. It can be presumed that, for whatever reason, all are prepared to transcend the bias of individual and group egoism, even if the role of prior religious, theological, or metaphysical assumptions is debated. However it would be named, there is some kind of moral transcendence stirring in human consciousness. To be human is to be involved, for better or worse, in a realm of the consciously chosen (or rejected) good. The quality of such choices affects, directly or indirectly, the social and cultural environment of human history. There is a moral imperative when it comes to being a member of the human race. Whatever the problems and conflicts, the sense of a shared natural law makes possible a discussion of the common good and the good ordering of society founded in justice. *Is this kind of pragmatic self-transcendence sufficient to ground a global ethic? Or is a transcendence of a more religious and philosophical kind ultimately necessary?*

Discussion around the meaning of "transcendence" in this context cannot be separated from problems with the notion of the "natural." After all, natural law inevitably presupposes some notion of nature. In its primary meaning, nature is what each human being is born with. In a larger sense, it is what, through the course of history, we, individually and collectively, become. Hence, some kind of working definition of nature as what we all share is necessary if a global morality-ethic is to be developed. Obviously, "nature," in such a context at least, is the field of communication in which we identify one another as human and collaborate to support and enhance our common humanity. It might be that the crucial issue is not a theoretical discussion of what constitutes human nature, but rather the humane praxis of collaborating for the common good at this critical juncture of global history. Our humanity is a given, a datum — what each of us is born with. But it is also a program — what we make of ourselves and our culture, and all the ways we can "mean the world" to one another. In this context, the witness of wise, dedicated, and often heroic men and women, embodying what is best in our humanity, gives striking evidence of the virtues and values that would give depth and direction to a global morality. Hence, the question arises: *How can the notion of "nature" in natural law extend to both the anthropologically essential and practical and programmatic considerations?*

Approaches differ, but all agree that there is little to be gained in presenting natural law as an external obligation, or an abstract norm, with no prior resonance within human consciousness itself. A universally applicable natural law typically appeals to the criteria of "reason" and "goodwill." But these criteria do not reside in the supra-temporal faculties of metaphysical psychology. Nor are they found simply by appealing directly to the particular experience of moral conscience, unrelated to the dynamics that shape human consciousness as a whole. In the complex discussions around this point, I argue that Bernard Lonergan's style of "intentionality analysis" proves effective and reasonably communicable. As is well known, Lonergan crystalizes the dynamics of consciousness in reference to four imperatives: Be attentive! Be intelligent! Be reasonable! Be responsible! These imperatives are basic for both personal development and large-scale collaboration. Conscience, then, is not in the first place a refined moral sentiment, but the act of consenting to the self-transcending outreach implied in being attentive to new data, in asking the questions that need to be asked, in deliberating over the evidence in order to judge the reality of the situation, and, in consequence, in being responsible in collaborative decision-making. Such an approach would see natural law as fundamentally being in tune with interior law of our conscious being. This would not only counter the sense of natural law as an external obligation, but also locate the activity of "reason" in a richer experiential context. Therefore, the question: *To what degree is it possible and desirable to set the traditional idea of "reason" within a large intentionality of consciousness and subjectivity?*

Such an approach gives a deeper meaning to the transcendence referred to above. Even to envisage a global moral responsibility suggests an attraction, however implicit, toward the good that is beyond all restrictions and exclusions. Here, there is an excess accessible to spiritual experience of a more contemplative kind. It tends to set all particular responsibilities in a context of collaboration with a transcendent will and purpose working throughout the universe — however this may be named. It may give rise to a shared sense of natural law at the most intimate and universal point of ultimate commitments and hopes. This spiritual dimension is at the apex of the interior participation in a shared natural law, even if it exposes particular differences in the areas of cultural and religious beliefs. In this respect, natural disasters are notably provocative — whether the events concerned are floods in Pakistan, or the earthquake in Haiti, or the tsunami disaster in the northeastern region of the Indian Ocean, or famines in central Africa. An implicit solidarity of helping the other seems to emerge — which in many ways clothes more theoretical imperatives with the flesh and blood of suffering humanity. *What is to be learned, then, from the emerging global solidarity in responding to natural disasters?*

All this is to suggest that natural law presupposes rather more than a thin notion of reason as a logical and deductive activity. A richer, many-leveled notion of rationality is implied, based in the imperatives of self-transcendence. As a result, experience, imagination, intelligence, reasonableness, and an affective response to values come into play. Such a notion of rationality allows for both a tacit sense of the values and a discernment of the concrete good in ways that elude complete propositional expression. To this degree, it is more akin to what is currently named "emotional intelligence," and previously termed "connaturality" in the vocabulary of the Thomistic tradition, as the intimate attunement of human nature to the realm of aesthetic and moral values. It is the source, latent in human consciousness itself, of the truths and values that renew cultures and counter the forces of decline. *In what sense, then, can a globally conceived natural law be presented as the law of genuine human progress?*

When it comes to speaking about the "global" context, it is not enough to keep repeating the now worn-out metaphor of the "global village" when a privileged minority of the world's people consume most of its produce, own most of the natural resources, and control the means of production. In its best connotation, the global context connotes a newly emerging stage in world history. Despite the differences and divisions inherited from the past — in relation to different geographical locations, nations, languages, cultures, and religions — a new consciousness is emerging. *What is the best way to align the natural law tradition of morality with the global?*

In the background there is a growing awareness of the larger cosmic story of planet Earth, and the emergence of our humanity out of a long evolutionary history spanning the immensity of space and time. Humanity can now situate itself within a 14-billion-year prehistory. To be aware of the uncanny emergence of the cosmos, and of the singularity of life on this planet, is to live with a new sense of proportion. Whatever our national, ethnic, cultural, or religious differences, we have a common origin within an unimaginably immense and fecund cosmic process. Given the sheer contingency of our existence, despite the infinitesimal insignificance of our physical being in the physical universe, human consciousness has a unique capacity to ask the big questions: What is the significance of human existence? How do we belong together? How should we collaborate to bring a distinctively human contribution to the history of life in which we participate? *How might this sense of our common emergence contribute to the classical natural law tradition?*

In today's global experience, the sense of our common human emergence is accompanied by new human capacities. The astonishing developments in electronic communications have brought a new intensity and immediacy to human contact. It is as though our senses have been immeasurably extended. In principle, each individual is newly embodied in an electronic network of communication, with striking consequences for social interaction, culture, business, and scientific collaboration — and a common ethical discourse. A common humanity is less a philosophical abstraction, and more something being actualized in the creativity of a living conversation. But new forms of communication, along with new modes of teaching and learning, are not reducible to the wizardry of transferring information alone. They promise a fresh step in the formation of the human milieu, not without its own profound moral sensitivity. (Tim Berners-Lee's donating the World Wide Web system to humanity, and refusing to patent it for his own profit, comes to mind.) *How, then, does this "global commons" of interconnectivity and reciprocity invite us to revisit the natural law tradition in a fresh way?*

Another range of questions has emerged over recent decades with the growth of ecological awareness and responsibility. Human existence is situated within the realm of nature, and indeed depends on the biophysical world for its survival. For its part, human intelligence and freedom can be understood as a dimension of the creativity and adaptability of nature as a whole in sustaining life in all its forms. The conflicts and problems that arise point to the need of some inner ecology of values. These would form human consciousness into a responsible care within, and for, the biophysical reality of the environment. In that sense, the environmental crisis is not unrelated to the ecology of human culture and its ability to respect a hierarchy of values — physical, biological, vital (health), political, economic, cultural, and religious — in their dynamic confluence within the common good. *Does this represent an opportunity for a fresh development of the natural law tradition — even if the two "ecologies" are analogously related?*

Then there is the further question of how our evolutionary emergence affects the notion of natural law. If we become too "spiritual," we may become oblivious to the generic "animality" of the human condition. Here, sociobiology, when detached from its ideologies, can teach us much about human behavior by setting humanity within its evolutionary emergence. By recovering the "animal" within us, we more adequately understand ourselves. The details are subject, of course, to wide-ranging debate. But balanced perceptions are beginning to emerge. We are not "disembodied intelligences tentatively considering possible incarnations," but concretely embodied human beings with "highly particular, sharply limited needs and possibilities."[2] Our capacities to bond, to care for our young, to feel for the whole group are rooted in our evolutionary animal nature. As Mary Midgley observes, "We are not just like animals; we *are* animals."[3]

Our kinship with the animal realm offsets an ethereal sentiment of both individual existence and global belonging unaware of the inherent limitations of each. Particular feelings and actual bondings are "given" in ways that demand to be respected. Neither interpersonal relations nor religiously inspired universal love can afford to bypass a natural ordering of relationships — as Stephen Pope has convincingly shown.[4] By owning our place in an evolutionary biological world, we are less inclined to think of the human self as a free-

---

2. Mary Midgley, *Beast and Man: The Biological Roots of Human Nature* (Ithaca, N.Y.: Cornell University Press, 1978), 71.

3. Midgley, *Beast and Man,* xiii.

4. See Stephen J. Pope, "The Order of Love and Recent Catholic Ethics: A Constructive Proposal," *Theological Studies* 52, no. 2 (June 1991): 255-88. For a full treatment, see Stephen J. Pope, *Human Evolution and Christian Ethics* (New York: Cambridge University Press, 2007).

floating consciousness. Our present responsibilities have a biologically based emotional constitution. They are shaped in a particular direction by the genesis of nature. There are "givens" in the human constitution, and these conditions precede freedom, never to be repudiated unless at the cost of denaturing ourselves in a fundamental manner. In sexuality, for instance, neither culture nor a person-centered spirituality is the only consideration. Primary relationships to family, friends, community, and society need to be recognized in their particularity as priorities in our concerns. We belong to the whole human family through a particular family. We enter the global community by being connected to a special place and time. Self-transcendence is possible only by way of the given limits. It cannot be detached from the kin-preference deriving from our animal nature. We are naturally and instinctually bonded to our own species. Through our common animal descent and genetic inheritance, innate affective and other-regarding orientations are bred into us. *How, then, does this appreciation of our evolutionary inheritance provoke its own way of revisiting natural law and interpreting this document?*

*   *   *

The accelerated sense of history may well be our best teacher in answering the questions that we have raised in reference to the ITC document. The global financial crisis has already been a harsh lesson on trying to live with the absence of values. Similarly, the prospects of global peace look dim, given the enormous military arsenals of many countries and new forms of terrorism. Only some new vision of a pacific global humanity and a revitalization of its enduring values can lead to the disarmament of the heart. That would mean new structures of mediation and reconciliation, and a new determination to overcome the political and economic evils that degrade so many. The question persists and intensifies: Does the human race live in a moral universe, or is it essentially adrift in an unalterable world of conflict and violence, governed by the law of "might is right"? Is there, then, a natural law of common morality that can make peace possible, and give peacemakers a language to speak?

The Situation of Natural Law in Catholic Theology

Russell Hittinger

In Catholic theology, discussion of natural law can lean in one of two different directions. When natural law is used as one of the resources for inquiry about practical matters, the discussion moves toward particular actions, cases, and classes of actions. This is moral theology in its fully practical office. When we ask how natural law stands within the economies of creation and redemption, our inquiry points toward the foundations of theology. The question "Is contraception forbidden by the natural law?" is the first kind of issue; the question "Does the sacrament of marriage include natural law requirements of marriage?" corresponds to the second. Debates about natural law can arise either way. Not infrequently debates begin in one line only to jump into the other, and a change in one line almost always causes an alteration in the other. This is exactly what we ought to expect for any tradition that takes natural law seriously. For example, for nearly three decades after World War II Catholic moralists were intently focused on disputed questions about sexual and biomedical ethics. With the pontificate of Pope John Paul II, however, the focus shifted to issues of normative anthropology, such as the meaning of human sexual differentiation.

Two recent Catholic documents lean more toward the sources than toward practical argument. Neither intends to resolve a particular moral dispute so much as to uncover foundations and starting points. *Veritatis splendor* (1993) is the first papal encyclical devoted exclusively to moral theology. The encyclical treats the nature and scope of human agency in light of both the natural and evangelical laws.[1] The International Theological Commission's

---

1. "Natural law" (or "moral law") is mentioned more than fifty times in the encyclical *Veritatis splendor.*

(ITC) study, *In Search of a Universal Ethic: A New Look at the Natural Law,* considers natural law as a common component of the great wisdom traditions. The exposition is heavily weighted toward perennial anthropological and metaphysical themes. *Veritatis splendor* looks *ad intra* to the coherence of moral theology, while the ITC looks *ad extra* toward extra-ecclesial dialogue. These two documents — one pontifical, the other a curial paper — give us an interesting picture of how natural law is situated in Catholic theology at the half-century mark from Vatican II.

The purpose of this essay is to situate and analyze the task of the ITC document. In the first section I continue the contextualization by situating the ITC document within contemporary Catholic moral theology. Given that the primary stated task of that document is dialogue, in the second section I then describe the sort of "sapiential" dialogue the document undertakes before examining in the third and final section two problems posed by that dialogue that the document leaves unresolved.

In Search of a Universal Ethic and Catholic Natural Law Thought Today

After the collapse of political Christendom — marked in the Catholic world by the year 1870 — the older division of labor in Catholic Christendom that informally distinguished between authority in public policy and authority in ecclesiastical order, corresponding to the competence of royal courts on the one hand and ecclesial tribunals on the other, had become defunct. Rome now had to speak about the moral dimensions of public policy across the board, and not just as occasional pontifical judgments concerning things about which Catholic sovereigns disagreed. Pope Leo XIII used natural law as an appeal (and sometimes as an argument) to resituate the problems of society and authority. His use of natural law was elegantly neo-Thomist, and it won the admiration of the Catholic world because he succeeded in balancing the disputed moral or political question with the deeper questions about the nature and end of man and the origin of authority. In the twentieth century, however, the list of disputed issues treated at least partially in terms of natural law multiplied, and came to include the "life" issues such as war and peace, abortion, contraception, and sexual conduct generally, as well as the ever burgeoning sector of problems that spun out of the postwar human rights project. Pope John XXIII's *Pacem in terris* (1963) enumerated some two dozen human rights grounded in natural law. To accommodate the expanding field of social doctrine, the revised *Code of Canon Law* (1983) states that "the Church has the right always and everywhere to proclaim moral principles, even in respect of the social order, and to make judgments about any human matter in so far as this is required by fundamental human rights or the salvation of souls."[2]

The cumulative effect of a century of teachings in the arena of moral theology and social doctrine left the subject of natural law appearing rather cluttered at the practical end of the spectrum. It became necessary to organize this bevy of moral and social teachings in compendia for handy reference. It was easy to lose sight of the coherence that ought to obtain between these particular moral teachings and the principal sources of moral theology. Thus, the problem of coherence needed to be reconsidered and repaired where it was found wanting. This is the context in which we should read *Veritatis splendor*.[3]

Veritatis splendor turned to the question of what kind of component natural law is in moral theology, and how it relates to the other sources of doctrine: sacred scripture, Christology, theological anthropology, ascetical theology, and ecclesiology. I make no effort to summarize this very rich encyclical. Instead, I call attention to *Veritatis splendor*'s claim that natural law forms an organic part of moral theology.

Why shouldn't the Church concern itself only with the habits and actions immediately ordained to salvation — for example, the theological virtues, the gifts of the Spirit, the Beatitudes, works of mercy, and sacramental actions? Some theologians raised the question from a slightly different angle. Why shouldn't the things belonging proximately to the natural law fall within the magisterium of scholars and experts whose expertise pertains to temporal matters? The two concerns held together rather tersely in the *Code of Canon Law* ("in so far as this is required by fundamental human rights or the salvation of souls") were being pulled from either end. The encyclical notes:

> In their desire, however, to keep the moral life in a Christian context, certain moral theologians have introduced a sharp distinction, contrary to Catholic doctrine between an "ethical order" which would be human in origin and of value, for "this world" alone, and an "order of salvation" for which only certain intentions and interior attitudes regarding God and neighbor would be significant. This has then led to an actual denial that there exists, in

---

2. c. 747, §2.

3. This also helps us to understand the ITC paper, which keeps in view a human rights movement that has gone awry, multiplying and changing the content of rights to such an extent that only an apophatic universal remains — a "negative anthropology." That is to say, we can affirm what man is not, but not what he is prior to self-defining liberty.

Divine Revelation, a specific and determined moral content, universally valid and permanent. (37)

The encyclical explains that moral truths — in principle accessible to human reason (29) — not only constitute a "preparation for the Gospel," but are also situated within it (3). The moral law, thus understood, is presupposed in two ways by moral theology: first, as principles of moral order are derived from human nature; and second, as those very same principles are clarified and integrated in the teachings of Christ. "The Magisterium does not bring to the Christian conscience truths which are extraneous to it; rather it brings to light the truths which it ought already to possess, developing them from the starting point of the primordial act of faith" (64).

Alasdair MacIntyre has astutely noted the importance of at least one facet of this position:

> It is not just that the natural law can be known by the exercise of the powers of reason, independently of revelation, but also that the knowledge of divine law afforded by revelation presupposes a prior knowledge of the precepts of the natural law. It is a revealed truth, that is to say, that the truths of the natural law can be known prior to and independently of any revealed truths, including this particular revealed truth.[4]

MacIntyre assures the reader "that in holding this I am not being theologically eccentric." He is not at all. Indeed, his brief treatment of Romans 2:14-15 is virtually the same as that of *Veritatis splendor* (59).[5] MacIntyre, however, might have drawn a more pointed lesson for moral theologians. Even if the institutions of a given culture — universities, courts, the media, other churches and religions — had no further use of natural law either as a supposition or as an explanatory framework, the Church nevertheless would be bound to teach and affirm the natural law. Furthermore, it would need to affirm it precisely as the natural, created measure of human acts.

This double commitment highlighted by *Veritatis splendor* (64) rules out reducing moral theology exclusively to grace or to experience untutored by

4. Alasdair MacIntyre, "From Answers to Questions," in *Intractable Disputes about the Natural Law: Alasdair MacIntyre and His Critics*, ed. Lawrence S. Cunningham (Notre Dame, Ind.: University of Notre Dame Press, 2009), 341.

5. MacIntyre, "From Answers to Questions," 344: "But we could not be rightly held responsible for those violations and that rebellion if we were not aware of God's law, simply *qua* human beings, and not only aware of the precepts that comprise God's law, but aware of the compelling character of their authority."

revelation. The complexity of sources makes for both the creativity and the difficulty of the Catholic tradition. St. Thomas Aquinas investigated natural law in his dual role as philosopher and theologian, for which there is no equivalent office or craft in our secular institutions, and increasingly less so in ecclesiastical ones. As Fergus Kerr puts it: "[Aquinas] is a philosopher and a theologian, and we are never going to agree on where to put the emphasis."[6] But the problem of emphasis and ongoing debates about it in interpreting Aquinas are set within, and can arise only within, a tradition that strives to be doubly articulate. *Veritatis splendor* requires the natural law component to be treated in just that fashion.

In Search of a Universal Ethic: A New Look at the Natural Law (2009) differs from *Veritatis splendor* not only in its curial pedigree and magisterial weight (a study paper allowed to be published by the cardinal prefect of the Congregation for the Doctrine of the Faith), but more relevantly, for our purposes, in the questions as well as the audience it addresses. The ITC study aims to orient and enrich a dialogue outside the immediate environs of moral theology: "we would like, in this document, to invite all those pondering the ultimate foundations of ethics and of the juridical and political order, to consider the resources that a renewed presentation of the doctrine of the natural law contains" (9). However, in shifting from sources of moral theology to the resources for dialogue, the ITC moves to even more difficult terrain than the one occupied by *Veritatis splendor*. *Veritatis splendor* of course also worries about negative anthropology and exaggerated notions of individual autonomy that disorient the natural law that theology presupposes. But it has the signal advantage of correcting and moderating claims of autonomy, as well as the array of different understandings of natural law, within the landscape of its own tradition. The ITC appears to tackle the issues on an open field with recourse only to natural law. It claims no more authority than being one wisdom tradition among others — albeit a tradition with centuries of experience in this field of inquiry.[7] The authors are surely correct that a discussion of natural law that puts reason, nature, and God into competition (74-75), or that refuses to give to each focus the salience that experience and reason will allow, if not demand, falls short of the Catholic tradition.

6. See Fergus Kerr, *After Aquinas: Versions of Thomism* (Oxford: Blackwell, 2002), chapter 6, "Natural Law: Incommensurable Readings."

7. The ITC treats natural law in the light of what the Catholic tradition has cumulatively discovered and formulated over the centuries, including what it has learned from shortcomings in its own experience (10, 38, 52, 56, 59, 99).

Sapiential Dialogue

Interestingly, the ITC does not situate its presentation and its understanding of dialogue in the fashion of a model UN plenary session. Rather, it puts its discussion of moral universals in the context of great wisdom traditions, both religious and philosophical:

> In offering our contribution to the search for a universal ethic, and proposing a rationally justifiable basis for it, we want to invite the experts and proponents of the great religious, sapiential and philosophical traditions of humanity to undertake an analogous work, beginning from their own sources, in order to reach a common recognition of universal moral norms based on a rational approach to reality. (116)

Wisdom traditions, on this view, recognize and make explicit (in different ways and in various degrees) (1) that there is a "common patrimony" of moral values, (2) that certain moral actions are required by human nature itself, and (3) that human persons must reckon in a creative and harmonious way with a cosmic or metaphysical order that transcends them. Wisdom traditions, in other words, are open to reality as a whole, even if their vision is partial in this or that aspect. As the ITC recalls, Catholic theology fed on the bread of sapiential traditions as a *praeparatio evangelicae,* and once assimilated to theology the two "function as one" in the Catholic mind (26).

The ITC does not mean by dialogue either the Habermasian or Rawlsian methods for reaching norms mutually acceptable to the parties of the discussion (8). It also eschews dialogue that is "a purely inductive search, conducted on the parliamentary model, for an already existing minimal consensus" (6). This is a dialogue, in fact, without a "search." As the authors remark, it has not proven adequate either to secure foundations for the post-1948 human rights project or to win support of religions and wisdom traditions, which need more than a "minimal ethic" (6). Thus the ITC envisages a dialogue rather different from what is usually meant by "public reason." Rather than holding back one's best considered reasons, it puts the mature line of reasons on the table, inviting others to do the same. Although the authors give due weight to the pre-philosophical experience and appropriation of the rudiments or seeds of moral truth, they do not pretend that a rationalistic reduction of morality to what is most primitive in experience is apt to yield a reliable consensus about the moral order (60). Appropriation of the "evidences" of natural law either by the individual or by a culture is a slow process, requiring action and reflection — in a wisdom tradition, an "apprenticeship" (53, 38).

This certainly has the aura of an interreligious rather than a legal or political dialogue. One is reminded of C. S. Lewis's illustrations of the Tao in *The Abolition of Man*, albeit with Thomistic glosses. Cardinal Ratzinger said in a speech at Cambridge: "Now the concept of a personal relationship between God the Creator and each individual person is certainly not missing from the religious and moral history of humanity; but it is limited in its pure form to the realm of biblical religion. *What was first of all common to all of pre-modern mankind,* however, lies really along the self-same line: the conviction that in man's being there lies an imperative, the conviction that man does not devise morality itself by calculating expediencies; rather *he comes upon it in the being of things.*" The most troubling sign of our times, he concluded, is "what is moral has lost its evidence."[8]

The idea is very attractive. Let those who have non-reductive anthropologies (open to reality as a whole) put their best understanding of human good and flourishing in common view, and then let us see where they "converge." The hope will be that this kind of discussion will achieve more than the "minimal ethic" in a very narrow and completely practical grounding, such as the one stipulated in the UN's *Universal Declaration of Human Rights* of 1948 (5-6, 115, and note 42). Even if we are not so naïve to believe that a dialogue of wisdom traditions could persuade, much less replace, the legal and political conventions governing human rights, it would still be of value. A few strong convergences in the fashion of Lewis's Tao would speak more effectively to human conscience than the dubiously abstract and highly politicized lists of rights that are continually multiplied and revised.

Limits of Sapiential Dialogue

There are two aspects of the ITC paper that I find disappointing. First, while the document affirms clearly enough, even insistently, the importance of pru-

---

8. In 1988 Cardinal Ratzinger gave the Fischer Lecture for the Catholic Chaplaincy at Cambridge University. Arguing that "the moral has lost its evidence" for the West, he noted C. S. Lewis's use of the Tao in *The Abolition of Man*. What marks a wisdom tradition is that it has not lost its sense of "evidence." Cardinal Joseph Ratzinger, "Consumer Materialism and Christian Hope," in *Teachers of the Faith: Speeches and Lectures by Catholic Bishops*, foreword by Cardinal Cormac Murphy-O'Connor, ed. Tom Horwood (Catholic Bishop's Conference of England and Wales, 2002), 87-88.

dence in judgments that make the natural law effective, its depiction of universal moral norms *prior to* prudence is not very clear. Second, it leaves out of the picture what kind of dialogue can be conducted with secular modernity.

Regarding universal moral norms, the ITC is reluctant to put a system of precepts in front of its proposals about human nature. For one thing, on anthropological grounds alone it rejects the notion of pure practical reason that can generate *a priori* such a system of norms. Quite reasonably, the authors also want to acknowledge contingencies of culture and history and the effects of sin — "ideologies and insidious propaganda, generalized relativism, structures of sin" (52). They are at pains to emphasize that a mature understanding of moral truth is an achievement dependent on the agent's formation in sound social institutions and acquisition of moral virtue. All of this reflects the paper's strategic decision to discuss natural law within time-tested wisdom traditions.

When we ask, however, what precepts of natural law are universally binding in a normative sense of the term, the document warbles somewhat. The paper quotes St. Jerome's remark on the Golden Rule: "Who does not know that homicide, adultery, theft and every kind of greed are evil, since one does not want them done to oneself? If a person did not know that these things were bad, he would never complain when they are inflicted on him" (51). Accordingly, there is no prudence, just as such, about whether to commit adultery. Provided that one can pick out the relevant facts (this is my neighbor's spouse), the negative precept suffices. Granting that negative precepts need to be completed within a larger moral project (24), it is very important to recognize that sound moral reasoning of the more complete kind depends on what agents can know at this simpler level.

To be sure, the ITC says strongly enough that there are "precepts and values that, at least in their general formulation, can be considered as universal, since they apply to all humanity" precisely because they are derived from anthropological constants (52). Here, the anthropological constant is immutable, for it is the ground for values and precepts that "can be considered" universal in their "generality." This does not quite capture what St. Jerome and others have wanted to say about the negative precepts. We also read that we must safeguard "the fundamental givens expressed by the precepts of the natural law that remain valid despite cultural variations" (54). It is difficult to know exactly what the paper means, but on my reading the "data" are the anthropological constants, while the precepts seem to be a kind of sign or expression of a good or value. It is less clear that a precept is a sign of a command or obligation. At paragraph 59, the paper states that moral science cannot furnish an acting subject with a norm to be applied adequately and almost automatically to concrete situations; only the conscience of the subject, the judgment of his practical reason, can formulate the immediate norm of action. But at the same time, this approach does not abandon conscience to mere subjectivity: it aims at having the subject acquire the intellectual and affective dispositions which allow him to be open to moral truth, so that his judgment may be adequate. Natural law could not, therefore, be presented as an already established set of rules that impose themselves *a priori* on the moral subject; rather, it is a source of objective inspiration for the deeply personal process of making a decision.

Some readers will sense that a step is missing in this very condensed account. Even if natural law should not be presented as an already assembled system of precepts, it does not follow that the natural law is only "a source of objective inspiration for [the agent's] deeply personal process of making a decision" (59). In what precise sense are the inspirations *precepts*? Are they just objective indicators en route to the discovery of adequate moral norms? Some sentences seem to suggest the latter. "Only the conscience of the subject, the judgment of his practical reason, can formulate the immediate norm of action" (59). "Prudence," as the ITC insists, "is a necessary element in the exercise of one's authentic moral obligation" (58). Is it the only one?

The quotation taken from St. Jerome requires an intermediate step — a small one, and rather thin, but important nevertheless. Between our grasp of the human good (anthropological constants) and fully practical judgments perfected by prudence, there are some moral norms of the natural law on which even prudence must rely. Precisely in this zone we might expect some initial but sturdy convergence of moral judgment among wisdom traditions regarding the negative precepts of the moral law. Without it, the dialogue is apt to remain in the anthropological sphere of "objective inspirations" that perhaps intimate, without explicitly reaching, specific precepts.

Another conspicuous problem is that the secularized institutions of the West are not organized within a wisdom tradition; nor do they constitute one. Whereas a wisdom tradition is open to reality as a whole — a natural transcendence, so to speak (97) — the modern, Western mind does not view nature or the "natural" as "impregnated with an immanent wisdom," but rather, to use the ITC's own language, it is "stripped of every teleology or finality" (72). This is to acknowledge that prior to choice and prior to satisfying procedures of consent "the natural" is *merely* immanent, along the lines of what Charles

Taylor has called "closed world structures."[9] On this view, purpose is assigned rather than discovered within the ordinary frame of things.

By shifting the problem of authority from the internal structure of a theological tradition to the moral authority of a "common patrimony" implicit in many wisdom traditions, the ITC will not relieve the misgivings of secular interlocuters. For example, when the ITC proposes that there are moral "messages" in the nature of things and that natural law is not imposed on creatures from without, but is inscribed in their very nature (11-12, 63), it summons a quite different meaning of the "immanent" than what will be obvious to most agents formed in the institutions of Western secular culture. For them, nature is not obviously a semiotic (a book or a ladder) in the sense that we have inherited from St. Paul, St. Bonaventure, or St. Thomas. The immanent rather is a domain of freedom just for the reason that it does not require transcendent messages, much less messages that arrive so intimately with authority. The immanent, for all practical purposes, is nothing other than what is bereft of, or perhaps still waiting for, authority. This is why the sciences and contemporary institutions of civic formation, education, and economic activity are deemed useful and indeed legitimate. Precisely by not requiring a sapiential philosophy or religion to interpret transcendent "messages" freedom is protected.

While the problem of liberty unseated from nature is more likely to be bridged in dialogue with wisdom traditions, it remains the tougher problem in the familiar world of secular modernity. The ITC remarks: "In order that the notion of natural law can be of use in the elaboration of a universal ethic in a secularized and pluralistic society such as our own, it is therefore necessary to avoid presenting it in the rigid form that it assumed, particularly in modern rationalism" (33). This prescription strikes me as a good way to facilitate dialogue among wisdom traditions, at least those that already regard modern rationalism as a dead end. It is much harder to see how the prescription has medicinal value for dialogue with a "secularized" society. Its denizens are not bothered by rationalism so much as by appeals in the public order to transcendent values — not only the supernatural, but also what the ITC means by natural law (97). For its part, the ITC makes clear enough that the Church often invokes natural law (moral truths antecedent to faith) defensively, against a belligerent secularism that dismisses a natural law foundation of moral choice and conscience as a purely confessional subversion of civic

---

9. Charles Taylor, *A Secular Age* (Cambridge, Mass.: Belknap Press of the Harvard University Press, 2007), chapter 15.

dialogue.[10] The ITC authors are anything but naïve about who is the main antagonist on questions of natural law. The question is how to help this antagonist become a dialogical partner on the question posed by the document, the search for a universal ethics.

The ITC is faithful to untutored common sense and to its own tradition in affirming that "apart from any theoretical justifications of the concept of natural law, it is possible to illustrate the immediate data of the conscience of which it wants to give an account" (37). Some rudiments of moral truth are so close to human experience that they are available to anyone. One can interpret and appropriate these "evidences" even against the grain of one's inherited explanatory frameworks. Yet the dialogue that an individual person can conduct in what *Gaudium et spes* calls the "sanctuary" of his own conscience is not a sufficient condition for the broader and more difficult dialogue envisaged by the ITC.[11] By grasping the first precepts of natural law one has already crossed the threshold into a world of social and intellectual formation, languages, and, for good or ill, informal and formal explanatory frameworks. We return therefore to the question of what to do or to say to the modern antagonist. This is the issue around which the ITC maneuvers all too carefully, and understandably, but disappointingly.

In a press conference during a trip to Portugal on May 11, 2010, Pope Benedict XVI expressed hope for a dialogue between religion and modern rationality.

> Today we see that . . . if European culture were merely rationalist, it would lack a transcendent religious dimension, and not be able to enter into dialogue with the great cultures of humanity all of which have this transcendent religious dimension — which is a dimension of man himself. So to think that there exists a pure, anti-historical reason, solely self-existent, which is "reason" itself, is a mistake; we are finding more and more that it affects only part of man, it expresses a certain historical situation but it is not reason as such. Reason as such is open to transcendence and only in the encounter between transcendent reality and faith and reason does man find himself. So I think that the precise task and mission of Europe in this situation is to create this dialogue, to integrate faith and modern rationality in a single anthropological vision which approaches the human being as a whole and thus also makes human cultures communicable.

10. In *In Search of a Universal Ethic*, 35, of the "four principal contexts" in which the Catholic Church invokes natural law today, three are clearly defensive.
11. *Gaudium et spes*, 16.

The "single anthropological vision" entertained by Pope Benedict XVI requires the secular civilization to either develop a wisdom tradition or to reattach itself to the one it abandoned. The pope surely had the latter option in mind. This hope moves the question beyond the specific problem of natural law groundings for a common morality to the prospects of what would have to be a profound intellectual, moral, and spiritual conversion. *Veritatis splendor* recounts the dialogue Jesus had with the rich young man (Matt. 19:16-22) in order to emphasize that the invitation to radical discipleship presupposed adherence to the moral law. Today, however, we can imagine the rich young man "going away sad" at the prospect of the moral law itself. The urgency of the dialogue will have to be moderated by the virtue of patience, more or less like it was taught by Pope Benedict XVI's namesake.

In Search of a Universal Ethic

On Islam and Islamic Natural Law: A Response to the International Theological Commission's *In Search of a Universal Ethic: A New Look at the Natural Law*

Anver M. Emon

The International Theological Commission's (ITC) document on universal ethics and natural law comes at a time when global dialogue on shared values across religious communities is increasingly viewed as both important and a *sine qua non* for global order, peace, and harmony. This particular document is also noteworthy given a series of events that have juxtaposed the Christian and Muslim worlds in an often tense relationship. Pope Benedict XVI's 2006 speech in Regensburg, Germany, prompted considerable outrage among Muslims, who considered the pope's remarks about Islam and its capacity for reasoned deliberation uninformed and stereotypical.[1] In response to the pope's speech, Muslim leaders, intellectuals, and clerics drafted a letter to initiate open dialogue and exchange. That letter, "A Common Word Between Us and You," has since been the subject of multiple academic conferences and articles, where the letter has been celebrated, criticized, and held up as a starting point for a more global conversation.[2]

---

1. For an analysis of the pope's remarks in light of Islamic intellectual history, see Anver M. Emon, "On the Pope, Cartoons, and Apostates: Shari'a 2006," *Journal of Law and Religion* 22, no. 2 (2006-7): 303-21.

2. The letter can be viewed at the official website of A Common Word: http://www

---

I would like to thank the editors of the volume for inviting me to contribute to this important volume. Robert Gibbs has been a wonderful dialogue partner on the ideas expressed herein. Aleatha Cox very ably copyedited earlier drafts of this essay and improved its readability. This essay benefited from the support of a grant awarded by Canada's Social Sciences and Humanities Research Council.

Four years later, the ITC issued the document that is the subject of this anthology of essays, in which it articulates in as inclusive a manner as possible a path to universal values and ethics. Far from positing particular values as shared, the ITC proffers "natural law" as a *theoretical framework* within which the global dialogue about universal ethics and values can take place. In other words, natural law provides a dialogic framework to guide a global dialogue on universal ethics.

To proffer natural law as such a framework, the ITC had to satisfy one preliminary burden, namely, to address whether the ideas and concepts that animate "natural law" exist in the various religious and wisdom traditions across the globe. In paragraph 17 of *In Search of a Universal Ethic,* the ITC offers its analysis of natural law in Islam:

> Islamic law, inseparably communitarian, moral and religious, is understood as a law directly given by God. The Islamic ethic is, therefore, fundamentally a morality of obedience. To do good is to obey the commandments; to do evil is to disobey them. Human reason intervenes to recognize the revealed character of the Law and to derive from it the concrete juridical implications.

The ITC continues by addressing two pre-modern theological movements, Muʿtazilism and Ashʿarism, which held opposing views on the authority of human reason to determine the law of God. The ITC represents these two theological traditions as follows:

> the Muʿtazilite school proclaimed the idea according to which "good and evil are in things," which is to say, that certain behavior is good or bad in itself, prior to the divine law that commands or forbids it. The Muʿtazilites, therefore, judged that man could by his reason know what is good and evil. ... But the Ashʿarites, who dominate Sunni orthodoxy, have upheld an opposing theory.... [T]hey consider that the divine positive revelation of God alone defines good and evil, right and wrong. (17)

Importantly, the ITC suggests that even the Ashʿarites ascribed to a set of rules that reflect the "moral patrimony of humanity," citing at length in footnote 13 a Qurʾanic passage that presents such basic rules. However, the lan-

---

.acommonword.com/. For analyses of the letter, see Yvonne Yazbeck Haddad and Jane I. Smith, "The Quest for 'A Common Word': Initial Christian Responses to a Muslim Initiative," *Islam and Christian Muslim Relations* 20, no. 4 (2009): 369-88; Daniel L. Migliore, "The Love Commandments: An Opening for Christian-Muslim Dialogue?" *Theology Today* 65 (2008): 312-30.

guage in the quoted paragraph does not bode well for an Islamic natural law tradition in contemporary Sunni orthodoxy. Natural law depends in part on human reason having an ontological authority to know, derive, or find the law of God. Without that authority, the capacity of natural law to offer a shared framework for dialogue loses its intelligibility. Indeed, the ITC is not entirely oblivious about this; one can infer from the ITC's representation of the Mu'ta-zilites a wistful nostalgia for an Islamic intellectual trend that could have led to a vibrant Islamic natural law tradition (but did not do so in the end). This perspective on the Islamic tradition was certainly present in Pope Bene-dict XVI's Regensburg speech, when he emphasized the voluntaristic nature of Islamic law.[3]

The ITC's attempt to understand the role and authority of reason in Islam raises important, but highly sensitive questions that Muslims have debated for centuries. The ITC should certainly be applauded for offering a frame within which communities of faith can consider shared values. But when that frame is natural law, which involves fundamental questions about reason, the ITC cannot ignore that in the case of Islam, there are important theological, phil-osophical, and political stakes involved. To make brief reference to a theolog-ical group such as the Mu'tazilites or to quote a Qur'anic verse without more information raises serious problems about the politics of orthodox belief and the implications of both theology and philosophy on fundamental questions of authority and reason in Islam. In short, the ITC's analysis of the Islamic tradition is either politically naïve or theologically imperialistic by implicitly advocating a contested theology for Muslims without understanding the phil-osophical, theological, and political dimensions of debates about reason in Islam.

The fact remains that there is a much more complex story to tell about the different natural law theories that were developed throughout Islamic legal history. This is not the place to go into substantive detail about the story of natural law in Islamic law. I have offered a book-length account of the history and jurisprudence of Islamic natural law theory in my *Islamic Natural Law Theories*.[4] This essay draws extensively on that work in order to outline com-

3. Pope Benedict XVI, "Faith, Reason and the University," 3-4. For the text of the speech, see http://www.vatican.va/holy_father/benedict_xvi/speeches/2006/september/documents/hf_ben-xvi_spe_20060912_university-regensburg_en.html. See also Emon, "On the Pope, Cartoons, and Apostates," 303-21, 304-8.

4. In the interest of space and readability, notes to this essay will be limited. Readers interested in a fuller account of the natural law theories outlined here can refer to chapters 2, 3, and 4 of my *Islamic Natural Law Theories* (Oxford: Oxford University Press, 2010).

peting Islamic natural law theories and their different juridico-theological justifications for the authority of reason in Islamic law. This essay shows that the ITC's representation of natural law in Islam is not only incorrect, but also suffers from overprivileging theology over jurisprudence as the primary medium of religious argument in Islamic thought. This essay concludes by looking at why getting the Islamic natural law story right should matter to the ITC, and the costs of failing to do so.

The Theology and Politics of Reason in Islamic Intellectual History

To search for a natural law tradition in Islam is to ask about the role and authority of reason in Islamic thought. Such a question is not merely an academic exercise; it has deeply political ramifications. The debates about reason in Islamic law occur alongside popular perceptions of Islamic law as legislated by God, to whom the devout are bound to obey.[5] In other words, Shari'a is perceived as involving arguments from authority and not arguments from reason.

Within the prevailing Sunni orthodox theology today, reason cannot be an authoritative source for divine obligations; at most, it can confirm or corroborate what is already established by authoritative source-texts. The historical counterargument to that position was offered by the pre-modern theological group called the Mu'tazilites, who are referred to in the ITC document. The Mu'tazilites, adherents of a theological movement founded in the early eighth century, were considered the early rationalists in Islam.[6] Their position on the authority of rational argument was intimately tied to their theology of God and God's justice. They held that God only does the good and avoids the evil: to put it more straightforwardly, God does X *because* X is good. By holding such a position they suggested that concepts like "good" and "just" are virtues that are separate from and prior to a divine act. As separate and distinct

---

5. For an overview of such views and how they operate in the public sphere today, see Anver M. Emon, "Islamic Law and the Canadian Mosaic: Politics, Jurisprudence, and Multicultural Accommodation," *Canadian Bar Review* 87 (2008): 391-425.

6. For the history of Mu'tazilite theology, see Richard C. Martin, Mark R. Woodward, and Dwi S. Atmaja, *Defenders of Reason in Islam: Mu'talism from Medieval School to Modern Symbol* (Oxford: Oneworld, 1999), 25-45; W. Montgomery Watt, *The Formative Period of Islamic Thought* (Oxford: Oneworld, 1998), 209-52. For thematic analysis of Mu'tazilite and other theological doctrines, see Harry Austryn Wolfson, *The Philosophy of the Kalam* (Cambridge, Mass.: Harvard University Press, 1976).

from God's will, they are virtues that can be reasoned about and rationally known; in other words, they are virtues that are susceptible to reasoned deliberation. Their position was criticized as unduly impinging on the omnipotence of God. In other words, to hold that humans can reason about the good and the bad implicitly suggests that God would not (in fact, cannot) act counter to that good or in furtherance of that evil; that humans could, through their reasoned deliberation, limit the scope of God's acts and will.[7] This implication of the Mu'tazilite theology of God and his justice fueled their critics, voluntarist theologians, who adamantly adhered to the absolute omnipotence of God — an omnipotence that made no room for the possibility that reasoned deliberation about the good could somehow limit God in any way.

For various reasons, Mu'tazilite theology was associated with heterodoxy sometime after it was repudiated as the official Abbasid theology in the ninth century. Instead, voluntarist theology occupied the dominant theological frame for understanding God and his omnipotence. Today, those who oppose the inherited orthodox view are deemed heterodox, and are often labeled as modern-day Mu'tazilites who fall outside the orthodox teachings of Islam.[8] Even more, whether or not a scholar is explicit about his Mu'tazilite sensibilities, any suggestion that reason offers an important source of guidance for the modern Muslim raises suspicions of heterodoxy framed in pre-modern terms. To theorize about reason, whether in terms of pre-modern theology, or modern debates about natural law, thereby begs highly fraught questions about the intellectual bounds of credible Shari'a-based argument and the political bounds of religious community and belonging.

7. Qadi 'Abd al-Jabbar, *Sharh al-Usul al-Khamsa* (Beirut: Dar Ihya' al-Turath al-'Arabi, 2001), 203-7. For further discussion on the relationship between God and justice, see Martin, Woodward, and Atmaja, *Defenders of Reason in Islam*, 71-81.

8. Martin, Woodward, and Atmaja, *Defenders of Reason in Islam*, 166-67. The apostasy case of Nasr Hamid Abu Zayd, an Egyptian intellectual deemed to have apostatized from Islam through his writings on the Qur'an, is a well-known case of an intellectual whose ideas were viewed by some as Mu'tazilite or as heterodox, and thereby contrary to prevailing Islamic norms. For an overview of the relationship between intellectual freedom and apostasy cases, and the Abu Zayd case, see Baber Johansen, "Apostasy as Objective and Depersonalized Fact: Two Recent Egyptian Court Judgments," *Social Research* 70, no. 3 (Fall 2003): 687-710; Susanne Olsson, "Apostasy in Egypt: Contemporary Cases of Hisbah," *The Muslim World* 98 (2008): 95-115. For a comparative study of Mu'tazilite ideas and those of Abu Zayd, see Thomas Hildebrandt, "Between Mu'tazilism and Mysticism: How much of a Mu'tazilite is Nasr Hamid Abu Zayd?" in *A Common Rationality: Mu'tazilism in Islam and Judaism*, ed. Camilla Adang, Sabine Schmidtke, and David Sklare (Würzburg : Ergon in Kommission, 2007), 495-512.

The Ontology of Reason: Reason and Philosophy in Contemporary Muslim Debates

Just because a call for natural law in Islam might invoke a certain politics of belonging does not mean, however, that modern Muslim thinkers avoid addressing the scope, role, and authority of reason in Islam.[9] However, they often fail to address a fundamental question about reason that is of crucial significance to natural law, namely, the ontological authority of reason in Islamic thought. For instance, when the Qatar-based cleric Yusuf al-Qaradawi writes in support of reason in Islam, he bases the authority of reason by reference to Qur'anic verses in which the Qur'an asks the reader to think or reflect.[10] This approach to the ontological authority of reason relies on the authority of the Qur'an, which indeed clothes the use of reason with a type of divine authority. The philosophical implication of this approach, though, renders the authority of reason derivative at best. If the Qur'anic references constitute the bases by which reason is an authoritative source of Shari'a, then reason does not stand as a separate and distinct source of Shari'a at all.

But if reason is a separate source and if the Qur'an merely corroborates what we already know by reason, that begs the question, How do we know? Tariq Ramadan, a European Muslim, suggests that the natural world offers insights about the workings of God's will. He writes:

> God always makes available to humankind tools and signs on the road that leads to recognizing Him. The first space that welcomes human beings in their quest is creation itself. It is a book . . . and all the elements that form part of it are signs that should remind the human consciousness that there exists that which is "beyond" them. This Revelation in and through space is wedded to Revelations in time, which, at irregular intervals, came as reminders of the origin and end of the universe and of humanity.[11]

Creation and source-texts offer two approaches to understanding the divine will. For Ramadan, both are "texts" that must be read and reflected on.

9. For a general overview of different modern Muslim reformists who contend with the nature and scope of reasoned deliberation, see Jasser Auda, *Maqasid al-Shariah as Philosophy of Islamic Law: A Systems Approach* (Herndon, Va.: International Institute of Islamic Thought, 2008), 144-53.

10. Yusuf al-Qaradawi, *al-'Aql wa al-'Ilm fi al-Qur'an al-Karim* (Beirut: Mu'assasat al-Risala, 2001), 11-68.

11. Tariq Ramadan, *Western Muslims and the Future of Islam* (Oxford: Oxford University Press, 2004), 13.

The created world, fashioned by God, is a sign of God's will if only we would look closely. Ramadan effectively fuses fact and value in the created world, thereby rendering it a foundation for the authority of reason as a source of Shari'a norms. He offers an approach to reason's ontological authority that may be sympathetic with natural law. But to render the natural world akin to a text that anyone can "read," he empowers the private individual while making the law vulnerable to massive idiosyncrasy and indeterminacy at a systemic level.

Islamic Natural Law Theories: An Overview

Muslims have, throughout history, contended with the role, scope, and authority of reason in a religious tradition that is fundamentally linked to a book (the Qur'an), which is believed to be God's word revealed to the Prophet Muhammad and a guide to humanity's salvation. Adhering to and satisfying God's will is an important factor in attaining salvation. Consequently, the Qur'an offers the most obvious source of God's will for Muslims to follow. However, Muslim jurists knew that the world of lived experience could not be totally captured between the Qur'an's two covers; as such, they debated whether and to what extent they could build on what they learned from the Qur'an. Hence we find the pre-modern genre of legal theory *(usul al-fiqh)* that offered theoretical reflections on the nature and dynamism of law and legal interpretation.[12] Since the late nineteenth century, much of the debate about reason has focused on whether, how, and to what extent Muslims can perform *ijtihad,* or renewed interpretation, on matters already addressed by historical precedent. In both the scholarly and popular literature, the doctrine of *ijtihad* offers theorists and reformists alike an important doctrinal site to address the scope of moral agency; the nature of epistemic authority; and the relationship between law, reform, and modernity.[13]

Importantly, a natural law inquiry frames the role of reason in a manner that is distinct from, though certainly not unrelated to, the question of *ijti-*

12. For scholarly treatments of Islamic legal theory, see Wael B. Hallaq, *A History of Islamic Legal Theories: An Introduction to Sunni Usul al-Fiqh* (Cambridge: Cambridge University Press, 1999); Mohammad Hashim Kamali, *Principles of Islamic Jurisprudence,* 3rd ed. (Cambridge: Islamic Texts Society, 2003); Subhi Mahmasani, *Falsafat al-Tashri' fi al-Islam,* 3rd ed. (Beirut: Dar al-'Ilm li'l-Malayin, 1961).

13. For scholarly works on *ijtihad,* see Shaista P. Ali-Karamali and F. Dunne, "The Ijtihad Controversy," *Arab Law Quarterly* 9, no. 3 (1994): 238-57; Wael B. Hallaq, "Was the Gate of Ijtihad Closed?" *International Journal of Middle East Studies* 16, no. 1 (1984): 3-41.

had. A key distinction is that an Islamic natural law inquiry concerns the *ontological* authority of reason as a source of law, as opposed to its *epistemic* authority in legal interpretation. In the Sunni *usul al-fiqh* literature, premodern jurists phrased the question as follows: In the absence of some scriptural source-text such as the Qur'an or the traditions of the Prophet *(hadith)*, can jurists utilize reason as a source of law? There were those who said yes, and others who said no.

Those who said yes — the hard natural law jurists — believed that God creates all things for the purpose of good and benefit. Any other option would mean that God might do something for evil purposes, which they rejected as an unacceptable possibility in their theology. If God only acts with goodness and justice, they argued, then all of his creation must also be vested with that goodness. To what end, they then asked, was this bountiful world created? Perhaps it might be for God's use and enjoyment. But since God is omnipotent and needs nothing, that option was theologically unacceptable. Instead, the created world, they argued, must be for the benefit and enjoyment of God's creatures, in particular human beings. The upshot of this theological argument is to render the created world fused with fact and value: the "is" is also the "ought." By fusing fact and value in the created world, hard natural law jurists invested reason with the ontological authority to analyze, investigate, and derive new norms.

Against the hard natural law jurists were those who disagreed with the theological view that God only does the good. According to these voluntarist theologians, there is no standard of justice that precedes God or in any way limits his omnipotence. Rather, the voluntarists held that the question about whether God can do only good or also evil fundamentally confuses human nature with God's nature. Human nature may be subject to reasoned deliberation about the good and the bad, but no one can presume to impose on God any obligation to do the good. Rather, this latter group argued that God does as he wishes; whatever he does is by definition good. Nonetheless, the voluntarists could not ignore the fact that as much as they looked to God for guidance in his sacred scriptures, those texts were limited. Consequently, they could not deny the need to engage in legal reasoning. In fact, they could not deny that at times, reason would have to be a source of the law itself.

To theorize reason's ontological authority, these voluntarist jurists developed a natural law theory that both fused fact and value in the created world and preserved their voluntarist commitment to God's omnipotence. Their natural law theory might be called soft natural law. Like the hard natural law jurists, soft natural law jurists argued that nature is fused with fact and value, thereby reflecting a presumption of the goodness of nature. But they argued that the fusion is not because God only does the good and cannot do evil. Rather, the fusion of fact and value in nature results from God's grace *(tafaddul)*. God chose to be gracious when creating the world. Once they held that nature is fused with fact and value, they effectively rendered reason an ontologically authoritative source of law. Grace also allowed them to preserve their voluntarist theology: if God exercised grace when creating the world, he can presumably choose to alter his grace. Soft natural law jurists granted reason ontological authority by fusing fact and value in nature on a theory of divine grace. *Theologically speaking*, since God can choose to change his grace any time, soft natural law is consistent with voluntarist theology. *Jurisprudentially speaking*, they upheld the ontological authority of reason because they maintained that after God created the world as a benefit, it would not seem that God has changed his mind. Because they felt that God's grace could change, though, their commitment to the fusion of fact and value was not nearly as hard and fast as the view held by the hard natural law, which explains why I call this second group *soft* natural law jurists.

The soft natural law jurists, having granted reason ontological authority, could not just leave it at that. They were worried about reason holding an unchecked ontological authority as a source of Shari'a. To let reason hold such authority, they worried, would make them seem like the hard natural law adherents, whom they disagreed with on theological grounds, but not necessarily on jurisprudential ones. So they devised an epistemic model of reasoning to limit the scope of reasoned deliberation. They held that there are various issues and interests that work to the benefit and detriment of society. Those issues may not be the subject of any source-text. In cases where no source-text governs, those interests *(maslaha)* can be subjected to reasoned deliberation and relied on to generate a norm of legal significance. As long as the interest at stake neither confirms nor negates a source-text, relates to one of the aims and purposes of the Shari'a *(maqasid)*, and concerns a social necessity (as opposed to any lesser value), then it can be the source of law.

The issue of social necessity is quite interesting to reflect on: it is one of three categories that delineate the significance of a *maslaha* for social well-being. Aside from necessity *(darura)*, there are needs *(hajiyyat)* and edificatory interests *(tahsiniyyat)*. While soft natural law jurists would give examples to demarcate these levels of significance from each other, the fact remains that they are not well defined. That is perhaps part of the draw they provide and the flexibility they offer. Notably, regardless of any definition of these three categories, soft natural law jurists held that only the *maslaha* that addresses a social necessity *(darura)* could be a basis for Shari'a norms. A *maslaha* that falls into the other two categories could not constitute a basis for legal norms that could presumably reflect the divine will. Certainly they may provide a basis for some normative ordering, but they do not assume the authority of a Shari'a norm. These three categories are important because, in the aggregate, they limit the scope of reason's authority.

Conclusion: The Upshot of Getting It Right

The different approaches to natural law in Islamic legal history reveal three important insights that might help the ITC craft a vision toward global interfaith engagement. First, *In Search of a Universal Ethic*'s paragraph 17 situates the Islamic debates on reason at the intersection of a theological dispute that has deeply political implications; this undermines the purpose of the ITC's effort. The historical fissure between the Ash'arites and Mu'tazilites still resonates today. When Muslim authors develop theories of law and politics that remotely smack of Mu'tazilite sensibilities, they are immediately criticized for stepping too far outside the bounds of inherited orthodoxy.[14] This is not to suggest that inherited orthodoxy should not be questioned. Indeed, contemporary Muslim writers constantly challenge views that are deemed orthodox. For the ITC to do so, though, needlessly fronts the politics of that theological dispute. *In Search of a Universal Ethic* thereby might raise speculation either about the ITC's political naiveté, or its capacity to act imperialistically in matters of theology pertaining to other faith communities.

Second, the ITC's recourse to early theological disputes in Islam, arguably, is needless if its intention is to posit natural law as a frame of reference for global engagement on pressing questions about values and ethics. As suggested above, one fundamental feature of natural law theories has to do with the ontological authority of reason. While contemporary Muslim authors seem to skirt the philosophical question about reason's authority, pre-modern Muslim jurists did not. They developed two theories of natural law that started from

14. For instance, Khaled Abou El Fadl makes a case for democracy in Islam. Mohammad Fadel criticizes Abou El Fadl's argument, however, for drawing on what he considers to be discredited Mu'tazilite views that are outside the pale of accepted orthodox Sunni beliefs. Khaled Abou El Fadl, *Islam and the Challenge of Democracy: A Boston Review Book,* ed. Joshua Cohen and Deborah Chasman (Princeton, N.J.: Princeton University Press, 2004), 3-48; Mohammad H. Fadel, "Too Far From Tradition," in *Islam and the Challenge of Democracy,* 81-86, 82.

competing theological positions, but ended up in similar jurisprudential positions. In other words, despite the fissure between Ash'arite and Mu'tazilite jurists, the irony is that their natural law models are quite similar. To get the Islamic natural law story right would enable the ITC to reorient its engagement with the Islamic tradition, shifting its focus from highly disputed theological issues to the area of legal philosophy and jurisprudence. From a purely strategic perspective, the ITC document would have greater purchase if it examined how Islamic soft natural law contributes to its renewed look at natural law.

Third, whether one sides with hard natural law jurists or soft natural law jurists, both camps rely on metaphysics to explain and justify their respective natural law theories. Consequently, a different strategy for finding a shared site for debate and engagement across faith traditions would be to ask whether and to what extent a global discussion about ethics can be framed in metaphysical terms. This is not only a question for members of faith traditions, but also one faced by liberal-secular theorists who contend with the role of religion in the public sphere.[15] The twenty-first-century global citizen lives in a world that may be skeptical of natural law theories that require metaphysical presumptions, whether informed by theology or liberal philosophy. To (re)present wisdom traditions without accounting for the presumptions that rendered certain views intelligible covers those presumptions in a new historical moment when they are now vulnerable to critique in light of prevailing theories of knowledge, philosophies of law, and theories of government. This essay does not, and cannot in the space provided, offer a post-metaphysical natural law framework. Nonetheless, this essay concludes by suggesting that the engagement sought by the ITC on questions of ethics may require people of different faith and philosophical persuasions to consider how shared commitments to order, ethics, and the good can be framed without, or in spite of, a commitment to one metaphysics or another.

---

15. See, for instance, Jürgen Habermas, "Religion in the Public Sphere," *European Journal of Philosophy* 14, no. 1 (2006): 1-25, who writes that to live in a post-secular society requires that citizens present their arguments about justice and ethics in terms that avoid metaphysical presumptions about truth and the good.

Some Questions for the International Theological Commission Document on Natural Law

David Novak

Natural law is a matter of both practical and theoretical concern. The practical concern of natural law is with the precepts that proponents of natural law take to be what all humankind is obliged to do. The theoretical concern of natural law is with the reasons theorists of natural law give as to why these precepts are to be kept. The theory of natural law that deals with principles is logically prior to natural law as a set of concrete norms. Natural law governs intelligent human action, and without theoretical explanation praxis is not intelligent action but only thoughtless behavior. Theory without praxis, though, can be coherently formulated. It can wait for the kind of praxis that needs its intelligent guidance and direction. Nevertheless, almost all of us experience being obliged to practice those deeds sooner or later prescribed by natural law precepts before the reasons for our being so obligated are thought of. That is the chronological priority of natural law as praxis. Therefore, what is usually needed for cross-cultural agreement on natural law qua praxis is to show that various traditions have in fact prescribed the same universal practical norms on basic moral questions. Medieval scholars designated this type of cross-cultural consensus by the late Roman legal concept of the "law of nations" *(ius gentium)*. It is natural law "on the ground," so to speak. Theoretical agreement, though, requires the formulation of a set of principles that have to be argued for rather than simply being what is readily at hand from general experience. Medieval scholars designated this type of cross-cultural rational discourse on morality by the concept of "natural right," which was their considerable re-working of the late Roman legal concept of *ius naturale.*

At the level of practical agreement, as a Jewish proponent of natural law

I find very few of the natural law precepts taught by the magisterium of the Catholic Church with which I disagree. (One of the few exceptions is the teaching of the Church on contraception, for short of permanent sterilization I do not think contraception is a subject of natural law legislation.) That is why I have been able to join together with Catholics (and other Christian proponents of natural law) in arguing for the legalization of some of the natural law norms we hold in common, such as the prohibitions of elective abortion and active euthanasia, and the positive injunctions to save human lives and alleviate human suffering whenever possible. However, the International Theological Commission's (ITC) document *In Search of a Universal Ethic: A New Look at the Natural Law* is primarily a statement of natural law theory. And here there is more divergence than our divergence over the actual teaching of the Church on issues of direct moral praxis. Nevertheless, my critical questions are those of one friend who has been invited to comment critically on the thought of some other friends; it is not the hostile criticism of a stranger who is not and does not want to be in intimate conversation with those whose house he has invaded uninvited. Indeed, the purpose of my critical questioning is to at least suggest what I think are better arguments for what we hold quite similarly regarding praxis.

My questions are political, philosophical, and theological. My political question pertains to the immediately normative public presentation of natural law in this document. It is appropriate since we share the same public space in our largely secular society, where all statements of public policy have to be made. My philosophical question pertains to the conception of metaphysics set forth in this document. It is appropriate since we share the same assumption of the necessary link between ethics (of which natural law theory is a type, just as natural law praxis is a type of morality) and metaphysics. And my theological question pertains to the portrayal of Judaism in this document. It is appropriate because Christian theology that is true to Christianity cannot be indifferent to Jewish theology, which the Church still regards to be a matter of its ongoing concern, since both theologies are rooted in the same scripture: the Hebrew Bible, about whose moral teaching there is much agreement between us.

Politics

I take the following to be a political statement: "Certainly, natural law is a law accessible to human reason . . . and the Church does not have exclusive rights over it, but since revelation assumes the requirements of the natural law, the

Magisterium of the Church has been established as the guarantor and inter-preter of it" (34). My question here is: "the guarantor and interpreter of it" *to whom?* If the Church claims to be the guarantor and interpreter of natural law for the world, and if in this world (i.e., the world of rational discourse or what we now call "public reason") the only moral proposals one can argue for are those based on reasons rather than on the authority of revelation, then it would seem that the magisterium of the Church is irrelevant here. For why would anyone accept the teaching authority of the Catholic Church unless she is al-ready a Catholic or planning to soon become one? But if the Church is saying that the same reason that obliges one to keep the precepts of natural law also obliges one to become a Catholic, then aren't the universal claims the Church is making for its version of natural law a key component of a covert prosely-tizing agenda? Yet the Church also claims that its natural law agenda and its evangelical mission are distinct public enterprises. And, from what I under-stand of Catholic theology, the faith claims the Church makes in its evangeli-zation mission (and its re-evangelization mission to its lapsed members) are not the same type of argumentation the Church makes when advocating its positions on matter of public morality in secular societies. In fact, was anybody ever argued into or out of faith?

It would seem, therefore, that the public to whom the Church is teaching natural law as both praxis and theory are the faithful people of the Church itself. They are the ones who accept the revelation from which the Church takes its moral warrant. But if they are the proper addressees of Catholic moral (i.e., practical) theology based as it is on revelation and traditions, then why do they need to be taught about natural law at all? (In fact, I remember reading a remark made by Pope Benedict XVI, when he was Cardinal Ratzinger, to the effect that the rhetoric of natural law has been quite ineffective in secular so-cieties, and that it might be more prudent for Catholic moral theology to simply represent natural law teaching straight out of its revealed sources to those who already accept the authority of those sources anyway.)

Nevertheless, it is stated that "revelation takes up the requirements of natural law" (34). It seems to me that this means that the Church recognizes that the acceptance of natural law morality is a prerequisite for the intelligent acceptance of its revealed teaching. In other words, persons who do not al-ready have a sense of universally binding morality, and who do not think in ethical terms, are in no position to rise to the level of faith (which is the per-sonal confirmation of revelation). Faith is super-rational, not sub-rational. In fact, without this rational prerequisite, faith becomes the kind of "blind faith" that G. K. Chesterton famously ridiculed when he quipped something like "people who begin by believing in nothing often end up believing in anything." That is why the Church should always emphasize that its moral teaching is more than natural law per se (grace being greater than nature), but it is never less than natural law. Thus affirming natural law as the necessary "bottom line" (the *conditio sine qua non*) of its full teaching saves that teaching from becoming irrational and fanatical. Yet it also saves the full teaching of the Church from being reduced to natural law alone (taking natural law to be its *conditio per quam*), which is the error of modern secular rationalism. (There is a similar strategy in Jewish theology.)

Moreover, acting rationally is itself an act of faith as belief. Could one sustain the search for the rational norms to live by and promote in the world unless one already believed such norms already exist? (In the same way, could a scientist proceed in his search for the laws of physical nature unless he *believed* the physical world is altogether intelligible — hence Einstein's famous belief that "God does not gamble with the world"?) And, if one holds that the most plausible ontological ground of these norms is best expressed by the belief that the Creator of the world wisely promulgated them for us, could this not be a spur to seek the type of personal intimacy with the Creator that only a historical revelation confirmed by faith as ultimate commitment can provide? Thus the objective side of the covenantal relationship with God is the personal presentation of God's commandments in revelation; the subjective side is the personal acceptance of that revealed content by faith. Accordingly, we must then distinguish between faith as belief, which rationality presupposes, and faith as ultimate commitment to which reason at best suggests. And the kind of rationality that discovers natural law, though having faith both behind it and ahead of it, must not be regarded as the necessary consequence or the sufficient ground of either kind of faith. Just as faith as belief makes rationality as a sustained mode of human discovery possible, so does rationality make faith as ultimate commitment possible. Belief is not potential for rationality, any more than rationality is potential for ultimate commitment.

Philosophy

Perhaps some of the lack of clarity in distinguishing between the claims of reason and the claims of faith are due to the philosophical conception of metaphysics employed in this statement. Thus I agree with the insistence here of the inadequacy of separating ethics from metaphysics. Yet, surely, Aristotelian metaphysics employed here makes more problems for a theology based on the

Bible, and for a post-Galilean/post-Newtonian philosophy of nature, than it solves. This comes out in the following statement: "To give the notion of the natural law all its meaning and strength as the foundation of a universal ethic, a perspective of wisdom needs to be promoted, belonging properly to the metaphysical order, and capable of simultaneously including God, the cosmos and the human person" (76). Thus it would seem that *nature* is what includes God, the cosmos, and the human person. As such, God, the cosmos, and the human person are seen to be functioning in a descending *natural* order (what some have called "the great chain of being").

From a biblical standpoint, however, how can one state that God is "included" — that is, contained — by anything or anyone else? Doesn't this imply that God participates in a reality greater than Godself inasmuch as the whole is greater than any of its parts, even if that part is its apex (as it is for Aristotle)? Nevertheless, "could it be that God dwells on Earth, since the highest heavens do not contain you [*ye-khalkkelukha*]?" (1 Kings 8:27). Furthermore, identifying wisdom and God will not solve this problem. Wisdom is still "God's wisdom," not wisdom that is itself divine, even though it is holy *(hagia sophia)*. Even Job's famous praise of wisdom *(hokhmah)* says that "God [alone] comprehends its way, and he [alone] knows its place" (Job 28:23). That means God knows wisdom *because* it is still God's creation, albeit God's greatest creation. But that certainly does not mean that wisdom itself is divine (even if holy as *hagia sophia*), let alone being what "includes" even Godself. (Indeed, this is the Achilles' heel of all the Muslim, Jewish, and Christian Aristotelian philosophical theologies, which might explain why some important modern Thomist theologians have tried to make Aquinas more and more independent of Aristotle and medieval Aristotelianism.)

Nevertheless, for Judaism and Christianity (and maybe for Islam) God does dwell on Earth, be that dwelling the *Shekinah* in the Temple and even in the synagogue for Jews, or be that dwelling Jesus Christ in Jerusalem or even in the Eucharist for Christians. But that dwelling is God's own choosing. And, just as God can choose to be present *with* us *in* the world, God can just as easily choose to absent Godself *from* us *out of* the world. "Claim the Lord [only] when he is present [*be-himats'o*]" (Isa. 55:6). Revelation is God's breaking into our world to reach us directly. (It is what my late revered teacher, Abraham Joshua Heschel, taught to be "God in search of man.") That is fundamentally different from God's being included by some overarching nature within which humans find their place by locating themselves via natural law within the intelligent cosmos, which then mediates the God-human relationship. Surely, the biblically presented covenantal relationship between God and God's people is unmediated. And, furthermore, already Galileo and Newton (both more beholden to the Bible than to Aristotle or Ptolemy or Dante) destroyed the old paradigm of a teleological ascending natural cosmos culminating in God as the end-of-all-ends. Clearly, this natural teleology is very problematic both theologically (in what it says about God) and philosophically (in what it says about the world).

I do not suggest here that Catholic natural law ethics (as a theoretical enterprise) eliminate teleology, for teleology as purposiveness is what distinguishes intelligent human action (the subject of ethics) from instinctive behavior (the subject of experimental psychology as an empirical science). However, I think both Christians and Jews can learn much from Kant, who saw rational persons as the ends toward *whom* human action is to be directed, primarily as a response to the justifiable claims other persons make on us (a point well made by the Jewish philosopher Emmanuel Levinas). Kant's (and Levinas's) limitation, however, is that he could not accept God as the supreme End to whom human persons together as members of a covenanted community can be directly related. That is because Kant had no place in his epistemology for divine revelation. He could only argue for the conditions that make ordinary experience possible. But divine revelation is not ordinary experience. It is a singular event, not a repeatable and predictable moment in a natural process regularly available for ready inspection. As such, though divine revelation occurs in the ordinary world, it is not of it; hence it requires the formulation of additional categories more adequate to its uniqueness. And since divine revelation primarily calls for our active response as the social-practical beings we naturally are (and only thereafter for our theoretical reflection thereon), it comes in the form of commandments as moral prescriptions.

We can only know the justifiable claims other human persons make on us as ends-in-themselves (*Zweck an sich selbst*) when they *reveal* to us what they justifiably want from us. Certainly in the Bible, God is a person — indeed, *the Person* — whose archetypal personhood is but reflected in humans as *imago Dei.* Now since a moral relationship with any other person is only possible *when* that other person reveals his or her claims on us in words, we can thus only know how to be related to God when God reveals to us *what* God wants *from* us and *that* God wants to be *with* us in the life of the covenanted community. The covenant does not enable us to participate in the life of God (though the Kabbalists thought otherwise); the covenant enables God to be *the* participant in our covenanted life. That is divine immanence — not immanence in the natural world, but only in the covenanted world. Divine transcendence is God's freedom to be either present or absent there as God so chooses. "I will be whenever and wherever I shall be" (Exod. 3:14). Clearly, this more biblically authentic ethical understanding requires a very different metaphysics than that which is still too beholden to Aristotelian metaphysics.

What this means for metaphysics by biblically based theologians, whether Jewish or Christian, might be as follows. The "meta" in *metaphysics* means what is "beyond," that is, what seems to ultimately underlie what for the Aristotelians was natural science, especially astrophysics. But the post-Aristotelian natural science, beginning with Galileo, seemed to no longer require metaphysical grounding. Rather than simply deny, though, the validity of metaphysics altogether (something done by positivists of all stripes, including theological positivists), Kant transferred metaphysics from speculation on physical nature per se to reflection on human nature per se. (And, whereas for Kant physical nature per se is constructed by human observers of phenomena, human nature per se is a *noumenon:* an intelligible reality.) For Kant, human nature or essence is to be a moral being. That is why Kant called his foundational work in ethical theory *Groundwork of the Metaphysics of Morals.* But, as noted before, Kant could not acknowledge that human persons defined by that nature are not only to be related to other human creatures, but also to be related to God on God's own terms, terms that could only be revealed since they are not to be found in the world of our ordinary experience. And human persons are ends-in-themselves only because they are the image of this revealing God.

I have made so much of Kant regarding metaphysics in order to show he correctly formulated his metaphysics to undergird ethics, rather than to undergird what had become by his time (and so much more by our time) an irretrievable cosmological paradigm. As such, he also restored the originally biblical priority of praxis to intellection (even if that was probably not his intention). But by making God, at best, a mere postulate of practical reason, Kant jettisoned the biblical emphasis on the primacy of the God-human covenantal relationship, which gives ethics its most coherent grounding. Therefore, the philosophical task of Jewish and Christian theologians is to formulate a metaphysics of revelation with a primarily ethical thrust. (I see this project getting very promising results in the work of the contemporary Catholic theologian Matthew Levering.)

Theology

When Catholic theologians speak of "first covenant" or of "the Law," they are speaking of Judaism. Clearly, Catholic theologians have to distinguish Christianity from Judaism inasmuch as the Christian church is no longer a Jewish sect. Jews understand that need and can respect it. Nevertheless, Jews can certainly question whether the Judaism from which Christianity is being distinguished has been accurately characterized here, and whether it is accurate from the perspective of the current magisterium of the Church. We do have our fundamental differences, but let theologians from each religious tradition get these differences right and for the right reasons.

The first theological characterization of Judaism I question in this document is where "the first covenant" (as in *vetus testamentum*) as "the law of the people of Israel" is distinguished from "the new covenant" (as in *novum testamentum*), which itself "introduces the distinction and the relative autonomy of the religious and political orders" (93). This follows from an earlier distinction (basing itself on Aquinas) where it is said that "medieval . . . Jewish philosophers . . . attributed an essentially political role to religious revelation" (26 n. 33). Here, it seems to me, Judaism is being characterized as the *nomos* of a particular people and its polity, being distinguished from the Church as the *nomos* of universal humanity, irrespective of whatever particular political order all of us are now living in before the full realization of the kingdom of God on Earth (as it is already in heaven). In other words, this looks like the relatively modern distinction (with ancient precedents to be sure) between Jewish "particularism" and Christian "universalism." That is why it is said by certain Christian supersessionists (more often by Protestants than by Catholics) that Judaism is the religion for only one people, but Christianity is the religion for all peoples. This is the type of "supersessionism" that assigns Judaism a definitely parochial role in the trajectory of human history as *Heilsgeschichte,* or salvation history. However, is this distinction true? Is it true about Judaism, and is it true about Christianity? I think not.

It is not true about Judaism because Judaism is a universal religion of an international people. For most of our history, we Jews have not had our own particular polity. And even since 1948, when most Jews have strongly identified with the Jewish state of Israel, the Jewish people itself transcends this particular (and extremely valuable) polity. Zionism for most of us is a part of our Judaism, but there is more to our Judaism than Zionism just as there is more to the Jewish people than the land of Israel and its present Jewish polity. Furthermore, our universality is evidenced by the fact that throughout our history we have accepted converts, those who were born into other peoples, yet who become "reborn" into the Jewish people. Jews are God's elect people, both collectively and individually, *wherever* we are to be found in the world. Moreover, the universal God we Jews serve and with whom we are forever covenanted has not lost his concern for all his human creatures, indeed with all his nonhuman creatures as well. The fact of the covenant does not mean our (the "our" here designating relation, not possession) God is exclusively concerned with the Jews alone. God is King over the whole universe, even though all humankind has yet to acknowledge that truth.

The statement quoted above is also not true about Christianity. The Christian church, though calling itself *catholic*, or "universal," is clearly not identical with all humanity, at least not with all humanity short of the arrival of the full kingdom of God on Earth. The universality of the church is a *desideratum* not a *factum*. And it is a desideratum that should not be realized by any kind of imperial expansion or conquest, a point that has emerged from Vatican II and from the teachings of the Pope John Paul II and Pope Benedict XVI. To assume otherwise seems to many non-Christians and to many Christians (and even to many Catholics I know as well) to smack of the type of Constantinianism that the Church should be wary of. The fact is that the Christian church is a particular people in the world just like the Jews are a particular people in the world. And just as Christian eschatology looks forward to the time at the end of history *(eschaton)* when all, universal humankind will become Christian, so does Jewish eschatology look forward to the time at the end of history *(ahareet ha-yamim)* when all, universal humankind will become Jewish, when the peoples of the world will say "let us ascend to the mountain of the Lord, to the house of Jacob's God, that he might teach us his ways so that we shall walk in his paths" (Isa. 2:3). Indeed, it is at the point of our not only distinct but truly different eschatologies with their respective modes of anticipatory praxis that our presently irreconcilable difference — *la différance même* — surely lies. That fundamental difference is greater than our many political, philosophical, and even theological commonalities.

There is a dialectic of the universal and the particular in both Judaism and Christianity. But it is not that one people and its Torah are universal and the other people and its Torah are only particular. After all, isn't the One God with whom we both take ourselves to be covenanted himself both the most particular of particularities in his singular uniqueness and the most universal of universalities in his governance and care of the universe?

Finally, we read the following: "Jesus Christ . . . did not hesitate to relativize, indeed to abrogate, certain particular and temporary dispositions of the law. . . . [T]he positive obligations of the law added on to the requirements of the natural law" (107). But didn't Jesus, who for Catholic theology instituted the sacrament of the Eucharist at the Last Supper for the Church to administer perpetually, thereby *add* to the natural law content of the Old Covenant that the Church has retained? As such, Jesus did not abolish the particularities of the Old Law; instead, Jesus' disciples replaced them with the sacraments of the Church. In other words, just as the particularities of the Old Law celebrate God's salvific acts with Israel (especially the exodus from Egypt leading up to the revelation at Sinai), so do the particularities of the New Law celebrate God's salvific acts in the life, ministry, death, and resurrection of Jesus. This actually follows a school of thought in pre-Christian Pharisaic theology that assumes that when the Messiah comes, his life and ministry will be celebrated in place of the earlier "sacraments" (the practice of the positive, commemorative commandments of the Torah is preceded by thanksgiving to God for our *sanctification* by God through them). The difference between us, then, is whether Jesus of Nazareth is the real Messiah who can warrant that sacramental displacement and replacement.

My questions above have been expressed in the spirit of the dialogical friendship I have enjoyed with a number of Catholic theologians over the years. I hope that our dialogue will continue and grow, and that these questions will stimulate the authors of this statement to ponder them and perhaps even respond to them.

Natural Law, Legal Authority, and the Independence of Law: New Prospects for a Jurisprudence of the Natural Law

Jean Porter

The International Theological Commission (ITC) was established in 1969 to serve as a kind of standing advisory committee to the Congregation for the Doctrine of the Faith. We might expect, therefore, that its reflections on natural law and the prospects for a universal morality would be directed inward, toward Vatican officials and ultimately to Pope Benedict XVI, whose interest in this topic was well known at the time. Yet in the introduction to its 2009 document, *In Search of a Universal Ethic: A New Look at Natural Law*, the ITC extends an open invitation to all those concerned with moral universalism and the origins of law to consider the natural law tradition as a resource for reflection (9). By implication, its target audience does not consist only of Church leaders or even Catholics, but "all persons of good will," whoever and wherever they may be, who are willing to enter into an open-ended conversation on these issues. Nor does this seem to be a rhetorical flourish. The document was clearly developed with this wider audience in mind, focusing on presumed common ground while offering a restrained, carefully qualified portrayal of the natural law tradition itself.

Thus, in order to lay the foundations for further dialogue on these issues, the ITC begins by surveying the religious traditions of the world, setting out the ways in which these reflect a wide consensus that normative claims are in some way grounded in a natural order that does not depend on individual or social choices (12-35). It goes on to argue that the natural law tradition offers a plausible way of accounting for this consensus in terms of an innate, pre-thematic sense of the natural values and operative structures proper to our existence as creatures of a specific kind (36-43, 79-80). Certainly, these natural givens need to be formulated and given explicit expression in order to serve as norms for action (52-54). Nonetheless, we can identify these natural principles, not perfectly but sufficiently to provide normative guidance for moral conduct and social practice. The ITC concludes by calling on the representatives of diverse traditions to engage in an analogous reflection, drawing on their own starting points, that might facilitate shared recognition of a common morality (116).

This is a reasonable and courteous invitation. It is by no means clear that it will reach the men and women of goodwill to whom it is directed, and it would be regrettable if it does not. The ITC's remarks on the natural law offer what is, taken as a whole, an appropriately modest and attractive entree into the natural law tradition, especially as appropriated in traditional Catholic thought. While the ITC does seem at some points to identify the natural law with specific, and sometimes controversial, moral norms, more often it stresses the pre-thematic and general character of natural law principles, and acknowledges that corresponding judgments will always be to some extent imperfect, context-dependent, and provisional (contrast, for example, 49, 80, 91 with 52-54, 90). This approach leaves room for development in our understanding of human nature and its appropriate expressions — a refreshing departure from the tendency to identify the natural law with a specific set of fixed norms. Even more refreshing, at least for this American reader, is the ITC's readiness to acknowledge the value of personal and communal autonomy, and to commend a robust doctrine of natural or human rights (5, 64-68, 77, 89-90, 92). These affirmations are qualified — as they should be — but they nonetheless open the door to conversation with our many fellow citizens who cherish these ideals.

In my own reflections, I want to focus on one topic that offers greater scope for mutual dialogue than the members of the ITC may have anticipated: the relation between the natural law and human law, especially formally enacted law. Near the beginning of its report, the ITC invokes a contrast between universal natural standards of conduct and legal positivism, arguing that the horrors of the early twentieth century discredited the latter, to the advantage of the former (5). There is some truth to this claim, but it is misleading as it stands, and similarly, misleading to suggest that contemporary secular lawyers and legal philosophers remain committed to a narrow positivism. When we look more closely at contemporary legal philosophy (at least within the Anglophone tradition) it becomes apparent that the situation is more complex. Leading figures in this field have long acknowledged the need to identify some kinds of normative constraints on legal systems, while also attempting to hold on to what is valid in legal positivism. For some time now, the sharp divisions between natural law and positivist approaches to jurisprudence have been eroding, so much so that prominent jurists today sometimes refuse to apply the terms of the division to their own work. To a really remarkable extent, contemporary jurisprudence, even in its most secular forms, has opened up possibilities for extensive and fruitful dialogue between legal philosophers and those who defend a traditional natural law approach to morality and law — as I show in what follows.

Legal positivism is commonly identified with the view that laws depend for their legal force solely on the authoritative will of a lawgiver, expressed though formal enactments in accordance with established procedures. On this view, even the most egregiously unfair or iniquitous law cannot be said to be deficient as a legal enactment, however lacking it may be in other respects. By the same token, even unjust laws are legally binding, implying that it is appropriate and even necessary, from a legal standpoint at least, to punish their infraction.

Understood in these stark terms, legal positivism is clearly problematic. As the ITC notes, whatever credibility it enjoyed at the beginning of the twentieth century was soon undermined by the almost universal revulsion at the horrors perpetrated — with perfect legality — by Nazi Germany, and then later by the Soviet Union, on their own citizens. After the war, the Allies prosecuted Nazi officials by appealing to customary international law and generally accepted standards of conduct, and creating a legal forum for adjudicating these claims. While this procedure could be, and was, criticized as "victors' justice," it could also be regarded more sympathetically as a belated and inchoate acknowledgment of a natural law more basic and authoritative than the formal laws of nation-states. Later, a similar felt need for recognized transnational standards of justice generated a doctrine of universal human — that is to say, natural — rights, and as Ronald Dworkin observed more than thirty years ago, such a doctrine is incompatible with a strict legal positivism.[1]

In contrast, natural law jurisprudence, as commonly understood, identifies the natural law with universal norms, accessible to human reason and precise enough to be put into practice without a great deal of specification or interpretation — a kind of natural law code, in other words, equivalent in its concreteness and comprehensiveness to the laws of a given polity. (This approach is closely allied to the modern rationalist model of natural law that the ITC rightly

---

1. See Ronald Dworkin, *Taking Rights Seriously* (Cambridge, Mass.: Harvard University Press, 1978), 184-205.

rejects; see 33.) Thus understood, the natural law is, or should be, a direct source for positive law, or at the very least, a readily accessible, fairly specific standard against which positive law can be evaluated, corrected, or overturned. A jurisprudence of the natural law, thus understood, played a prominent role in legal thought and practice throughout the modern period, until it began to be supplanted by positivist approaches in the nineteenth century. We might expect that the same circumstances that undermined the appeal of legal positivism would have led to a revival of natural law jurisprudence. Yet jurists and legal philosophers, by and large, did not attempt to revive natural law jurisprudence in its early modern form — that is to say, they did not attempt to ground or evaluate specific laws in terms of their conformity to natural moral principles. The widespread dissatisfaction with strict forms of legal positivism, profound though it was, did not do away with the pervasive uneasiness with natural law jurisprudence that had motivated early positivists in the first place.

It is easy to see why so many modern and contemporary jurists have been uncomfortable with natural law jurisprudence. If the moral law as such had direct legal force, there would be little or no place left for the diverse practices of inquiry, reflection, discussion, and negotiation through which laws are not only formulated, but formulated in such a way as to be embedded in a communal way of life. This approach would therefore render any kind of political procedure, not just democratic procedures, otiose, and by so doing, it would undercut the very processes through which the laws emerge out of some kind of communal consensus and secure general acceptance. Once we take account of these considerations, the significance of authoritative enactment appears in a different light. Certainly, there is something problematic about the early positivist construal of legislative authority as an absolute power, operating without any kind of normative or practical constraints. But seen from another perspective, lawmaking authority serves to safeguard key social ideals — it offers a way to express the judgments of the community in democratic societies, or shared judgments arrived at through some equivalent process of mutual consultation.

Even more fundamentally, we are suspicious of attempts to bring together law and morality too closely, to "legislate morality," for what are, paradoxically, normative considerations. We cherish ideals of equity and mutual forbearance that imply the greatest possible tolerance for differing convictions and ways of life, and a corresponding reluctance to impose the ideals of the majority on an unwilling minority. Even more fundamentally, we know how vulnerable individuals are in relation to state power or public opinion, and therefore safeguard individual rights through guarantees of due process and opportunities to mount one's own defense, in accordance with the ideal that even the worst among us is entitled to a certain respect and forbearance. (Or that is the ideal — it has been badly eroded in recent years, especially in the United States, but that fact only underscores its fragility and its importance.) Law thus depends for its proper functioning on norms of due process and proper procedure that sometimes require us to bracket wider moral considerations — in the name of safeguarding deeply held ideals of respect for all persons, ideals that cannot otherwise be expressed and preserved.

These norms of equity, fair treatment, and respect for individual dignity are expressed through deeply entrenched institutional forms, reflecting what sociologists sometimes describe as the autonomy of law. Thus, Western legal systems typically operate in accordance with their own internal structures, which function more or less independently of other institutions or wider social processes. What is more, the autonomy of law is closely tied to widely shared social values, expressed in ideals of independence of law and proper legality — that legislation and adjudication *should* be carried out without regard to extra-legal considerations, that the validity of these processes *does,* or at any rate *should,* depend on authority or correct procedure and not on considerations of probity or intrinsic reasonableness, and that adjudication *should* be guided by authoritative laws and not exclusively by general considerations of morality or expediency. This last observation reminds us once again that authoritative enactment has a positive normative role to play in any legal system. Apart from some kind of authoritative enactment, the forms and procedures necessary to safeguard the independence of the laws could not be put into place. What is more, formal processes of authoritative enactment themselves express the ideal that the laws should be reflections of communal will and shared interests, in contrast to the oppressive decrees of an overlord or a ruling class on subordinates. Again, it is all too plain that these ideals do not always inform our actual political and legislative processes, but nonetheless, they can be attained, albeit imperfectly, and we cannot afford to give up on them if we want to preserve any semblance of a free society.

It might seem that contemporary jurists and legal philosophers are thus faced with two unsatisfactory alternatives — a legal positivism that offers no check on arbitrary power, on the one hand, or a natural law jurisprudence that undermines democratic procedures and the ideals of integrity of law and due process, on the other. It seems that the members of the ITC have this standoff in mind when they characterize contemporary jurisprudence by a positivist reliance on authority, leaving no space for broader normative considerations. Yet the ITC itself does not advocate a return to natural law jurisprudence in its familiar modern form either. At some points, it comes close — for example, the general natural law principle forbidding homicide is said to imply, as an immediate conclusion of this principle, a law prohibiting abortion (91). But in general, the ITC emphasizes the general and open-ended character of natural values, and acknowledges that specific formulations of these will typically be imperfect and to some extent provisional. By implication, the ITC would reject the kind of natural law jurisprudence that moves directly from natural norms to formal laws.

At any rate, legal positivism and natural law jurisprudence, understood in these unqualified terms, do not today represent the only alternatives. Faced with these options, early twentieth-century jurists began to ask whether the alternatives themselves had been correctly understood, and especially, whether they were necessarily mutually exclusive. They generally agreed that the earlier legal positivists had been right on one critical point. That is, formal laws and legal systems are dependent on social facts — meaning that they are the product of communal choices, whether explicitly (through legislation) or implicitly (through interactions giving rise to customary law). However, beginning with the great legal philosopher H. L. A. Hart, jurists began to argue that formal laws need not — and indeed, cannot — be understood in the simplistic terms of earlier positivism. Hart regarded himself as a kind of positivist, but legal positivism as he understood it implies a sophisticated account of the ways in which laws emerge out of a matrix of social processes, which are themselves shaped and constrained by normative considerations in a variety of ways. Hart recognized that any viable legal system will at least take account of the fundamental aims and limitations of human life, thus defending what he described as the core of truth in the doctrine of the natural law.[2] The American jurist Lon Fuller went still further in this direction, arguing that any legal system will necessarily observe what he called "the inner morality of the law," composed of the formal and procedural constraints that must be followed if the law is to serve as a set of rules for action.[3] And as I noted above, Fuller's distinguished student Ronald Dworkin has for some time argued that the recognition of human rights — analogous to the natural rights defended by the ITC — is incompatible with strict legal positivism.

These jurists converged on one critical point. That is to say, they all af-

2. See H. L. A. Hart, *The Concept of Law*, 2nd ed. (Oxford: Clarendon Press, 1994), 153-84; he introduces the term "soft positivism" in his postscript, 250-54.

3. The main lines of the argument are developed in Lon L. Fuller, *The Morality of Law*, rev. ed. (New Haven, Conn.: Yale University Press, 1969), 33-94.

firmed that formal laws depend on social facts, implying that they are conventional rather than natural, and yet they also agreed that the conventional status of the laws does not necessarily rule out normative constraints on legal authority. Thus, they collectively open the door to a reconsideration of traditional natural law jurisprudence, even though they also preserve the key positivist insight that human laws are dependent on communal choices in some way, rather than directly expressing a fixed, predetermined natural order. Subsequent legal philosophers have continued this trajectory. In his seminal essay on legal authority, Joseph Raz observes that legal positivists have traditionally made three distinct claims about formal law, which he describes in terms of a social, a moral, and a semantic thesis, respectively:

> In the most general terms the positivist social thesis is that what the law is and what it is not is a matter of social fact (that is, the variety of social theses supported by positivists are various refinements and elaborations of this crude formulation). Their moral thesis is that the moral value of law (both of a particular law and of a whole legal system) or the moral merit it has is a contingent matter dependent on the content of the law and the circumstances of the society to which it applies. The only semantic thesis which can be identified as common to most positivist theories is a negative one, namely, that terms like "rights" and "duties" cannot be used in the same meaning in legal and moral contexts.[4]

Raz goes on to observe that none of these necessarily entails the others. While he affirms the thesis that all laws are dependent on social facts, he goes on to say that neither of the other two claims necessarily follows from this fundamental thesis:

> The claim that what is law and what is not is purely a matter of social fact still leaves it an open question whether or not these social facts by which we identify the law or determine its existence do or do not endow it with moral merit. If they do, it has of necessity a moral character. But even if they do not, it is still an open question whether, given human nature and the general conditions of human existence, every legal system which is in fact the effective law of some society does of necessity conform to some moral values or ideals.[5]

4. Joseph Raz, *The Authority of Law: Essays on Law and Morality* (Oxford: Clarendon Press, 1979), 37-38.

5. Raz, *The Authority of Law*, 38-39.

Raz's essay anticipated, and to a considerable extent fostered, what is today a remarkable revival of natural law jurisprudence, or at least, a new openness to take it seriously as a resource for jurisprudence today. This openness goes together with a growing conviction that positivist and natural law approaches need not be exclusive — they can, instead, be regarded as two valid perspectives on law, mutually conditioning each other as they jointly point toward fundamental elements of legal authority. Raz himself defends a "moderate" version of legal positivism because he holds — rightly — that the conventional character of law presupposes that it rests on some kind of authoritative enactment, which is in some carefully qualified sense final and unqualified in its deliberations. At the same time, however, he insists that legal authority, thus understood, is justified because, and only insofar as, it serves (directly or indirectly) to promote the rational functioning of those subject to it. In this way, Raz defends a broadly positivist account of legal authority in terms of ideals of purpose and rationality central to earlier natural law jurisprudence.

Raz's approach thus illustrates a more general point. That is, the revival of interest in natural law jurisprudence does not reflect a rejection of legal positivism, so much as the recognition that we are now in a position to move beyond earlier divisions to incorporate what is best in both approaches. The jurist Neil MacCormick makes this point very well. After referring to the interpretation of legal positivism defended by Hart and Hans Kelsen, which he broadly accepts, he goes on to observe that "various contemporaries have pretty convincingly established that there is a need for improvement and correction to some of the tenets of Hartian or Kelsenian positivism. . . . It is better to reject the aforesaid dichotomy as based on a misleading account of the history of legal ideas than to trouble responding to the question: 'Are you a positivist or a natural lawyer?' . . . The 'natural' character of institutional normative order is not here in issue, though it is certainly natural at least in the sense of being neither miraculous nor unusual."[6] Elsewhere, he defends the stronger claim that a legal enactment can fail to attain legal validity if it does not meet a minimum threshold of morality, justice, or equity:

> Disputable as most deep moral questions are, it is not disputable that some orientation to justice and the common good is . . . essential to legitimate participation in legislative and judicial law-making and law application. Moreover, the fact, if it be one, that reasonable people can reasonably differ

6. Neil MacCormick, *Institutions of Law: An Essay in Legal Theory* (Oxford: Oxford University Press, 2007), 278-79.

about many questions concerning justice by no means entails that there are no outer limits of what can be reasonably represented as justice. . . . It is therefore perfectly possible and reasonable to set outward limits to what can be accepted as moral law. Provisions that are unjustifiable by reference to any reasonable moral argument should not be considered valid as laws.[7]

I turn now to my final point. Recent developments in contemporary jurisprudence were anticipated by key representatives of the pre-modern natural law tradition that the ITC commends. Admittedly, this is not immediately apparent because we tend to read Catholic natural law thinking in particular through the prism of modern formulations. But our medieval forbears came closer to our own contemporaries than these later formulations would suggest, and thus, they open up fruitful possibilities for the kind of shared reflections the ITC commends.

Medieval society in Western Europe in the late eleventh and twelfth centuries was marked by rapid growth, increased mobility, and institutional transformation.[8] As we might expect, social expansion and transformation were reflected in the legal systems, which progressed rapidly from small-scale, localized, mostly customary systems to the kind of complex, formal, self-sustaining legal systems familiar to us today. Institutional forms that we associate with modernity, including relatively autonomous legal systems, can in fact be traced to this period.[9] By the same token, early medieval natural law jurisprudence was not so different, in its key concerns and guiding assumptions, from our own. Like our own contemporaries, medieval jurists, whether canon lawyers or experts in civil law, did not accept the view that the precepts

---

7. MacCormick, *Institutions of Law,* 241-42.

8. These developments have been extensively documented and analyzed by historians over the past several decades; for an excellent entree into this discussion, focusing especially on the complex interconnections among social change, institutional creation, and the expansion of intellectual life, see R. W. Southern, *Scholastic Humanism and the Unification of Europe,* vol. 1, *Foundations* (Oxford: Blackwell, 1995).

9. In addition to Southern, *Scholastic Humanism,* and with particular emphasis on the history of law in this period, see James A. Brundage, *The Medieval Origins of the Legal Profession: Canonists, Civilians, and Courts* (Chicago: University of Chicago Press, 2008); Kenneth Pennington, *The Prince and the Law, 1200-1600: Sovereignty and Rights in the Western Legal Tradition* (Berkeley: University of California Press, 1993); Brian Tierney, *The Idea of Natural Rights* (Atlanta: Scholars Press, 1997); R. C. van Caenegem, "Government, Law and Society," in *The Cambridge History of Medieval Political Thought: c. 350–c. 1450,* ed. J. H. Burns (Cambridge: Cambridge University Press, 1988), 174-210, and van Caenegem, *An Historical Introduction to Western Constitutional Law* (Cambridge: Cambridge University Press, 1995).

of the natural law have direct legal force. They recognized the necessity for authoritative promulgation of formal laws, and they also saw that the formulation of laws requires interpretative judgment, through which general principles can be given the necessary degree of concreteness and relevance.

Most important, medieval jurists gave great weight to the ideal of the independence of the law, and they insisted on norms of due process and proper legality.[10] In the words of the distinguished legal historian James Brundage, by the middle of the twelfth century, a "romano-canonical procedural system" began to emerge, in response to "a mounting deluge of legal actions."[11] Twelfth-century canon lawyers claimed that God himself established the foundations of canonical procedure in Paradise, "when he summoned Adam and Eve, questioned them about eating the forbidden fruit of the tree of the knowledge of good and evil, found their testimony inconsistent, their excuses unconvincing, and in consequence banished them from Paradise (Gen. 3:9-19)."[12] Of course, God knew that Adam and Eve were guilty, but that was the point — rather than pronouncing summary judgment, he gave them their due, the opportunity to defend themselves in court, in accordance with impartial procedures. In a way, God himself acts as if bound by procedural constraints, independently of his own knowledge of the facts of the case. This does not exactly fit with popular images of our medieval forebears as defenders of an uncomplicated religious and moral ideal — inspiring or unsophisticated, depending on one's point of view. Historians of this period have long known better — we have much in common with our medieval forebears, and much to learn from their distinctive approach to a jurisprudence of the natural law. The members of the ITC have placed us all in their debt by calling for the renewal of this ancient, yet perennially vital tradition.

10. See Pennington, *The Prince and the Law*, 148-64, and Brundage, *The Medieval Origins of the Legal Profession*, 126-63, 430-51, for details.

11. Both phrases are taken from Brundage, *The Medieval Origins of the Legal Profession*, 126.

12. Brundage, *The Medieval Origins of the Legal Profession*, 152.

The Role of Natural Law and Natural Right in the Search for a Universal Ethic

Tracey Rowland

Natural Law as a Lingua Franca

In his *Values in a Time of Upheaval,* Joseph Ratzinger wrote:

> Natural law has remained — especially in the Catholic Church — one ele-
> ment in the arsenal of arguments in conversations with secular society and
> with other communities of faith, appealing to shared reason in the attempt
> to discern the basis of a consensus about ethical principles of law in a plu-
> ralistic society. Unfortunately, this instrument has become blunt, and that
> is why I do not wish to employ it to support my arguments in this discussion
> [about the moral foundations of a free state]. The idea of the natural law
> presupposed a concept of "nature" in which nature and reason interlock,
> nature itself is rational. The victory of the theory of evolution has meant the
> end of this view of nature.[1]

In this passage one finds reference to a problem not often acknowledged by
Catholic scholars. Put simply, the argument is that if one's interlocutors no
longer believe that there is any inherent rationality within nature, there is not
much point positing a natural law argument. In such contexts references to
natural law become a "blunt instrument" rather than a lingua franca or "common ethical language." Thus, one preliminary observation upon reading *In
Search of a Universal Ethic: A New Look at the Natural Law* is that there is no

---

1. Joseph Ratzinger, *Values in a Time of Upheaval* (San Francisco: Ignatius, 2006),
38-39.

engagement with this problem by the International Theological Commission (ITC). There seems, on the contrary, to be a presumption that the idiom of natural law is an ethical Esperanto.

While references were made in *In Search of a Universal Ethic* to analogues in the "wisdom traditions" (61) and religions of the world for the principles of the natural law, and here specific mention was made of traditional African, Confucian, Hindu, Buddhist, Taoist, Islamic, and Judaic traditions, the social opposition that Catholics face in most countries of the developed world is *not* generated by conflicts between Catholics and members of these traditions. The most fundamental conflict is with cultural elites who are the heirs of the eighteenth-century philosophers who extolled the value of a rationality severed from all theological presuppositions, or cultural elites who are the heirs of the nineteenth-century Romantic reaction against the rationalism of the previous century for whom the whole category of a universal "human nature" is problematic.[2] As was acknowledged in *In Search of a Universal Ethic*'s paragraph 72, "With the eclipse of the metaphysics of being . . . Nature is no longer considered as an epiphany of the *Logos* . . . [it] ceases being a teacher of life and of wisdom, in order to become the place where the Promethean power of man is asserted." While there may well be points of convergence between the Catholic understanding of natural law and elements in the "wisdom traditions," these points are much harder to locate with the proponents of the liberal and Romantic or genealogical traditions wherein the Promethean potency of man asserts itself.[3]

Those from the Romantic tradition are usually opposed to the notion of pure reason. This is so for those anti-Kantian theists at one end of the spectrum and atheistic types at the other. While Romantics eschew the idea of a pure rationality, most contemporary liberals no longer believe in a universal human nature with particular goods of human flourishing attached to that nature. Nor do they believe in rationality in anything other than an instrumental sense. Like the postmodern Romantics, they tend to reject the idea that there are

2. While this is the primary fault line, the rise of militant Islamic movements signals the emergence of a further battlefield. The public debates in the United Kingdom over the possible recognition of Shari'a law is one example of this developing battle zone. In this context the ITC document refers to a movement in ninth-century Islam toward something like a natural law position, though no reference is made to any contemporary Islamic scholarship akin to the Stoic or Christian notion of a *logos* in creation.

3. The terms "Romantic" and "genealogical" are often used interchangeably, though "Romantic" is clearly broader than "genealogical," which tends to refer to the Nietzschean-inspired branches of the Romantic movement.

stable essences. They categorize essentialist thinking as outdated Aristotelianism — something that our knowledge of evolutionary processes has rendered redundant. Arguably the most famous liberal theorist of the twentieth century was John Rawls, and he totally rejected the idea that there is a range of goods linked to the flourishing of human nature. He argued that if a person wants to spend his life counting blades of grass, then that is the good life for him, and no one else can challenge this vision of a good life. There can be no hierarchical ranking of the goods, or "lifestyle options." The life of the grass blade counter and Mother Teresa are on par with each other. This is a radically different approach to political philosophy from that described in paragraphs 83-85 of the *In Search of a Universal Ethic* document, which is developed around the notion of there being a common good. Paragraph 85 acknowledges that societies can be defined by the type of common good they seek to promote, but it does not address the problem of a society built on the premise that there is no common good.

In the latter half of the twentieth century there was a convergence of the values to be found in the liberal and Romantic traditions. The point of intersection between the two is the notion that human life is a project, a work of art, and that a good society is one that gives the individual the maximum amount of freedom to pursue whatever project appeals. For Friedrich Nietzsche the elite are those whose lives offer the most original artistic creations. Christians and Jews are by this definition members of the herd since their lives are patterned on a model to be repeated again and again until the end of time. Christians face the Nietzschean charge that Christianity is a crime against individual freedom, happiness, and life itself and that all it offers the world is boring, bourgeois conservatism. Instead of carrying on a discussion on the ground of "nature" or "the laws of nature," when these terms are themselves a field of intellectual controversy, it may be better to move the discussion to the territory of alternative conceptions of human dignity, freedom, and self-development. Otherwise, it is a little like facing a twenty-first-century army with an eighteenth-century arsenal.

Rights Rhetoric as a Lingua Franca

A subsidiary issue within the general question of whether natural law is a lingua franca is the issue of whether the rights rhetoric is a lingua franca. The two are linked because from the perspective of Catholic conceptions of natural right, rights are defined by reference to the natural law. Paragraph 88 of *In*

Search of a Universal Ethic describes natural law as the anthropological category to which the natural right doctrine corresponds as a juridical and political category. In this context of the role of the natural right doctrine in the search for a universal ethics, *In Search of a Universal Ethic* describes the *Universal Declaration of Human Rights* (UDHR) as "one of the most beautiful successes of modern history" (5), but then it goes on to list a series of problems with it: (1) "certain countries have contested the universality of these rights, judged to be too Western"; (2) some have devalued the rights by seeking to harness them to the satisfaction of "the disordered desires of the consumerist individual" or of "the demands of interest groups"; (3) some rights have been "disconnected from the moral sense of values, which transcend particular interests"; (4) "the multiplication of procedures and juridical regulations leads into a quagmire, which, when all is said and done, only serves the interests of the most powerful"; and (5) "above all, a tendency comes to the fore to reinterpret human rights, separating them from the ethical and rational dimension that constitutes their foundation and their end, in favour of pure utilitarian legalism" (5).

With reference to this list of problems there are a couple of significant observations to be made. First, at the time of the drafting of the UN's UDHR in 1948 there was no consensus among those on the drafting committee on the theoretical foundation(s) of natural right. It was not a case of there being a golden age when the rights jurisprudence had "Christian-friendly" foundations that subsequently got undermined. There *never were* any commonly accepted philosophical or theological foundations for the rights that were recognized in 1948. The whole project was unstable from the beginning. Sumner B. Twiss has summarized the events of the time as follows:

> The development of the UDHR was a year and a half long process involving delegates from no fewer than fifty-six countries representing quite diverse cultural, moral, political, philosophical, and religious traditions, ranging across such systems and traditions as, for example, forms of Western liberalism (from Europe and America), socialism (from Soviet Russia and the Eastern bloc), Christianity (Catholic, Protestant and Orthodox), Hinduism, Buddhism, Islam (conservative and progressive forms), and Confucianism, among others. There were in fact some delegations (principally from South America) which wanted to build into the UDHR explicitly justificatory appeals to some of these systems. Prominent here were attempts to invoke theistic concepts and even Thomistic versions of natural law. In the actual debates of the Third Committee, these efforts were vigorously discussed and thoroughly aired with the final outcome, spearheaded by the Chinese, In-

dian and French delegates, being this: while the delegations could and did reach pragmatic agreement on a set of essential human rights norms, it was also recognised that, given the diversity of the world's cultural and philosophical systems and traditions, no deeper theoretical agreement would be possible, and so the delegates self-consciously chose to eschew the use of contestable metaphysical language and appeals.[4]

Most significant were the judgments of Jacques Maritain, who was of the view that it was possible to "adopt a practical viewpoint and concern ourselves no longer with seeking the basis of philosophic significance of human rights but only their statement and enumeration."[5] Twiss notes that Maritain's views were explicitly invoked by the French delegate to the Third Committee debate to support the Chinese delegate's position on maintaining metaphysical and justificatory neutrality.[6]

An important question to be put to those who support the justificatory neutrality stance is, What would motivate someone, for example, a Maoist, to respect the inviolability of human life, if one's anthropology is thoroughly materialistic? The Chinese delegates signed the declaration and then their government somehow managed to murder 35 million people between 1949 and 1975, with the ultimate Chinese communist death toll, including all the babies aborted as a result of the one-child policy, unknown. Other signatory states also acquired appalling human rights records, while the countries with the best records tended to be those where the Ten Commandments were most deeply embedded in their cultures. One might argue that the problem with the Nazis was not that they had no concept of natural right, but that their leader had explicitly rejected the Ten Commandments, referring to them as a "device to protect the weak from the strong."[7]

Second, the current legislative and judicial decisions that prevail in Western liberal democracies support the claim of Michael Ignatieff that the ideology of secularism is the lingua franca, or underlying "mythos," of the rights industry in the same way that the English language is the lingua franca of the

---

4. S. B. Twiss, "History, Human Rights and Globalisation," *Journal of Religious Ethics* 32, no. 1 (2004): 39-70, at 57.

5. Jacques Maritain, "Foreword," in UNESCO, *Human Rights: Comments and Interpretations: A Symposium with an Introduction by Jacques Maritain* (Paris: UNESCO, 1948), i-ix.

6. Twiss, "History, Human Rights and Globalisation," 58.

7. Hermann Rauschning, "Preface," in *The Ten Commandments: Ten Short Novels of Hitler's War Against the Moral Code*, ed. Armin L. Robinson (New York: Simon and Schuster, 1943), xiii.

global economy.[8] This is notwithstanding the attempts of Catholic philosophers and theologians to undergird the unstable edifice with an anthropology that includes the cornerstone of a non-rationalist natural law. Paragraph 92 of *In Search of a Universal Ethic* asserts that to acknowledge the existence of natural right is also to acknowledge the objective order of human relations based on the natural law. But this is precisely what the UN delegates found impossible to accept in 1948, and the chance of such a consensus emerging would seem to be even less hopeful in post-1968 conditions.

It might therefore be worth considering whether the unborn and elderly are best defended by the rights rhetoric or by an explicit statement to the effect that all human life is sacred. Direct appeals to the notion of the sacrality of human life may not persuade the liberal intellectuals any more than the references to rights, but they may have the effect of changing the ground on which the battles are fought in such a way that the liberals and the relativist postmoderns are forced to concede the materialistic foundations of their own anthropology. If human life is not sacred then it is a commodity of some kind over which some people have control and others do not. To fight on a pro-sacrality and anti-commodity platform might be better than getting bogged down in the mire of competing interpretations of rights. The political history of the post-1968 period would seem to suggest that the UDHR's consensus, achieved at the expense of any attention to the foundations of its practical claims, rendered it ineffective as an instrument for the protection of human dignity understood in a Christian sense.

Toward a Non-Rationalist Account of Natural Law

While the *In Search of a Universal Ethic* document does not offer advice on how the natural law or rights rhetoric may be deployed in dialogues with proponents of the liberal and postmodern or genealogical traditions, and is in this sense limited in its pastoral practicality, paragraph 33 does acknowledge that "in order that the notion of natural law can be of use in the elaboration of a universal ethic in a secularized and pluralistic society such as our own, it is therefore necessary to avoid presenting it in the rigid form that it assumed, particularly in modern rationalism." The recognition by the ITC that this has been a problem is a very positive development. Catholic intellectuals have of-

---

8. M. Ignatieff, *Human Rights as Politics and Idolatry* (Princeton, N.J.: Princeton University Press, 2001), 53.

ten marketed the natural law idiom as a way of talking about ethics without mentioning God. The suggestion has often been made that while the natural law is embedded in a much richer theological context, for the purposes of dialogue with non-Catholics it is best to keep the discussion strictly in the territory of philosophy, leaving the theological aspects as non-necessary Catholic "extras" to be consumed in private by those who want them.

In his 1969 essay on the treatment of human dignity in *Gaudium et spes*, Joseph Ratzinger was critical of this sort of strategy. He described the notion that "it is possible to construct a rational picture of man intelligible to all and on which men of goodwill can agree, the actual Christian doctrines being added to this as a sort of crowning conclusion" as "a fiction" and one that has the effect of making the Christian part of the puzzle of the human person a special "take" on anthropology that "others ought not to make a bone of contention but which at bottom can be ignored."[9] More generally, Ratzinger complained that a certain amount of ambiguity had arisen because *Gaudium et spes* did not offer a "radical enough rejection of a doctrine of man divided into philosophy and theology" — "the text was still based on a schematic representation of nature and the supernatural viewed far too much as merely juxtaposed."[10]

Thus the question arises: In the presentation of the Church's teaching on natural law, how much of the theological foundations should be laid bare? Should Catholics come out of the closet and acknowledge that their particular version of natural law presupposes a Trinitarian Creator God? The Ratzinger of 1969 would seem to reply, "rather a lot of it" and "yes." The current trajectory of natural law scholarship, consistent with paragraph 33 of the *In Search of a Universal Ethic* document, is also moving in this direction.

A prominent example of this shift may be found in *Aquinas, Ethics and Philosophy of Religion: Metaphysics and Practice* by Thomas Hibbs. Hibbs suggested that one needs to acknowledge that for Aquinas "reason is a participant in an order that encompasses it and exceeds its grasp" and that "there is an intimate connection in his theology between the Trinity as exemplar of human action and the development of a social ontology of individuals-in-relation, and the construal of ethics itself as a mimetic practice."[11] Similarly, in his *Biblical Natural Law* Matthew Levering argued that "no matter how nuanced

---

9. Joseph Ratzinger, "The Dignity of the Human Person," in *Commentary on the Documents of Vatican II*, ed. H. Vorgrimler, vol. 5 (New York: Herder and Herder, 1969), 119.

10. Ratzinger, "The Dignity of the Human Person," 119.

11. T. Hibbs, *Aquinas, Ethics, and Philosophy of Religion: Metaphysics and Practice* (Bloomington: Indiana University Press, 2007), 2.

the schemes for exhibiting basic requirements of human flourishing or however much one attempts to provide an autonomous role for human practical
reason apart from natural teleologies implanted by the Creator there are insu-
perable difficulties: the 'human flourishing' answers reduce to sophisticated
pragmatism rather than real 'law'; the 'practical reason' answers appear to be
a premature restriction of the possibilities of human freedom in ever evolving
history."[12]

As an alternative to a theologically neutered account of natural law,
Eberhard Schockenhoff recommended that the Christian churches "bear
witness to the inherent rationality of the high ethical teachings contained in
the biblical history of revelation" and put them on offer in an "open contest
about the *humanum*, where the various world religions, political utopias and
secular humanisms challenge each other."[13] In such a contest one can ask:
What effect does your vision of rationality, God, nature, and creation have
on your conceptions of human freedom, dignity, marriage, sexuality, death,
and conception?

The groundwork for these newly emerging presentations of the natural
law that are more overtly biblical and Christocentric was laid by the Belgian
Dominican Servais Pinckaers. In his account of Catholic morality Pinckaers
argued that "there is no real separation between the moral part of the *Summa
theologiae* of Aquinas, and its two dogmatic parts: the doctrine on the Trinity,
in particular on the Word and on the Holy Spirit, found in the *prima pars*,
pertains to the morality set forth in the *secunda pars* that we can thus identify
as Trinitarian and spiritual."[14] Similarly, "the doctrine of the *tertia pars* on
Christ and the mystical Body is intimately linked to Aquinas's moral teaching,
which is Christological and ecclesial."[15] Moreover, Pinckaers well understood
the problem with presenting natural law in what *In Search of a Universal Ethic*
called "the rigid form assumed in modern rationalism" (33). He emphasized
that in moral theology, "the point is not to observe the commandments of the
Decalogue materially, to obey them so as to fulfil one's obligations or through
a sense of duty; the point is to observe them out of love, with the heart."[16]

---

12. M. Levering, *Biblical Natural Law* (Oxford: Oxford University Press, 2008), 17.

13. E. Schockenhoff, *Natural Law and Human Dignity: Universal Ethics in an Historical
World* (Washington, D.C.: Catholic University of America Press, 2003), 284.

14. S. Pinckaers, "The Body of Christ: The Eucharistic and Ecclesial Context of Aquinas's
Ethics," in *The Pinckaers Reader: Renewing Thomistic Moral Theology*, ed. J. Berkman and
C. Titus (Washington, D.C.: Catholic University of America Press, 2005), 26-45, at 28.

15. Pinckaers, "The Body of Christ," 29.

16. S. Pinckaers, "Scripture and the Renewal of Moral Theology," in *The Pinckaers Reader:*

Pinckaers noted that this is "precisely the work of the Holy Spirit, infusing charity in our hearts, and forming the New Law within us as an interior law."[17]

Once one brings in the role of the Holy Spirit, including the effect of the gifts of the Spirit within the various faculties of the soul, one moves into the territory of linking affectivity with intellectual judgment, the will with the memory and intellect. Here it would seem to be significant that paragraph 54 of the *In Search of a Universal Ethic* document acknowledged the importance of the "wisdom of experience" and paragraph 57 of "emotional intelligence" for the morality of human actions, while paragraph 55 noted that "the moral subject must be endowed with a certain number of interior dispositions that allow him . . . to be open to the demands of the natural law." These insights were summarized in paragraph 59 with the statement that "it aims at having the subject acquire the intellectual and affective dispositions which allow him to be open to moral truth, so that his judgment may be adequate." These various paragraphs are consistent with the desire, expressed in paragraph 10, to "set out the traditional doctrine of the natural law in terms that better manifest the personal and existential dimension of the moral life." This is a significant and very positive development in the ITC presentation.

In this context it is also significant that Pope Benedict XVI stressed that "love *and* reason" are the "twin pillars of all reality." *In Search of a Universal Ethic* recognizes this theme in paragraph 69. A theological anthropology that pays due regard to the intellectual and affective dimensions of human action is now in the course of development. Here the mid-twentieth-century work of Dietrich von Hildebrand is a valuable source of insights on what the document calls "emotional intelligence."[18] The contemporary work of Robert Sokolowski has also drawn attention to this neglected element in presentations of the natural law. With reference to the notion of the law being written on the hearts of the Gentiles, Sokolowski has argued that the word *kardia* in the passage from St. Paul's Letter to the Romans (usually translated in the Vulgate as *cor*) does not connote the separation of heart and head that we take for granted in a world shaped by Descartes.[19] He concurs with Robert Spaemann's

---

Renewing Thomistic Moral Theology, ed. J. Berkman and C. Titus (Washington, D.C.: Catholic University of America Press, 2005), 46-63, at 51.

17. Pinckaers, "Scripture and the Renewal of Moral Theology," 51.

18. D. Von Hildebrand, *The Nature of Love* (South Bend, Ind.: St. Augustine's Press, 2007), and *The Heart: An Analysis of Human and Divine Affectivity* (South Bend, Ind.: St. Augustine's Press, 2006).

19. R. Sokolowski, *Christian Faith and Human Understanding* (Washington, D.C.: Catholic University of America Press, 2006), 230.

claim that in the New Testament the heart is taken to be a deeper recipient of truth than even the mind or intellect in Greek philosophy since it deals with the person's willingness to accept the truth.[20] These insights of von Hildebrand, Spaemann, and Sokolowski are consistent with what Aidan Nichols discerned as Pope Benedict XVI's desire to unite "philosophy and theology in a single, internally differentiated but also internally cohesive, intellectual act."[21] What one finds in Pope Benedict XVI's many publications is "a convergence of the mainly philosophical disclosure of *logos* with the chiefly theological revelation of love."[22]

Conclusion

In conclusion, the *In Search of a Universal Ethic* document recognizes the problems inherent in a rationalist account of natural law and the need to include a role for prudence and emotional intelligence in the discernment of, and receptivity to, the principles of natural law. These recognitions are welcome developments. However, when dealing with the question of the search for a universal ethics the document points to harmonious elements across the various wisdom traditions and religions of the world but does not address the "elephant in the room," that is, the value of the natural law and natural right idioms when dealing with contemporary liberal and postmodern interlocutors who reject the whole notion of creation and a stable and intelligent order within it. Perhaps part of the problem here is that the Church is dealing with a complex array of issues that transgress disciplinary boundaries. The ITC is concerned with the theological dimensions of the issue, but a strategic plan for dealing with the array of issues would require a supplementation of the theological work with the insights of intellectual and social historians as well as political and linguistic philosophers. It would also require the theologians to work on the issue of just how much of the theological dimensions of the natural law doctrine need to be exposed. How one answers this question depends on how one understands the relationship between nature and grace,

20. R. Sokolowski, "What Is Natural Law? Human Purposes and Natural Ends," *The Thomist* 68 (2004): 507-29, at 525. This section of the essay is a summary of ideas presented in T. Rowland, "Natural Law: From Neo-Thomism to Nuptial Mysticism," *Communio: International Catholic Review* 35 (Fall 2008): 374-96.

21. A. Nichols, *From Hermes to Benedict XVI: Faith and Reason in Modern Catholic Thought* (Leominster: Gracewing, 2009), 228.

22. Nichols, *From Hermes to Benedict XVI*, 222-31.

and the relationship between faith and reason. Currently there is not one Catholic version of natural law, but several, running on different nature and grace, and on different faith and reason, foundations. The *In Search of a Universal Ethic* document does not buy into these foundational issues, which will need to be resolved before there can be any common Catholic account of natural law. As it stands, however, the document's call to move beyond a rigidly rationalist account of natural law is sympathetic to the kinds of approaches fostered by Pinckaers, Hibbs, Levering, Schockenhoff, Sokolowski, von Hildebrand, and Ratzinger, which may at least mean that references to natural law might be less of a blunt instrument when dealing with those who believe that there is a *logos* within creation. In contrast, the mid-twentieth-century bracketing of theological commitments to engage with others on the basis of natural law tended to acquiesce to a central liberal and Romantic-Nietzschean move that in effect subverted (rather than simply bracketed) those commitments.

The question of how best to engage the proponents of the liberal and Romantic and/or genealogical traditions remains an urgent work in progress. For those who have been formed within these traditions the idioms of natural law and natural right are not a lingua franca shared with theists but the very battlefield on which their fight for a culture of death will be fought. For as long as Catholic scholars keep their heads firmly in the sand over this, the younger generation of Catholic leaders will be without a game plan.

Hume and Moore: An Ambiguous Legacy

Fergus Kerr, O.P.

Adversaries or Allies?

At the present time, in the British academic scene, both philosophically and theologically, those of us who endorse natural law ethics as expounded by St. Thomas Aquinas (not that we all agree about what precisely that covers!) need to find allies where we may or at least refrain from caricaturing our adversaries. The story that the International Theological Commission (ITC) sketches of the erosion of natural law ethics since the late Middle Ages under the impact of nominalism, voluntarism, and Prometheanism, dissolving finally into "the idea of a completely arbitrary human creation of values," even "pure and simple nihilism" (71-72), culminates in condemnation explicitly of David Hume and G. E. Moore (73):

> In this context, where nature no longer contains any immanent teleological rationality and seems to have lost all affinity or kinship with the world of the mind, the passage from knowing the structures of being to the moral obligation that seems to derive from them becomes effectively impossible and falls under the criticism of the "naturalistic fallacy," denounced by David Hume and then by G. E. Moore in his *Principia Ethica* (1903). The good is in effect disconnected from being and the true. Ethics is separated from metaphysics.

In effect, even the possibility of discussion between the heirs of Hume and Moore and natural law moralists is refused in advance.

One recent development in Anglo-American ethical theory — especially in bioethics — is the emergence of the concept of common morality. The idea is that all humans — well, all morally competent humans — have a pre-theoretical awareness of certain moral norms. We simply know, without needing to be reasoned into it, as if there were room for doubt, that there is something uncontrovertibly right (say) about certain acts of self-sacrifice and something likewise intrinsically wrong about telling lies, breaking promises, or killing innocent people. These purportedly universal judgments provide the raw data from which ethical theories may be constructed if such are felt necessary, though sometimes the theories only undermine confidence in the validity of the natural reactions so that what philosophers with Christian commitments may be required more often to do is to undermine the plausibility of such theories in order to leave us to act naturally.

In any case, the defense of natural law ethics requires us to stake out as much common ground with our opponents as we can. In this light, need Hume and Moore be picked out and written off so negatively? Given the immensely generous hospitality that the ITC document shows toward Hindu, Buddhist, Chinese, African, Muslim, and other traditions that, whatever their diversity and (one might think) sometimes implausible and bizarre paraphernalia, are credited with holding the fundamental elements of what we might label "common morality," it seems (to say the least) remarkably ungracious to be so dismissive of widely influential thinkers (for better or worse) in one extensive region of post-Christian secular culture. Hume and Moore have each exercised so much influence in the analytic-philosophical tradition that dominates in British universities and spreads its diverse assumptions, ideals, and doctrines throughout the social and political order that it seems defeatist to take for granted that no interaction is possible with either Hume's non-reductive naturalism or Moore's ethical non-naturalism (as we may characterize their positions).

Catholic theologians, however, often have a blind spot about analytic philosophy. Even in the encyclical *Fides et ratio,* which includes a masterly survey of the threat to rationality in contemporary philosophy, the focus is evidently on the Continental tradition (Nietzsche, Husserl, Heidegger, and so on, to name the unmentioned key figures), and on the problems that it creates for the metaphysical and moral realism that we should regard as consonant with and even fundamental to Catholic doctrine. The assumption — which is widely shared by Thomists — seems to be that the "analytic" tradition (Frege, Russell, Wittgenstein, Quine, and so on), dominant in English-speaking universities, remains so stuck in logical positivism, or at any rate in British empiricism and Oxford ordinary language philosophy, that no interaction is worthwhile or even possible. Of course St. Thomas Aquinas did not shy away from contending with philosophical positions that were radically incompatible with the metaphysical and ethical presuppositions that he took as essential for Catholic doctrine — indeed, he was sometimes able to deepen and clarify his own views as a result of engaging with what he clearly regarded as absurd views. It need not only be for apologetic reasons that we might be motivated to debate with the nonbelieving philosophers who are the majority in our neighborhood. To do so in ways that might stir their interest would of course run the risk of speaking their language and thus perhaps of distorting or even surrendering the essentials of our own philosophy. For those who regard Frege's doctrine that existence is a second-level concept as sacrosanct it is, for example, difficult to make sense of the metaphysics of being. However, analytic philosophy has been open to moral and metaphysical realism at least since two famous seminal papers, "Modern Moral Philosophy" (1958)[1] and "Truth" (1959),[2] by G. E. M. Anscombe and Michael Dummett, respectively, both much indebted to Frege and both (as it happens) devout Catholics: the former giving rise to neo-Aristotelian virtue ethics and the latter to the debate about anti-realism, which have occupied center ground in the analytic-philosophical agenda for half a century. Most Catholics who are professionally engaged in philosophy in the English-speaking world are (as Anscombe and Dummett were) astonished that Catholic theologians prefer post-Nietzschean philosophers as their favored interlocutors. Of course there is no agreed position either in virtue ethics or about the realism–anti-realism debate — philosophy, after all, is dialectic; yet it seems premature to assume that Catholic thinkers have nothing to learn or to teach in conversation with typical analytic philosophers.

Moore's Naturalistic Fallacy

We should at least be clear about what philosophers whom we regard as our adversaries actually maintained. For a start, should Hume and Moore be lined up together at all? For some of their heirs, it is true, especially in mid-twentieth-century Oxford, they jointly legitimized emotivism, prescriptivism, and other forms of non-cognitivism in ethics; but is this the best reading of their work?

1. G. E. M. Anscombe, "Modern Moral Philosophy," *Philosophy* 33, no. 124 (1958): 1-19.
2. Michael Dummett, "Truth," *Proceedings of the Aristotelian Society* 59 (1959): 141-62.

The "naturalistic fallacy" was so named by G. E. Moore in his *Principia Ethica*:[3] goodness, which we discern intuitively to be the fundamental ethical value, is not susceptible of being defined in terms of anything natural or non-moral, in terms of either Darwin's biological hypothesis (chapter 2) or Jeremy Bentham's egoistic hedonism (chapter 3). The fallacy is not well named since, for Moore, what is good in itself should not be defined in terms of "a supposed supersensible reality" (chapter 4). Moore's main concern evidently was to refute Herbert Spencer's then extremely influential attempt to found ethics on the evolution-hypothesis ("certain kinds of conduct are more evolved than others") and Bentham and John Stuart Mill's even more influential hedonism ("pleasure alone is good as an end or in itself"). Goodness is *sui generis,* unanalyzable into anything allegedly more elementary: "one of those innumerable objects of thought which are themselves incapable of definition, because they are the ultimate terms by reference to which whatever is capable of definition must be defined."[4] There are certain natural phenomena that are intrinsically good, such as friendship and appreciation of beauty; but, if his favorite examples reveal his pre-1914 English leisure-class ideals, Moore was, of course, just as ready to speak of "great intrinsic evils," giving as examples cruelty and lasciviousness (chapter 6).

Moore knew little about Christian theology (though he and Wittgenstein once tried to read St. Paul's Letter to the Romans together but soon gave up). When he rejects any metaphysical or religious definition of the good this is because he conceives metaphysics as a quasi-science of the supersensible. Good actions are good in themselves, not in need of determination by divine revelation, which means that he would have rejected any form of divine command ethics. In what he opposes, that is to say, we might find ourselves allies. On the other hand, with goodness understood as a directly intuited property, could we be so happy with the epistemology? Moreover, for Moore, as for many British philosophers at the time, Aristotle's analysis of goodness in terms of happiness equates eudemonism with hedonism (chapter 5).

After completing the manuscript, Moore discovered in Franz Brentano's *Origin of the Knowledge of Right and Wrong* "opinions far more closely resembling my own than those of any other ethical writer with whom I am acquainted" (as he notes in the preface). Thus one of the founders of analytic philosophy recognized some affinity with one of the founders of the phenomenological movement. Brentano (formerly a Catholic priest) incorporated

3. G. E. Moore, *Principia Ethica* (Cambridge: Cambridge University Press, 1903).
4. Moore, *Principia Ethica,* 61.

Thomistic ideas into his work, notably the idea of the intentionality of the mental. In his moral philosophy, Brentano saw the directedness of emotions as distinguishing between their correct and incorrect objects, which of course ensures moral objectivity. Little if anything has ever been made of the possible effect on Moore of Thomistic ideas via Brentano.

Things went badly astray, however. In *The Meaning of Meaning* (1923), an extremely influential intervention, C. K. Ogden and I. A. Richards mocked Moore's concept of intuitively discerning good or evil as (in their phrase) "purely emotive." This soon gave us the term "emotivism," or what C. D. Broad, another Cambridge philosopher, scornfully called the "hurrah-boo" theory of moral language. Non-cognitivists in ethics claim that if you adopt a non-cognitivist account of value judgments, it need make no difference to first-order ethical talk: that can go on just as it does, even if ethical sentences are really exclamations, disguised imperatives, or whatnot.

While few would now regard Moore's arguments for the objectivity of good and evil as satisfactory, or his case for immediate access intuitively to these allegedly intrinsically justified values, his concern to defend the principles of ethics and the objectivity of moral judgments against evolutionism and hedonism remains an issue on the agenda. In this respect Moore is even among the precursors from whose mistakes we might learn.

Hume's Law

Hume's law (as philosophers at Oxford in the 1950s labeled it) runs as follows: no sentence containing the word "ought" can be derived from a sentence containing the word "is."

This famous remark comes in an afterthought at the end of Hume's attack in the *Treatise of Human Nature* (III.I.I) on moral rationalism.[5]

> In every system of morality, which I have hitherto met with, I have always remark'd, that the author proceeds for some time in the ordinary way of reasoning, and establishes the being of a God, or makes observations concerning human affairs; when all of a sudden I am surpriz'd to find, that instead of the

5. The first two volumes of the *Treatise*, though not the third *(Of Morals)*, were completed in 1737, when Hume was twenty-six. He chose to settle for nearly three years at La Flèche, in Anjou, to have access to the magnificent library of the Jesuit college. He discussed philosophy with no one but some of the Jesuit fathers. Unfortunately, we have no record of their conversations.

usual copulations of propositions, is, and is not, I meet with no proposition that is not connected with an ought or an ought not. This last change is imperceptible; but is, however, of the last consequence. For as this ought, or ought not, expresses some new relation or affirmation, 'tis necessary that it should be observed and explain'd; and at the same time that a reason should be given, for what seems altogether inconceivable, how this relation can be a deduction from others, which are entirely different from it. But as authors do not commonly use this precaution, I shall presume to recommend it to readers; and am persuaded, that this small attention wou'd subvert all the vulgar systems of morality, and let us see, that the distinction of vice and virtue is not founded merely on the relation of objects, nor is perceiv'd by reason.[6]

Concern with this remark dates from the 1950s: Hume's contemporaries made no big deal of it. The is-ought passage is not mentioned in Norman Kemp Smith's massive *The Philosophy of David Hume* (1941), the pioneering study in the retrieval of what he taught us to call Hume's naturalism.

Hume's argument against rationalism is that moral distinctions cannot consist of relations between ideas, and therefore are not discoverable by reason since "reason or science is nothing but the comparing of ideas and the discovery of relations." Morality, for Hume, is founded on feeling and sentiment, on our reflective impressions:

Take any action allow'd to be vicious; Wilful murder, for instance. Examine it in all lights, and see if you can find that matter of fact, or real existence, which you call vice. In which-ever way you take it, you find only certain passions, motives, volitions and thoughts. There is no other matter of fact in the case. The vice entirely escapes you, as long as you consider the object. You never can find it, till you turn your reflexion into your own breast, and find a sentiment of disapprobation, which arises in you, towards this action. Here is a matter of fact; but 'tis the object of feeling, not of reason. It lies in yourself, not in the object. So that when you pronounce any action or character to be vicious, you mean nothing, but that from the constitution of your nature you have a feeling of sentiment or blame from the contemplation of it.[7]

On the modern reading Hume's is-ought distinction is taken to mean that no ethical or evaluative conclusion whatsoever may be validly inferred from

6. David Hume, *A Treatise of Human Nature*, ed. L. A. Selby-Bigge (Oxford: Clarendon, 1888), 469.

7. Hume, *Treatise*, 468-69.

any set of purely factual premises. For "hurrah-boo" moralists, Hume became a patron of the fact-value distinction, which has a grip ubiquitously in British culture ("These are the facts, it is up to you what to make of them"), far beyond university philosophy faculties. According to this version of Hume's legacy, ethical value is detached altogether from the world and becomes a function of arbitrary individual decision — a state of affairs that would have horrified Hume, a politically and socially conservative thinker. Even on this melodramatic interpretation, however, Hume's is-ought distinction does not coincide with Moore's naturalistic fallacy. Unintentionally, Hume and Moore left the way open for emotivist-noncognitivist ethics, but Hume's attempt to liberate morality from rationalism was a quite different project from Moore's desire to protect the intrinsically good from would-be explanation in terms of evolution, hedonism, and (not that he knew much about it) divine command ethics.

The "hurrah-boo" reading of Hume's remark has been controversial from the outset. Contending that Kant is the one who discovered the supposedly unbridgeable gap between moral judgments and factual judgments, Stuart Hampshire commented en passant that Hume "never denied that our moral judgments are based on arguments about matters of fact, he only showed that these arguments are not logically conclusive or deductive arguments."[8] Similarly, Alasdair MacIntyre, in a detailed analysis,[9] concludes that Hume was not suggesting that morality lacks a basis in nature: he was refusing to found morality in reason alone or in religion at all, founding morality instead in human nature, understood as including human needs, interests, and desires as well of course as reason. And this conclusion Hume regarded as grounded on experience and observation — not on any metaphysical hypothesis, which he assumed to be the only alternative.

Remarks by Hume, as by Moore, or by any philosopher for that matter, are best read in context. Hume regarded himself as the first, "in our philosophical researches," "to march up directly to the capital or center of [all] the sciences, to human nature itself."[10] He challenged the long-established assumption that reason and passion are always in combat, with reason required to rule over our contrary passions. Rather, "reason alone can never be a motive to any action of the will." Reason "is, and ought only to be the slave of the passions," an opinion

---

8. Stuart Hampshire, "Fallacies in Moral Philosophy," *Mind* (1949), reprinted in *Freedom of Mind and Other Essays* (London, 1972), 42-62.

9. Alasdair MacIntyre, "Hume on 'Is' and 'Ought,'" *The Philosophical Review* (1959), reprinted in *Against the Self-images of the Age: Essays in Ideology and Philosophy* (London: Duckworth, 1971), 109-24.

10. Hume, *Treatise*, xvi.

which, as he says, "may appear somewhat extraordinary" (*Treatise* II.III.III)[11] — Hume's would-be witty rebuttal of philosophers for whom our knowledge of good and evil is discovered by reason alone (Hobbes, Locke, and especially Samuel Clarke), at least as Hume understood them. Reason discovers the facts (he believed) but is insufficient to yield a judgment that some situation or action is virtuous or vicious — that requires an emotional response. Moral judgments are grounded not in reason alone but in human nature, holistically understood as embodied, affective, and social. Given the kind of creatures that we are, with the dispositions for pain and pleasure that we have, and the kinds of social interdependence that constitute our life together, we are quite naturally engaged in making moral judgments. Once we have a set of moral concepts we may reach moral conclusions by inference from factual premises, say about the effects of a person's character traits. Hume makes such inferences frequently. Having refuted rationalism (Clarke held that moral judgments can be as certain as those in mathematics), Hume is simply saying that while we move from factual to evaluative judgments, as we commonly and perfectly legitimately do, our motivationally active passions as well as our reasoning capacities are always involved. "Since vice and virtue are not discoverable merely by reason, or the comparison of ideas, it must be by means of some impression or sentiment they occasion, that we are able to mark the difference betwixt them." "Morality, therefore, is more properly felt than judg'd of."[12]

The paradigm of reasoning for Hume is always in mathematics, as so often for philosophers in the tradition since Plato. Of course, we should not want to endorse Hume's remark about reason as "the slave of the passions" (which, like the is-ought remark, is not repeated in the *Enquiry*). On the other hand, we might well envisage an attempt to rebalance the relationship between reason and the passions, and in particular an affirmation of the place of affectivity in moral judgments, which, while not expecting them completely to agree, would provide the common ground to enable Hume and St. Thomas at least to have a conversation.

Hume and Natural Law

Natural law dominated in moral philosophy courses in the Scottish universities in Hume's day. Hume never doubted the existence of natural law. In the *Treatise*

---

11. Hume, *Treatise*, 415.
12. Hume, *Treatise*, 470.

the rules of justice may be called "laws of nature." He specifies property and its transfer by consent and keeping promises. Such laws rest, he insists again, not on reason but on the constancy of human nature:

> The interest, on which justice is founded, is the greatest imaginable, and extends to all times and places. It cannot possibly be serv'd by any other invention. It is obvious, and discovers itself on the very first formation of society. All these causes render the rules of justice steadfast and immutable; at least as immutable as human nature. And if they were founded on original instinct, cou'd they have any greater stability?[13]

Like languages the rules of justice are gradually established by convention. But they are not established by mutual promises or any kind of contract, and they are not arbitrary:

> To avoid giving offence, I must here observe that when I deny justice to be a natural virtue, I make use of the word, natural, only as oppos'd to artificial. In another sense of the word; as no principle of the human mind is more natural than a sense of virtue; so no virtue is more natural than justice . . . Tho' the rules of justice be artificial they are not arbitrary. Nor is the expression improper to call them Laws of Nature; if by natural we understand what is common to any species, or even if we confine it to mean what is inseparable from the species.[14]

Hume and his contemporaries did not think of natural law as a theory: natural law and morality were synonymous. Hume would have been astonished to hear that, according to some commentators, his "no ought from an is" remark would exclude ever appealing to natural law.

Moore's Legacy: Ethical Otherworldliness

Elizabeth Anscombe contended that, in a post-Christian culture, philosophers should cease talking of law, obligation, and so on since these concepts depended (as she thought) on Christian doctrine; they would do better to return to Aristotle and learn how to relate goodness and the virtues to human flourishing *(eudaimonia)*. Since her intervention, there has been a massive renewal

13. Hume, *Treatise*, 620.
14. Hume, *Treatise*, 484.

of Aristotelian ethics. For both Alasdair MacIntyre's *After Virtue* (1981) and Philippa Foot's *Natural Goodness* (2001), to take two obvious examples, there is an intimate relation between virtue and human happiness: between the notions of a good person, of that person's good, and of the good for the human species.

This neo-Aristotelian ethical naturalism does of course attract criticism. In *Good and Evil*, widely recognized as one of the most important contributions to ethics in recent years, Raimond Gaita resists such construals of the human good.[15] Fairly or otherwise we have no space to discuss here, but Gaita regards Foot as reducing ethics to biology: "we could account for the virtues and why we prized them by extending, in ways suggested by Aristotle, our understanding of what is good for the life of a plant."[16] Gaita is equally suspicious of MacIntyre's "non-reductive teleology of the virtues," which is "canonically legitimated and, at certain points, discursively underwritten as a requirement for any sound account of the self and of action"[17] — which, in effect, for Gaita, ties the ethical to the biographical.

These would be new forms of the naturalistic fallacy, not that Gaita uses the phrase. Nor does Gaita mention Moore. His worry is about "an ethic for the relatively fortunate," the "defining concepts" of which are "autonomy, integrity, courage, nobility, honour and flourishing of self-realisation." With this Gaita contrasts "an ethic of renunciation" — the only one, he contends, that "can find words to keep fully amongst us those who suffer severe, ineradicable and degrading affliction or those who have committed the most terrible deeds and whose character seems fully to match them." This ethic of renunciation, Gaita argues, was expressed first by Socrates when he said to his incredulous interlocutors that it is better to suffer evil than to do it. Later, in the Western Christian tradition, Gaita goes on, this philosophy was deepened by an affirmation that every human being is infinitely precious. This may be easy enough when facing human beings who are "flourishing"; it is much more difficult, however, when we have to do with people who are severely damaged mentally or physically, or who are black-hearted criminals. Here Gaita points to "the wondrousness of saintly love" (he himself has no religious commitment), which he finds in Mother Teresa of Calcutta[18] and in a nun whose compassion he witnessed among desperately damaged people in a hospital in which he

15. Raimond Gaita, *Good and Evil: An Absolute Conception* (London: Routledge, 1991; 2nd ed., 2004).

16. Gaita, *Good and Evil*, xxix.

17. Gaita, *Good and Evil*, 83.

18. Gaita, *Good and Evil*, 204-6.

himself worked as a young man. For Gaita there is an "absolute goodness" that even a "non-reductive humanism" does not comprehend; he goes so far as to speak of "a kind of ethical other-worldliness" (but regrets having done so, according to the second edition). Gaita's book certainly exhibits what ethical non-naturalism might mean, going much deeper than Moore.

Hume's Legacy: "Two Faces of Naturalism"

Peter Strawson taught at Oxford from 1947 until retirement in 1987. No one was more typical of Oxford philosophy. After the hostile reign of logical positivism he re-created metaphysics in the analytic mode; in somewhat idiosyncratic readings of Kant he developed a kind of non-Cartesian philosophical anthropology; but he also rehabilitated Hume as an exponent of moral naturalism.

One of the classics of analytic philosophy is Strawson's lecture "Freedom and Resentment":[19] without mentioning Hume, he discredits the attractions of determinism (and its consequences for moral obligation and responsibility, punishing and blaming, and so on) by reminding us of "commonplaces," insisting in particular on what it is like "to be involved in ordinary interpersonal relationships, ranging from the most intimate to the most casual."[20] These "reactive attitudes," as he labels them, are clearly descended from Hume's "moral sentiments." Strawson contrasts adopting an "objective" attitude to other persons, seeing them to be "managed or handled or cured or trained," and a "participant" attitude, granting the other a status that engages "resentment, gratitude, forgiveness, anger, or the sort of love which two adults can sometimes be said to feel, reciprocally, for each other."[21] This contrast may be a variant on Kant's opposition between treating persons as means and as ends. For Strawson, anyway, these diverse types of attitude are rooted in our human nature and our membership in human communities: the thesis of determinism, like Samuel Clarke's moral rationalism for Hume, fails in credibility when we remind ourselves of the ordinary phenomena of the moral life. We need no arguments to refute determinism, any more than we need reasons to justify the mass of reactive attitudes that constitute morality.

19. P. F. Strawson, "Freedom and Resentment," *Proceedings of the British Academy* (1962), reprinted in *Freedom and Resentment and Other Essays* (London: Methuen, 1974), 1-25.
20. Strawson, "Freedom and Resentment," 5.
21. Strawson, "Freedom and Resentment," 6.

In *Skepticism and Naturalism* (1985) Strawson contrasts two types of naturalism: hard, or scientific; and soft, or humanistic. We need not choose between them; indeed, on many issues we switch. There is, however, a temptation to take a naturalistic or objective or even reductive view of human beings and human behavior, which undermines the validity of moral attitudes and reactions. Non-reductive naturalism does not offer would-be arguments, appealing to putative metaphysical and non-natural foundations for our general disposition to moral responses and passing moral judgments — Strawson explicitly rejects the ethical intuitionists (though not naming Moore). Rather, the non-reductive naturalist simply insists that "it is simply not in our nature, to make a total surrender of those personal and moral reactive attitudes, those judgments of moral commendation or condemnation, which the reductive naturalist declares to be irrational as altogether lacking rational justification."[22] There can be a lack only where there is a need. Here Strawson cites the later Wittgenstein, not Hume; but he has made it abundantly clear throughout the book that he is happy to inherit Hume's non-reductive naturalism.

Of course, all of this, including their legacy in the wonderful work of Gaita and Strawson, does not mean that Hume and Moore would persuade, or ever be persuaded by, natural law moralists — but it is hard to believe that the conversation would be fruitless.

22. Strawson, "Freedom and Resentment," 40-41.

Ecocide and Christian Natural Law

Michael S. Northcott

In this essay I lay out grounds for believing that we are in the midst of a grave ecological crisis which, without rapid and serious reparative actions, will see the end of most presently living species; I explore the links between this crisis, industrialism, and the nominalist revolution in Christian theology in the late Middle Ages; I examine the alternative to the nominalist cosmology that the medieval synthesis of Augustinian metaphysics and Aristotelian natural law represents; and I explore the case made by the International Theological Commission (ITC) for an ecological repristination of natural law, and its intersections with the writings of important twentieth-century ecologists, including the English polymath Herbert Massingham and the Norwegian ecosophist Arne Naess.

The Ecological Crisis

It is becoming hard to exaggerate the threat industrial civilization now represents to the future of life on Earth and to future generations of humans. The abundance of life with which humans have shared this planet throughout the 100,000-year history of *Homo sapiens* is now collapsing in the oceans with 90 percent of life fished or hunted out of the oceans in the past fifty years.[1] The abundance of life on land is also in dramatic decline. One-fifth of plant species,

---

1. John C. Briggs, "Marine Extinctions and Conservation," *Marine Biology* 158 (2011): 485-88.

one-third of amphibians, and one-sixth of large mammals are threatened with extinction in the wild. Already the extinction rate is higher than in any previous geological event, and this is the first major extinction event caused by one species.[2] The principal cause of extinction is the destruction of the remaining tropical forests, which are the greatest terrestrial residue of biodiversity as well as major sources of oxygen and freshwater. Forest burning and land use change — principally for conversion to soya and oil palm crops — contributes 20 percent of humanly produced greenhouse gases annually. But forest destruction continues apace in the last surviving tropical forests in the Amazon, in the Congo, and in Sumatra and Borneo, driven by rising demand for biofuels, cooking oil, animal feeds, and tropical timber in the developed and developing worlds. As a result of land-use changes, rising temperatures, and increasing drought in many areas global plant production went into decline for the first time in the decade 2000-2010.

The most immediate environmental threat to millions of human beings presented by the unsustainable nature of industrial civilization concerns their access to potable water. Subterranean continental aquifers that store thousands of years of rainwater are being drained so fast to feed an insatiable and still rising industrial demand for water that they will be all but empty in a few decades. A considerable proportion of the ground water so extracted is being used to grow crops to turn into biofuels to substitute for fossil fuels in luxury cars and to run air conditioning systems and furnaces. The consequences for poor communities are already grave, while others will pay the price for this extravagant waste of a once abundant resource in future decades.

Far from responding to these natural signs as indicative of human error, governments and industrial corporations are seeking out ever new wild areas to mine and drill for fossil fuels, emissions from which the planet cannot absorb without serious harm to human communities already suffering from increasingly frequent extreme weather events. The melting of land and sea ice in the Arctic region represents the greatest present danger from fossil fuel and forest burning. There are many meters of sea level rise in the Arctic and Greenland combined. Summer sea ice has declined so rapidly in recent years that ships can now circumnavigate the Pole in the summer as both Northeast and Northwest Passages are open for the first time in recorded history.[3] As more

---

2. Gerardo Ceballos, Andres Garcia, and Paul R. Ehrlich, "The Sixth Extinction Crisis: Loss of Animal Populations and Species," *Journal of Cosmology* 8 (2010): 1821-31.

3. Julienne C. Stroeve, Mark C. Serreze, et al., "The Arctic's Rapidly Shrinking Sea Ice Cover: A Research Synthesis," *Climatic Change* 110 (2012): 1005-27.

ice melts and more ocean replaces it the dark ocean absorbs more heat from the sun than the reflective white ice and the Arctic warms faster still. In addition, the frozen subsoils and subarctic oceans contain vast quantities of carbon and methane that will be released into the atmosphere as the soils melt and ocean temperatures rise. This process has already begun with the Arctic region having become a net producer of carbon dioxide since 2000, while significant quantities of methane are also being released from the Barents Sea and the once frozen soils of northern Siberia and Canada.[4]

While the nations deliberate over climate and biodiversity treaties, they devoted trillions of dollars of public monies, in the wake of the financial crash of 2007-8, to support the banks that lend the money that fuels excessive consumerism, habitat destruction, and climate change. But they require no change in the ecological sustainability of bank lending practices in exchange for this public largesse. International treaties are so much hot air when governments spend their resources on subsidizing business as usual.

Industrial civilization is not the first civilization to be so resistant to natural signs. Neglect of natural signs that ecological limits were being exceeded led to previous civilizations collapsing: archaeologists believe that the collapse of the Mayan civilization of Central America and of the Roman Empire were in part attributable to ecological destruction. But the present form of industrial civilization is the first to have spread destruction into every habitat on Earth from the deep ocean and once impenetrable tropical forests to the gases in the atmosphere. And yet there is a widespread refusal to acknowledge that there are limits to economic consumption of natural resources, or to pollution and destruction of habitats. And there is a related refusal to acknowledge that changes in the climate that bring increasing drought and flood, and strengthening storms to many regions, is indicative of human abuse of the Earth.

The refusal to acknowledge human responsibility for the significant and discernible global growth in "natural" disasters that is observed, for example, by insurance companies as well as natural scientists is a consequence of the abandonment since the scientific revolution of the traditional Christian account of natural law. The reasons for this abandonment are in part in the scientific revolution itself and in part in the European Enlightenment. The scientific project to manipulate and re-engineer life on Earth began in earnest in the seventeenth century and was described in salvific terms in Francis Bacon's *New Atlantis*. It is in response to the claim of science to discern and de-

---

4. A. Vaks, O. S. Gutavera, et al., "Speleothems Reveal 500,000-year History of Siberian Permafrost," *Science* 1228729 (2013): 1-6.

sign the purposes and structure of biological and physical life that rationalist philosophers from David Hume and Immanuel Kant until the present have abandoned the metaphysical project that had led Plato and Jeremiah, St. Augustine and St. Aquinas, to hold that there is a law-like character to life on Earth that governs the lives of creatures — and of the creation itself — as well as the moral actions and spiritual destinies of human beings. It is this metaphysical perspective that meant that when the land of Israel was turning to desert at the end of the Hebrew monarchy Jeremiah attributed it to human greed, idolatry, and rebellion against the divine law. Similarly, when Plato in *Critias* laments topsoil disappearing from the hillsides of Attica so that the land had become like a skeleton, and when he speaks of the destruction of the once fertile city and region of Atlantis, he indicates that these things happened because those who lived there grew weak in their cultivation of the divine nature and were morally debased.[5] For Jeremiah and Plato ecological destruction of the Earth and moral disorder in the human heart, and in society, are related. As Jeremiah puts it:

> But this people has a rebellious and defiant heart, they have rebelled and gone their own way. They did not say to themselves, "Let us fear the Lord our God, who gives us the rains of autumn and spring showers in their turn, who brings us unfailingly fixed seasons of harvest." But your wrongdoing has upset nature's order, and your sins have kept from you her kindly gifts. (Jer. 5:23-25)

The sense of the intertwining of natural and human purposes and intents, and of a transcendent anchoring and origin of that intertwining, is fundamental to classical, Jewish, and Christian cultures, as it is also to Taoism, Buddhism, Islam, and Hinduism. And in classical and Christian tradition this transcendent anchoring comes to be understood as an essential part of the natural law.

Jürgen Habermas argues that it was in response to the claims of science to order and re-engineer life that modern philosophers abandoned the metaphysical synthesis:

> Modern science compelled a philosophical reason which had become self-critical to break with metaphysical constructions of the totality of nature and history. With this advance in reflection, nature and history became the

---

5. Plato, *Timaeus*, cited in Richard M. Pasichnyk, *In Defence of Nature: The History Nobody Told You About* (Lincoln, Neb.: Writer's Club Press, 2003), 60.

preserve of the empirical sciences and not much more was left for philosophy than the general competences of knowing, speaking, and acting subjects.[6]

Habermas is of course right that the Enlightenment — and first of all David Hume and Immanuel Kant — responded to the rise of science by arguing for a division of labor between philosophers and natural scientists. It is this situation that has brought us to a place where it is hard for philosophers to resituate their moral discourses and logics in the larger than human world without considerable mental gymnastics. In the case of Heidegger and some others, these gymnastics involved the effort to recover the category of being as an ontological order, and the effort — albeit unsatisfactory — to reinstate metaphysical claims against the anthropocentric and immanentist personalism of modern philosophy. However a fuller genealogy, such as may be found in the ITC's report *In Search of a Universal Ethic: A New Look at the Natural Law,* as in the work of Hans Blumenberg[7] or John Milbank,[8] traces the antecedents of the modern break with metaphysics in Western Europe to the late Middle Ages.

The Nominalist Revolution

The great Western medieval metaphysical synthesis — which reached its fullest flowering in St. Thomas Aquinas and which is also manifest in great medieval achievements in architecture, agriculture, politics, and technology — linked God, humanity, and created order in a purposive web of relationships accessible to reason and imbued with the divine Spirit. This synthesis was a result of a new integration between Augustinian Christianity and the newly recovered and translated works of Aristotle that rebalanced the Augustinian heritage with a greater emphasis than St. Augustine achieved on human powers, and loves, in this world. This synthesis not only was a result of a new integration between Western Christian and classical Greek philosophy but also reflected an era, from the eleventh to the thirteenth centuries, in which Europe experienced a particularly benign physical climate, now known as the "medieval

6. Jürgen Habermas, "An Awareness of What Is Missing," in Jürgen Habermas et al., *An Awareness of What Is Missing: Faith and Reason in a Secular Age,* trans. Ciaran Cronin (Cambridge: Polity Press, 2010), 19.

7. Hans Blumenberg, *The Legitimacy of the Modern Age* (Cambridge, Mass.: MIT Press, 1985).

8. John Milbank, *Theology and Social Theory* (Oxford: Blackwell, 1991).

warm period."[9] The resultant crop surpluses not only fostered a theology of a benign cosmic provider but also gave rise to surplus income that led to the great cathedral-building enterprises of the Gothic era.

The benign Middle Ages came to an end with a series of cataclysmic events — the Hundred Years War, the Black Death, and what climatologists now call the Little Ice Age — which saw dramatic declines in crop outputs and the depopulation of whole towns and villages across northern Europe.[10] These events significantly unsettled life in Western Europe, and Western theologians increasingly began to doubt the traditional claim that the purposes of God as Creator could be read off the physical forms of created order or that the Creator Spirit inhabits and sustains creation. Hence the idea of a harmonious cosmic order in which humans play a pivotal role gives way to a stronger emphasis on the omnipotence of God in which there is less room for efficacious human action and in which the sustaining activity of God as Creator is increasingly set apart from the activity of God as Redeemer. These theological moves are first evident in the work of John Duns Scotus and Henry of Ghent and reach their fuller flowering in William of Ockham and the nominalist movement, which, though suppressed by the Church, becomes the dominant theology of the fifteenth century.[11] The nominalists emphasized contingency over order and suggested that every being is an object of special divine creation since all that exists does so by the direct will of God alone. In this view there are no universals set into the structure of being by the Creator other than the will and power of God, and names point only to the particular nature of each being — or "thisness."

The Demise of Metaphysics and Modern Sins against Nature

Nominalist theology produced a new cultural emphasis in Western Europe on human powers in this world, an emphasis that was underlined by the Renaissance. Renaissance philosophers went beyond the nominalists in their recovery of classical humanism, and in particular in the claim that man, and not God, is "the measure of all things." In emptying nature of moral connection

9. Michael S. Northcott, *A Moral Climate: The Ethics of Global Warming* (London: Darton, Longman & Todd, 2007).

10. Michael Allen Gillespie, *The Theological Origins of Modernity* (Chicago: University of Chicago Press, 2008), 15, 29.

11. For a fuller treatment, see Michael S. Northcott, *The Environment and Christian Ethics* (Cambridge: Cambridge University Press, 1996).

with the purposes of a beneficent Creator, while setting humanity up as the supreme being within creation, nature became available for human reordering through the new modalities of capitalism and natural science. The result, as the ITC suggests, is that "the nature of things ceased being law for modern man and is no longer a reference for ethics" (71). Instead of the Creator Spirit being understood as immanent within created order, and the incarnate *Logos* being seen as the one in whom "all things hold together" (Col. 1:17), human reason alone becomes the source of meaning and order in Renaissance thought, and thence in modern science and philosophy. Consequently, nature is no longer encountered as "an epiphany of the Logos," and this loss of the Christian "metaphysics of being, alone capable of founding on reason the differentiated unity of spirit and of material reality," results in a radical opposition between spirit and matter. This in turn sustains an increasingly mechanistic account of nature that supplants the medieval view of Earth as mother and God as father of all being. The results are growing dualisms between spirit and matter, nature and culture, that are clearly enunciated in the *Meditations* of Descartes and in the physics of Newton:

> Cartesian physics, then Newtonian physics, have spread the image of an inert matter, which passively obeys the laws of universal determinism that the Divine Spirit imposes on it and which human reason can perfectly know and master. Only man can infuse sense and design into this amorphous and meaningless mass that he manipulates for his own ends with technical skill. Nature ceases being a teacher of life and of wisdom, in order to become the place where the Promethean power of man is asserted. (72)

There follows a disconnection of the good from the structure of being as narrated in Christian metaphysics, and it no longer seems to moderns that there is any relationship between natural law and the flourishing — morally and spiritually — of life, including human life. Hence an "objective norm" for human behavior gradually disappears in modern European moral philosophy. This disappearance finds philosophical substance in the fact-value and is-ought distinctions of David Hume and G. E. Moore.[12] For Hume and Moore the moral life is no longer set into the structure of life itself. And hence nature, animals, ecosystems, all lose moral significance in societies shaped by Cartesianism, modern science, and rationalism. Hence animals have no endowment of the divine spirit and are consequently subjected to increasing

12. See further my critique of the is-ought distinction in Northcott, *Environment and Christian Ethics,* 71, 245-46.

and systematic cruelty, and perversions of their natural behaviors, in modern factory farms. At the same time wild habitats are increasingly degraded so that non-domesticated creatures from beetles and birds to small mammals and the higher primates all experience a rate of decline in numbers unprecedented in human history.

The ITC recognizes the profundity of the ecological crisis when it speaks of "sins against nature" that manifest the inability or unwillingness of modern humans to recognize the "moral significance of natural pre-rational dynamisms" (80, 79). This inability is linked to the autonomous claims of reason once recognition of the eternal law disappears. Consequently, "the plan of God regarding creation" ceases to have significance for modern man, and moderns increasingly emphasize their autonomy from the given laws that constitute creation (42). Hence the possibility of a shared morality revealed in the divine *Logos* as part of the structure of being — and as affirmed by the Christian natural law tradition — is rejected.

The modern demise of the idea of a shared morality across cultures and traditions occurs precisely at the moment when science, technology, and capitalism link human beings across cultures in unprecedented fashion. The technological and economic interconnectedness of contemporary life creates a sense of human beings across the world belonging to a "single community":

> A local event can have an almost immediate worldwide repercussion. The consciousness of global solidarity is thus emerging, which finds its ultimate foundation in the unity of the human race. This finds expression in the sense of planetary responsibility. Thus, the question of ecological balance, of the protection of the environment, resources and climate, has become a pressing preoccupation faced by all humanity, and whose solution extends far beyond national boundaries. (1)

This global community is also manifest in the shared intentions of citizens, politicians, and religious representatives for poverty eradication and respect for the environment, which are manifestations of "common ethical values" and the common good.

> However, these efforts cannot succeed unless good intentions rest on a solid foundational agreement regarding the goods and values that represent the most profound aspirations of man, both as an individual and as member of a community. Only the recognition and promotion of these ethical values can contribute to the construction of a more human world. (2)

The inability of modern Western philosophers to arrive at such agreement arises from the claimed autonomy of secular reason from the created order and from divine law. Hence the environmental crisis that characterizes modernity is directly related to the nature-culture and matter-spirit dualisms that are set into the foundations of modern Western philosophy.

It is in this context that the ITC proposes a recovery of a natural law account of basic human goods that not only defines those goods in relation to human ends but also recognizes that these goods — since they are the eternal law that also guides the cosmos toward its divine destiny — ought also to shape the interaction between humans and nature.

In the absence of a spiritual foundation for, and appropriation of, fundamental human goods, modern societies have constructed a legal positivism that underwrites an "arbitrary use of power" sustained by the state and by economic corporations, which has produced a form of dominion over the created order that is ecologically destructive (7). A key form of this arbitrariness, in terms of the present ecologically unsustainable direction of industrial civilization, is the modern refusal to recognize that there are natural limits to the manipulation and re-engineering of the human body and the larger created order. The neglect of such limits by the modern powers of science and technology, as mobilized by the corporation and the nation-state, reflects the nominalist and voluntarist character of reason and law, and of cosmology, when shorn of their foundations in natural law. And key to the repair of this neglect of limits is therefore a recovery of the conception of the Earth as a divine creation that, in its stability and life-sustaining character, is a true reflection of the beneficence of divine being, and not merely a randomly evolved arrangement of atoms and cells.

The revival of the medieval Christian tradition of natural law by modern scholars both Catholic and Protestant, as well as by the ITC, therefore represents a significant contribution to the recovery of a form of global civilization that is more ecologically benign. One of the first proponents of such a recovery was the English agrarian H. J. Massingham, who argued that the synthesis of Christian cosmology and liturgy realized in Celtic and Catholic Christianity in the Middle Ages sustained a "religious friendship with nature" that was the most socially just, and the most ecologically benign, form of civilization in Christian history.[13] In Celtic Britain this synthesis promoted the tribal ownership of land and "a unique fusion" between "the Church and Celtic tribal society."[14] And it

---

13. H. J. Massingham, *The Tree of Life* (London: Chapman Hall, 1943), 23.
14. Massingham, *The Tree of Life*, 25.

promoted the gradual end across medieval Europe of the institution of slavery. Hence Catholic Europe, and more especially the Cistercian order, before growing wealth corrupted them both, sustained a liturgically ordered way of life that interweaved agriculture and craftsmanship with the hours of prayer, the seasons of the church's year, and scholarly study:

> The Cistercian idea of wholeness as inseparable from holiness faithfully translated into action the recognition of Christ both as transcendental Godhead and the Peasant Craftsman on earth who expressed a cosmic wisdom in the terms of peasant speech.[15]

The passing of whole villages into monastic hands in the Middle Ages promoted the end of slavery — which had endured from Roman times — while it deepened the liturgical shaping of the agricultural year and the craftsman-guilds of the towns where freed slaves found a living. The Christian humanism of the late Middle Ages therefore had its origins in a natural law–shaped civilization in which every person came to be seen as a holder of natural rights in the land described by Gregory the Great as the "common property of all men" whose fruits "are yielded for the common use of all."[16]

The corruption of the papacy under the Borgias, and the corruption of the Cistercian order as the monks grew wealthy on the success of their agricultural enterprises, led to a break with this conception of property and use rights. It produced a growing alienation between trade and the land, and the emergence of a monarchic, and papal, relation to the people in which lie the first glimmerings of the totalizing powers of the modern nation-state and economic corporations. And it is in this context that the natural law synthesis gives way to nominalist scholasticism.

The ecological crisis can therefore be seen as having its historical roots, and sources for its resolution, in the natural law tradition of the Celtic and Catholic Middle Ages. Instead of the modern materialist mentality, which views nature as an inchoate bank of resources available for reordering by those who are most successful in purloining it, there is the need for a recovery, as the ITC suggests, of "a philosophy of nature, which takes note of the intelligible depth of the sensible world, and especially a metaphysics of creation" that can enable the overcoming of "the dualistic and Gnostic temptation of abandoning nature to moral insignificance" (78). In this perspective the ecological crisis is intricately related to the inability of modern scientists

15. Massingham, *The Tree of Life*, 38.
16. Massingham, *The Tree of Life*, 45.

and economists to treat of material resources as symbolic of a divinely cre-ated realm of being in which the parts are related to a larger divine purpose and order that is logos immanent in the structure of being. The ratio of human will and scientific reason detached from logos represents a uniquely disembodied and ahistorical guiding logic of modern industrial civilization that explains the all-pervasiveness of its destructive relation to the natural order. Against this the ITC's recovery of the natural moral law affirms "the central role of reason in the actualization of a properly human plan of life, and the consistency and the proper meaning of pre-rational natural dyna-misms" (79).

This affirmation of pre-rational as well as rational natural law is fully consistent with St. Thomas Aquinas's account of natural law, and clearly sets the ITC against the neo-Kantian rationalism of the "new natural law" as pro-pounded by John Finnis and Germain Grisez.[17] For the ITC ecological de-struction is therefore appropriately understood as sin against nature,

> insofar as it is opposed to right reason and hinders the authentic develop-ment of the human person. However, some behaviors are described in a special way as sins against nature to the extent that they contradict more directly the objective meaning of the natural dynamisms that the person must take up into the unity of his moral life. (80)

The ITC concludes its ecological consideration with a warning against the danger of absolutizing nature and the neglect of "its intrinsic vocation to be integrated into a spiritual project" (81). While commercial exploitation of na-ture is by human agents who exploit the biosphere exclusively for commercial profit, the biocentric egalitarianism of deep ecology is mistaken precisely be-cause it weakens "the responsibility of man for the biosphere of which he is a part" (81). And the worst extremity of this weakening is manifest in those who argue that humanity is a "destructive virus" on the biosphere since this results in a "totalitarianism that excludes human existence in its specificity and con-demns legitimate human progress" (81).

In this critique the ITC is close to feminist critiques of deep ecology, such as that of the Australian philosopher Val Plumwood.[18] But in response deep

---

17. For a critique of Finnis and Grisez along these lines, see Michael S. Northcott, "The Moral Standing of Nature and the New Natural Law," in *The Revival of Natural Law,* ed. Nigel Biggar (Aldershot: Ashgate, 2000), 262-82.

18. Val Plumwood, "Nature, Self and Gender: Feminism, Environmental Philosophy, and the Critique of Rationalism," *Hypatia* 6 (1991): 3-27.

ecologists such as Arne Naess[19] might argue that the Catholic natural law tradition has itself sustained at various points in its history an ecclesiastical totalitarianism that promoted rather than restrained the subjugation of many humans to an elite few, and the purloining of the land by the few at the expense of the many. This subjugation begins with the domestication of the Mass in the late Middle Ages and the increasing exclusion of those laity who could not afford private chapels from reception of the elements except at Easter. Hence there is a need not only for a recovery of the medieval synthesis, but for a more self-critical recovery than we find in *In Search of a Universal Ethic* that includes recognition of the seeds of the demise of the medieval synthesis in the internal corruption of the Catholic Church in the late Middle Ages. Since that time the totalitarianisms that have often arisen in the modern age have not always been resisted by the Catholic Church, and in certain places and eras — and not least in Latin America — the Church was complicit, and not merely passive, in response. Nonetheless at the heart of this important document are the lineaments of an ecologically situated natural law that speaks powerfully to the modern ecological crisis and that resonates in significant ways with the attempts to critique the roots of this crisis in the disorder of a disembodied reason — and the atomistic individualism and atavistic materialism this reason has promoted — by environmental philosophers and theologians, including deep ecologists such as Arne Naess.

19. For a synthetic account of his thought, see Arne Naess, *Ecology, Community and Lifestyle,* ed. and trans. David Rothenberg (Cambridge: Cambridge University Press, 1989).

In Search of a Universal Ethic: A New Look at the Natural Law by the International Theological Commission

David Burrell, C.S.C.

Some decades ago the impeccably literate commentator of St. Thomas Aquinas Josef Pieper explained succinctly why Thomism had failed to do the work that Pope Leo XIII envisaged it doing: offering a thoroughly rational, hence utterly persuasive, presentation of key facets of Catholic metaphysics and ethics. His disarming remark that the "hidden element in the *philosophy* of St. Thomas is [free] creation" (emphasis added and "free" presumed) corroborated the suspicion of secular philosophers: that the touted distinction between philosophy and theology was quite porous.[1] Yet that very distinction had already been molded into a sharp separation of faculties of Catholic universities, so the damage was done: generations of students would be misled into presuming that the operative core of their faith was available to untrammeled reason. Philosophy, and notably the philosophy of St. Thomas Aquinas, was to mediate between believers and unbelievers because that philosophy was presumed innocent of propositions depending on faith. To their credit, the International Theological Commission (ITC) reflects Pieper's insight throughout their clear and seamless presentation of a traditional Catholic view of natural law. What is more, they range well beyond the philosophy of St. Thomas to make points similar to his, emphasizing how Creator and creation are germane to ethical reasoning:

1. Josef Pieper, *The Silence of St. Thomas: Three Essays* (New York: Pantheon, 1957): "The Negative Element in the Philosophy of St. Thomas," 47-67. For a critical look at traditional lines of delineation between philosophy and theology, see my "Theology and Philosophy," in *Blackwell Companion to Modern Theology,* ed. Gareth Jones (Oxford: Blackwell, 2004), 34-46.

Natural law is understood as the rational creature's participation in the eternal, divine law, thanks to which it enters in a free and conscious manner into the plans of Providence . . . with the recognition of the consistency of nature, in part linked to the rediscovery of the thought of Aristotle, the scholastic doctrine of the natural law considers the ethical and political order as a rational order, a work of human intelligence. The scholastic notion of natural law defines an autonomous space for that order, distinct but not separated from the order of religious revelation. (27)

So the Creator presumed is provident and free, just as the "consistency of nature" is clarified by adding to Aristotle what he could never have conceived: a free Creator. In fact,

it is above all essential to develop a non-competitive conception of the connection between divine causality and the free activity of the human subject. The human subject achieves fulfillment by inserting himself freely into the providential action of God and not by opposing himself to this action. It is his prerogative to discover with his reason the profound dynamisms that define its nature, and then to accept and direct these dynamisms freely to their fulfillment. In fact, human nature is defined by an entire ensemble of dynamisms, tendencies and internal orientations within which freedom arises. (77)

Yet how might these logical and ontological premises guide the "search of a universal ethic" when the key affirmations are embedded in faith? I argue that faith premises do not militate against a kind of shared understanding that could be called universal, using portions of the ITC document to suggest why this is so, though claiming at best indirect support of the document itself. Yet in so arguing, I highlight ways in which this presentation of natural law exemplifies the highly analogous syntax needed for a proper grasp of that multivalent expression. Simply put, be prepared for an understanding of natural law at once theological (though hardly partisanly so) yet also quite ordinary, like that elaborated in Julius Kovesi's slim masterpiece *Moral Notions*.[2] The relevant portion of the ITC document, entitled "Convergences," occurs very near the beginning; it displays how the search for natural law can elicit variegated cultural expressions:

---

2. Julius Kovesi, *Moral Notions* (London: Routledge and Kegan Paul; New York: Humanities Press, 1967).

in diverse cultures, [human beings] have progressively elaborated and developed traditions of wisdom in which they express and transmit their vision of the world as well as their thoughtful perception of the place that man holds in society and the cosmos. Before all conceptual theorizing, these wisdom traditions, which are often of a religious nature, convey an experience that identifies what favors and what hinders the full blossoming of personal life and the smooth running of social life. They constitute a type of "cultural capital" available in the search for a common wisdom necessary for responding to contemporary ethical challenges. (12)

Hindu, Buddhist, Taoist, African, and Muslim traditions are then detailed (13-17) before even mentioning the Western patrimony, "classic Greek culture," presented here with "the exemplary figure of Antigone" (18). Only then are Hellenic developments sketched and named, precisely as bearing witness to the wisdom tradition in the Hebrew scriptures:

In many ways, man is made a participant in this wisdom that comes from God. This participation is a gift from God, that one must ask for in the prayer: "I prayed, and understanding was given to me; I called upon God, and the spirit of wisdom came to me" (Wis. 7:7). (23)

And since this is a Christian document, it will proceed to affirm how, in the fullness of time, Jesus Christ preached the coming of the Kingdom as a manifestation of the merciful love of God made present among [us] through his own person and calling for conversion and the free response of love on [our] part. (24)

The argument implicit here, I suggest, is that each of these religious traditions offers ways that can be construed, analogously, to confirm that

the Creator is not only the principle of creatures but also the transcendent end towards which they tend by nature. Thus creatures are animated by a dynamism that carries them to fulfill themselves, each in its own way, in the union with God. This dynamism is transcendent, to the extent to which it proceeds from the eternal law, i.e., from the plan of divine providence that exists in the mind of the Creator. But it is also immanent, because it is not imposed on creatures from without, but is inscribed in their very nature. (63)

By suggesting how widely divergent cultural expressions can converge on critical points touching human dignity, the document doubtless intends to correct a narrowly Western view of natural law as embedded in a set of specific philosophical strategies. Yet by affirming how such disparate traditions can be understood relative to one another, the document neatly avoids the shibboleth of relativism by presuming that comparative considerations pertain centrally to this sort of inquiry. A new kind of universalism indeed!

Some of the linkages will be highly analogous, of course, as the affirmation of a *Creator,* so central to the traditions this document elaborates, will hardly find a clear resonance in Buddhist or Taoist thought. So we are invited to acknowledge cognate affirmations rather than seek a coherent *notion* of a Creator. Yet it may well be that an analogous notion of *nature* could lead to grasping the gist of such disparate affirmations, finding inverse corroboration in Jean-Paul Sartre's insightful observation that without a maker there can be no nature. So the converging testimony of two sharply divergent witnesses, Pieper and Sartre, may be said to inspire this fresh treatment of natural law, suggesting how *creaturely* it must be if it can be said to be *natural.* And if Josef Pieper's succinct observation — that the "hidden element in the *philosophy* of St. Thomas is [free] creation" — spelled the demise of a Thomism tailored to philosophical modernism, this document offers a benignly postmodern account of natural law, reflective of John Henry Newman, Hans-Georg Gadamer, Bernard Lonergan, and Alasdair MacIntyre, respectively, for whom any inquiry originates in trust by utilizing a tradition critically. And since most such traditions will be religious, and if properly religious, stem from an abiding, if intellectually critical, faith, natural law reasoning will turn out to be as natural as anything else human, reflecting stark variations in human nature together with surprising convergences, yet without benefit of a general theory and absent the specter of pure reason. That conclusion may feel as unsatisfying to many as Wittgenstein's *Philosophical Investigations* initially must have, yet reference to the disarming thesis of Julius Kovesi's *Moral Notions* can help underscore the profundity of Wittgenstein's manner of inquiry, as well as that of this document. I give body to that strategy by calling on witnesses to the way grammar and beauty have the inherent capacity to display the *structure* of a created world, once we learn how to interpret the role they play in our lives and thought.

Kovesi simply reminds us that language itself, when properly used, embodies a grammar that displays a demanding ethic. This grammar can, of course, be violated in slogans, like "pro-choice," for the action of aborting a human fetus can hardly be compared to choosing Coke or 7UP. Our grasp (or not) of the reality proper to undertakings will be revealed (whether we wish to or not) in the way we speak of them, as casual sparring about life-or-death situations displays so clearly. Herbert McCabe's telling example of an intrinsically evil action — "roasting babies alive" — elicits spontaneous revulsion akin to the gang rape executed to Beethoven's *Ninth Symphony* in *Clockwork Orange*. The natural repulsion is elicited by a use of language that can unwittingly reveal the ethic endemic to discourse itself. Nor need we turn to recondite modes of expression to display the normativity embedded in ordinary language. As children we often failed to fathom the zeal our mothers showed for proper grammatical expression until we came across Ezra Pound's powerful observation that "when language corrupts, crime abounds." Indeed, Aristotle's insistence that enunciating a declarative sentence commits us to the truth of what we say is daily confirmed negatively by a habit often adopted by young people: "Well, it is, like, raining." Are they trying to avoid the commitment endemic to an unadorned statement?

Yet does this mode of reflection not sound much like natural law reasoning, though blessedly devoid of theory and animated by fittingness and beauty — two intercultural "universals" of this analogous sort. Yet how can we access what is "natural" in our lives and reflection, when so much of both is constructed? Let me suggest that attention to grammar as an inherent vehicle of what is true and beautiful can remind us forcibly of the polyvalent senses of "natural" in natural law. In this way, the quite disparate work of Olivier-Thomas Venard, O.P., Terry Eagleton, and David Bentley Hart can enhance the rich suggestiveness of this ITC document. The "linguistic turn" here is natural enough to classical philosophical discourse, though enhanced attention to language inspired by the work of the later Wittgenstein has helped us see how classical philosophy was carried by language. Think of the examples Aristotle uses in his *Metaphysics* to introduce as well as establish salient philosophical distinctions, a practice that must have inspired Aquinas's observation in his commentary on the text that "the mode of metaphysics is logical" — read "grammatical." Attending to language need never imply that one ends with language; language is rather a privileged vehicle for any journey beyond the obviously empirical.[3] Three recent works by Venard conspire to celebrate the "poetics" of St. Thomas Aquinas, offering an incisive analysis of the way his acute attention to language gives his arguments *in divinis* their critical edge as well as their celebrated clarity.[4] The works, successively, offer a sensitive

---

3. A point neatly missed by Francesca Murphy in her oddly polemical critique of the strategies many of us have employed in an effort to parse discourse about divinity responsibly: *God Is Not a Story: Realism Revisited* (Oxford: Oxford University Press, 2007).

4. *Litterature et theologie: une saison en enfer* (Geneva: Ad Solem, 2002), *La langue de l'ineffable: essai sur le fondement théologique de la métaphysique* (Geneva: Ad Solem, 2004),

delineation of the central role that Aquinas gives to language in the care he takes in composition in pursuing his intellectual inquiry. By suggesting a way of aligning "medieval" modes of inquiry with "postmodern," Venard's oeuvre brings to light the inescapable role that the language of religious expression plays in the way Aquinas leads us to understand those matters that he avows we are able at best to "imperfectly signify." All of this contributes to the strategy of *manuductio* for which his work is celebrated, as well as accounts for the chiseled clarity of expression that never fails to impress readers of his work, and clearly distinguishes him from his erstwhile peers. This manner of expression itself bears witness to that radical intellectual asceticism celebrated by Pierre Hadot, a benign "postmodern" himself.

Terry Eagleton displays an early and profound formation in classical philosophical theology when he takes on Richard Dawkins in the *London Review of Books*.[5] A piquant taste of his criticism, astutely literary and linguistic, follows:

> Imagine someone holding forth on biology whose only knowledge of the subject is the Book of British Birds, and you have a rough idea of what it feels like to read Richard Dawkins on theology. Card-carrying rationalists like Dawkins, who is the nearest thing to a professional atheist we have had since Bertrand Russell, are in one sense the least well-equipped to understand what they castigate, since they don't believe there is anything there to be understood, or at least anything worth understanding. This is why they invariably come up with vulgar caricatures of religious faith that would make a first-year theology student wince. The more they detest religion, the more ill-informed their criticisms of it tend to be. If they were asked to pass judgment on phenomenology or the geopolitics of South Asia, they would no doubt bone up on the question as assiduously as they could. When it comes to theology, however, any shoddy old travesty will pass muster. These days, theology is the queen of the sciences in a rather less august sense of the word than in its medieval heyday.[6]

Notice how the literary critic uses his finely honed skills to call attention to what "it *feels like* to read Richard Dawkins on theology." The cultural critique

Pagina Sacra: le passage a l'écriture sainte à l'écriture théologique [Postface de John Milbank] (Paris: Editions du Cerf–Ad Solem, 2009); see my "A Postmodern Aquinas: The Oeuvre of Olivier-Thomas Vénard, O.P.," *American Catholic Philosophical Quarterly* 31 (2009): 331-38.

5. Terry Eagleton, "Lunging, Flailing, Mispunching," book review of *The God Delusion* by Richard Dawkins, *London Review of Books* 28, no. 20 (October 19, 2006): 32-34.

6. Eagleton, "Lunging," 32.

that follows suggests why someone today might not feel it incumbent to attend to the niceties of theological discourse, but the rest of the critique does just that, showing how craft-specific attentiveness can identify Dawkins's criticisms as jejune, if not sophomoric. (The book-length sequel melds Dawkins with Christopher Hitchens as "Ditchkins," using acidic humor throughout to illustrate how blunt are the points they purport to make against religion or theology.)[7] Again, it is a relentlessly negative display of the coherence proper to a mode of discourse, specifically by calling attention to the way these "critics" prove unable to "hear" the tensive tonalities in theological assertions. As Wittgenstein succinctly put it: "grammar tells us what a thing is," so will grammatical howlers indicate how we have missed the target.

David Bentley Hart has taken on today's "cultured despisers" of religion and theology as well, in an extended "apologetic" that pulls few punches, yet it is his expository work on *beauty* that better illustrates my point here.[8] For writing *about* beauty can be a snare and delusion, as anyone trying to negotiate the prose of art critics can testify. Recall how painters, when asked what the painting is *about,* have the ready riposte: "If I could say it, I would not have had to paint it!" Hart takes a middle way, exposing by examples how properly theological discourse communicates when it conveys the beauty of its subject by the muted elegance of the prose employed. Similar to Venard's extended illumination of the lucidity of Aquinas's crafted prose, we are reminded that discourse that purports to operate in the stratosphere of the "transcendental" cannot afford to be pedestrian, lest it betray the subject it hopes to expound.

All of which returns us to the intercultural paragraphs of the ITC document, which I have treated as an invitation by the authors to extend a treatment of "natural law" beyond their elegant yet seamless exposition of strategies reflecting Aquinas at his best. Let us add a closing reminder that the "universality" intended is a thoroughly analogous one, open to illumination from disparate cultures, much as Aquinas himself relied on Jewish and Muslim interlocutors to help keep him from speaking nonsense about divinity. His observation, in parsing "naming God," that at best we "imperfectly signify" divinity (*ST* I, q. 13, a. 4), shows how acutely aware he was of that risk, and offers just the space we need for employing some form of Wittgensteinian therapy in matters theological, in metaphysics, and in ethics. For whatever else

---

7. Terry Eagleton, *Reason, Faith, and Revolution: Reflections on the God Debate* (New Haven, Conn.: Yale University Press, 2009).

8. David Bentley Hart, *Atheist Delusions: The Christian Revolution and Its Fashionable Enemies* (New Haven, Conn.: Yale University Press, 2009), and *The Beauty of the Infinite: Aesthetics of Christian Truth* (Grand Rapids: Eerdmans, 2003).

"imperfectly signify" might mean, it clearly implies that we get it wrong much of the time! And that is what we must be prepared to do in intercultural inquiry, so the bold humility that this document displays seems just right. Muslim tradition makes a great deal of the "inimitability" of the Qur'an, the inherent ability of its Arabic to speak to human hearts, yet properly grammatical prose of any sort can remind us of the aesthetic structure of the universe, and so intimate those transcendentals that bind diverse traditions together without having to collapse them into one.

A New Look at the Natural Law

Natural Law as Source of Inspiration: Unpacking *In Search of a Universal Ethic: A New Look at the Natural Law*

Jennifer A. Herdt

The 2009 International Theological Commission (ITC) document on natural law offers a major restatement of the Catholic natural law tradition as a "common moral patrimony" of the world's wisdom traditions (11). This ambitious undertaking is apt to be received in different ways by different audiences, as the authors of the document clearly anticipate; in its opening exploration of convergences among the wisdom traditions and religions of the world, *In Search of a Universal Ethic: A New Look at the Natural Law* addresses itself to Hindu traditions, Buddhism, Chinese thought, African traditions, and Islam. Intramural Christian debates over natural law teaching are addressed less overtly. Yet the document clearly aspires to attract not only those for whom the natural law is a new and unfamiliar way of construing received moral wisdom, but also those who for various reasons have long been suspicious of the language of natural law. How successful is the document in responding to the concerns about natural law discourse typically raised by Protestant Christians?

The openly particularist, fallibilist, and Christocentric way in which *In Search of a Universal Ethic* sets out the natural law as a framework for the search for universal ethics goes a long way in responding to Protestant charges that natural law teaching underestimates the impact of the fall on our capacity to know and do the good. However, there are a few instances in which the document speaks of the discovery of the precepts of natural law in a way that feeds negative stereotypes about natural law thought — stereotypes that regard claims about the natural law as cloaking the contestable character of particular moral teachings by suggesting that they derive in some direct and obvious way from empirical observations of human experience. If these instances are taken as highly compressed summaries of lines of argument that have been or could be developed elsewhere, then they are not worrisome. In particular, if they are read in harmony with the document's overall recognition of the essentially normative and discursive character of the task of distinguishing fundamental inclinations of human nature from mere impulses of desire, and that of reflecting on the range of ways in which these fundamental inclinations can be realized so as to constitute genuine human flourishing, then these moments can be reconciled with the overall grain of the document.

The overall tone of the document is set in its opening paragraphs: Christianity has "*a* teaching on natural law" and not *the* teaching on natural law; Christianity "does not have the monopoly on the natural law" (9); Christians, "engaged in a patient and respectful dialogue with all persons of good will, . . . participate in the common endeavor to promote human values" (3). While clearly rejecting legal positivism, a purely inductive search for a least-common-denominator universal morality, and a Habermasian formalism focused on the necessary conditions of open and free dialogue, the document is careful not to claim that natural law offers a "closed and complete set of moral norms" (27), a "code entirely made of intangible prescriptions" (11), or a "list of definitive and immutable precepts" (113). While the document thus distances itself from the relativism, minimalism, and formalism of dominant secular approaches, it is clearly most concerned to distinguish its own approach from some influential past and present understandings of the natural law. In particular, the document helpfully distinguishes its own interpretation of the natural law from both physicalism on the one hand and rationalism on the other. Physicalism is seen as having attempted to move too directly from biological inclinations to ethical prescriptions and proscriptions, failing to see that natural inclinations become fully intelligible in a normative sense only in relation to the unity of the human person as a rational embodied creature summoned by the love of God (79). On the other hand, the document rejects as rationalistic those approaches that understand the natural law as generated wholly from reason without reference to "pre-rational natural dynamisms" (79 n. 75).

In Search of a Universal Ethic regards both of these misinterpretations of the natural law as results of the secularization of natural law thought in the early modern period (33). As the document narrates these developments, natural law reflection in the early modern period revolted against voluntarist tendencies within late medieval thought, which had deprived both law and nature of any intrinsic intelligibility. In the face of confessional conflicts, natural law thinkers looked to reason as a source of a necessary, eternal, and immutable natural law (30-31). Contemporary rationalistic presentations of the natural law are latter-day instantiations of this modern, secularized understanding of natural law, which was insufficiently historicist and contextualist, inadequately attentive to sin and grace, and falsely deductive in method and comprehensive in ambitions (33). Physicalist interpretations, meanwhile, attempted over against rationalism to recover the significance of pre-rational nature, but failed to grapple with the naturalistic fallacy.

In Search of a Universal Ethic seeks, then, to articulate an understanding of the natural law that can avoid both the Scylla of rationalism and the Charybdis of physicalism. While it holds that one can legitimately speak of an unchanging essence of human nature (52), it conceives of this essence as being realized in a host of different ways throughout human history. Thus it takes natural law to be universal only on a very general level; natural law is culturally and historically variable in concrete application to contingent and changing realities (53). It argues, moreover, that the specification of natural law takes place not deductively, but through a dialectical reflection on tradition and experience (54). And it insists that sin can obscure or even erase even the most general and immutable precepts of the natural law (52). Thus, while one can legitimately speak of the natural law as universal and immutable, the document specifies the universality of the natural law as a universality of *application*: "we find a set of precepts and values that, at least in their general formulation, can be considered as universal, since they *apply* to all humanity" (52; emphasis added). Repeatedly, the document characterizes the natural law as "a permanent and normative guiding principle" (11), a "source of constant guidance" (27; see also 113).

This is a remarkably chastened understanding of the natural law. In fact, it is so modest that it offers ample room for fruitful rapprochement with Protestant thought. The core of the Protestant critique of natural law thinking has been that it fails to recognize the gravity of sin and the fall, and is thus too confident about the possibility of clearly grasping created human nature and/or reading ethical guidance off fallen human nature.[1] Natural law thinking is taken to be insufficiently reliant on revelation and insufficiently Christocentric. But it was Karl Barth, more than earlier Reformed or Lutheran thinkers, who sought to close the door completely to natural law thinking.

---

1. See Stephen J. Grabill, *Rediscovering the Natural Law in Reformed Theological Ethics* (Grand Rapids: Eerdmans, 2006), and Daniel Westberg, "The Reformed Tradition and Natural Law," in *A Preserving Grace: Protestants, Catholics, and Natural Law,* ed. Michael Cromartie (Grand Rapids: Eerdmans and the Ethics and Public Policy Center, 1997), 103-17.

Luther and Calvin themselves were both so preoccupied with the task of excluding any human contribution to or cooperation in justification that they simply did not offer a fully developed account, whether positive or negative, of natural law. What we have are hints capable of being developed in each direction. It is telling that Barth, in his famous dispute over natural theology with Emil Brunner, was driven to say that "we are not in a position to-day to repeat the statements of Luther and Calvin without at the same time making them more pointed than they themselves did."[2] Calvin did not really know St. Thomas Aquinas, notes Barth, but was responding rather to late medieval nominalism; his position does not therefore exclude a possible rapprochement with Aquinas. "It is therefore not physically and mechanically impossible to precipitate oneself into that little corner which has been left uncovered in Calvin's treatment, and to supplement his rejection of Cicero's natural theology by putting forward a dialectical theology of nature and grace," as Brunner effectively did.[3] Barth argues that to do so is a distortion of the overall thrust of Calvin's thought, which is to emphasize the utter incapacity of fallen humanity, but he is forced to admit that his own reading is "more pointed" than what Calvin himself says.

The ITC document's one reference to Protestant thought respectfully seeks to identify the open door to the possibility of a Protestant account of natural law. In a footnote, the document notes that the position of the Reformers "was not monolithic," that Calvin recognized the existence of natural law, and that Protestants drew on natural law thinking in jurisprudential thought for several centuries (31 n. 36). The document goes beyond this to claim that "only with the secularization of the natural law did Protestant theology, in the 19th century, distance itself from it" (31 n. 36). Thus, the document suggests that both Protestant and Catholic thinking on the natural law were warped, though in distinct ways, by modern secular rationalism and its conception of the natural law. With these false ambitions cleared away, the footnote implies, common ground can now appear.

While these claims are not uncontroversial, they are defensible. Calvin does recognize the existence of a natural law.[4] Of course, it is necessary to note

2. Emil Brunner and Karl Barth, *Natural Theology, Comprising "Nature and Grace" by Professor Dr. Emil Brunner and the Reply "No!" by Dr. Karl Barth,* introduction by John Baillie (Eugene, Ore.: Wipf and Stock, 1946), 101.

3. Barth, "No!" 103.

4. On Calvin's understanding of nature and the natural law, see Susan Schreiner, *The Theater of His Glory: John Calvin and the Natural Order* (Durham, N.C.: Labyrinth Press, 1991; Grand Rapids: Baker Book House, 1995), and Schreiner, "Calvin's Use of Natural Law," in *A*

his insistence that the *purpose* of natural law is to render fallen humanity in-excusable. That is, sinful human beings have sufficient understanding of right and wrong in order to be justly held responsible for their actions, but not more than this.[5] More specifically, Calvin argues that when it comes to the "rule for the right conduct of life," as opposed to knowledge of God and the way of salvation, fallen human beings are often capable of correctly framing general principles, but less so of applying them justly to particular cases (*Inst.* II.II.23). The power of understanding earthly things (things having to do with the present life, including government and household management) has been less af-fected by sin than the power of understanding heavenly things. So fallen hu-man beings remain capable of fostering and preserving society, according to "universal impressions of a certain civic fair dealing and order," the seeds of which have "been implanted in all men" (*Inst.* II.II.13). Calvin speaks of this as a kind of "instinct" appropriate to a "social animal." It is sharply distinct from the knowledge of God's will and the rule by which we conform our lives to that rule since these belong among heavenly things.

When it comes to the will, Calvin downplays the significance of the first precept of the natural law, to do good and avoid evil. This, too, is simply an instinct, held in common with nonhuman animals, not to rationally pursue what is truly good, but to follow inclination without reason or deliberation. "Good" here, moreover, argues Calvin, "refers not to virtue or justice but to condition, as when things go well with man" (*Inst.* II.II.26). It is only through Christ's incarnation that grace is restored to fallen humanity, and only through the regeneration of the Holy Spirit that human beings become capable of lov-ing what is truly good. The image of God radically corrupted at the fall can only be restored by Christ, the most perfect image of God, and this is the "end of regeneration" (*Inst.* I.XV.4).

The thrust of Calvin's argument is to disclose fallen humanity's utter de-pendence on redemptive grace, not to identify a universal objective ethic. But genuine common ground between Calvin and *In Search of a Universal Ethic* nevertheless exists. In both, claims about the universal recognition of certain very general moral norms having to do with life in society are placed alongside claims about the difficulty of descending to particulars and about the profound effects of sin on the human heart. Both, moreover, place their account of the

---

Preserving Grace: Protestants, Catholics, and Natural Law, ed. Michael Cromartie (Grand Rap-ids: Eerdmans and the Ethics and Public Policy Center, 1997), 51-76.

5. John Calvin, *Institutes of the Christian Religion,* ed. John T. McNeill, trans. Ford Lewis Battles (Louisville: Westminster John Knox Press, 1960), II.II.22.

natural law emphatically within the context of salvation history, grace, and the work of Christ.

This Christological frame of the ITC document comes to the foreground only in its culminating chapter. Prior to this point, only a brief paragraph adverts to Jesus Christ as making the love of God personally present in humankind and as taking up the Golden Rule (24). Chapter 5, in contrast, is squarely centered on Christ, as its title, "Jesus Christ, the Fulfillment of the Natural Law," suggests. The chapter begins with a significant qualification of the autonomy of the natural law; nature "is not foreign to the order of grace" (101). This is developed through a *Logos* Christology; the Son of the Father is the *Logos,* the image of God in whom all things were created. Man "bears in himself a very special imprint of this personal Logos" (103), but this image has been "seriously obscured" by sin (104). Sin's perversion of human nature is not so grave that human beings are incapable of recognizing the traces of God in creation, but they "do not recognize the profound meaning of the world and interpret it in terms of pleasure, money or power" (104). Jesus Christ, the incarnate *Logos,* restores the image of God to humanity. Thus, he is both "the ultimate criterion for correctly discerning the authentic natural desires of man" (105) and the Savior "who gives us the real possibility of putting the law of love into action" (110), revealed in his teaching and most fully in his passion.

This is certainly still an ethic of continuity rather than disruption; grace does not destroy but perfects nature; only Christ reveals the fullness of the human, but this "confirms elements already present in the rational thought of the wisdom traditions of humanity" (114). But it is only because human nature is in a special way made according to that image that is the *Logos* that the natural law exists in human beings as a participation in eternal divine law. And it is only due to the restoration of the image of God through the incarnation, through the *Logos* uniting itself with the humanity of Jesus, that the moral intelligibility of human nature is manifest; "only in the mystery of the Incarnate Word does the mystery of man become clear" (105, quoting from *Gaudium et spes,* 22). Moreover, the gravity of sin is acknowledged to be such as to preclude the possibility of either adequately grasping or living out the natural law apart from grace. Thus, both ontologically and epistemologically, the autonomy of the natural is denied. Ontologically, the natural law rests on the special relation of the *Logos* to human nature, realized most perfectly and fully in the incarnation. Epistemologically, ethical guidance cannot be read in any straightforward way off fallen human nature, and created human nature can be fully grasped only in and through Christ. This is both an epistemologically humble and an emphatically Christocentric statement of the natural law, one that will be acceptable, even attractive, to many who stand in the tradition of the Reformers, even as it must be conceded that Protestant thinkers suspicious of the kind of continuity associated with *Logos* Christology, or emphatic that the saving work of Christ can be appropriated only through explicit personal faith, will be resistant to its approach.[6]

Up to this point I have emphasized what I take to be the primary face of *In Search of a Universal Ethic,* one that articulates a rather modest account of the natural law as a "spring of inspiration" rather than a source of concrete action-guiding norms. On this account, affirming the natural law amounts to a way of committing oneself to moral realism; dialogue across traditions; and ongoing casuistic reflection drawing on tradition, scripture, and concrete experience (including scientific and social-scientific investigation). It is a distinctive way of committing oneself to these things, one that offers a theological and metaphysical account of how they all hang together coherently, of why it is that we may cherish a reasonable hope that dialogue will be productive, and of why it is that the ethical categories received from casuistic tradition can and should be extended and developed in such a way as to respond to the findings of scientific and social-scientific investigation, but without losing their theological bearings. It is not, though, a source of action-guiding moral norms derived purely from rational reflection on the fundamental inclinations of human nature, since "reason" is always already formed and informed by particular traditions of reflection, and the identification of "fundamental inclinations" and of "human nature" as such is likewise conditioned and mediated by our grasp of reality as a whole.

But there are also moments at which *In Search of a Universal Ethic* speaks of natural law not as a "source of guidance" but rather as a source of "objective and universal" precepts that constitute a "permanent critical instance" (9). At such times, which come to the foreground in chapter 2, the document is at risk of feeding stereotypes about natural law thought as seeking to short-circuit debate over particular, highly contestable moral teachings by rooting them in what is "natural."[7] A question-begging slide from a set of "natural inclinations"

---

6. Kathryn Tanner develops a vibrant contemporary statement of this Christocentric understanding of human nature in a way that shows their ecumenical potential, in chapter 1 of *Christ the Key* (Cambridge: Cambridge University Press, 2010).

7. I set to one side the document's heavily Kantian interpretation of Aquinas's comments concerning the first principle of practical reason, which here appears as a moral obligation imposed immediately by reason on itself. I suspect that an elision here of the distinction between the first principle of practical reason (describing the intentional character of human agency) and the first precept of the natural law (that good is to be done and pursued and evil

to concrete action-guiding precepts obscures the fact that the very process of distinguishing "simple blind impulses of desire" from "fundamental inclinations" of one's nature is already carried out with reference to one's understanding of what is, finally, perfective of that nature and what can serve as a final *telos* of one's activity (45). In gliding over these distinctions, *In Search of a Universal Ethic* appears not to acknowledge how theologically and metaphysically laden its account of both the fundamental inclinations of human nature and the precepts of natural law actually is.

At a variety of points in chapter 2, the document appeals to the pervasiveness of certain impulses and immediately experienced perceptions as though these in and of themselves yield normative conclusions. For instance, the impulse of self-preservation, which *In Search of a Universal Ethic* identifies as "a spontaneous reaction," is taken as a reason for affirming physical life as a "fundamental, essential, primordial good" (48). But an impulse or spontaneous reaction as such does not deserve, on the document's own terms, to be considered a fundamental inclination, so more would need to be said to ground the conclusion that physical life is a fundamental good. Turning from the inclination to self-preservation to the inclination to survival of the species, *In Search of a Universal Ethic* announces that "the good of the species appears . . . as one of the fundamental aspirations present in the person" (49). But how do we move from the sexual impulse to some purported concern for survival of the species, and from this to some purported aspiration to serve the *good*, as opposed to the mere survival of the species?

If these claims are made on the basis of empirical observation, they are surely open to dispute; the sexual impulse may in fact, as it operates over whole populations, contribute to the survival of the species, but it need not do so by way of any conscious aspiration on the part of the human person. The document speaks of "the natural inclination that leads man to woman and woman to man" as "a universal datum recognized in all societies," together with "the inclination to care for one's children and educate them" (49). But is it the *universality* of these impulses that renders them genuine inclinations of human nature? Surely not this alone; just as the fact that most participants in Stanley Milgram's notorious authority experiments were willing to comply with an apparently scientifically authorized command to administer electrical shocks to innocent persons does not render this a moral as opposed to a statistical

---

avoided) helps to prepare the ground for a further slide from (purportedly) universal aspects of human experience to claims about basic inclinations of human nature, and from basic inclinations to action-guiding precepts. I, however, confine myself to the latter.

norm. Furthermore, the inclination that brings man to woman and woman to man is recognized in all *societies,* yet it is not universal on the level of individual experience. The document is silent on this fact, and on the matter of how one might nevertheless conclude which form or forms of human sexual orientation constitute a fundamental inclination, rather than a blind impulse of desire. Having pointed to the universality of the inclination to sexual union and to raise children, the document states that "these inclinations imply that the permanence of the union of man and woman, indeed even their mutual fidelity, are already values to pursue" (49). But the implication is in no way spelled out, nor is there any acknowledgment of the fact that this implication has not itself been universally drawn.

There is one point in its account of the fundamental inclinations of human nature and the precepts that flow from them at which *In Search of a Universal Ethic* acknowledges that its account of these might be open to dispute. This comes in the discussion of the third set of inclinations, which have to do with the rational, spiritual, and relational character of properly human existence. In this context, the document notes that the desire to know and live in communion with God "can be denied by those who refuse to admit the existence of a personal God," even as it goes on to claim that "it remains implicitly present in the search for truth and meaning, experienced by every human being" (50). A broader admission of the highly compressed and contestable character of this discussion of the fundamental inclinations and precepts of the natural law would have been salutary here.

The document does acknowledge that the fundamental inclinations of human nature are different from "simple blind impulses of desire" (45). But it suggests that this distinction makes itself available with a kind of immediacy and universality that many will fail to see reflected in their own observations. The document also acknowledges that discursive reason is involved in the move from fundamental inclinations to the goals and precepts that "the human being" proposes for the sake of contributing "to the harmonious and responsible development of his own being and which, as such, appear to him as moral goods" (48). But in lieu of exemplifying discursive reason's work here, the document appears merely to assert that certain desires count as inclinations and that certain apparent goods are in fact perfective. It is indeed illuminating to see these ethical precepts as responsive to fundamental inclinations, and to construct an account of fundamental inclinations that reflects observed experience. But the process of moving between precepts and inclinations is much more dialectical than the document acknowledges, with both being fully informed by one's holistic grasp not only of human nature, but also of the nature of reality as such. At this point, the note of epistemological modesty repeatedly sounded by *In Search of a Universal Ethic* seems to ring hollow. These precepts do not in fact constitute "the common foundation for a dialogue in search of a universal ethic," even if those who hold them may consider them to be universal in the sense of applying to all of humanity (52).

The most charitable way to read this section is as a kind of shorthand, a promissory note inviting elaboration rather than seeking to exclude the need for it. When read in such a way, it can be brought into harmony with the dialogical and fallibilist tone of the document as a whole. Read thus, the compressed character of the comments properly draws attention to, rather than hides, the need for a fuller theologically and metaphysically informed account of the pathways of reflection linking self-preservation and the right to work, sexual inclination and a permanent marital bond between man and woman. What would emerge from such an account would be the complex ways in which traditional teachings, social changes, scientific observations, and ordinary experience come together in reflection and are interpreted through theological and metaphysical lenses that lend them unity and intelligibility and that justify their universality of application.[8] When developed at such a level of detail, natural law thinking admittedly loses some of the caché and authority that seems to accrue to the "natural"; its contestability becomes evident. But by virtue of its transparency it gains in credibility and can indeed become, not a common foundation, but a flexible and resilient framework for dialogical encounter with other traditions of ethical reflection.

---

8. Jean Porter's *Nature as Reason: A Thomistic Theory of the Natural Law* (Grand Rapids: Eerdmans, 2005) develops such a project in exemplary fashion. Porter defends a broadly Aristotelian account of human nature against strong constructionist accounts, but this does not directly give rise to properly ethical norms. The latter "emerge through an ongoing process of reflection and articulation, through which men and women become aware of the natural patterns of activity structuring their lives, and begin to guide their lives in accordance with these structures." "A Response to Martin Rhonheimer," *Studies in Christian Ethics* 19, no. 3 (2006): 391. This process of reflection and ongoing specification is carried out in the context of all sorts of contingencies and in the light of an overarching theological or metaphysical understanding of reality (393).

Seeing the Whole: How Protestants Help Us Read the Natural Law

David Cloutier

The natural law has long presented vexing challenges for what James Gustafson describes as the possible "rapprochement" between Protestant and Catholic ethics.[1] The Vatican II instruction for moral theology to become more scriptural and focused on vocation and discipleship[2] inspired Catholic debates over "faith and ethics"[3] and also led to the increasing influence of Protestant ethics, including Catholics studying at ecumenical institutions. Does the International Theological Commission's (ITC) articulation of the natural law contribute to this rapprochement? This essay addresses this question by engaging classic Protestant objections to natural law ethics, exemplified by sharpened versions in the work of Stanley Hauerwas. I suggest that the ITC's document does display a rapprochement with Hauerwas's work (properly understood; he is not quite the antithesis of a natural law thinker that some assume), and that his versions of classic Protestant critiques help Catholics read all of the ITC document's chapters as a unified, interdependent whole, culminating in the treatment of the New Law. However, such a reading may call into question the document's aspirations for a natural law that secures a common foundation for harmony among traditions, nations, and peoples.

---

1. James Gustafson, *Protestant and Roman Catholic Ethics: Prospects for Rapprochement* (Chicago: University of Chicago Press, 1978).

2. See *Optatam totius,* 16.

3. See the review of the "distinctiveness" debate and discussions of scripture in chapters 4 and 5 of Paulinus Odozor, *Moral Theology in an Age of Renewal* (Notre Dame, Ind.: University of Notre Dame Press, 2003).

Protestant Critiques of Natural Law

Protestant criticisms of natural law ethics, for the purposes of this essay, may be grouped into three categories. First, as Gustafson notes, Radical Reformation thinkers called into question the whole notion of a natural law by reading the law of the gospel as strikingly "new" and in fact overturning the notion of a continuity between a given order and the order of the gospel.[4] This "discontinuity" criticism calls into question any connection between a natural moral order and the Christian life. A second set of criticisms, by far the most influential, are epistemological concerns about the supposed access to a rigid, given, immutable "order."[5] For these thinkers, natural law represents an overconfidence in reason's ability to make clear determinations of right and wrong, often instead naming what turn out to be "the sinful pretensions of the age."[6] Such a "sub-Christian" principle can even distort the Christian life itself, by "correcting the defects" of scriptural codes.[7] Finally, a third set of criticisms concerns the political effects of natural law, namely, that such a concept can offer arbitrary support and comfort to the state, as well as justification for its use of coercion, and thereby mute the necessary Christian witness to the inadequacy of the state's actions.[8]

Hauerwas's work, while influenced by all three concerns, focuses on the latter two. Despite the influence of the Radical Reformation on Hauerwas's work, his approach does not reject a "natural law," in the sense affirmed by Aquinas of the human creature's rational participation in the eternal law. I am not aware of any place in his work where Hauerwas seriously denies the existence of a "human nature" common to all persons, nor does he embrace a version of so-called divine command ethics, whereby reasoning about moral action is somehow excluded. He "certainly . . . would not deny that [natural knowledge of God] may exist," and he rejects the idea that a "specifically reli-

---

4. Gustafson, *Protestant and Roman Catholic Ethics*, 15-17.

5. Such a concern is voiced throughout Gustafson's text, most primitively as Luther's critique of the law as promoting a destructive presumption of self-confidence in one's goodness. Note also Paul Ramsey's suspicions that it had to end up naming either "a new form of legalism" or "an ethic of intuition." *Basic Christian Ethics* (New York: Scribner, 1950), 340.

6. Reinhold Niebuhr, *The Nature and Destiny of Man* (New York: Scribner, 1964), 281-82; cf. Gustafson, *Protestant and Roman Catholic Ethics*, 62, 144.

7. Ramsey, *Basic Christian Ethics*, 76.

8. A criticism exemplified in the twentieth century by Karl Barth; see Nigel Biggar, *The Hastening That Waits: Karl Barth's Ethics* (Oxford: Clarendon Press, 1995), 52-62. Barth shares the epistemological concern as well.

gious morality implies that we worship and serve a God who arbitrarily issues commands for no reason."[9]

Hauerwas's concerns about natural law, then, are not of the "discontinuity" sort, but rather can be divided into epistemological and political concerns. Let us address each in turn. First, he sharpens the epistemological concern about the "alleged transparency" of the natural law tradition, worrying that it, "rather than indicating agreement between Christian and non-Christian, served to note agreements within a widely scattered and pluralistic Christian community,"[10] and it "was intelligible only so long as Catholicism presupposed a social order whose practices had been formed by Catholic habits."[11] Thus, what it represents is actually "the means of codifying a particular moral tradition."[12]

But Hauerwas extends this epistemological critique to moral psychology. Natural law ethics "creates a distorted moral psychology" by assuming that moral acts can be described in a "neutral" fashion, abstracted from both "the dispositions of the agent" and the agent's conviction-shaped identity. It ignores both vision and virtue — indeed, even the very description of acts is dependent on one's virtues (or vices) and one's conviction-shaped character. Ethics is about vision, and "seeing" is not merely a neutral act; yet natural law ethics lulls its adherents into ignoring this.[13]

This distorted moral psychology is disguised by the homogeneity of subculture Catholicism, but once that age ends, Hauerwas sees revisionist Catholic moralists (McCormick, Fuchs, Gula, O'Connell) as the consequence. He

---

9. Stanley Hauerwas, *The Peaceable Kingdom: A Primer in Christian Ethics* (Notre Dame, Ind.: University of Notre Dame Press, 1983), 69. As Michael Cartwright notes, he critiques not "Thomistic" but "Kantian" accounts of natural law because of the latter's abstraction from social location and character formation. See *The Hauerwas Reader*, ed. John Berkman and Michael Cartwright (Durham, N.C.: Duke University Press, 2001), 639. Cf. Hauerwas, *With the Grain of the Universe* (Grand Rapids: Brazos, 2001), 36; and also his exposition of Aquinas and Luther on the Decalogue in "The Truth About God," in *Sanctify Them in the Truth* (Nashville: Abingdon, 1998), 37-59.

10. Hauerwas, *The Peaceable Kingdom*, 51.

11. Hauerwas, "The Importance of Being Catholic," in *In Good Company: The Church as Polis* (Notre Dame, Ind.: University of Notre Dame Press, 1995), 96.

12. Hauerwas, *The Peaceable Kingdom*, 51.

13. For a Catholic account that Hauerwas evaluates *positively*, see his comments on Martin Rhonheimer in "Gay Friendship: A Thought Experiment in Catholic Moral Theology," in *Sanctify Them in the Truth* (Nashville: Abingdon, 1998), 105-21. He approves of Rhonheimer's refusal to abstract acts from the consideration of relevant circumstances and of the agent's virtue-shaped practical reason.

quotes Timothy O'Connell's summary of natural law ethics as the command to "Be human," thus using the natural law tradition to contend that what "Be human" means must be something available in the experience of all agents, and (even more important) from the supposedly neutral data of the social sciences.[14] Such "autonomous ethics" — "natural law ethics by another name"[15] — took advantage of the growing sense of human autonomy and cultural pluralism in society to argue that what was "truly human" must be regarded as true since, according to Aquinas, revelation did not add any new moral precepts.[16]

While Hauerwas has little sympathy for these thinkers, neither does he believe that moral clarity can be remanufactured by assertions about "objectivity" from ecclesial authorities. He points out acerbically that the claim that natural law is an alternative to ecclesiastical authoritarianism "seems doubtful in light of the history of the use of 'natural law' by church authorities to support authoritarian positions. Indeed, I would suggest that part of the difficulty with the moral reasoning supporting some of the church's sexual ethics is that by attempting to give them a 'natural law' basis devoid of their theological basis they appear arbitrary and irrational — thus requiring authoritarian imposition."[17]

Using sexual ethics as an example, Hauerwas claims "bluntly" that "there is no way that the traditional Christian insistence that marriage must be characterized by unitive and procreative ends can be made intelligible unless the political function of marriage in the Christian community is understood."[18] Characteristically, the claim here is about "intelligibility," not about the infinite malleability of human sexuality; indeed, he acknowledges on the previous page that "broad anthropological analysis has shown us that we are fundamentally

14. Both O'Connell and Gula have developed richer accounts of the moral life in their later work. See Richard M. Gula, *The Call to Holiness* (New York: Paulist, 2003), and Timothy E. O'Connell, *Making Disciples* (New York: Crossroad, 1998).

15. Odozor, *Moral Theology*, 116, referencing the claims of Bruno Schuller, *Wholly Human*, trans. Peter Heinegg (Washington, D.C.: Georgetown University Press, 1986).

16. Odozor, *Moral Theology*, 112, following the claims of Joseph Fuchs. But note that Aquinas's natural law ethic is not freestanding: all law, including natural law, is of God, "the external principle moving to good, . . . Who instructs us by means of His law" (*ST* q. 90, intro.), instruction we need precisely because of the problem of sin, dealt with in the questions immediately prior (qq. 71-89). At a minimum, Aquinas presumes the context of a God who instructs and a situation (sin) where instruction is needed.

17. Hauerwas, *The Peaceable Kingdom*, 64.

18. Hauerwas, "Sex in Public: How Adventurous Christians Are Doing It," in *The Hauerwas Reader*, 483.

sexual beings, and that is indeed a good thing."[19] But such an account does not get us very far ethically. And specifying that one can do so via "natural law" generates even more confusion: Is what is "natural" a particular structure of the "marital act," or is "the natural" found in broader experiences of human sexual flourishing? Hauerwas compares natural law to Reinhold Niebuhr's attempt to justify various sexual norms, such as monogamy, on the basis of the "cumulative experience of the race."[20] But whose experience? Such hand-waving then leaves one without resources when the culture changes and/or when the claim is falsified by the study of other cultures. When they continue to be pressed as "natural law," the effect amid a pluralism of practices is to render them *less* persuasive, not more. What is needed, instead of repeated assertions about an objective moral order assumed to be universally intelligible, is for the natural law tradition to recover crucial psychological and social elements of act description and agent formation to replace this "view from nowhere."

But if the ability to make universal claims is lost, might a "located" natural law lead to a sectarian politics that would portray those outside the tradition as simply lost in sin and darkness? As Gustafson particularly charges, doesn't such epistemological specificity entail a withdrawal from collaborative projects in a pluralistic society and world?[21] This charge is the flipside of the Barthian concern that the natural law approach is dangerous precisely because it tempts us to collaborate politically and remain "relevant" only by serving as a support for political power that is contrary to the gospel.

The political problem, it would seem, is to provide enough common ground for collaboration, while also narrating the natural law with sufficient connection to the gospel witness so that one can identify where such collaboration is refused. Hauerwas proceeds in a subtle way amid these concerns. First, he points out that for Catholics, "our culture's persistent failure to find an adequate substitute for Christianity has presented theologians with a temptation almost impossible to resist. Even if they cannot demonstrate the truth of theological claims, they can at least show the continued necessity of religious attitudes for the maintenance of our culture."[22] On Hauerwas's reading, this

19. Hauerwas, "Sex in Public," 482. Elsewhere, he says he is "unsympathetic" to "the peculiarly modern presumption that our sexual conduct has no purpose other than the meanings we give it and so are able to derive from it." See Hauerwas, "Gay Friendship," 118.

20. Hauerwas, *With the Grain of the Universe*, 64.

21. Hauerwas, "Why the 'Sectarian Temptation' Is a Misrepresentation," in *The Hauerwas Reader*, 104.

22. Hauerwas, "On Keeping Theological Ethics Theological," in *The Hauerwas Reader*, 52.

has already proven a disaster for Protestant ethics (as exemplified by his career-long criticisms of Reinhold Niebuhr), and he thinks that the work of Catholic natural law thinkers like John Courtney Murray and the Catholic neo-conservatives represent a similar attempt to maintain "relevance" by portraying the natural law as the necessary and only alternative to "the destructive individualism [and positivism] of Locke and Hobbes."[23]

But such an approach leads to one of two ends, both problematic: either one acts coercively and violently in order to impose such views, or (what Hauerwas sees as the far more likely outcome) one ends up neglecting the very theological claims and community formation Christians actually need to survive such cultures. If the former path is pursued, natural law proves to be *more* triumphalistic than Hauerwas's ethic, not less. Why? Because the natural law approach "tempts us to coerce those who disagree with us, since its presumptions lead us to believe that we always occupy the high ground in any dispute."[24] This is of course a hangover from "the habits and practices of a Constantinian ethic," which was the crucible in which natural law was developed.[25] With a Christian prince ruling a society made up almost exclusively of Christians, this was problematic enough, but in a pluralistic society it tempts us "to imagine that those who do not share such an ethic must be particularly perverse and should be coerced to do what we know on universal grounds they really want to do."[26] Whether in "anti-Burqa" laws made by "neutral" elites in Europe or in the kind of violence that infects debates over abortion in the United States, the presuppositions of the universality of "our" moral knowledge may not lead to a more harmonious and peaceful world, but in fact to a world with much more violence.

But ironically this political temptation then also neglects the real Catholic task in pluralistic societies: formation in discipleship for witness. Hauerwas's work has always warned that, in the U.S. context, the "anyone" of the natural law tradition "turned out to be . . . the 'individual' of the Enlightenment, whose very being depended on the refusal to acknowledge or spell out his/her particular history."[27] The problem with an "ethics for everyone" is how it is unable to "imagine the visibility of the Gospel after Christendom."[28] The most important "involvement" that a Christian has in any society is "being the Church," not coerc-

---

23. Hauerwas, "Sex in Public," 467. Hauerwas notes his preference for Pope John Paul II over Murray on faith and reason in *With the Grain of the Universe*, 226.

24. Hauerwas, *The Peaceable Kingdom*, 63-64.

25. Hauerwas, "The Importance of Being Catholic," 97.

26. Hauerwas, *The Peaceable Kingdom*, 61.

27. Hauerwas, "The Importance of Being Catholic," 101.

28. Hauerwas, *With the Grain of the Universe*, 240.

ing the Enlightenment individual. This task of witness and conversion, plainly authorized as primary by the New Testament commissions, is *harmed* by attempts at coercion, and even further endangered when attempts to use state coercion to secure certain natural law claims require compromises with existing arrangements. Such a problem is exemplified by the odd and destructive allegiance of U.S. Catholic leaders with the pro-military, pro-market political party, though one might equally cite compromises made on the opposite side.[29]

By contrast, Hauerwas's approach is politically more humble. He notes that "emphasis on the distinctiveness of Christian ethics does not deny that there are points of contact between Christian ethics and other forms of the moral life."[30] Such ad hoc points of contact provide ample opportunity for Christians to be involved in many efforts that are pluralistic in composition, while acknowledging the necessary limits of such involvement depending on circumstances.[31] What is crucial here is a balance between recognizing overlap and yet not allowing such an overlap to rest on an ethic independent of the gospel.

Reading the International Theological Commission Document

Is the ITC articulation of the natural law tradition susceptible to these criticisms? I think the answer is no, if the document is read a certain way — in particular, as long as chapter 2 is not abstracted from the entire document. However, read this way, one cannot help but wonder whether the desiderata listed in the opening document — a natural law theory aimed at consensus and world harmony amid pluralism — can really be obtained by rehabilitating natural law.

The Protestant epistemological suspicion of the abstract "view from nowhere" that does not attend to the psychology and social formation of the agent, and retains overconfident access to the details of an objective order, from which norms can be deduced, does not reflect how the ITC document

---

29. See Hauerwas's concerns about the "bind" in which the U.S. bishops find themselves in their letter *The Challenge of Peace,* in "Should War Be Eliminated? A Thought Experiment," in *The Hauerwas Reader,* 401. This bind between a gospel vision of peace and (especially U.S.) military action supposedly based on natural law is indicated in the divergence between magisterial and U.S. Catholic discourse about Iraq.

30. Hauerwas, *The Peaceable Kingdom,* 60.

31. Hauerwas, "Why the 'Sectarian Temptation' Is a Misrepresentation," 102-4: "I see no reason why such stark alternatives [complete involvement and complete withdrawal] are necessary."

proceeds. While the first two chapters offer a series of cross-cultural examples to support the epistemological plausibility of the existence of the natural law — surveying traditions in order to identity "a largely common moral patrimony" (11) and reflecting on how humankind "experiences an interior call to do good" (39) — they do not add up to the kinds of objective, rigid abstractions on which the Protestant critique focuses. Instead, "only the recognition of the metaphysical dimension of the real can give to natural law its full and complete philosophical justification" (62). This claim, which begins chapter 3, introduces the document's true theoretical foundations, which are treated in chapters 3 and 4. What are those foundations? Chapter 3 presents a noncompetitive relation of agency between the divine and the human (77),[32] which places human freedom not only within God but also within the providentially established cosmic order of the eternal law and thus within "nature." This ontology is then paired, in chapter 4, with a noncompetitive account of the human political order oriented by the pursuit of the common good (85).

The combination of an account of agency positioned within a *theological* cosmology, and then acting within a particular kind of political order, responds to Hauerwas's key epistemological criticisms: the failure to recognize the natural law's dependence on customary arrangements within a particular type of social order, and the abstraction of agency from any sort of theological vision. Both the vision and the eschatologically limited social order fulfill his desire for a natural law that "only makes sense against a theological background."[33] The document thereby throws into doubt all Catholic theologies — whether they rely on the "experience" distilled from social science data or "pure reason" (e.g., "new natural law" theory) — which attempt to make arguments apart from metaphysical and political claims. It moves beyond what Oliver O'Donovan calls "the unacceptably polarizing choice between an ethic that is revealed and has no ontological grounding and an ethic that is based on creation and so is naturally known."[34]

Moreover, by recognizing both the continuity with and the necessity of the New Law, the "deeper perspective on God's plan" offered by salvation history (103), for these natural law claims, the document responds to the *ecclesial and political* Protestant critiques. It corrects any idea that the natural law rep-

---

32. Cf. *Veritatis splendor,* 38-45.

33. Stanley Hauerwas and Jana Bennett, "Catholic Social Teaching," in *Oxford Handbook of Theological Ethics,* ed. Gilbert Meilaender and William Werpehowski (Oxford: Oxford University Press, 2005), 520-46, at 522.

34. Oliver O'Donovan, *Resurrection and Moral Order,* 2nd ed. (Grand Rapids: Eerdmans, 1994), 19.

resents a "minimalistic" ethic that waters down and neglects the real ethic of the gospel.

The New Law is in fact the fulfillment of the natural law, such that love of God and neighbor are the internal *telos* of the natural law. The document emphasizes that the natural law "is not foreign to the order of grace," but that grace "heals [nature], strengthens [it], and leads it to its full realization" (101). Such an ordering follows Hauerwas's claim that nature cannot be understood apart from God's action in Jesus and the church, but neither can Jesus and the church be understood properly without the "natural dimension."[35] The natural order is already an order of love, or at least is intended to be such. The law revealed in the Old Testament is not inferior, but is already the law of the love of God and neighbor (Leviticus 19), the law of the Golden Rule (Tob. 4:15) (108). The justice to be established in society is already one of solidarity, in which love is *interior* to justice, not simply added.[36] The love command, already present, "becomes with Christ the commandment to love without limit" (108). It is placed in the more radical context of enemy-love, mercy, and a "challenge . . . to take the initiative in a love that is a gift of self," illustrated by the parable of the good Samaritan (108). Love thus "acquires a universal dimension and a matchless strength," and so breaks down existing barriers with a new eagerness (108).[37] The natural law is thus not only theological, but also Christological.

This "Christological fulfillment" is also a "Christological necessity" because of sin, by which humans have "made bad use of [their] freedom" (104). Due to sin, humans "do not recognize the profound meaning of the world and interpret it in terms of pleasure, money or power" and even try to hide their actions and "elaborate false theories to justify their sins" (104). Jesus reveals the fully human, and shines this light in his life (105), and his existence makes it impossible to hide. Yet this necessarily harsh light is "good news" because Jesus is also revealed as the one who forgives sin, so long as the hiding and self-justifying are abandoned. By recognizing this problem and Jesus' compassionate response to it, the document allays concerns about a potential minimalism that, as Barth feared, could lead to support for forms of fascist oppression (e.g., Hitler), but simultaneously moves against the concern Hauerwas raises about triumphalism and coercion: the document's admirable emphasis on the tragic blindness caused by sin, and the subsequent necessity of Chris-

35. Hauerwas, "The Truth About God," 45.

36. This is very consistent with the place of love in Catholic social thought established by *Caritas in veritate*.

37. One might here imagine much recent literature on vocation to be a characterization of this wholehearted dedication to the cause and practice of love.

tians to act in self-sacrificial ways for all, invites us to imagine the world as in need of service and healing, not coercion.

One might object to my close linking of the chapters by noting that chapter 2's object "is precisely to show how the common moral values that constitute natural law are grasped" (37). How does sin affect this experience? This "freedom" encounters the good, but is "weakened by sin" (41), the chapter tells us. But chapter 5 takes a stronger line on the problems sin introduces. First, due to sin, persons "hate the light and elaborate false theories to justify their sins" (104). Second, they fail to recognize the "profound meaning of the world" because they "interpret it in terms of pleasure, money or power" (104). Sin gives us bad theory and inflates the importance of certain kinds of selfish goods. If sin makes humans "so gravely affected" (104 — not just "weakened"!), then some recognition of the limited effectiveness of natural law arguments must be acknowledged. In particular, sinners need the invitation of forgiveness, rather than the rod of coercion, in order to acknowledge such sin.

But even apart from the discussion of sin in chapter 5, chapters 3 and 4 also remind us not to read chapter 2 in isolation. The theo-political vision offered there raises questions: Does the person with "immediate experience" in chapter 2 need at least the experience (if not the theory) of living noncompetitively with God, nature, and her neighbor if she is to understand rightly her interior experience of the law? And does she also need to live in a political order directed toward the "common good," understood as "the good of all and of each one in particular" (85), and "open to the perpetual search for God, truth, and justice" (96)? It would seem so. Yet achieving some semblance of these apart from revelation is a tall order. Not impossible, of course. A non-eschatological politics of the common good is certainly possible, but it is far from the standard politics of the secular, individualistic state. And noncompetitive ontologies populate secular environmental movements, often drawing on Asian religious traditions, though, as the document warns, this kind of holism can "risk . . . absolutizing nature," such that the proper place of the human person and the personal character of the transcendent end is lost (81).

Given this kind of piecemeal overlap in vision and politics, the document would seem to substantiate Hauerwas's piecemeal, ad hoc approach to political engagement. As with chapter 1's appeal, not simply to the Western tradition, but to many world traditions, the document outlines natural law as a vision that we are likely to encounter in incomplete versions in political reality. It thus redescribes natural law in a way that is less likely to tempt Christians to coercion, but also in a way that retains the importance of witness to the New Law as the completion of any natural order encountered.

The Search for "Common Values": Still an Open Question?

In response to the Protestant criticisms, exemplified by Hauerwas, I have suggested that the ITC has moved toward a richer, more contextualized, more theological account of natural law, insofar as we read the document's five chapters as a unified whole. But in so doing, I conclude by noting that the document's "search for common ethical values" for addressing such global challenges as the environmental crisis, terrorism, and biotechnology (all mentioned in the opening paragraph) is rather quixotic (1). It is interesting to juxtapose this hopefulness with Alasdair MacIntyre's comment that defenses of the natural law will commit us "not just to continuing disagreement, but to continuing conflict with those who reject the precepts of the natural law and with those who uphold the authority of positive law that is at odds with the natural law. And commitment to this kind of conflict is incompatible with the norms of the liberal state."[38] And we might add, the norms of the capitalistic economy. MacIntyre's writings suggest that defenses of the natural law, far from bringing people together, will instead create inevitable and intractable *conflict* with the dominant institutions and intuitions of our contemporary world. That is not an argument for abandoning natural law. But it calls into question the idea that natural law can represent "common values" if the development of such values requires a cosmology and a politics so at odds with dominant ideas.

Of course, some commonalities will be found, especially in the large pieces of the Catholic world that remain less than fully instantiated into liberal individualism. But in modernized contexts, Hauerwas represents a reminder that in addition to seeking commonalities amid pluralism, even "natural law" points forward to its fulfillment in a New Law addressed to a world of sin. Common language and pluralistic structures may sometimes work, but perhaps it is Hauerwas's gift to the Catholic world to be a constant antidote to the Church's temptation to spend much time and energy trying to speak to "all people of good will," while neglecting the task of forming and disciplining its own people. When it tries — and unfortunately, there is no shortage of examples of this failure within Catholic ecclesial life! — the most beautiful arguments in the world tend to fall on deaf ears.

---

38. Alasdair MacIntyre, "From Answers to Questions: A Response to the Responses," in *Intractable Disputes about the Natural Law,* ed. Lawrence S. Cunningham (Notre Dame, Ind.: University of Notre Dame Press, 2009), 313-51, at 341.

Can't We All Just Get Along?

Gilbert Meilaender

In Search of a Universal Ethic: A New Look at the Natural Law is a clearly written, though not especially exciting, presentation of natural law theory as it has developed in the Roman Catholic tradition. Perhaps those concerned to examine the intricacies of intra-Roman Catholic debates about natural law can find places where the document tilts in one direction or another, but I find relatively little that is new in the overall presentation. Nor is that comment intended as criticism. It is perfectly appropriate to attempt a restatement of the basic structure of natural law theory.

More striking, at least to me, is what appears to be the animating spirit of the document — a belief and hope that getting clear on the structure of the natural law will help us all to get along. This is the admirable, though touchingly naïve, starting point of the document. The search for natural law is characterized as the search for a universal ethic that can bring people together, securing peace and happiness for them. It can help achieve global solidarity, a shared planetary responsibility, and ecological equilibrium (1). The hope — as Rodney King plaintively expressed it in the midst of rioting that followed acquittal of the police officers who had beaten him — is that "we all can get along."

There are at least three reasons why one might question whether *In Search of a Universal Ethic* makes such hope plausible: (1) The International Theological Commission's (ITC) depiction of natural law has simultaneously too much theory and too little anthropology. (2) The document does not sufficiently recognize the need for virtue if one is to discern the natural law. (3) The document does not think through to the end the implications of its assertion that Jesus Christ is the fulfillment of the natural law.

I

It is always a bad idea to carry more theoretical baggage than is actually needed, especially perhaps when traveling to a destination as remote as a "global solidarity" (1) in which "the total human community" will "transcend egotistical and partisan tendencies" (10). *In Search of a Universal Ethic* gives what I take to be a relatively standard theory of natural law — beginning with the precept to do good and avoid evil, moving to certain fundamental inclinations that lead us to perceive three "natural dynamisms," from which one reasons to secondary precepts, which prudential reason then applies to the various circumstances we encounter in life.

Perhaps this essentially Thomistic theory, "belonging properly to the metaphysical order" (76), does, in fact, unpack the underlying structure of the objective moral law. Yet it seems, at least to me, to lack the metaphysical ground of which it speaks. While rejecting voluntarism and anthropological dualism, the document does relatively little to describe what it calls "the human in the human being" (36). It might have been wise to begin lower to the ground, with basic reflection on the nature of human life. The fundamental character of organic life is a work of self-preservation carried out through an activity (metabolism) that both works to preserve the organism and, simultaneously, to open it to the surrounding world. That openness involves a desire to mate and, at least in human organisms, the capacity to reflect on what is not immediately given. The entire character of such organic life is purposive, which means that we cannot talk of nature without also talking of destiny. Thus, if we could think a little more about what the nature of human beings actually is, the basic structure of the natural law might appear less as theoretical baggage and more as a description of the most fundamental features of human organic life from which all traces of anthropological dualism would already be eliminated.[1]

In any case, I would not put forward the theory developed in the document as a promising way to achieve shared — much less, universal — moral agreement. And, in fact, at a number of places the ITC document itself seems implicitly to suggest that such theoretical baggage is more likely to follow agreement than be a path to it.

Thus, the document begins with "convergences" (11). The great moral and philosophical traditions of our history "witness to a largely common moral patrimony" (11). Most human cultures have recognized the excellence of (for ex-

---

1. I have developed this anthropological perspective in greater detail in chapter 2 of *Neither Beast Nor God: The Dignity of the Human Person* (New York: Encounter Books, 2009).

ample) courage, patience, compassion, and moderation, even as they have regarded as vicious (for example) murder, theft, greed, and avarice. Different religious and philosophical traditions may ground these virtues and vices in different explanatory theories, but they share "common moral values" (37). Versions of Golden Rule reasoning abound in human history. "Who does not know that homicide, adultery, theft and every kind of greed are evil, since one does not want them done to oneself?" (51). If agreement is what we are seeking, we are far more likely to find agreement that such precepts are deliverances of reason than we are to agree on a theory that explains their rationality. This common moral patrimony — what C. S. Lewis, in *The Abolition of Man*, called the Tao — shines by its own light. We reason from these shared values, not to them.

This was, in fact, the experience of those who worked to frame the *Universal Declaration of Human Rights,* which the ITC document characterizes (perhaps a little too effusively) as "one of the most beautiful successes of modern history" (5). In the process of preparing the declaration, UNESCO convened a committee of philosophers to examine the theoretical ground for claims about human dignity and rights. Jacques Maritain, one of the participating philosophers, later recounted how "at one of the meetings of a UNESCO National Commission where human rights were being discussed, someone expressed astonishment that certain champions of violently opposed ideologies had agreed on a list of those rights. 'Yes,' they said, 'we agree about the rights *but on condition that no one asks us why.*'"[2]

There is, I repeat, nothing wrong with attempting to develop a theory that adequately outlines a universal theory of objective moral law, although doing so requires a richer anthropology than this document provides. If, however, our aim is to achieve some mutual understanding among those of different cultures and faiths, too much theoretical baggage may be more harm than help along the way. It may make it harder, rather than easier, for us all just to get along.

II

Although he had described the first principles of the natural law as self-evident, St. Thomas added that they are "self-evident only to the wise."[3] Evil habits and passions might often hide from us truths that ought to be evident to our nat-

2. Jacques Maritain, "Introduction," in *Human Rights: Comments and Interpretations,* ed. UNESCO (New York: Columbia University Press, 1949), 9.
3. *ST* I-II, q. 94, a. 2, resp.

ural reason, and St. Thomas offered as an example the ancient Germanic raiding and marauding tribes, who had failed to recognize robbery (an explicit violation of natural law) as unjust. Living largely from plunder in a world kept in relative order by Roman imperial power, they had, as E. A. Goerner noted, no need to develop certain (naturally) virtuous habits of behavior.[4] Only as Roman power waned and they were forced to live with the consequences of a way of life based on plunder were the Germanic tribes also forced to become people of a certain sort — for whom robbery was self-evidently a violation of the natural law.

Thus, even some of the more basic principles of the natural law, which constitute reason itself, are not just obvious to anyone who looks. Only the virtuous see them. The ITC recognizes that those who engage in "dialogue . . . must learn to distance themselves from their own particular interests, in order to be open to the needs of others, and to allow themselves to be summoned by the common moral values" (52). Put forward as this claim is, in a calm and sober tone, we are likely to nod our agreement. What it calls for and requires is, however, a monumental task — nothing less than the disciplining of what Iris Murdoch called the "fat relentless ego." Reflecting on an image such as Socrates's famous myth of the cave, she wrote that "in opening our eyes we do not necessarily see what confronts us. We are anxiety-ridden animals. Our minds are continually active, fabricating an anxious, usually self-preoccupied, often falsifying *veil* which partially conceals the world."[5]

If there is anything to Murdoch's claim — and anyone who has read and been instructed by Plato and St. Augustine is likely to think there is — those hoping to forge agreement on a universal ethics should probably regard the development of virtue as far more essential than the full-blown theory of natural law the ITC gives us. I repeat yet again that I do not denigrate the theory; I simply find it several steps removed from what is needed if even a faint semblance of the agreement for which the ITC hopes is to be achieved. This is why Aristotle said that ethics is a branch of politics. This is why attention to and support for families as places for moral initiation is essential. This is why churches must try to be places where the Christian way of life is not just affirmed but actually transmitted. Only in communities in which virtuous habits of behavior are inculcated are we likely to find people really in a position to "see" the precepts of the natural law.

4. E. A. Goerner, "On Thomistic Natural Law: The Bad Man's View of Thomistic Natural Right," *Political Theory* 7 (February 1979): 114ff.

5. Iris Murdoch, *The Sovereignty of Good* (New York: Schocken, 1971), 84.

To be sure, the ITC document (especially in section 2.6) recognizes this, but I do not see that the recognition plays a major role in shaping the document. Recognizing it would mean less concern about universality, global solidarity, and planetary responsibility, and more concern for epistemologically particular starting points — families, churches, schools, workplaces, communities — in which character may be shaped in ways that enable us to see when we open our eyes rather than to fabricate falsifying veils that partially conceal the world. The way to a universal ethic may be circuitous rather than direct. The direct route of universal moral theory may make it harder, rather than easier, for us all just to get along.

III

For Christians, of course, the epistemologically particular starting point for talk of what it means to be human must be Jesus, who, as the document states, "brings the original plan of the Father for humanity to fulfillment and by this very fact reveals man to himself" (105). Still more, "In his person Jesus Christ . . . manifests an exemplary human life, fully conformed to the natural law. He is thus the ultimate criterion for correctly discerning the authentic natural desires of man, when these are not concealed by the distortions introduced by sin and disordered passions" (105). Such affirmations simply develop the statement in Ephesians (4:13) that becoming "mature" as a Christian is growing "to the measure of the stature of the fullness of Christ."

How exactly beginning here in our search for a picture of mature, flourishing humanity can contribute to the universal ethics that the ITC aims to outline is, however, far from clear. The document itself indicates the difficulty, though it does not seem (to me, at any rate) to realize the implications of what it acknowledges. Charity, as Jesus depicts it, "reveals the profound meaning of the golden rule" (108). It turns out, however, that this profound meaning "becomes with Christ the commandment to love without limit" (108). Going well beyond commutative justice, it asks us "to take the initiative in a love that is a gift of self" (108). Indeed, "the practice of love overcomes every closure and every limitation" (108).

How does this contribute to the search for a universal ethic? If we want to develop a universal ethic on which all can agree, making Jesus central to our vision of mature humanity — however obvious for Christians — may create as many problems as it solves. For the Jesus we know from the stories in the New Testament Gospels often expresses views that seem, at least on the face of it, contrary to some widely shared moral understandings. If, for example, the full meaning of our humanity is displayed in Jesus, it is displayed in one who must be in his Father's house even at some cost to the normal meaning of filial piety, in one whose notion of justice to those who labor may seem unjust to many people, and in one whose readiness to forgive may seem offensive to the moralist in each of us.

If a self-giving love without limit that overcomes every closure is really to be put forward as a grace that does not destroy but brings to full realization our shared human nature (101), we may, again, need a somewhat richer anthropology than the document itself provides. We will have to see embedded in the organism's work of self-preservation an openness to the surrounding world that involves risk, and that may mean sacrifice. Only if that is true can Jesus be one who "brings the original plan of the Father for humanity to fulfillment" (105). And then an epistemologically particular starting point may lead us to moral truth that is ontologically universal because truly human.

But the particular starting point in Jesus is not given by reason, nor are the virtues needed to become people able to see the objective moral law. Hence, something more than a theory of natural law, however otherwise insightful and useful it may be, is needed if we are all just to get along — something less like theory and more like witness. Nor is this witness directed only to those who do not share Christians' starting point in Jesus as the image of mature humanity. It is directed also — again and again — to Christians themselves, as they seek to grow into "the stature of the fullness of Christ" (Eph. 4:13).

Any hope that moral theory alone — or primarily — can bring people together, securing peace and happiness for them, is naïve. Nor, I think, does such hope take the ITC's own document seriously enough. "The search for a common ethical language is," we are told, "inseparable from an experience of conversion" (4). We are divided internally within ourselves; we are divided externally among ourselves. If the condition for what the document calls "true dialogue" (4) is that this clash of competing voices within the self and among ourselves must first be overcome, then the document is right to see that this requires conversion: the heart of stone transformed "under the action of the Spirit" into the heart of flesh that is "sensitive to wisdom that calls us to compassion" (4).

All honor, then, to the theory outlined in *In Search of a Universal Ethic*. It is careful, thorough, and instructive. What it is not, however, is the path toward helping us all just to get along. That is given in the one "who is our peace" and who has broken down the walls of hostility that divide us internally and externally (Eph. 2:14). Until the day when his reconciled body is brought to its fruition, our hopes for peace and happiness will almost surely rest less on moral theory than on learning again from St. Augustine to honor the need for force to secure the temporal — and always fragile — peace that is the tranquility of order and that is the best semblance we can manage of a way for us all just to get along.

From a Heart of Stone to a Heart of Flesh: Toward an Epideictic Rhetoric of Natural Law

M. Cathleen Kaveny

What is most striking about *In Search of a Universal Ethic: A New Look at the Natural Law* is its rhetorical style. On the one hand it is startling because it clearly undermines the preconceptions that many people, including many Catholics, have about the characteristic style of official Catholic teaching on the natural law. More specifically, it does not proceed in bloodless, syllogistic fashion by applying clear, exceptionless rules to a fixed set of facts in order to produce an unequivocal moral assessment of the issues under consideration. It does not invoke magisterial authority in order to bring discussions of complicated issues to certain closure. It does not read, in short, like most people's conception of a deliverance of law, natural or not.

Yet there is also something oddly familiar about the style. The document emphasizes questions rather than answers, facilitates conversations rather than confrontations, and calls for cooperation in a pluralistic society. This rhetorical style is also an important part of the Church's official communicative tradition, albeit a part that has a rather more recent pedigree. It is the style that characterizes the official documents of Vatican II, particularly *Gaudium et spes,* the *Pastoral Constitution on the Church in the Modern World.*

This conjunction of natural law and the rhetoric of Vatican II is a particularly noteworthy aspect of *In Search of a Universal Ethic.* Although Vatican II issued specific documents of relevance to other theological disciplines, it did not do so with respect to moral theology, which has centrally been articulated in terms of natural law. Obviously, certain documents are extremely relevant to the discipline, including *Gaudium et spes, Dignitatis humanae, Lumen gen-*

tium, and *Dei verbum.*[1] Nonetheless, they leave a gap: we have no opportunity to see what magisterial reflection on the natural law would look like in the key of Vatican II, so to speak. Why not? At the time, dealing with questions of natural law would have meant dealing with the emerging issues raised by the birth control pill. The council fathers decided to prescind from those questions in view of Pope Paul VI's intention to convene a group to study the matter at a later date.[2] The firestorm surrounding the issuance of *Humanae vitae* doubtless consumed any other immediate intentions to produce other, more systematic studies of the natural law.

Drawing on recent work of John O'Malley, S.J.,[3] I articulate more precisely what constitutes the distinctive rhetorical tone of Vatican II, using that articulation to illuminate key features of *In Search of a Universal Ethic.* In my view, however, rhetoric is not ultimately separable from substance. By choosing to cast their discussion of natural law in a particular rhetorical style, the International Theological Commission (ITC) also and inevitably facilitated a particular substantive approach to natural law. In my view, both the rhetorical and the substantive turns are welcome developments in the discussion.

The Rhetorical Developments of Vatican II

According to O'Malley, the rhetorical style of the council carried its meaning as much as the theological propositions embedded in its documents. "The literary style, that is to say, was but the surface expression of something meant

1. *Dignitatis humanae,* the *Declaration on Religious Freedom,* makes important statements on the dignity of the human person and the respect due to individual conscience in fundamental matters such as religious belief. *Lumen gentium,* the *Dogmatic Constitution on the Church,* addresses the prophetic authority of the magisterium in interpreting the natural law. *Dei verbum,* the *Dogmatic Constitution on Divine Revelation,* offers guidance on how to interpret scripture, including its ethical implications.

2. The pre-conciliar Theological Commission prepared two texts for inclusion in the volume of materials distributed to the bishops in preparation for the council's first session. These texts, one on Christian moral order and the other on sexuality and the family, never made it onto the council's agenda and did not significantly inform conciliar documents. Many thanks to Joseph A. Komonchak for this information.

3. John O'Malley, S.J., *What Happened at Vatican II* (Cambridge, Mass.: Belknap Press of Harvard University Press, 2008), and John O'Malley, *Four Cultures of the West* (Cambridge, Mass.: Belknap Press of Harvard University Press, 2004). In *Four Cultures of the West,* O'Malley argues that there are four basic rhetorical cultural sensibilities that have shaped the West: the prophetic, the academic-legal, the humanistic, and the artistic.

to sink into the very soul of the church and of every Catholic. It was much more than a tactic or strategy, much more than simply the adoption of a more 'pastoral language.' It was a language event. The language indicated and induced a shift in values or priorities."[4]

What was that shift? O'Malley claims that the documents of earlier councils largely exemplify a broadly academic or legal way of approaching problems. It is the language of case analysis and analytical precision — the characteristic discourse of those who believe they are responsible for ordering and controlling society.

> Although allowance must be made for many differences, the councils from Nicaea to Vatican I had a characteristic style of discourse. That style was composed of two basic elements. The first was a literary genre — the canon or its equivalent. The second was the vocabulary typical of the genre and appropriate to it. It consisted in words of threats and intimidation, words of surveillance and punishment, words of a superior speaking to an inferior — or to an enemy. It consisted in power-words.[5]

In contrast, O'Malley argues that the characteristic discourse of Vatican II was the "epideictic" language most at home in humanistic culture. "Its goal is the winning of internal assent, not the imposition of conformity from outside. It teaches, but not so much by way of magisterial pronouncement as by suggestion, insinuation and example. Its instrument is persuasion, not coercion."[6]

A style, of course, cannot be clinically described; it must be evoked in order to be communicated. O'Malley does a marvelous job of evoking that style throughout his book on Vatican II. For my purposes, however, I need to limit myself to one illustration, which also vividly indicates how rhetoric and substance are ultimately inseparable.

> In its general orientation, as articulated especially in its most characteristic vocabulary, the council devised a profile of the ideal Christian. That ideal, drawn in greatest length in *Gaudium et spes,* is more incarnational than eschatological, closer to St. Thomas Aquinas than to Karl Barth, more reminiscent of the fathers of the Eastern Church than of St. Augustine — more inclined to reconciliation with human culture than to alienation from it,

4. O'Malley, *What Happened at Vatican II,* 12.
5. O'Malley, *What Happened at Vatican II,* 45.
6. O'Malley, *Four Cultures,* 12.

more inclined to see goodness than sin, more inclined to speaking words of friendship and encouragement than of indictment. The style choice fostered a theological choice.

The result was a message that was traditional while at the same time radical, prophetic while at the same time soft-spoken. In a world increasingly wracked with discord, hatred, war, and threats of war, the result was a message that was countercultural while at the same time responsive to the deepest human yearnings. Peace on earth. Good will to men.[7]

The tension between the academic-legal rhetoric of the Council of Trent and the humanistic rhetoric of Vatican II is likely to be sharp in every field of theological inquiry. In no case, however, is it as likely to veer as close to actual contradiction as it is in the case of moral theology. Why? Because moral theology, as a discipline, is largely if not exclusively the child of the Council of Trent.[8] That council emphasized the essential role played by the sacrament of reconciliation in the Christian life, as well as the need for an educated cadre of priests to administer it.

Over the centuries, religious orders such as the Dominicans, Jesuits, and Redemptorists took responsibility for producing manuals that could structure seminary courses designed to prepare young priests to hear confessions, a sacramental ritual requiring them to act *in persona Christi* as both judges and healers of penitents' sins. In characteristically academic fashion, these manuals proceeded in an orderly and deductive manner, typically organizing the range of possible sinful behavior under the general prohibitions articulated by the Ten Commandments. And in characteristically legal fashion, they precisely identified sinful acts according to the requisite mental state of the agent (in criminal law, *mens rea*) and the requisite component parts of the physical act *(actus reus)*. They also precisely identified the aggravating and mitigating circumstances relevant to assessing a penance and applying appropriate spiritual medicine.

Of course, academic and legal rhetoric are not the same. But in many cases, they do have two important elements in common: the speaker's claim of authority vis-à-vis certain members of the audience, and a certain didactic quality of presentation drawing from and reinforcing that authority. In certain modes, both academics and lawmakers are teachers, charged with the task of imparting knowledge to those who are ignorant in an orderly fashion. On the academic side, the manner of presentation is meant to communicate a clear

---

7. O'Malley, *What Happened at Vatican II*, 310-11.

8. For a helpful overview of the history, see John Mahoney, *The Making of Moral Theology* (Oxford: Clarendon Press, 1987), chapter 1.

and defined body of knowledge from teacher to students. On the legal side, it is designed to convey a clear and comprehensive body of authoritative action guides from ruler to subjects.

Moreover, both teachers and lawyers are likely to adopt a particular attitude toward questions: ideally speaking, they are to be minimized. A careful presentation of basic material or a thorough statement of the law will answer all questions before they are asked. In a basic lecture, too many questions will derail the step-by-step presentation of the material. In a piece of legislation, too many questions may suggest that the law is hopelessly vague, and cannot function as an action guide. Within this framework, rhetorical questions are permissible as a way of ordering the material, but *real* questions are a threat. As we will see, the same is not true of *In Search of a Universal Ethic.*

The Rhetorical Challenges of the "Search for Universal Ethics"

The rhetorical tone of the ITC document is set by both its title and the first sentences of the introduction. A search implies questions. Not surprisingly, therefore, the first sentences of the document place the emphasis on questions:

> Are there objective moral values which can unite human beings and bring them peace and happiness? What are they? How are they discerned? How can they be put into action in the lives of persons and communities? These perennial questions concerning good and evil are today more urgent than ever, insofar as people have become more aware of forming one single world community. (1)

The questions are not merely rhetorical; they are agonizingly real. They are essential to address, according to the ITC, because of two facets of globalization. First, the problems threatening human beings are global in nature; they include terrorism, organized crime, and new forms of violence and oppression, as well as new forms of biotechnology such as genetic manipulation and cloning, which even threaten the very identity of human beings. Second, none of these problems — or potential solutions — can be hermetically sealed in one area or culture of the world. Thanks to new forms of communication such as the Internet, information and opinions travel quickly between cultures, and even between different cohorts of the same culture. Echoing *Gaudium et spes,* the ITC recognizes that global problems are going to require global solutions.

And by their very nature, global problems cannot be didactically identified from on high, with the corresponding solutions then legally imposed from the top down. As the ITC recognizes, they must be identified and addressed in the context of a mutually respectful dialogue. Crucially, however, the ITC does not abandon its own identity or moral commitments in the course of this recognition. The introduction to the document articulates straightforwardly and nondefensively three key concerns of the Vatican.

First, while appreciating the goals of the "global ethics movement" to identify shared values, the ITC wonders whether its purely inductive, empirical method will allow it to achieve its own goals. "Does a purely inductive search, conducted on the parliamentary model, for an already existing minimal consensus, satisfy the requirements for basing law on what is absolute? Moreover, does not this minimal ethic lead to relativizing the strong ethical requirements of each of the religions or particular schools of wisdom?" (6).

Second, the ITC worries about the ascendency of juridical positivism, where legislation operates only as power broker seeking a workable compromise among various interests. In its view, "juridical positivism is notoriously insufficient, for a legislator can only act legitimately within certain limits, which derive from the dignity of the human person, and in service to the development of what is authentically human" (7). Politics and the civil law cannot be separated from ethics and a higher moral law.

Third, while acknowledging that dialogue is an indispensable means to the recognition of moral truth, the ITC cautions that it cannot by definition *constitute* moral truth. The ITC resists an entirely constructivist account of morality. A Habermasian "discourse ethics" is procedurally helpful, but it is unable to produce "new substantial contents." The substance it generates risks being reduced to the fruits of a strategy of compromise. Consequently, the ITC affirms that "dialogue and debate are always necessary for obtaining an achievable agreement on the concrete application of moral norms in any given situation, but they could not relegate moral conscience to the margins. A true debate does not replace personal moral convictions, but it presupposes and enriches them" (8).

We are now in a position to perceive the not insubstantial rhetorical and substantive challenges that the ITC has set for itself. On the one hand, the ITC clearly intends to proceed in an inductive, dialogical manner, gathering insights from other religious traditions as well as the Roman Catholic tradition. The first chapter of the document is devoted, for example, to identifying "convergences" between world religions, the ancient Greeks and Romans, the insights of sacred scripture, and the Christian tradition, particularly its Catholic branch, on moral values. It aims to respect complexity, nuance, and insights from different perspectives and cultures. On the other hand, it does not want to endorse a purely constructivist notion of morality, which *defines* moral truth as the product of a consensus among differing parties.

From Rhetoric to Method: Moral Realism and Epistemological Inductivism

Both the rhetorical tone and the substantive commitments expressed by the ITC in the introduction shape the method of *In Search of a Universal Ethic*. Accordingly, the fulcrum of the document is chapter 3: "The Theoretical Foundations of the Natural Law." The document recognizes that the condition for the possibility of its desired global discussion on the moral law turns on a universal human capacity to perceive moral norms, albeit frequently imperfectly. It honors the need, in short, for a metaphysical conception of human nature that accounts for the reliable contact of human beings with the normative ordering of the universe, as well as the experience of acting in accordance with those norms in particular situations. It also honors the need to provide a theory of error, accounting for large and small misperceptions of moral norms, as well as evident decisions to refuse to follow them when doing so does not accord with some perceived self-interest.

Here, the ITC echoes the concerns of St. Thomas Aquinas. By viewing the natural law as a "participation" in the eternal law, which in the end is God himself, demand for moral realism is secured. In every moral judgment they make, human beings are rooted in and shaped by the divine ordering of things, simply by virtue of the fact that they are human beings, and the minds of human beings are so structured to perceive and participate in the eternal law, the mind of God. This participation in the eternal law is part of what it means to be a human being.

The ITC's moral realism, rooted in a Catholic anthropology, grounds the possibility of the conversation it desires and nourishes the hope to continue even in difficult circumstances. It does not, however, circumvent the need for that conversation, or supply in advance a list of its correct results. Realism is not angelism; it does not endorse the attempt to escape the limitations of the human perspective in order to obtain a superhuman vantage on moral norms. As the ITC recognizes, one such limitation is entailed by the fact that all human beings are temporally and socially situated beings. We have no pure example of human nature abstracted from the conditions of time, space, tradition, and family. Even Jesus Christ, whom chapter 5 unequivocally proclaims as the fulfillment of the natural law, was not merely the *Logos,* the eternal ordering of the mind of God, but was also a human man shaped by his life in a particular era and culture.

The ITC's moral realism, in other words, furnishes the basis for fruitful and hopeful dialogue about the moral law; it does not obviate the need for such dialogue. How, then, do we approach such a dialogue? How do we collectively come to recognize the existence and importance of the natural law? The method modeled by the document is not deductive, but rather inductive: the case for natural law is made in part by an appreciative attention to its operations in the lives of both individuals and communities. Both method and tone are signaled early in the document: "By their wisdom, their generosity and sometimes their heroism, men and women give active witness to these common ethical values. Our admiration for such people is a sign of a spontaneous initial grasp of moral values" (2).

More generally, four aspects of the ITC method for discerning both the existence and requirements of the natural law are worthy of note. First, the document clearly roots its case for natural law not only in general human experience, but also in the experience of particular human beings. It emphasizes, for example, the moral competence of ordinary men and women to make judgments about what the requirements of the natural law are in practice, whether or not they have the philosophical competence to articulate the basis of those judgments: "the moral subject can put into practice the orientations of natural law without being capable — by reason of his particular intellectual formation — of explicitly discerning their ultimate theoretical foundations" (60).

Second, the ITC clearly recognizes the influence of culture and historicity not only on the perception of natural law, but also on the actual requirements in specific cases and situations. It recognizes that most people are introduced to morality in an enculturated way, not as a list of abstract principles, but in the context of communal and familial practices. Sometimes, of course, that enculturation can lead to tragic moral blindness, even within the Church itself. The ITC forthrightly admits that some socially endorsed practices such as slavery were accepted by the Church despite the fact that they could have been seen to be violations of the natural moral law much earlier than they were in fact acknowledged to be so.

Third, the ITC recognizes that a full account of natural law's operations will require the integration of virtue theory into the picture. Closely tracking St. Thomas Aquinas, the ITC acknowledges that it is the virtue of prudence, or practical wisdom, which applies the general principles of natural law to particular cases. In fact, it recognizes that the primary task is to form virtuous persons, persons who are capable of recognizing the requirements of natural law in particular cases. Such recognition requires both knowledge of general norms and patterns and insight into the particularities of the situation at hand. Rules are important, precisely because they reflect the general ordering of the moral life. At the same time, good judgment is necessary to apply them wisely to the specific circumstances of individual cases.

Fourth, the document recognizes the need to integrate natural law into a metaphysical framework that is also a thoroughly theological framework. Obviously indebted to *Lumen gentium,* the ITC works out what those three roles of Jesus Christ as prophet, priest, and king can mean with respect to the natural law. As the incarnation of the *Logos,* the living law in the eternal mind of God, Jesus Christ participates in the divine ordering of the universe, including its moral ordering. At the same time, his life on Earth offers a model of a human being who conforms perfectly to the divine order. The ITC emphasizes that Jesus Christ "is thus the ultimate criterion for correctly discerning the authentic natural desires of man, when these are not concealed by the distortions introduced by sin and disordered passions" (105). Finally, Jesus Christ reconciles humanity to God, not only revealing the law of love in his saving self-sacrifice, but also overcoming the bondage and delusion of sin. The ITC stresses that "Jesus Christ is not only an ethical model to imitate, but by and in his paschal mystery, he is the Savior who gives us the real possibility of putting the law of love into action" (110).

The ITC, then, offers a vision of an approach to natural law that is open to the insights of people of diverse backgrounds, religions, and cultures, while at the same time firmly rooted in the Christian commitment to Jesus Christ (112). In fact, it is a singular virtue of this document that its openness to the wisdom of all traditions and cultures is in fact anchored in its Christian anthropology and soteriology. Precisely because Catholics believe that all human beings participate in the eternal law, the same mind of God that was perfectly revealed in Jesus Christ, we can have the courage of continuing the dialogue even in difficult times.

Conclusion

In Search of a Universal Ethic is not blindly optimistic. The ITC fully recognizes the effects that sin and even simple error can have on human perception of moral norms, particularly when magnified by the effects of social structures and cultural entrenchment. Nonetheless, it rightly points to a significant global achievement as a source of pride and encouragement. A little more than fifty years ago, a world ravaged by war came together to endorse a *Universal Declaration on Human Rights,* which emphasizes the inalienable dignity of each and every human being. In both substance and rhetoric, the ITC aims to further the objectives of the *Universal Declaration.* It provides a framework in which fundamental Catholic Christological commitments can sustain a dialogue regarding the "fundamental values of our common humanity" (116). In so doing, it invites us all "to work together for understanding, mutual recognition and peaceful cooperation among all the members of the human family" (116). To put it another way, the ITC invites us all to move from a heart of stone to a heart of flesh (4).

The Natural Law, Global Justice, and Equality

Lisa Sowle Cahill

The International Theological Commission (ITC) is on target and even prophetic when it calls for the renewal of natural law ethics to support "planetary responsibility" and "global solidarity" (1). An ethics of the natural law is a resource to combat the destruction of the natural environment, ongoing poverty and oppression, and constant cycles of war and violence. The ITC is right that actual human lives testify that the most basic human values and moral goals are shared. Goods such as adequate food and water, freedom from disease and violence, and a say in local government are easily recognized everywhere.

Academic philosophers and scholars of postcolonialism theorize moral incommensurability out of the facts of cultural variety and imposed value systems that serve global inequities. But human moral unity is precisely the basis on which evil systems and inequities can be identified for what they are. Around the world, those who suffer the most severe effects of sexism, racism, militarism, and free-market capitalism call out for respect, protection, and opportunity on the basis of their and our shared humanity. At its most basic, natural law is simply the idea that human beings are similar enough in their needs and priorities to agree at a fundamental yet politically potent level about what constitutes good or bad treatment of other people, and good or bad organization of society.

The defense of natural law given in *In Search of a Universal Ethic* makes room for cultural pluralism by stipulating that all readings of "universals" are contextual and experience-based (6). To grant that natural law reasoning is always historical creates tension with the defense of natural law in a specifically Catholic ecclesial context. The consequences of historicity for moral reasoning are easier for the tradition to absorb regarding social justice than in areas once termed "personal" morality, such as sexual ethics and bioethics.

The present discussion first treats the inductive character of natural law, substantiated by the ITC's analysis, then turns to possible objections and the ITC's responses. Then, using peacebuilding as an example, I show how ground-up discernment of common values can be a meeting place for different religious and cultural traditions. Finally, using gender ethics, I demonstrate how partiality in the discernment process can result in bias, disagreement, and even oppression. In conclusion, however, natural law is a valuable ethical approach despite its limits.

The International Theological Commission's Inductive Epistemology of Natural Law

The ITC affirms that what justifies natural law is "reflective observation of the anthropological constants" (61), a term it borrows from Edward Schillebeeckx (whom the ITC does not cite directly). In other words, the ITC proposes not that natural law is a deduction from self-evident first principles or revealed truths, but that it is essentially an appeal across cultures for consensus about actual, experienced human values.

Schillebeeckx's own list of seven "anthropological constants" includes human corporeality and relation to the ecological environment; relationships with other people; social and institutional structures; conditioning by time and space; reciprocity of theory and practice; religious and "para-religious" consciousness; and the reality of human culture as a synthesis of the first six.[1] These constants present us with values that we discern within social and political circumstances, and with the help of the symbols, archetypes, models, and theories that make experiential phenomena intelligible. Human experiences, critically reflected on, gain authority as disclosures of reality and of what constitutes "truth and goodness, . . . justice and human happiness."[2] The derivation of specific norms, however, is not given imme-

---

1. Edward Schillebeeckx, *The Schillebeeckx Reader*, ed. Robert J. Schreiter (New York: Crossroad; Edinburgh: T&T Clark, 1984), 28-39; selected from *Christ: The Experience of Jesus as Lord*, trans. John Bowden (New York: SCM Press, 1980), 733-43.

2. Schillebeeckx, *The Schillebeeckx Reader*, 43-44.

diately with the anthropological constants, but depends on creative inter-pretation of "true and livable humanity" in "the changing process of history."[3]

The ITC reappropriates the natural law theory of St. Thomas Aquinas as its main theoretical resource, but it reads Aquinas through a historically ori-ented lens, similar (but not equal) to that of Schillebeeckx. From such a per-spective, basic principles of natural law are authoritative because they are the products of critical, communal reflection on the experience of what contrib-utes to human flourishing and what does not. Though humans necessarily know as a matter of general principle that they ought to do good, it takes time and experience to recognize what the good actually is.

Humans come to similar basic understandings about good and evil be-cause there are some basic facts about the human reality that do not change. These facts have most obviously to do with the human body and its survival needs, but they also include the need for cooperative and trustworthy relations to other people and to social institutions. Such facts ground Aquinas's appeal for consensus about the basic principles of the natural law.

Following Aquinas,[4] the ITC identifies three specific areas of human ex-istence in which human goods and obligations to protect them are recognized de facto in all societies: human life itself and the goods necessary for survival; reproduction, intergenerational families, and the education of the young; and life in community, especially political community and (inquiry about) com-munion with God (48-50). The ITC does not state as explicitly as Schillebeeckx that specific norms must be geared to changing circumstances, but they do maintain that, even in its scholastic version, natural law was never "a closed and complete set of moral norms" (27). The ITC also grants, again with Aqui-nas, that the more detailed prescriptions of the natural law will be less certain because they address contingent situations (53).[5]

Beyond Aquinas's three basic goods with their correlative obligations, the ITC further specifies that justice entails "the recognition of the equal dignity of every individual of the human species, beyond the differences of race and culture, and a great respect for humanity wherever it is found, including that of the smallest and in the most despised of its members" (51). Here the ITC reflects its own modern, even "Western," context. Justice as equality, and equal-ity as requiring remedial action on behalf of those who have suffered past

---

3. Schillebeeckx, *The Schillebeeckx Reader*, 29, 44.
4. St. Thomas Aquinas, *ST* I-II, q. 94, a. 2.
5. Citing *ST* I-II, q. 94, a. 4.

exclusions, are modern values characterizing democratic societies and political philosophies.

What is sometimes termed "the preferential option for the poor" is also a recent development as far as official Catholic social teaching is concerned. As will be shown, one problem with the ITC's program is that it is not so easy as it assumes to convince people that all enjoy basic equality at the practical rather than merely rhetorical level. It is even harder to get universal consent to special treatment of the "most despised of [society's] members."

Common Objections to Natural Law and the International Theological Commission's Replies

Citizens of modern, Western democracies resist the idea of natural law for three main reasons. First, they associate the term with hidebound and socially conservative moral systems, perhaps backed by religious authority, that are virtually unresponsive to today's world, its values, and its needs. Second, modern media present us with such a dizzying array of cultures, religions, and ideologies that it is easy to conclude that culturally different life experiences and worldviews are in deep ways unintelligible to each other, even if objects of mutual curiosity.

Third, some people have lost interest in the whole of idea of planetary collaboration because today's society seems so transient, unstable, and unreliable. Even the fortunate citizens of "first world" nations feel under threat and politically impotent. Many seek meaning, identity, and security in local communities where a shared lifeworld serves as anchor and buffer against uncontrollable external forces and the unknown future. A religious version of this inward-turning and tribal reaction is the formation of churches (or temples or mosques) with strong group identity and boundaries, emphasis on local unifying symbols and rituals, and divestment from the larger social order.

In Search of a Universal Ethic responds to these three rejections correctly and persuasively. First, natural law is not the exclusive property of Catholicism or religious traditions, nor is it impervious to new insights and change. The ITC cites parallel efforts to define common ethics such as the *Universal Declaration of Human Rights* (UDHR), produced after World War II and the Shoah. Moreover, it acknowledges that even the UDHR is regarded as "too Western" by some (5), opening the door to the need for constant revision of any specific lists of goods, norms, or rights in light of cross-cultural exchange. If natural law is to serve as a moral and political compass in secular and pluralistic societies, then it is "necessary to avoid presenting it in the rigid form" that it has sometimes assumed in the past (33). The formulation of norms of the natural law calls for modesty, prudence, and dialogue (52).

Second, despite cultural and religious diversity, the ITC insists that some virtues and ways of life are quite widely shared around the world. The world's great religious traditions converge on essential moral points, especially the ideal of treating others as we would want to be treated, as well as nonviolence, harmony with nature, and respect for life. When the Church or Christians in public life invoke the natural law to insist on "the defense of the rights of the oppressed, justice in international relations, the defense of life and of the family, religious freedom and freedom of education," their arguments are not merely "confessional," but derive from the requirements of care for the common good (35). The requirements can be and are affirmed in many traditions.

Third, *In Search of a Universal Ethic* retains a large place for the cultivation of a specifically Christian religious identity, but that identity should direct one's vision past the church and into the world. Commitment to the global common good is integral to Christian identity. The answer to personal, political, and economic instability is not communalistic retreat but a renewed commitment to enact the law of love, and to express it socially in the form of justice. The ITC calls Christians and others to "work together for understanding, mutual recognition and peaceful cooperation among all the members of the human family" (116). This cooperation and its historical possibilities are validated theologically by the doctrine of creation of all, through the *Logos,* in the image of God (104); by the restoration of this image in the work of Jesus Christ as the new Adam (105); and by the transforming presence of the Spirit (110-12).

Natural Law Contributions: The Case of Peacebuilding

The merits of a natural law approach to global social problems are clear if we consider cases such as war, civil conflict, and the challenges of building peace. Even though there will be immense variation in the specific ways conflicts are settled and peaceful social life resumed, the natural law rhetoric of common humanity, dignity of all persons, mutual rights and duties, just government, and the common good is a priceless heritage with which to encourage a social ethos of equality, solidarity, and accountability.

The theory of "just war" was devised precisely to set limits on violence, to establish peace as the only legitimate cause for war, and to ensure that the conduct of war will result in the least loss of life possible. Its philosophical rationale is wide agreement on these aims. No one would say that natural law norms concerning respect for life and nonviolence are always followed before, during, or after violent conflict. Critiques of the specific criteria for justifying war, of the possibility of justifying war at all in an era of massively destructive weapons, and of deception and self-interest in the deployment of the theory are all well placed, as is the proposal that a greater emphasis should be placed on building peace than on justifying war. Yet the values of life and peaceful coexistence are recognized even by people who prevent others from their enjoyment, signaling that a natural law basis exists for work to reduce conflict and enhance peace.

The natural law need not marginalize the role of religion in politics, for religious communities can both form participants for compassion, solidarity, and justice, and sponsor social practices that move closer to a just society. For instance, Christian organizations and other religious groups are active in situations of violent conflict to mediate between opposing sides, advocate for civilians, and encourage a return to peaceful coexistence. In so doing, they rely on the universal human desire to live under conditions of peace and social stability. Religious peacebuilding work is often interreligious, especially important where conflict has been part of bigger religious divisions.[6]

The modern papal social encyclicals and other social teaching constitute a long tradition uniting Christian religious conviction with the confidence that people can work together across cultures, nations, and religions to seek the universal common good. Pope Benedict XVI titled his 2009 World Day of Peace message "Fighting Poverty to Build Peace." His words illustrate the common values necessary to promote peace and human well-being in the twenty-first century:

> One of the most important ways of building peace is through a form of globalization directed towards the interests of the whole human family. In order to govern globalization, however, there needs to be a strong sense of *global solidarity* between rich and poor countries, as well as within individual countries, including affluent ones. A "common code of ethics" is also needed, consisting of norms based not upon mere consensus, but rooted in the natural law inscribed by the Creator on the conscience of every human being (cf. *Rom* 2:14-15).[7]

6. For examples and literature, see the website of the Catholic Peacebuilding Network (http://cpn.nd.edu/).

7. Pope Benedict XVI, "Fighting Poverty to Build Peace," 2009 World Day of Peace mes-

Problems with the Natural Law: The Case of Sex and Gender

Now on to some problems. Though I find the ITC's basic proposal compelling, I discern some complications that are either not addressed explicitly by the ITC, or are addressed but not fully confronted. These already begin to come up with the example of war and violence; they will become even more obvious when we turn to the status of women.

Despite the ITC's successful defense of the basic idea of natural law and its merits as a rallying call against evils such as violent conflict, problems remain in at least three areas. These are all related in some way to the fact that the natural law is a historical reality, known inductively through variable local processes. The problem areas are: (1) uncertainty about how to recognize the "right" interpretation; (2) the effects of sin on fulfilling the natural law; and (3) the relation of reason and religion in knowing the natural law.

To get a concrete sense of the significance of these difficulties, think about how to define the "nature" and status of women. The first problem is that perceptions of gender originate in the history and experiences of particular communities, and change as those experiences change. Though there are certainly human "constants," such as men's and women's different reproductive capacities, the meaning and value of these constants is mediated through a rich and intricate set of symbols, practices, and discourses, replete with constant contestations and innovations. The ITC acknowledges this when it notes that moral knowledge is acquired by "thoughtful experience, conveyed by the wisdom traditions, by philosophies or by human sciences" (61). The epistemological range of any one person or group will necessarily be limited, perspectival, and evolving.

We have only to consider the history of Catholic natural law assessments of the nature and roles of women to find a number of once authoritative positions whose credibility was undermined by changing philosophies, sciences, and mores, and which therefore transitioned into different forms. In 2009 the ITC cited the UDHR, article 16, as evidence that the natural law is universal (49). But the provisions of this article name goals or ideals that have been disputed, both historically and today. For instance,

(1) Men and women of full age, without any limitation due to race, nationality or religion, have the right to marry and to found a family. They are entitled to equal rights as to marriage, during marriage and at its dissolution.

---

sage, 8 (http://www.vatican.va/holy_father/benedict_xvi/messages/peace/documents/hf_ben-xvi_mes_20081208_xlii-world-day-peace_en.html; accessed June 25, 2010).

(2) Marriage shall be entered into only with the free and full consent of the intending spouses.[8]

St. Thomas Aquinas viewed women not only as physically weaker than men, but also as less rational and in need of male control, and even as resulting from some sort of mishap in the development of the embryo.[9] In our time, the popes have moved past the idea of women's natural inferiority to men, and in fact have defended women's basic equality and social and domestic rights.[10] Whereas as recently as 1930, Pope Pius XI opined that women should be subject to their husbands and not be allowed to manage their own financial affairs, Pope John Paul II in 1995 acclaimed "the great process of women's liberation."[11]

These developments are no doubt due in large part to the modern ethos of equality and democracy, and to the gradual social emancipation of women at the practical level. These factors in turn informed and even changed the reading of the religious tradition — for example, scriptural testimony to the ministry of Jesus — making possible a theological defense of basic gender equality.

However, women's nature is still seen to be complementary to that of men, so women's highest and most important roles are wife and mother. By contrast, men seem better suited for public roles outside the family.[12] Given the perspectival character of normative assertions about gender, to establish that the sexes are equal and to arrive at a consensus about what that means practically requires a historical, critical, dialogical, and gender-inclusive process of discernment, negotiation, and renegotiation.

A related problem area for natural law is the effects of sin on knowing what is morally good, and particularly on recognizing the basic human equality that the ITC affirms. Disputes about equality and equal treatment are not abstract; they reflect actual social arrangements and the power dynamics embedded in them. To argue that another group is unequal in relation to certain goods is to try to control allocation of goods so that some group or groups benefit more than others. When the purported inequalities either do not exist or are not relevant to the goods at stake, then to use them to define status in access to the goods is unjust.

8. *Universal Declaration of Human Rights* (http://www.un.org/en/documents/udhr/index .shtml; accessed June 25, 2010).

9. St. Thomas Aquinas, *ST* I, q. 92.

10. Pope John Paul II, *Familiaris consortio (On the Family)* (1981), 22-24.

11. Pope Pius XI, *Casti connubii*, 26-29, 74; Pope John Paul II, *Letter to Women*, 6.

12. Pope John Paul II, *Familiaris consortio*, 23.

Catholic social teaching, as based on the natural law, tends to downplay the staying power of injustice. Natural law is relatively confident that the social effects of sin, group bias, and domination can be overcome gradually by those who cooperate in goodwill. References to the gospel, charity, and truth in the social encyclicals aim at conversion to this end. Catholicism's natural law view of social justice, and now of the global common good, is progressive, evolutionary, even optimistic.

Though the ITC's primary theological authority is Aquinas, St. Augustine's memorable contribution to Christian social ethics is his conviction of the deep-seated character of human evil. He describes political society as constituted as much by "miserable necessities" and "dirty hands," as by "tranquility of order" and "well-ordered concord."[13] Deep in the human heart is the *libido dominandi* ("lust for domination"), which is of the essence of sin.[14]

In light of the clear and present contemporary dangers of political cynicism and moral despair, the ITC's recovery of the constructive potential of a "universal ethics" is salutary. It is right to insist that, although the kingdom of God will not be established on Earth, the political order "can anticipate the kingdom by advances in the area of justice, solidarity, and peace" (95). Nevertheless, the Augustinian tradition provides a useful corrective to naively progressivist readings of natural law.

In Search of a Universal Ethic concludes by urging the following:

> Beyond the differences of our religious convictions and the diversity of our cultural presuppositions, we must be capable of expressing the fundamental values of our common humanity, in order to work together for understanding, mutual recognition and peaceful cooperation among all members of the human family. (116)

This work cannot erase the specter, not only of partiality, but also of willful if self-deceived bias, in allocating access to human goods. All offers to the common endeavor must be subject to the same rules of respectful receptivity to different viewpoints (especially of "the poor"), of self-criticism, and of openness to revise some formulations of the past. This is not to say that absolute condemnations can never and should never be tenaciously held: killing of the innocent, sexual violence, and depriving other human beings of basic survival needs would be among the more obvious.

The necessity for Catholic natural law teaching itself to be subject to dia-

---

13. For the former, see *City of God,* XIX.4 and 6; for the latter, see XIX.13.
14. *City of God,* I, preface.

logical reevaluation is certainly underplayed in *In Search of a Universal Ethic*. For example, the document alludes to magisterial teaching about gender, sex, procreation, contraception, and family as evidence that basic norms of the natural law are recognized (34, 49). It leaves aside the numerous allegations that these teachings do not adequately capture the nature of the goods at stake or justice in enjoyment of them. Perhaps the authors were aware of these problems, but chose strategically to sideline them, lest the reception of their defense of natural law be derailed by polarized, intransigent in-house Catholic debates over sex and gender. The ITC's focus is on the viability of a renewed natural law ethic to sponsor efforts toward global justice, and this is as it should be. Yet ultimately sex and gender must be part of any adequate consideration of global justice, and certainly of human dignity as entailing basic equality.

The ITC makes its strongest and most persuasive case for natural law when it emphasizes that natural law is a realist ethic that deals in the human "constants" and their moral consequences in an open and dialogical way, inviting the critical and self-critical participation of all peoples and cultures. The emphasis is not on particular moral norms, but on common vision, solidarity, and commitment to combat worldwide crises whose seriousness admits of little doubt. The ITC advocates for essential human equality, and the access of all to basic goods, without barriers of sex, race, class, or nationality. The case is weaker where the ITC does not develop its own proposals to their logical conclusion: even in the hands of the Catholic Church, the natural law is still an inductive, historically situated mode of inquiry, whose more specific provisions must remain open to change, not least of all regarding sex and gender justice.

A final set of complications concerns the interdependence of reason and faith. Sometimes reason is presented as though it can operate in the abstract; sometimes religion, too, is treated as a sphere immune to the other spheres in which believers engage. Along these lines, the ITC asserts that "the natural law which is the basis of the social and political order does not demand the adherence of faith, but of reason" (99). This implies a distinction between faith and reason that is too strong. People of faith do not — and in fact cannot — operate with a reasoning capacity that is somehow cut off from the other dimensions of their existence that constitute their identities. Faith and reason operate together.

Aquinas stipulates that it is the practical, not speculative, reason that knows the concrete moral good. Practical reasoning processes are interdependent with bodily experiences, natural environments, personal relationships, education, imagination, emotion, and formation in virtue. Reasoning is interactive with all the other factors and forces that constitute our particular lives and connect us at the practical level with other human beings. Participation in a religious tradition awakens one's moral imagination and sensitizes one's sense of values in relation to the transcendent. But even for those who avow allegiance to no faith, reason is never neutral and tradition-free. Everyone approaches issues of common concern, even in the public sphere, on the basis of formative communities, traditions, and commitments, be they religious, cultural, political, philosophical, or ethical. The challenge or task, then, for natural law social ethics is not to vacate the public square of all particular traditions, but to encourage the discernment of the common goods and goals that mark our common humanity, and to facilitate interactions among traditions that better realize goods at the practical and political levels.

Despite the fact that religion can be corrupted by bias and unjust power — as can the family, the economy, education, or government — religion also connects us to the divine. An important ethical contribution of Christianity, and of all religions that teach compassion, mercy, and redemption, is the faith that God wills inclusive love and active justice for all (Matthew 25). Religious communities aspire to educate members in practices that embody these virtues, so also forming citizens of "the world" who can begin to change the status quo. Christianity teaches that humility, repentance, and sacrifice are necessary counterparts of compassionate action, and that those who sacrifice rightly hope that their action will bear fruit.

In conclusion, then, the ITC's Catholic interpretation of natural law is a tradition-based approach to global ethics that aims to identify basic goods and values that people in all cultures recognize and respect. Natural law ethics is necessarily inductive and perspectival, but it also provides a basis for global cooperation in the face of shared human problems, such as sexism, racism, poverty, war, and climate change. Natural law does not provide a set of clear solutions to such problems. Instead, it encourages a process of common discernment and debate toward consensus. That process must be self-critical and more inclusive than it has been in the past. Nevertheless, the ITC is right to hope that, despite cultural diversity, all peoples recognize their "common humanity," and can work together toward solutions that are equitable, attractive, and politically feasible (116).

The Political Common Good:
From the Nation-State to a Global Perspective?

Joseph Capizzi

Despite its political emphasis on "unit[ing] human beings and bring[ing] them peace and happiness" (1), which culminates in a long section entitled the "Natural Law and the City," the International Theological Commission's (ITC) document *In Search of a Universal Ethic: A New Look at the Natural Law* mentions the state only a few times and in those few instances does so critically. This critical and slight attention is remarkable when considered from the perspective of the United States, where despite a nearly decade-long "Great Recession," the institutions and aspirations of the state remain robust and where, unlike in Europe, any regional multistate relationships make little impression on the civic consciousness. If there is a "demise of the state," one would not know it in a state that recently carried on military operations in four distinct theaters, the total costs of which crept to more than 1.5 trillion dollars.[1] In addition, the slight attention is remarkable in part because the state has been and continues to be a significant political actor, in particular at the international level. Does the ITC document exhibit the wish-casting of European cosmopolitans, or is there a theoretical, and natural law, justification for the document's slight attention to the state?

In my reflections on the ITC document, I make the case that the document's inattentiveness to the state, seen clearly in chapter 4, reflects a theoret-

1. On the "demise of the state," see Vito Tanzi, "The Demise of the Nation-State," IMF Working Paper 98/120, August 1998; on the costs of U.S. wars, see "Cost of Wars a Rising Issue as Obama Weighs Troop Levels," *The New York Times*, June 21, 2011, http://www.nytimes.com/2011/06/22/us/politics/22costs.html, accessed June 23, 2011.

ical, natural law justification for resisting the temptation to equate "political reflection" with "reflection on the activities of the State." I make this case in three steps: in step 1, I briefly discuss the "common good" in its classic use and place the common good in contact with the political principle of subsidiarity; in step 2, I look to the ITC document to make the case that it considers the global common good a genuine and political good indicating a scope of the common good that transcends the responsibility of the state; in step 3, I make the case for a politics at the level of the global common good. I conclude with some caveats to my argument that may anticipate a couple of objections.

Step 1: The Common Good and Subsidiarity

The ITC document identifies "four principal contexts" in which Church teaching invokes the natural law, of which three are manifestly political and address the natural law's relationship to the common good. The last of these three principal contexts concerns in particular the "threats of the abuse of power, and even of totalitarianism" of the contemporary state (35). The document thus draws our attention to the close relationship between natural law reflection and political concerns, including the common good. Reflection on the natural law often accompanies reflection on the common good, so it is appropriate to turn our attention there.

The document alludes to the magisterial definition of the common good found in Vatican II's *Gaudium et spes* (26). According to the document, "by the fact that human beings have the vocation to live in society with others, they have in common an ensemble of goods to pursue and values to defend. This is what is called the 'common good' " (85). But this is not the only sense of the common good; the common good can also name the final cause of political life.[2] The common good is thus a regulating end of political activity — what the ITC document acknowledges as the "second level" of the common good (85).[3] As the final cause of political life the common good is the end, or purpose, of political acts. The common good permits us to evaluate political activity, thus the document states that societies can even be "defined by the type of common good they intend to promote" (85). We are able to see both whether the political act achieved what it pursued and, because of its connec-

---

2. St. Thomas Aquinas, *ST* I-II, q. 90, a. 2.

3. "The common good is that which assigns an end to the political order and the city itself." *In Search of a Universal Ethic*, 85.

tion to the natural law, whether what it pursued ought to have been pursued at all.

The political common good is the end of coordinated action that serves the good of both the community as a whole and the goods of each member of that community in particular. Thus, the common good does not identify some end of collective activity to which some individuals' ends must be sacrificed as though the good in common can only be pursued at the expense of the goods of some. The document thus calls the common good the "good of all and of each one in particular" (85). The common good is both "one," in the sense of indivisible, and "universal," in the sense of serving the good of every particular member of that community. When political communities fail to pursue the common good, they diminish their members' flourishing; likewise, when the members of political communities fail to order their activities toward the common good, not only do they undermine their own flourishing, but they also diminish the community of which they are a part.

The many different forms of human association have distinct "common goods." There is general agreement that the use of the term "common good" in application to the many different levels of human association is analogical, ultimately on analogy to the highest and perfect "good in common" for the human person, God, but analogically more immediately to the common good of the *polis*, as that which orders all those particular goods relative to it. The point to be brought forward, building on the prior claims, is that individual goods and common goods are not rivals, but correlates.[4] Thus V. Bradley Lewis: "the good of the individual human person is particular in relation to the common good of the family or the larger community. But the good of the family is also particular relative to that of the city, as is the good of the town, the province, the postal service, or ministry of defense."[5] The common goods of these plural levels of human association can be viewed from different perspectives — from above or from below, as it were — and from either of these perspectives, they require coordination. Their coordination is the work of politics and a critical principle of the coordination of these goods is the principle of subsidiarity.

First appearing in the encyclical *Quadragesimo anno* (1931), the principle of subsidiarity states, "a community of a higher order should not interfere in the internal life of a community of a lower order, depriving the latter of its functions, but rather should support it in case of need and help to coordinate

---

4. Cf. V. Bradley Lewis, "The Common Good in Classical Political Philosophy," http://faculty.cua.edu/lewisb/Common%20Good3.pdf, 1-21.

5. Lewis, "The Common Good," 6.

its activity with the activities of the rest of society, always with a view to the common good."[6] Often commentators stress the principle's respect for lower levels of political and social organization and their rights and duties to do their "functions." Given the context of *Quadragesimo anno,* when the Church resisted the rise of authoritarian states in Europe, this "devolutionary" emphasis makes sense. Contained in the principle, however, and in fact helping make better political sense of the principle, is the notion of right order. Subsidiarity does not merely (or always) emphasize pushing functions down to more immediate levels of state bureaucracy; it affirms the plural forms of political organization and their respective functions, including both the form of the state, and, arguably, levels of organization *beyond* the state. The principle of subsidiarity orders not only the different levels of communal organization internally but also the correlative goods of social life externally. The principle emphasizes that the place of the state in ordering politics is only partial: the state has a limited good for which it, and it alone, is responsible. To take on greater responsibility (the totalitarian impulse) or to have increased responsibility thrust on it (the welfare impulse) burdens the state to its own detriment and to the detriment of the goods and persons served by other levels of political life.[7] "Subsidiarity" limits the state to its legitimate functions and to those alone.

The case being made by the ITC document draws on the principle of subsidiarity (admittedly mentioned by name only once in the document [99]) to argue the place for a "global" political good, in relationship to which the good of any state is only particular and which, therefore, has rights and obligations specified by the principle of subsidiarity and on which the state cannot encroach. The case requires, however, the claim that there is a "community" at the global level, and it is to that we turn.

Step 2: A Global Community?

Does the ITC document affirm the existence of a global community beyond the state? The opening lines of the document announce its animus and scope: the pursuit of moral objectivity in the context of problems of international

6. Pope Pius XI, *Quadragesimo anno* (1931), 79-80. See also *Catechism of the Catholic Church,* 1883.

7. The language of "welfare" in this context has precedent in the tradition of Catholic social doctrine; cf. Pope Benedict XVI, *Caritas in veritate* (2009), 57.

— indeed, global — scope. The backdrop to this is the document's claim of a growing "awareness" among peoples that they are forming "one single world community" (1). The document thus directs our attention to global concerns it claims animate increasing awareness of a global community. In so doing, the document contextualizes the place of the state that it later will claim is insufficient — even if necessary — in its capacity to meet these concerns. At least some of these concerns do not seem resolvable at the level of the nation-state. So, the document states with confidence that "the question of ecological balance, of the protection of the environment, resources and climate, has become a pressing preoccupation faced by all humanity, and whose solution extends far beyond national boundaries" (1). In other words, not only do we have an emerging sense of our global community, but that community also faces questions the state cannot solve.

Mentioned among the problems of international scope are maintaining "ecological equilibrium," responding to terrorism and organized crime, and evaluating developments in biotechnology. In *Caritas in veritate*, Pope Benedict XVI adds to this the ongoing financial crisis.[8] Problems like these, the document claims, are bringing people into awareness of theological realities Catholic social doctrine has long affirmed: the unity of the human family and the interdependence of individuals and peoples with each other. The document states, "global solidarity is thus emerging, which finds its ultimate foundation in the unity of the human race" (1). Often Catholic social doctrine speaks of the awareness of "interdependence," a term that signals a sociological given about the increased interrelationship of modern economies.[9] Solidarity is the moral response of people to the fact of interdependence.[10] Interdependence and solidarity are intelligible because of the prior reality of the "unity of the human race." In emphasizing interdependence and solidarity at this point, the ITC document joins recent documents of Catholic social tradition affirming the increased perception of a global community. The perception is fueled by global social problems, but the reality of a global community is a theological one based on the unity of all peoples as children of God.

The document insists on the unity of the human family that is not abstract but real. The document claims the human community increasingly perceives

---

8. See, for instance, paragraphs 21, 24-25, 27, and 36.

9. See Pope John XXIII, *Pacem in terris* (1963), 130.

10. See Pope John Paul II, *Sollicitudo rei socialis* (1987), 26: "At the same time, in a world divided and beset by every type of conflict, the conviction is growing of a radical interdependence and consequently of the need for a solidarity which will take up interdependence and transfer it to the moral plane."

this unity, in part because of the global scope of certain contemporary problems. But that perception of unity speaks to a more fundamental unity, the unity of a human nature that "indicates . . . a totality that embraces all human beings who share the same destiny. The simple fact of being born *(nasci)* puts us in enduring relations of solidarity with all other human beings" (n. 66). There is a unity, then, both at the level of the human person's origin and at the level of his destiny. Christians "know that Jesus Christ, 'our peace' (Eph 2:14), who has reconciled all human beings to God by his cross, is the principle of the most profound unity towards whom the human race is called to converge" (3). Among humanity's tasks, then, is the task to respond by instantiating into society our natal relations with other persons (87).[11] And just as this responsibility presents itself to each qua individual, so it does to all in common. There is, the introduction explains, a "planetary responsibility" to embrace and foster solidarity with others (1, 87, and 95). Our global problems provide the foundation for deepening political relationships with each other.

Thus the document shows how as a social being the person finds himself in the midst of a series of relationships that relate to his flourishing. "The person is a social being by nature, not by choice or in virtue of a pure contractual convention. In order to flourish as a person, he needs the structure of relations that he forms with other persons. He thus finds himself at the centre of a network formed by concentric circles: the family, the sphere of life and work, the neighborhood community, the nation, and finally humanity" (84). The document invokes the language of the common good at this point, as both means and end: the common good is both "the ensemble of conditions that allow a person to be a more human person," and "that which assigns an end to the political order and to the city itself" (85).[12] The common good is a means, or efficient cause, by which the person achieves his flourishing and the end (in the sense of final cause) of political action. Placed back to back in this manner, the document compels us to recognize as Catholic social doctrine had before that there are "common goods" at multiple levels of human asso-

---

11. The document reads, at paragraph 87, "Finally, it is necessary for society to be regulated by a kind of solidarity which assures mutual assistance and responsibility for others, as well as the use of society's goods in response to the needs of all." I think the language of "regulated by a kind of solidarity" unnecessarily suggests a legal or statutory regime that might be off-putting to the American ear. "Regulated by a kind of solidarity" should be read more broadly than that, keeping in mind that Catholic social doctrine understands solidarity as a fundamental principle of political and social organization akin to "friendship" (cf. Pope John Paul II, *Centesimus annus* [1991], 10).

12. Again the document cites *Gaudium et spes*, this time at paragraph 26.

ciation, including the association of the human family as a whole. There is, then, a "common good" of and for humanity.

The moves made in the document mirror the moves made by Pope Benedict XVI in *Caritas in veritate,* where he writes, "In an increasingly globalized society, the common good and the effort to obtain it cannot fail to assume the dimensions of the whole human family, that is to say, the community of peoples and nations, in such a way as to shape the *earthly city* in unity and peace, rendering it to some degree an anticipation and a prefiguration of the undivided *city of God."*[13] Pope Benedict XVI and the ITC document are thus pointing to the current ways political reflection must focus on a good beyond the ambit of the state: there are political needs surpassing the authority of the state that impinge on the goods of all persons. Subsidiarity requires a politics to match these goods. We are not startled, then, when the ITC document claims a "common good of humanity" (5) and "the common good of the planet" (38).

Step 3: The State and the Global Common Good

The document places its political reflections in the context of a broader reflection on the natural law in the light of our age's increased interdependence and increased sense of the diversity of values. Chapter 4, devoted specifically to political analysis, contains eighteen paragraphs (83-100), only three of which mention the state and all three of which describe limitations on the state.[14] Prior to chapter 4, there are only three mentions of the state, one of which is very brief, when the document applauds the *Universal Declaration of Human Rights* (1948) and states that human rights transcend "the positive laws of states" (5). The paragraph notes that legislators did not create these rights and by implication positive law cannot deny them, positive law having merely made "manifest" what objectively existed. The other two mentions, again where "state" is not capitalized and which thus seems to indicate a non-technical analysis, are quite important and relate to this first mention. Both occur in paragraph 28, in which the document exemplifies the relationship of the natural law to the international law that "regulates the relations of peoples and states among themselves" (28). The example invoked is the intervention

13. *Caritas in veritate,* 7.

14. On the other hand, there are some thirteen mentions of the "city" in chapter 4, including in the title, "Natural Law and the City."

by Spanish theologians on behalf of the native peoples of the Americas against "imperialist ideology." The natural law is posited as grounding international law to challenge the pretenses and activities of actual states, as they did the Catholic states of Portugal and Spain. Vitoria and other theologians appealed to the natural law to challenge the existing positive laws and defend the rights of the indigenous American populations. Natural right, which anchors human law to the natural law (89), demanded respect for the rights of the native peoples. And, the document adds, "the idea of natural law also allowed the Spanish theologians to establish the foundations of an international law, i.e., of a universal norm that regulates the relations of peoples and states among themselves" (28). The use of the term "ideology" in paragraph 28 echoes later in the document's more systematic reflections on the state.

The first mention of the state in the document's systematic political analysis in chapter 4 comes at paragraph 95, where, much as in those three initial mentions the activity of the state was limited by law, we are told what the state cannot do:

> The State, therefore, cannot set itself up as the bearer of ultimate meaning. It cannot impose a global ideology, nor a religion (even secular), nor one way of thinking. In civil society religious organizations, philosophies and spiritualties take charge of the domain of ultimate meaning. . . . The political order is not called to transpose onto earth the kingdom of God that is to come. It can anticipate the kingdom by advances in the area of justice, solidarity, and peace. It cannot seek to establish it by force.

The paragraph warns against the totalitarian temptation of states, when they consume the space that should be left to civil society where men freely can associate and order their lives.

The second mention occurs in the following paragraph and again limits the aspirations of the state. The document states, "If the political order is not the sphere of the ultimate truth, it must, nevertheless, be open to the perpetual search for God, truth, and justice. The 'legitimate and sound secularity of the State' consists in the distinction between the supernatural order of theological faith and the political order. This latter order can never be confused with the order of grace to which all persons are called to freely adhere" (96). In the first of these limitations on the state, we hear the echo of concerns about Spanish and Portuguese imperialist ideology: states cannot bear "ultimate meanings"; doing so violates the coordination of social order and rises to the level of ideology. The second limitation adds to this the point that the state's inability to bear "ultimate meaning" nonetheless requires its openness to ultimate truth. States may not "bear" ultimate meanings; instead, they surrender to the religious, philosophical, and spiritual institutions of civil society the space to "take charge of" the domain of ultimate meaning.

The final mention comes in the penultimate paragraph of chapter 4 and ties these insights together. Thus paragraph 99:

> But constant reference to natural law presses for a continual purification of reason. Only in this way does the political order avoid the trap of the arbitrary, of particular interests, organized lying, and manipulation of minds. The reference to natural law keeps the state from yielding to the temptation to absorb civil society and to subject human beings to an ideology. It also avoids the development of the paternalistic state that deprives persons and communities of every initiative and takes responsibility away from them. Natural law contains the idea of the state, based on law, structured according to the principle of subsidiarity, respecting persons and intermediate bodies, and regulating their interactions.

Once again, the passage emphasizes the place of the political order in its service to "persons and communities." The natural law "purifies" the state of ideology, much as the Spanish scholastics attempted in the sixteenth century, and it keeps the state within the just bounds set by subsidiarity. Somewhat obliquely the passage refers positively to an *idea* of a "state of rights." Given that the structure of the chapter is to specify the relationship of the natural law to the common good and that it does this first by specifying the limitations placed by the natural law on the political order (including in particular, the state), we can only then speak constructively of an ideal of that political order, bound by rights and subsidiarity to serve the goods of people and the communities they form. The "state of rights" coordinates the political activities of "persons and mediating bodies" according to the natural law. There is no indication in the document that this "state of rights" could not operate at the international level of organization, nor, of course, that it must or can only operate at that level. We must assume that the theoretical warnings made to the state apply as well to some kind of international or world government: it serves a discrete and limited political good and does so in service to that good, the goods of all other levels of human association, and ultimately the goods of all the members of the human family.

Conclusion

The ITC document shows, then, an increased perception of a global community, a perception that is the awareness of the theological given of a human family by origin in God's creation and by destination in Christ's redemption. There is, then, a community that possesses a good, a final cause of a politics attentive to increasingly globalized problems that reveal the state's practical limitations and allow clearer vision of its theoretical limitations. The modern state simply cannot, and should not, take on or be given tasks exceeding its just limits. International law, drawing on natural law and expressed so well in the example of the Spanish scholastic response to imperialism, should be directing human activity toward this global common good.

I finish with two caveats to this argument. Turning the focus of politics toward a "global common good" is a requirement of Christian political thinking, and on this score the ITC document is right to expand the scope of its natural law political analysis beyond the contemporary state. There are at least two reasons, however, to chasten such talk.

The first is a theological reason. There have been many "millennial" temptations in Christianity, where historical developments were read eschatologically. One might thus be tempted to see "increased awareness" of global interdependence as a sure and inevitable step toward God's kingdom and thereby be emboldened to embrace global political authority as a step closer to Christ's rule. The document warns against this temptation in the paragraph quoted above, that "the political order is not called to transpose onto earth the kingdom of God that is to come" (95). Nonetheless, within Catholic political reflection there has been at times a failure to distinguish political developments from progress toward the kingdom. Perception of increased interdependence is largely driven by reversible contemporary technological and economic developments. Even those that do not depend on technology and economics, however, can quickly reverse course or have built into them the seeds of their own demise. The point is not just that progress of this sort can have positive and negative aspects, but the broader point that recalls the tension between the kingdom of which we have a taste and the kingdom of God not yet present. So long as the kingdom is not present in its fullness, all political authority — global, national, and otherwise — stands equally under the judgment of God.

The second reason is the secular temptation to view the emergence of a global common good with millennial hope. This can happen; if "God and all transcendence were . . . excluded from the political horizon, only the power of man over man would remain" (97). The document thus alerts us to the temptation to invest the political order with more significance — and ultimately more authority — than it can or should bear. As the document states quite clearly, one piece of the Christian patrimony to political thought is the desacralization of the political order (93). Whatever shape the governing authority associated with a global common good takes, its tasks as outlined in the document's reflections on the natural law are real, significant, and yet limited. They are of the sort mentioned by the document itself: the discrete yet necessary tasks that supersede the capacity of any state. By reference to the natural law and the political principle of subsidiarity, Catholic political reflection can contribute to a social order of vibrant and interrelated forms of human association that serve the good of each person and the good that pertains to all persons.

Teleology, Divine Governance, and the Common Good: Thoughts on *In Search of a Universal Ethic: A New Look at the Natural Law*

Steven A. Long

The International Theological Commission's (ITC) document on natural law — *In Search of a Universal Ethic: A New Look at the Natural Law*[1] — manifests a rich awareness of the speculative and essentially teleological foundations of the natural law. It likewise displays a deep understanding of the history of metaphysical obscuration that has marginalized and distorted proper understanding of the natural law, engendering a false ethos of absolute autonomy of the human moral agent vis-à-vis divine providence: an apotheosis of arbitrary will criticized in *Veritatis splendor.*

In what follows, I address two strategic *foci* of the ITC document. First, I engage the document's teaching inasmuch as it vindicates the primacy of the speculative in relation to the practical — a judgment focally articulated in its stress on the centrality of metaphysical wisdom for moral judgment, and its corresponding judgment of the essential moral import of natural teleology. Second, I address the ITC document's affirmation of the strategic importance of a noncompetitive account of divine and human causality for the understanding of natural law as a mode of the divine providence.

---

1. In accord with the standardization of the usages of the present volume, this essay proceeds citing the official translation available on the Internet at the Vatican website: http://www.vatican.va/roman_curia/congregations/cfaith/cti_documents/rc_con_cfaith_doc_20090520_legge-naturale_en.html.

The Primacy of the Speculative and the
Normative Role of Natural Teleology

The document unequivocally affirms the priority of the speculative vis-à-vis the practical in moral theology and philosophy, chiefly through its unremitting stress on the definitory importance of metaphysical truth (surely a speculative rather than practical science, and indeed naturally speaking the principal speculative science), but also by its clear and unequivocal affirmation of the essential ethical import of natural teleology. For without metaphysically realistic normative natural teleology nothing is genuinely ordered to anything qua fulfillment or end, and so no natural wisdom regarding human flourishing will be possible. It observes "two levels of coherence and depth" in the "philosophical justification of natural law" (61). Thus "the idea of a natural law is justified first of all on the level of the reflective observation of the anthropological constants that characterize a successful humanization of the person and a harmonious social life" (61). Yet it continues to note that the defining character of the natural law is a function of metaphysical judgment:

> Nevertheless, only the recognition of the metaphysical dimension of the real can give to natural law its full and complete philosophical justification. In fact metaphysics allows for understanding that the universe does not have in itself its own ultimate reason for being, and manifests the fundamental structure of the real: the distinction between God, subsistent being himself, and the other beings placed by him in existence. God is the Creator, the free and transcendent source of all other beings. (62)

Thus, it continues:

> The Creator is not only the principle of creatures but also the transcendent end towards which they tend by nature. Thus creatures are animated by a dynamism that carries them to fulfill themselves, each in its own way, in the union with God. This dynamism is transcendent, to the extent to which it proceeds from the eternal law, i.e., from the plan of divine providence that exists in the mind of the Creator (62). But it is also immanent, because it is not imposed on creatures from without, but is inscribed in their very nature. Purely material creatures realize spontaneously the law of their being, while spiritual creatures realize it in a personal manner. In fact, they interiorize the dynamisms that define them and freely orientate them towards their own complete realization. They formulate them to themselves, as fundamental norms of their moral action — this is the natural law properly stated

— and they strive to realize them freely. The natural law is therefore defined as a participation in the eternal law. (63)

The definition of a thing is not accidental to it, and natural law is according to St. Thomas Aquinas (*ST* I-II, q. 91, a. 2) "nothing other than a rational participation of the eternal law." A definition more theocentric and metaphysical in character would be hard to imagine: if there is no eternal law, there is no natural law. This is quite contrary to accounts of natural law that view it as essentially practical, for its very definition is speculative and metaphysical: it is *nothing* other than a rational participation of eternal law, which rational participation of course *presupposes* the passive participation of this same law in the creature's reception from God of its being, nature, and natural ordering toward the good.[2]

As St. Thomas teaches in *ST* I, q. 79, a. 11, the only difference between acts of speculative and practical intelligence is that in the latter knowledge is further ordered to the good of an operation — something accidental to knowledge as such, which is essentially defined by the adequation or conformity of the mind to the real. For knowledge to be ordained to the good of an operation, one must of course will the operation; as a human act, this presupposes rational desire — the motion of the will; and the motion of the will presupposes knowledge

2. Human reason is for St. Thomas a "measured measure" which, in order adequately to serve as a rule and measure of our conduct, must first be measured *by* the teleological order impressed on human nature by God from creation. Only the rational reception of this order as articulating precepts, reasons to do or not to do, is natural law. But it is from the normative teleological ordering of human nature that these precepts are derived, not by getting a "value" out of a "fact" but by rationally receiving this teleological ordering (*ST* I-II, q. 91, a. 3): for if a natural end is not a reason for action, then what is? The sub-rational inclinations — granted that they are connaturally known, yet in a way itself still analogically speculative — must be placed in the wider rational framework of the universal good through contemplation before they are ethically directive because only so does one know their ends as integrated within the hierarchy of ends that defines the good for man. This contemplation is always normed by an essentially speculative knowledge of the order of ends. Granted that good action is action rectified by conformity to right appetite, *right appetite itself presupposes prior knowledge of the end and indeed of the hierarchy of ends.* And this knowledge of the ends defining the nature of the good for man has a speculative character *as a condition* of the will ever being moved by these ends since prior to the motion of the will and the consequent intention of ends and deliberation of means, there must first be the knowledge of that which comes to be desired as good. The effort to live in an excluded middle with respect to the priority of the speculative to the practical is a grandiose error, as is the denial of the normativity for reason of the teleological ordering impressed by God on nature, and through whose rational reception man is *preceptively* governed.

that is prior to and that specifies the motion of the will toward the desired good. Thus a speculative knowledge — a *speculum* — is implicitly and actually present in every practical cognition. It could not be otherwise: judgments regarding the nature of reality necessarily define and structure one's moral vision — moral life cannot momentarily detach from the nature of reality later to return. This is not a function of deriving reasons for action from propositions lacking reasons for action:[3] because good — in all its analogical modalities, ethical as well as culinary, athletic, technical, and so on — is nothing other (cf. *ST* I, q. 5, aa. 1-3) than being with a conceptual relation to appetite as perfective.

Knowledge of being as such, apart from any further direction toward action, is speculative, and knowledge of good — of every modality of good, both specifically ethical and other modes — considers being *with a conceptual relation* to appetite as perfective. But it is *being* that is thus known as perfective. Knowledge as such is essentially speculative — a matter of the conformity of mind and thing: *it is accidental to knowledge qua knowledge that it be further ordered to the good of an operation.* Although in practical knowing one orders the known truth to the good of an operation, *whether* it is truth that is so ordered is a function of conformity or nonconformity to the real: it is a *speculative* function. *It is hardly the case that merely because I order some judgment to my operation that therefore that judgment is true: to the contrary, its truth is a function of adequation to the real irrespective of whether I wish to apply it to action. Whereas sciences are denominated practical or speculative according to whether their objects concern doing or making, acts of the mind are denominated practical or speculative by their ends.*

This leads to the realization of the normative moral role of unified teleology, for to know being qua perfective is to know it as *end*. The document acknowledges that "the concept of natural law presupposes the idea that nature is for man the bearer of an ethical message and is an implicit moral norm that human reason actualizes" (69). It comments on the disastrous implications for ethics that ensue insofar as "the world of bodies is identified with extension, certainly regulated by intelligible mathematical laws, but stripped of every immanent teleology or finality" (72). The point could not be clearer in the document's affirmation that

> in this context, in which nature no longer contains any immanent teleological rationality and seems to have lost all affinity or kinship with the world

---

3. Cf. Robert P. George, "Natural Law and Human Nature," in *Natural Law Theory*, ed. Robert P. George (Oxford: Clarendon Press, 1992), 38.

of spirit, the passage from knowledge of the structures of being to moral duty which seems to derive from it becomes effectively impossible and falls under the criticism of "naturalistic fallacy" denounced by David Hume and then by George Edward Moore in his *Principia Ethica* (1903). The good is actually disconnected from being and from truth. Ethics is separated from metaphysics. (73)

But the role of the speculative in practical affairs — of being, nature, and natural teleology — is essential: the capacity to *abstract* from natural teleology does not establish its nonexistence or practical irrelevance. The human mind is a *measured measure* — it is measured, or "normed," by an order antecedent to its own judgment, an order prior to rational appetite, deliberation, and choice. Knowledge of the order of ends is presupposed by virtuous desire for the end. Granted that lower teleologies (e.g., toward food and water) are known directly by natural inclination, their place in a moral life (and with respect to choice) requires judgment in the light of the actual knowledge of the wider order of ends: a rational contact with the good necessary for and prior to rational appetite. For example, although both nutrition and friendship are goods, friendship is a loftier good, and it is truer to say that nutrition is ordered to friendship than the converse. We desire lower goods both in themselves and for the sake of higher goods — as we desire life both in itself and for the sake of friendship, truth, justice, beauty, wisdom, and communion with God.

The Absolutization of Human Autonomy

The ITC document's insight into the roots of moral antinomianism in the erroneous treatment of human and divine freedom as competitive — as though the divine causality were no different from a finite causality, or other than the very *cause* of human free acts themselves — is strategically crucial. It is subtle, and stated as cautiously and prudently as one can imagine — because this issue was the core of the *de auxiliis* disputations before the Holy See, the most difficult and profound set of disputations ever to be taken up by the magisterium.[4] Here the document's teaching is wholly correct. If one pursues the specu-

4. This of course refers to the congregation established by Pope Clement VIII to judge the issues that arose regarding grace and freedom near the close of the sixteenth century and continued into the reigns of Pope Leo IX and Pope Paul V in whose presence seventeen debates occurred. Twenty years of discussion and eighty-five conferences in the presence of the popes

lative etiology of the eclipse of metaphysics, one finds there a neuralgia that derives from the arguments regarding God and human freedom, from the Church's failure to judge the doctrine of Molina, and from a consequent skepticism about the role of causal metaphysics within theological method. After all, consequent on the failure to judge Molina's teaching, causal metaphysics became associated with what came widely to be viewed as a paralogism of speculative reason regarding divine and human agency. But a direct implication of the Molinist account is that the agency of the human will stands without the divine efficiency, and therefore stands without the divine causal providence.

Molina of course taught that the will is only free when, all requirements being retained, the will could will otherwise.[5] But if among the "requirements" is the divine causality, the result is that human free acts must then be held to stand outside the divine causality. As St. Thomas puts the matter *expressly regarding the divine agent causality and providence* (ST I, q. 22, a. 2, resp.):

> For since every agent acts for an end, the ordering of effects towards that end extends as far as the causality of the first agent extends. Whence it happens that in the effects of an agent something takes place which has no reference towards the end, because the effect comes from a cause other than, and outside the intention of the agent. But the causality of God, Who is the first agent, extends to all being, not only as to constituent principles of species, but also as to the individualizing principles; not only of things incorruptible, but also of things corruptible. Hence all things that exist in

---

did not lead to an authoritative resolution of the question, although the Dominican and Augustinian positions were considered conformable to tradition, and the Jesuit position (of Molina, as well as the congruism of Bellarmine) was considered permissible as it had never finally been judged. Cf. the words of Pope Benedict XIV: "The Thomists are proclaimed destroyers of human liberty and as followers, not to say of Jansenism but even of Calvinism; but, since they meet the charges with eminent satisfaction, and since their opinion has never been condemned by the Holy See, the Thomists carry on with impunity in this matter." Pope Benedict XIV likewise points out regarding the Augustinians that "since their opinion has not been condemned by the Holy See, there is no one who does not see that there can be no effort on the part of anyone to cause them to relinquish their opinion"; and that "the followers of Molina and Suarez" can "continue" in defense of their teaching while noting that "the Roman Pontiffs thus far have not passed judgment on this system of Molina." So this pontiff (and this is of course *after* the controversy *de auxillis*) holds that the Thomist position has been adjudicated as meeting the charges with eminent satisfaction and so not condemned by the Holy See, whereas the Molinist position is literally unadjudicated. Cf. Henry Denzinger, *Enchiridion Symbolorum*, 43rd ed., para. 2564, p. 520; para. 1997, p. 453.

5. Cf. Molina's *Concordia* q. 14, a. 13, disp. II.

whatsoever manner are necessarily directed by God towards some end; as the Apostle says: "Those things that are of God are well ordered" (Romans 13:1).

The ordering of effects toward the end extends as far as the causality of the first agent extends, and it is quite clear that the causality in question is *agent* causality. If human freedom is *subtracted* from the effect of divine agency, then of course human freedom lies outside the divine providence, and accordingly wholly outside the eternal law, outside the divine providential ordering. Thus natural law would be impossible because natural law is nothing other than the rational participation in eternal law, and eternal law and divine governance generally extend only so far as divine agency extends. As St. Thomas puts it in *ST* I-II, q. 91, a. 2, resp.:

> Wherefore, since all things subject to Divine providence are ruled and measured by the eternal law, as was stated above (Article 1); it is evident that all things partake somewhat of the eternal law, in so far as, namely, from its being imprinted on them, they derive their respective inclinations to their proper acts and ends.

Remove human freedom from the divine providential government, and one has absolutized human freedom, rendering it *a se*,[6] and rendered the very idea

6. That God is *a se* affirms that God is Pure Act, or as St. Thomas puts it, is *ipsum esse subsistens per se*. Accordingly, it affirms that God is his own reason for being, thus being subject to no reciprocal causality on the part of beings that owe their existence to God, as God has no dependent origin (hence *ens a se non ens ab alio*). For St. Thomas only Pure Act really independent and transcendent of all other being is able to constitute its own sufficient reason (a phrase that does not, as with Leibnitz, pertain to something wholly of the analytic order, but which is analogous). As St. Thomas says in *Summa contra gentiles* II, ch. 15: "that which has no cause is something first and immediate; hence it is necessary that it be by reason of itself and in consequence of what it is." It follows that all other beings are not by reason of themselves and in consequence of what they are — they are not their own sufficient reason. The analogical principle of sufficient reason of course is also taught by *Humani generis*, 29: "For this philosophy, acknowledged and accepted by the Church, safeguards the genuine validity of human knowledge, the unshakable metaphysical principles of sufficient reason, causality, and finality, and finally the mind's ability to attain certain and unchangeable truth." In any case, God being the end and not really related to or dependent on any other reality, the divine action *ab extra* with respect to creation is not necessitated or *entailed*; whereas in created beings, when the conditions are such as to be objectively causal with respect to action, action occurs (minus any impeding causality or, alternately, minus any impeding deprivation in the agent: all of which is simply again to say, when the conditions for causality are met). By contrast, God is causally adequate for the creation of countless beings, but the existence of these cannot be said to be

of natural law an impossibility. This is the effect of defining human freedom in relation to God — who as cause of universal being is cause both of the necessary and the contingent — rather than by its rational nature. Precisely such a freedom is articulated by the absolute autonomist libertarian account of freedom that is present in seedling form in Molina's formulation. God is not merely a finite cause, but the source of all other causality that accordingly is inscribed within the effect of his agency. Inasmuch as the proper object of God's causality is being, to say that a thing possesses "liberty of indifference" to the divine causality is to speak of something as standing outside of being, to speak of it as not existing. But not existing is neither freedom nor any other real attribute.

The noncompetitive view of divine and created agency and causality — that is, that God's causality is inclusive, not exclusive, of human freedom, because human freedom is a providential divine gift — is essentially intellectualist as St. Thomas Aquinas develops it. The ITC document is wholly correct in cleaving to this account (cf. 75 and 77). For St. Thomas, freedom of the will with respect to any finite object, inclusive of revealed truths, follows from the very nature of intellect and will. The intellect is ordered to the universal true, and the will is natively ordered toward the universal good, good in general. But no finite good can compel the will because no finite good *is* the universal good.[7] Hence even grace, construed *as an object of choice,* cannot compel the will. Only were man to see God would his will be wholly perfected and fulfilled in such a manner that nothing save cleaving to God would be possible. But regarding all terrestrial objects of volition, man is free. Thus man's freedom is defined, not by a spurious liberty of indifference to divine causality that nothing real possesses or could possess, but by the nature of the rational will in relation to its finite terrestrial objects.

Yet, man is not *a se.* As the ITC document puts it, "Freedom is therefore not an absolute creator of itself, but is rather an eminent property of every human subject" (77). As St. Thomas Aquinas puts it, just as one may be cause of a thing without being the first cause, so one may cause one's own free act without being the first cause of one's own free act. As nothing moves itself from potency to act save by virtue of that which is first in act, and man is not always proceeding to apply the natural motion of the will to act, God moves us from

---

necessitated by the divine essence because God possesses infinite blessedness in himself and creation does not proceed by a necessity of the divine essence: creation of creatures *ad extra* is utterly free and gratuitous.

7. Cf. *ST* I, q. 82, a. 2.

potency to act with respect to our own self-determination in freedom. Indeed, the divine simplicity is such that God has no real determined relation to the creature, whereas the creature is really determined toward and dependent on God. The only difference between God willing X and God not willing X is the being of X, for there is no change in God. Thus, while grace as an object of choice is subject to our freedom — as we are free, say, to reject a grace calling us to prayer, or worship, et alia — grace *in relation to the divine simple will* is simply efficacious because either God does or does not will the effect. The perfection of our freedom in free acts is thus a gift, and even a gift for which we may and should pray. Hence in the composite sense, insofar as God moves me freely to will, I am not not-freely moving to will because I cannot freely move and not-freely move at the same time and in the same respect, and freedom is not a denial of the law of noncontradiction. What makes the act free is that we are ourselves interiorly the source of the act, and no finite object of our free choice can compel our choice — but nothing prevents this interior act, uncompelled by the finite object, from being itself in its positive ontological dimensions an effect of the divine goodness. Thus as an act the free choice stands within and not without the divine causal providence.

Considered from the most formal and metaphysical perspective, the question is whether God is genuinely the first cause of every perfection of being. If so, then God must be the first cause of the perfection of our free acts of self-determination, and this is indeed the teaching of Aquinas. Hence he writes in *De malo,* q. 3, a. 2, ad 4, that

> when anything moves itself, this does not exclude its being moved by another, from which it has even this that it moves itself. Thus it is not repugnant to liberty that God is the cause of the free act of the will.

St. Thomas famously argues (*ST* I-II, q. 109, a. 1) that no creature, no matter how noble, can even proceed to its act unless it first be moved by God, and that the action of any created being depends on God in two ways, "first inasmuch as it is from Him that it has the form whereby it acts; secondly, inasmuch as it is moved by Him to act."

If we remove the positive substance of man's free acts from the transcendent divine causality, it will follow as a necessary corollary that the positive substance of these free acts is alike removed from divine providence. *And that which lies outside divine providence is not subject to the direction of eternal law.* From this point on, that which for St. Thomas *defines* the natural law — namely, that it is a *rational participation* in the *eternal law* — will become something *extraneous* and *alien*.[8] On this supposition, finite human creatures roam the Earth creating *ex nihilo* the added perfection or reality of their free determinations, entirely outside the divine causality, the divine providence, and the eternal law.[9] The volitional agent is thus removed from the divine jurisdiction in being removed from the divine causality. *This directly implies a way of understanding the natural law that St. Thomas's philosophy and theology prohibit — a way that treats nature and natural law not as manifestations of divine government but as demarcating a zone of independence from divine governance.*[10]

Nature and reason go from being manifestations and expressions of normative divine order to being antipodes of divine order to which one may appeal in order to "safeguard" human freedom from divine authority. God moves from being the author and perfector of human liberty and virtue to being a threat to authentic human freedom and an alien distortive influence on morality. The symmetry of these implications with Kantian autonomism is arresting, yet this aspect of the Kantian teaching is a late and secular effect of what is originatively an intra-Catholic error. Practically speaking it is an error that removes both moral law and grace from any authoritatively directive role in human life. It is not difficult to see how, given the perspective of such an absolutization of human freedom, the magisterium of the Church with respect

8. If the volitional act is not subject to divine causality, it is alike not subject to divine providence. This inference is absolute. St. Thomas does not, of course, envision this causality as violent or external. Rather, the divine causality of the acts of the will is precisely that whereby they are naturally constituted as volitional acts. God causes necessary things necessarily, and contingent things contingently, and the will is denominated as "free" because it is not an operative power prefixed to only one effect, but has for its formal object the universal good as specified by reason. St. Thomas holds that no finite good may compel the rational will, so that the will is objectively free with respect to its natural finite objects. Yet he also maintains that the rational will cannot proceed to its own act of free self-determination unless moved from potency to act with respect to this act of free self-determination by God.

9. The citations possible for this doctrine of St. Thomas are numerous. But, for instance, see *Summa contra gentiles* 3b.89-90. The title of chapter 89 is quite clear: "That the Movement of the Will, and Not Only the Power of the Will, is Caused by God."

10. For St. Thomas, the rational creature both passively and actively participates in the eternal law. It passively participates in this law because its very own nature, act, object, and end are established by the eternal law and received from God as first cause. Yet unlike the case of lower creatures who also participate in the divine government in a merely passive way — precisely *because* the rational creature is created, sustained, and actuated as such — it actively participates in the eternal law and shares in its own government. Because its passive participation includes the possession of reason, the rational creature receives its ordering from God not merely passively but also rationally and *preceptively,* as giving it *reasons* to do and not to do. Cf. *ST* I-II, q. 91, a. 2.

to moral life subsequently comes to be received with hostile skepticism as nothing other than an inherently futile and falsifying exertion of raw power over an interiority and freedom natively transcendent of such merely external exactions — or as the ITC document puts it:

> Furthermore, on account of the emergence of a metaphysical conception in which human and divine action are in competition with each other — since they are conceived in a univocal fashion and placed, wrongly, on the same level — the legitimate affirmation of the autonomy of the human subject leads to the exclusion of God from the sphere of human subjectivity. Every reference to something normative coming from God or from nature as an expression of God's wisdom, that is to say, every "heteronomy" is perceived as a threat to the subject's autonomy. The notion of natural law thus appears as incompatible with the authentic dignity of the subject. (75)

The magisterium's directions come to be viewed rather as though one's bowling league started to issue pronouncements on proper use of the generative faculties: at best *ultra vires* and at worst comically pathetic. Such an error at the root of the spiritual life is manifestly not finally compatible with the Catholic ethos. Yet many, through concessions to modernity and postmodernity on this fundamental point, have exposed the Catholic life to this foundational and destructive error.[11] Eventually, the project of mere rhetorical and irenic accommodation of mutually exclusive propositions will require that the project of theology as wish fulfillment give way to theology as *scientia* and *sapientia*. The ITC document does well to prompt theologians toward the realization that the first — *scientia* — is essential and necessary, and cannot be replaced by even the most elevated rhetoric.

---

11. Some authors seem to suppose that the reality of human freedom as lying within rather than without divine causal providence should absolutely require God to overcome every defect of each and every created liberty. But God does not in justice owe it to the defectible creature to overcome every defect even in the proportionate natural order — any more than God owes it to every pear tree that it yield perfect fruit — much less in the order of supernatural fruition whose attainment is the very reality of God himself. Yet some are more willing implicitly and actually to relativize and reduce to created proportions the exalted perfection of the beatific vision — which is proportionate to no creature whatsoever — than to stress to the wayward wills of men the absolute priority of divine grace and the lesson of humility. It cannot be denied that this unfortunate tendency, articulated in doctrinal terms, has real implications finally inconsistent with acknowledgment of the governance of divine providence and eternal law, whether in the mode of man's rational participation (the natural law) or man's graced participation (the life of faith, hope, and charity, and finally of beatific vision).

Natural Law as a "Work of Reason": Understanding the Metaphysics of Participated Theonomy

Martin Rhonheimer

In a crucial passage, the International Theological Commission (ITC) document on natural law *In Search of a Universal Ethic* says that "while in St. Thomas Aquinas the law was understood as a *work of reason* and an *expression of wisdom,* voluntarism leads one to connect the law to will alone, and to a will detached from its intrinsic ordering to the good" (30; emphasis added). In the following I wish to comment on how such an understanding of law as a "work of reason" bears on Aquinas's understanding of natural law and why it is so important.

The Best of Natural Law Tradition: "Law" as "Something Pertaining to Reason" and a "Work of Reason"

The Christian tradition of natural law thinking is characterized by overcoming the one-sidedness of the Stoic conception of natural law as a cosmic law, which often erroneously is held to be the blueprint for Christian natural law thinking. As *In Search of a Universal Ethic* points out, "the Fathers of the Church, however, do not purely and simply adopt the Stoic doctrine. They modify and

---

A substantially expanded version of this article has been published as "Natural Law as a 'Work of Reason': Understanding the Metaphysics of Participated Theonomy," *American Journal of Jurisprudence* 55, no. 41 (2010). It contains a much more detailed account of the present topic, including several important points that in this brief essay could not be treated at all, or not with all the precision required.

develop it" (26). Most important is the Christian idea that the human person — not the cosmos as a whole — is the bearer of the *imago Dei*. Therefore, following the moral law fundamentally means following the dictates of one's own reason. Adopting a theological view, *In Search of a Universal Ethic* grounds this anthropology in a wider Christological perspective: "To conduct oneself in conformity with reason amounts to following the orientations that Christ, as the divine *Logos,* has set down by virtue of the *logoi spermatikoi* in human reason. To act against reason is an offense against these orientations" (26).

At least since St. Augustine's affirmation that the moral life is based on "the impression in us of the knowledge of the eternal law,"[1] the Christian perspective has been that the natural moral law is *a cognitive power impressed in the human soul* by the work of the divine Creator, a participation in and impression of the divine *Logos* in our intellect and, thus, participation in knowledge of the eternal law *through* the created reason of the human person. It is this patristic tradition that was retrieved and developed by the high medieval Church lawyers[2] and continued by philosophers and theologians from William of Auxerre — who conceived of the natural law as the *precepts of natural reason,* self-evident practical principles[3] — to the immediate predecessors of Aquinas like Alexander of Hales, who called the natural law a "natural dictate of reason."[4]

Aquinas depends on this tradition. He, too, understands natural law as a natural and most basic form of *moral knowledge.* It is the preceptive knowledge or discernment of good and evil as it naturally, meaning spontaneously and necessarily, unfolds by the acts of human reason. For Aquinas, natural law is a set of normative and preceptive (i.e., practically compelling) judgments or propositions that are *naturally known.*[5]

This follows from Aquinas's general account of law, which "is a rule and measure of acts, whereby man is induced to act or is restrained from acting." Now "the rule and measure of human acts is the reason" so "*it follows that law*

---

1. "aeternae legis notio, quae impressa nobis est" (*De libero arbitrio* 1.6.5.1). See also the quote of St. Augustine's *De Trinitate* XIV.15, referred to in *In Search of a Universal Ethic,* note 31; and St. Ambrose, *De Paradiso* 8, 39.

2. Cf. the landmark studies by Brian Tierney, *The Idea of Natural Rights: Studies on Natural Rights, Natural Law, and Church Law 1150-1625* (Grand Rapids: Eerdmans, 1997), especially 58-69.

3. See Lottin, *Psychologie et morale aux XIIᵉ et XIIIᵉ siècles,* vol. 2, 75-77; Michael Wittmann, *Die Ethik des Hl. Thomas von Aquin* (Munich: Max Hueber Verlag, 1933), 329.

4. Lottin, *Psychologie,* 86-90.

5. See *ST* I-II, q. 58 a. 4; *Q. disp. de virtutibus* q. 1, a. 8.

is something pertaining to reason.[6] Aquinas applies this concept of law to the natural law. In a definition of natural law, he writes that

> the law of nature [*lex naturae*] is nothing other than the light of understanding infused in us by God, whereby we understand what must be done and what must be avoided. God gave this light and this law to man at creation.[7]

In the final sentence of his account of natural law presented in *ST* (I-II, q. 91, a. 2), Aquinas states that what is called the natural law "is nothing other than the participation of the eternal law in the rational creature." In the course of the article, he describes natural law as natural reason's capacity of discerning good from evil, a divine light that through creation has become part of human nature. For this, Aquinas quotes Psalm 4:6: "Many say, Who showeth us the good?" The Psalmist's answer is: "The light of thy countenance, O Lord, is signed upon us," and continues "thus implying that the light of natural reason, whereby we discern what is good and what is evil, which is the function of the natural law, is nothing else than an imprint on us of the Divine light."[8]

According to Aquinas, therefore, the natural law, like every law, is "something pertaining to reason,"[9] "something established by reason,"[10] and "a work of reason."[11] It is such a "work of reason" not only in the sense that it is the work of divine reason that created the rational creature, but also because it is itself a work and ordinance of created human reason. To be truly both *law* and *natural*, this law must be formulated or — as *Veritatis splendor* says (42) — promulgated by human reason. At the same time, in a metaphysical perspective that considers the first cause, it is equally and originally to be understood as an effect of divine wisdom, which, however, comes to bear through a created, natural, and secondary cause: human reason. Human reason's truth-attaining judgments participate in the divine wisdom, which is thus revealed in the created order of secondary causes.[12]

Yet to say that natural law is essentially the work of reason, and as such

6. *ST* I-II, q. 90, a. 1; emphasis added.

7. *In duo praecepta caritatis et in decem legis praecepta expositio,* Prologus. This text is referred to several times in the encyclical *Veritatis splendor,* most importantly in 40.

8. *ST* I-II, q. 91, a. 1. See also *Veritatis splendor,* 42.

9. *ST* I-II, q. 90, a. 1; q. 91, a. 2.

10. *ST* I-II, q. 94, a. 1.

11. *ST* I-II, q. 94, a. 1.

12. For a thorough treatment of this doctrine, see my *Natural Law and Practical Reason: A Thomist View of Moral Autonomy* (New York: Fordham University Press, 2000).

"something established by reason," is to speak of the natural law in the most *formal* way. It is not sufficient for explaining the *material contents* of natural law, and how the "constitution" of the natural law through reason takes place — two questions often confused by scholars who intend to emphasize the ontological foundation of natural law in human nature.[13]

Only the formal consideration of natural law provides the decisive outlook, helping us not to seek the natural law where no *law*, in the proper and most formal sense, can be found: in nature as such, in "natural inclinations," "natural teleology," or "natural ends." In other words, even though the material content of natural law — *what* it prescribes and directs to — is ontologically grounded and even in a sense predetermined by nature, and has much to do with the intrinsic teleology and ends of the natural inclinations, *the natural law itself* — formally considered — is not simply an ontological given, but a cognitive reality in the human soul. It is a set of practical judgments regarding doing good and avoiding evil. Failing to distinguish between *formal* and *material* consideration of the natural law causes enormous, ongoing confusion.

"Participated Theonomy": The Rational Creature's Possession of the Light of Divine Reason

Emphasizing that natural law is a "work of reason" is not smuggling into the teaching of Aquinas a modern conception of practical reason and natural law. The opposite is true: it corresponds to the Christian tradition of natural law thinking, starting with the fathers and culminating in Aquinas. The typically modern conception is to *deny* that any law is a work of reason. As *In Search of a Universal Ethic* rightly points out, the modern way is to understand law as a work not of reason, but of the will (30-33).

Conversely, natural law as conceived by Aquinas does not reproduce an order of nature, but rather an order of reason that is natural for man, coextensive with the order of the virtues. This order of reason and of the moral virtues is the true expression of what corresponds to human nature, indicating its proper perfection. As such a created and fully *natural* reality, the natural law is — as Aquinas says in *ST* I-II, q. 91, a. 2 — nothing other than "the partici-

13. One example of this confusion is found in Steven A. Long, "Natural Law or Autonomous Practical Reason: Problems for the New Natural Law Theory," in *St. Thomas Aquinas and the Natural Law Tradition: Contemporary Perspectives*, ed. John Goyette, Mark S. Latkovic, and Richard S. Myers (Washington, D.C.: Catholic University of America Press, 2004), 165-93.

pation of the eternal law in the rational creature." It is, thus, "participated theonomy."[14] Notice that for the rational creature to really *participate* in a law — here, the eternal law of God — does not simply mean "to be subject to this law," or "to learn the law and apply it to concrete acts," but rather to *formally possess* and even *to be* the law: to possess the very reason that properly is the law because it *formulates* the law, promulgates it, and imposes it through reason's own obliging force.

This is what Aquinas explains in his *Summa theologiae,* mainly in the two key articles I-II, q. 91, a. 2 and q. 94, a. 2. The first of them contains the proper definition of what natural law essentially is: *"the light of natural reason, whereby we discern what is good and what is evil."* This, Aquinas says, *"is the function of the natural law,"* and it is "nothing else than an imprint on us of the Divine light."[15]

This is why the natural law is truly the eternal law, *not as it is in God's mind, but as it is in the rational creature.* For the rational creature, natural law as a participation in the eternal law means to possess the light of reason that actively orders one's acts to the good and is, thus, a true participation in God's providence. Natural law is part of the cognitive equipment of the human person as a moral subject. "Natural law" is not simply an object of the human intellect "to be known," but is itself the "work" of this created intellect: it is properly and formally *law,* and as such a "work of reason." The very essence of natural law, and the focal meaning of the term "natural law," is to be found in its most formal definition as "the light of natural reason, whereby we discern what is good and what is evil."

The Origin of Natural Law in Practical Reason: Understanding Practical Reason as Moral Reason

In Search of a Universal Ethic does not give a one-sidedly "naturalistic" or "ontologistic" understanding of natural law, but fully recognizes the *cognitive* character of natural law as the most basic element of moral knowledge. *In Search of a Universal Ethic* provides us with a balanced exposition of the main features of the Thomistic doctrine in which the cognitive-epistemological (for-

14. *Veritatis splendor,* 41.

15. This has been taught by Pope Leo XIII in his encyclical *Libertas praestantissimum,* referred to also in the encyclical *Veritatis splendor,* 55. The same doctrine can be found in many classical manuals of moral theology, mainly of the Dominican School and faithful to Aquinas, as, for example, B. H. Merkelbach, *Summa Theologiae moralis ad mentem D. Thomae et ad normam iuris novi,* I (Paris: Desclee 1931, 1938), 227.

mal) aspects of natural law, its (material) ontological grounding, and its posterior (metaphysical) interpretation are harmoniously integrated.

Most important, *In Search of a Universal Ethic* situates the origin of the natural law in man's *cognitive interiority*, in his genuine moral experience, based in "an interior call to do good" that has its root in practical reason (39). This is because

> he discovers that he is fundamentally a moral being, capable of perceiving and of expressing the call that, as we have seen, is found within all cultures: "One must do good and avoid evil." All the other precepts of the natural law are based on this precept. *This first precept is known naturally, immediately, by the practical reason,* just as the principle of non-contradiction (the intellect cannot at the same time and under the same aspect both affirm and deny the same thing about something) which is at the base of all speculative reasoning, is grasped intuitively, naturally, by the theoretical reason, when the subject comprehends the sense of the terms employed. (39; emphasis added)

This is Aquinas's teaching in *ST* I-II, q. 94, a. 2. *In Search of a Universal Ethic* continues to claim that by this knowledge through practical reason of the "first principle of the moral life," which is the first precept of natural law, "we find ourselves immediately in the sphere of morality" (40). This is the reason why the doctrine, mentioned in the above quotation, of the parallelism of theoretical and practical reason is of such crucial importance: the first notions of morality and the constitution of the acting subject as a *moral* subject are not derived from theoretical knowledge, but spring *naturally* and *immediately* from basic insights of practical reason.

This is possible because practical reason is reason embedded in the natural inclinations; it is in these inclinations that the source of its activity is to be found. The first notions of the good as *moral* and thus *practical* values are not derived from any previous knowledge or principle. These natural acts of practical understanding are directed to grasping aspects of reality — mainly the reality that we are constantly striving after some good, and the goods *as the goals of this striving*. Thomistic practical reason is not Kantian practical reason, which is essentially *constructivist* and turns out to be nothing other than a will independent from all "empirical" constraints.

Why is it so important to emphasize the origin of natural law in practical reason? It is important because only by understanding the origin of the process of practical reason can we also understand why practical reason is essentially *moral* reason, genuinely directed to the good. Moral reason is reason prescribing the good, forbidding evil, and generating the moral "ought" or moral obligation. Thus, being essentially moral reason, practical reason constitutes the subject as both an *acting* and a *moral* subject.

Practical knowledge, thus, is not something *added* to natural law or *referring* to it. Rather, natural law is itself an exercise of the practical reason and a result of this exercise: the practical principles or precepts regarding the good to be done and the evil to be avoided. As *In Search of a Universal Ethic* points out, "*The spontaneous grasp of fundamental ethical values,* which are expressed in the precepts of the natural law, *constitutes the point of departure* of the process that then leads the moral subject to the judgment of conscience, in which he formulates the moral requirements that impose themselves on him in his concrete situation" (60; emphasis added).

This is perhaps the main reason why natural law in fact is not only a, but *the* only possible basis of a "universal ethics": because it is not a philosophical *doctrine* or an *interpretation* of nature, but an *intrinsic anthropological reality,* belonging to human nature, a cognitive reality inserted in the human soul that unfolds through the first and spontaneous judgments of practical reason itself.

The Ontological Basis of the Precepts of Natural Law: The Natural Inclinations

I understand the concerns of those who emphasize that natural law must be understood as an order of good that has an ontological foundation. Yet disregarding the differentiation between the formal and the material aspects of natural law easily leads one to confusion. In order to safeguard the objective ontological basis of natural law and to prevent subjectivism, those who share this concern promote the idea that natural law is something previous to the exercise of practical reason, and therefore different from it. So, Steven Long says that "natural law is not merely the *product* of practical reason but the *precondition* of its right exercise."[16] This is true for the relation between natural law and *deliberate* reason, which deals with concrete actions to be performed here and now; natural law provides the *principles* for deliberate practical reason and is therefore a precondition of its right exercise.[17]

16. See Steven Long, "Reproductive Technologies and the Natural Law," *National Catholic Bioethics Quarterly* (Summer 2002): 221-28, at 221.

17. See for this my *The Perspective of Morality: Philosophical Foundations of Thomistic Virtue Ethics* (Washington, D.C.: Catholic University of America Press, 2011), part 5.

This "alternative view," however, fails to understand what natural law formally is as an anthropological and cognitive reality. Formally speaking, natural law is not a set of natural ends or teleological patterns, but the naturally formulated precepts of human practical reason, and thus the principles for any subsequent exercise of practical reason. Hence, to say that natural law is *generally* a precondition of the right exercise of practical reason is to misunderstand what natural law essentially is: the *natural* exercise of practical reason, and therefore not "subjectivist" but objective and truth-attaining *knowledge of the good.*

Practical reason unfolds its knowledge of the goods in and through the natural inclinations. An account of natural law as a "work of reason" does not forget what Steven Long — adopting terminology I originally used in my *Natural Law and Practical Reason*[18] — calls the "passive participation of the eternal law." The natural inclinations are an expression of this *passive* participation (see *ST* I-II, q. 91, a. 2). This participation, however, does not constitute what is properly called a "law"; it is called "law" only analogically.[19]

If we speak about natural law *formally* — assigning its essence — we have to say that it is "something pertaining to reason." Thus "the sense that 'natural' has in 'natural law' always includes reason. The inclinations St. Thomas lists in *IaIIae.94.2* are only the basis of precepts of natural law and not in themselves precepts."[20] But reason *alone* is not able to form what we call the natural law. For this, reason must focus on the goods that are the goals of the natural inclinations.

The Metaphysical Unity of Reason and Nature

A complete account of natural law is a piece of metaphysics, and of metaphysically grounded anthropology, which fully includes the "highest part" of the human soul: its rationality. It does not exclude from "nature" the spiritual part of the human person, but sees the human person as a body whose principle of life or substantial form is a *spiritual* soul and which, therefore, is a substantial unity of body and spirit. Here "nature" is neither the body nor the soul

18. Chapter 2, 66-68; chapter 5, 246.

19. *ST* I-II, q. 91, a. 2.

20. Ralph McInerny, "On Knowing Natural Law," in *The Ethics of St. Thomas Aquinas,* ed. Leo J. Elders and Klaus Hedwig (Vatican City: Libreria Editrice Vaticana, 1984), 133-60, at 140. See also Russell Hittinger, *The First Grace: Rediscovering the Natural Law in a Post-Christian World* (Wilmington, Del.: ISI Books, 2003), 97.

alone, but the compound of both, the *animal rationale*. The body only reveals its truth through the spirit, while the spirit cannot attain truth by disregarding the body.

The metaphysical structure of Aquinas's doctrine of natural law as a participation of the eternal law in the rational creature — as "participated theonomy" — thus adequately presupposes and reflects what *In Search of a Universal Ethic* calls "the idea that nature is for man the bearer of an ethical message and is an implicit moral norm that human reason actualizes" (69). This "implies therefore the reasoned conviction that there exists a harmony among the three realities: God, man, and nature. In this perspective, the world is perceived as an intelligible whole, unified by the common reference of the beings that compose it to a divine originating principle, to a *Logos*" (69). *In Search of a Universal Ethic* emphasizes, however, that not every creature participates in this *Logos* in the *same manner*.

> Man, since he is defined by reason or *logos,* participates in it in an eminent manner. In fact, by his reason, he is capable of freely interiorizing the divine intentions manifested in the nature of things. *He formulates them for himself under the form of a moral law* that inspires and orients his action. In this perspective, man is not "the other" in relation to nature. On the contrary, he maintains with the cosmos a bond of familiarity founded on a common participation in the divine *Logos*. (70; emphasis added)

This is why "reason" must never be excluded from or opposed to "nature." By saying that man is not "the other" in relation to nature, the human person is not reduced to (irrational) nature, but the spiritual or rational part of his being is included in the natural. "The natural" is not, for man, equal to "the pre-rational." This is the whole point of Aquinas's doctrine on natural law (and a real antithesis to the Kantian bifurcation between nature and reason, nature and freedom).[21]

Therefore, *In Search of a Universal Ethic* provides us an authentic Thomistic way to understand this doctrine. Key for this understanding is that, although natural law is a "work of reason," this is a reason embedded in the natural inclinations of an essentially bodily-spiritual being, the human person.[22] "Person is not opposed to nature" (68): there is no human freedom and no exercise of human reason that is not the freedom and reason of a bodily

---

21. See about this Thomas Hibbs, "A Rhetoric of Motives: Thomas on Obligation as Rational Persuasion," *The Thomist* 54 (1990): 293-309.

22. See my *Natural Law and Practical Reason*, 95-103.

constituted being. In the term "human nature," nature connotes both the body and the spirit, which is its substantial form. Therefore, it would be wrong to reduce, as some interpreters of Aquinas inspired by Kant have tried to do, the natural law to the command of "acting in a rational manner, that is, to applying to the totality of behaviors a univocal ideal of rationality generated by practical reason alone" (79 n. 75). This would be tantamount to "wrongly identifying the rationality of the natural law with the rationality of human reason alone" (79 n. 75).

As I have stressed elsewhere against such "Kantian" interpretations,[23] it is impossible to understand the unfolding of practical reason as "natural law" independently from the dynamics of the natural inclinations that partly spring from the pre-rational level of human nature. There can be no actualization of reason — no knowledge — without an intelligible object. Thus, *In Search of a Universal Ethic* states the *complete* picture without falling into one-sidedness: "The doctrine of the natural moral law must, therefore, maintain at the same time both *the central role of reason* in the actualization of a properly human plan of life, and the consistency and the *proper meaning of pre-rational natural dynamisms*" (79; emphasis added).[24] On the other side, however, *In Search of a Universal Ethic,* as quoted above, states that it is *man* who formulates "the divine intentions manifested in the nature of things . . . under the form of a moral law" (70). The natural moral law is, thus, constituted *as law* by human reason; it is truly a "work of reason." Nothing pre-rational or non-rational can be properly called a "law" and impose moral obligation. This belongs to reason alone, prescribing to do good and to avoid evil.

23. See chapter 5 of my *The Perspective of the Acting Person: Essays in the Renewal of Thomistic Moral Philosophy,* ed. William F. Murphy Jr. (Washington, D.C.: Catholic University of America Press, 2008).

24. Which come to bear especially, as is noted in the following (80), on the traditional doctrine of "sins against nature." See for this also my extensive treatment in *Natural Law and Practical Reason,* 94-109, and *The Perspective of the Acting Person,* chapter 6.

Part of the "New Look" at the Natural Law: The Use of "Orientation" alongside "Inclination"

William C. Mattison III

Natural law discussions have traditionally attended to what are commonly called "natural inclinations." Inclinations are stable characteristics that identify some being, such as a human person.[1] As suggested in the scholastic dictum *agere sequitur esse* ("action follows being"), what an entity is, and how that entity does or should act, are closely related.

There are actually different types of questions in play when examining natural inclinations. One set concerns precisely identifying the natural inclinations so as to better specify natural law norms, or how one acts in accordance with that nature. For instance, if there is a natural sexual inclination in human persons, is it toward monogamous marriage as "natural"? Is homosexuality "natural"? Is celibacy "natural"? If there is a natural human inclination to live in society, or be communal, is the life of a religious hermit "natural"? What forms of government are and are not "natural"? This first set of questions entails identifying what natural inclinations the human person possesses, and what acts are in accord with those inclinations. This first set of questions is not the focus of this essay.

A second set of questions is how natural inclinations function in a person living in accordance with the natural law. In particular, this set of questions concerns what role inclinations play in practical reasoning, especially since

---

1. Though this term could be used more broadly, what is generally assumed here is that we are discussing natural *human* inclinations.

Thanks to Joseph Capizzi, David Cloutier, John Berkman, and Siobhan Riley Benitez for their helpful suggestions on an earlier version of this essay.

such reasoning is itself an expression of a natural human inclination. Are natural inclinations a "given" or set of "givens" discovered by the person, with which the person can then choose to live in conformity? Or are the natural inclinations that very process or activity of human practical reasoning? As one contemporary theologian asks:

> Is natural law *discerned* by human reason as a normative order inscribed in nature? Or is natural law *constituted* by the judgments of practical reason, which transform and elevate (humanize) inclinations found in nature by reorienting these inclinations to the personal ends known by spiritual creatures?[2]

On the one hand, proponents of natural law as something *discerned* "out there" are rightly concerned lest any human reasoning process be considered natural. They are right to insist that practical reasoning should conform to the natural law.[3] On the other hand, proponents of natural law as something *constituted* by the judgments of reason rightly note that practical reasoning is not a human capacity whereby we consult the natural law out there and then choose to act, but rather practical reasoning is itself an expression of natural human inclinations. The capacity to grasp and act in accordance with the true and the good (which simply is practical reasoning) is itself a natural inclination, and doing this human activity well *is* the natural law.[4]

Though the ITC document addresses both of these sets of questions, the purpose of this essay is to examine how it addresses the second set. It is clear that the "new look at natural law" referenced in the document's title is particularly concerned to reject a view of natural law as a "static given," something that can be readily apprehended by observations of (particularly biological) nature and then implemented or not (113; cf. 64). In that sense, the document seems to side more with those who affirm that natural law is constituted by practical reasoning rather than those who affirm natural law is discerned by human reason. But this is actually too quick a conclusion. The argument here is that the ITC document affirms natural law as *both* constituted by and discerned by human reason. Natural law is an activity of human practical reason-

---

2. Matthew Levering, "Natural Law and Natural Inclinations: Rhonheimer, Pinckaers, and McAleer," *The Thomist* 70 (2006): 155-201, at 156.

3. For an example of this approach to natural law in this volume, see the essay by Steven A. Long.

4. For an example of this approach to natural law in this volume, see the essay by Martin Rhonheimer.

ing rather than something simply prior to that reasoning; but this practical reasoning must also proceed in conformity with inclinations that are in some sense prior to practical reasoning in order to be truly "natural." Achieving this balance is obviously no small task. Assessing the success of the document in doing so is not the primary task here. The task of this essay is identifying *how* the document affirms the natural law as something both discerned by and constituted by human practical reasoning.

To achieve this task, this essay tracks the use of several terms in the document which all roughly mean "inclination," including the term "inclination" itself. The term "inclination" is a mainstay in traditional discussions of natural law. But as referenced above and in the document, a conception of natural law has arisen over the past few centuries (albeit with late medieval roots), commonly called "physicalism," in which natural inclinations supply the "given" for the natural law in what most now view as a problematic manner. Since the term "inclination" is associated with this problematic view of natural law, the document's authors seem to have two choices. They could repudiate the term "inclination" as no longer useful, or contribute to its rehabilitation by "stretching" it back to its original meaning as something not only given, but also dynamic and pointing toward some goal that includes human activity. This essay argues that the ITC document adopts the latter route. And it does so by implementing the term "inclination" alongside other terms that are not only bereft of problematic connotations, but also connote a more active and teleological role for the inclinations. The most obvious such term is "orientation,"[5] though the terms "dynamism" and "tendency" are also employed. These terms are used to indicate not only what is given in practical reasoning, but also how the activity of practical reasoning, toward the goal of human flourishing, constitutes the natural law. It is argued here that the use of "orientation" (and the other terms) does not replace the use of "inclination" but complements it, perhaps ultimately in order to rehabilitate that traditional term to its fuller meaning.

The Term "Inclination" in the Document

How is the term "inclination" used in this document?[6] It will first help to observe where, or in what context, the term is most commonly used in the

5. Despite the common usage of "orientation" today to refer to sexual orientation, this term has a far broader meaning in the document, as explained below.

6. The term "inclination" is used thirty-one times in the English version of the docu-

document. Two such contexts stand out. In both, the term "inclination" is used primarily to refer to those "givens" discerned by practical reasoning.

First, more than half of the term's appearances in the document are found in the span of several paragraphs (45-52), in chapter 2's examination of the precepts of the natural law. The concentrated usage of the term "inclination" there is unsurprising given the virtual necessity in Catholic discussions of natural law to treat St. Thomas Aquinas's classic *ST* I-II, q. 94, a. 2 text, where he discusses, among other things, natural inclinations. The document, citing this very text, states that

> one traditionally distinguishes three great sets of natural dynamisms that are at work in the human person. The first, which is in common with all substances, comprises essentially the inclination to preserve and to develop one's own existence. The second, which is in common with all living things, comprises the inclination to reproduce, in order to perpetuate the species. The third, which is proper to the human person as a rational being, comprises the inclination to know the truth about God and to live in society. From these inclinations, the first precepts of the natural law, known naturally, can be formulated. (46)

Each of three ensuing paragraphs (48-50) further describes one of these inclinations and suggests some basic moral norms that are distilled from each inclination. Two immediate observations about the term "inclination" are suggested by the above extended quotation. First, "inclination" is used synonymously with the term "dynamism." The term "dynamism" functions synonymously with "inclination" in this document for reasons mentioned below.[7] Second, and most important, natural inclinations are presented here as the source of the first precepts of natural law that are known naturally. In these paragraphs the inclinations supply the "givens" for practical reasoning. As the document itself claims in its summary of these paragraphs:

---

ment. "Inclination" is used thirty-two times in the original French (see n. 13 below on the discrepancy). The English citations are: 29, 45, 46 (4x), 48 (4x), 49 (4x), 50 (3x), 52, 63, 71, 74, 80, 86, 87, 115 n. 48.

7. The term "dynamism" appears sixteen times in the English version of this document: 42, 43, 46, 49, 63 (3x), 69, 77 (3x), 79 (2x), 80 (2x), and n. 75 (to paragraph 79). Given its synonymous use with "inclination," there is much overlap in where the two terms appear. It is also noteworthy that, as evident in the above quotation, each of the three levels of inclination is referred to at times as a "set" of inclinations, and at times as a singular inclination. Similar variation is evident in the use of "dynamism" as both plural (42) and singular (43). No explanation of this variation is offered in the document or here.

> After this brief exposition of the moral principles that derive from reason's consideration of the fundamental inclinations of the human person, we find a set of precepts and values that, at least in their general formulation, can be considered as universal since they apply to all humanity. (52; also 48)

Passages like this one reveal that the term "inclination" refers to something discerned by practical reasoning.[8]

The second context where the term "inclination" is particularly prominent in the document is paragraph 79, which explicitly addresses physicalism and attempts to differentiate this degraded similitude to natural law from an accurate vision of natural law. Most relevant for this essay, "inclination" appears five times. In four of those five usages it is employed to identify the inadequate way of appealing to natural inclinations. The document decries those who view the human person as a collection of various "diverse and autonomous natural inclinations":

> Neglecting to consider the unity of the human person, they absolutize the natural inclinations of the different "parts" of human nature, juxtaposing these inclinations without placing them in a hierarchy and omitting to integrate them into the unity of the overall, personal plan of the subject.[9]

By failing to regard the human subject as "a substantial and personal whole," "some modern presentations of the natural law" marred by physicalism fail to heed Pope John Paul II's claim that "natural inclinations take on moral relevance only insofar as they refer to the human person and to his authentic fulfillment."[10] As evident in this quotation, the term "inclination" can be used to describe a more accurate view of natural inclinations than that found in

---

8. See also paragraph 74, where the document decries "radical anthropological dualism . . . manifested in the refusal to recognize any human and ethical meaning in the natural inclinations that precede the choices of the individual reason."

9. Those familiar with recent Catholic debates in natural law may read this quotation as a rejection of incommensurability theorists, that is, those who derive natural law precepts from inclinations and who insist those inclinations cannot be hierarchically integrated. There is some irony in this critique appearing in a paragraph primarily devoted to rejecting physicalism since those theorists similarly attempt to avoid the raw reading of natural law norms off physical (especially biological) processes. But the location of this critique suggests that the natural law of the physicalists (an extreme version of those who view natural law as discerned by practical reason) and the natural law of the incommensurability theorists (an extreme version of those who view natural law as constituted by practical reason) are opposing errors that nonetheless share something in common.

10. See *Veritatis splendor,* 50.

physicalism. But it is noteworthy that four of five uses of "inclination" in paragraph 79 are to a physicalist version of natural law. If paragraph 79 contains a description of an inadequate view of natural law followed by a more adequate one, it is evident that the term "inclination" features far more prominently in the former than the latter, where instead the terms "orientation" and "tendencies" are preferred.[11]

In sum, in the two contexts where the term "inclination" features most prominently in the document, the term is used to identify what is supplied to and discerned by practical reasoning. The document never repudiates the importance to natural law of inclinations understood as such. Yet even when it emphasizes that the natural law is not only discerned by practical reasoning but also constituted by practical reasoning, the term "inclination" is used in reference to what practical reasoning "interprets."[12]

The Terms "Orientation" and "Orient" in the Document

What is the sense of the term "orientation" in this document?[13] The document uses the term on occasions where it is attending to the relationship between characteristics of the human person and actions that are "inspired" by those characteristics.[14] These are normally the occasions in Catholic natural law

11. The term "tendency" (or "tendencies") appears eleven times in the English version of the document, with five of those usages occurring in a nontechnical manner (5, 10, 33, 81, n. 72) and the remaining six being synonymous with inclination (49, 50, 51, 77, 79[2x]), evident (as with "dynamism") in the locations of the term being similar to those of "inclination." In every case the English "tendency" is used for the original French *tendance*, with the exception of the second usage of "tendency" in paragraph 79, which is used for the French *inclination*. This latter observation means there is a discrepancy between the original French and officially translated English versions of the document. Though the argument made here about the shift in paragraph 79 from using "inclination" to using "orientation"/"tendency" is striking in the English version, it is less evident (though still present) in the French version since the French *inclination* is once translated into English as "tendencies" toward the end of paragraph 79.

12. See the crucial paragraph 63, discussed below, for this term.

13. The term "orientation" (including the verb form "orient") appears twenty-four times in the document. See paragraphs 8, 9 (2x), 16, 26 (2x), 29, 38, 43, 51, 60, 63, 64, 68 (2x), 69 (2x), 70, 77, 79, 82, 112 (3x). Six of these are nontechnical and/or unimportant uses of the term (16, 29, 38, 51, 82, and the third usage in 112).

14. For the description of natural law as a principle of "inspiration," an interesting phrase whose closer examination is beyond the scope of this essay, see paragraphs 59 and 113. In the original French this phrase appears four times (11, 27, 59, 113). In English two of the four are translated "guidance."

thought where the term "inclination" is employed. And indeed, at times "orientation" is used in a manner that could simply be a style-driven alternative to "inclination," in that "orientation" refers what is given to and discerned by human practical reasoning.[15]

However, in other instances the term "orientation" also has what I call here a more "active" connotation in the document than that of "inclination," in that it is presented as actively moving the person toward fulfillment or flourishing.[16] For instance, the term appears in verbal form at the document's discussion of the basic concepts of "nature" and "essence":

> This essence takes the name of nature above all when it is envisaged as the internal principle of movement that orients the subject towards its fulfillment. Far from referring to a static given, the notion of nature signifies the real dynamic principle of the homogeneous development of the subject and of its specific activities. (64; see also 68)

The word "orient" has an active and teleological sense here, influencing a person and moving the person toward fulfillment. It is "far from" a "static given." In this quotation "orient" is the verb and the person is the object. The only stated subject of the verb is the "internal principle of movement" itself. In other passages the verb "orient" is used with "person" as the object of the verb, but God is the subject of the verb.

> By the dynamisms that the creator Word has inscribed in the innermost part of beings, he orients them to their full realization. This dynamic orientation is none other than the divine government that realizes within time the plan of divine providence, i.e., the eternal law. (69; cf. 26)

Here again we have "orientations" (used synonymously with "dynamisms") actively moving the person toward fulfillment, with God explicitly at the helm. Thus the term "orientation" (and "orient") has an active and teleological context, with a ready openness to naming God as the agent of the activity.

Yet whereas in the above quotations the "dynamic orientation" is happening *to* a person, even more noteworthy is the document's use of the terms "orientation" and "orient" to describe the person' own activity. In other words, at times the person is the subject of the verb, either actively choosing (or not) in accordance with the given dynamisms, or at times actually orienting the

---

15. See also paragraphs 9, 26, and 68.
16. This is partly, but not wholly, due to the possibility of using the verbal form "orient."

given dynamisms toward one's fulfillment. This usage, while not repudiating that orientations are something "given," also emphasizes that orienting is something that persons do. This latter usage suggests the natural law understood as constituted by practical reasoning.

For instance, the document speaks of how "the human person, in the free choices by which he responds in the concrete of his 'here and now' to his unique and transcendent vocation, assumes the orientations given by his nature" (68). Indeed, these orientations are in an important sense a source of (not obstacle to) human freedom, as when the document states: "human nature is defined by an entire ensemble of dynamisms, tendencies and internal orientations within which freedom arises" (77).[17] In perhaps the most active usage of this term, at times in the document it is the person who is the subject of the verb "orient," and the dynamisms themselves that are the object: "In fact they [i.e., spiritual creatures such as human beings] interiorize the dynamisms that define them and freely orient them towards their own complete realization" (63).[18] In what might be understood as a foreshadowing of paragraph 79's rejection of physicalism, the document's introduction states:

> It is true that the expression of the "natural law" is the source of numerous misunderstandings in the present context. Sometimes it only evokes the resigned and totally passive resignation to the physical laws of nature, whereas man seeks rather — and properly so — to master and direct [French *orienter*] these elements [French *determinisms*] for his benefit. (10)[19]

In these latter uses, the term "orient" signals both the presence of "given" (at times explicitly God-given) dynamisms directing the person toward fulfillment, and the person's active self-direction toward fulfillment in freedom, indeed a freedom only existent because of these orientations toward fulfillment. There is a balance between the "givenness" of orientations that are discovered by human reason, and a person's active orienting of given dynamisms

17. Here we have an explicit equation of the terms "orientation," "dynamism," and "tendency."

18. See also paragraph 70: "In fact, by his reason, he is capable of freely interiorizing the divine intentions manifested in the nature of things. He formulates them for himself under the form of a moral law that inspires and orients his own action."

19. This is the only place in the document where the French term *orientation* or *orienter* is not translated into English as "orientation" or "orient," but rather as "direct." Furthermore, this is the only use of the odd term "determinism" (from the French cognate *determinisme*) in the document, and it appears synonymous with "dynamism."

toward fulfillment. Both of these senses are evident in the document's introduction:

> This [natural] law, in substance, affirms that persons and human communities are capable, in the light of reason, of discerning the fundamental orientations of a moral action in conformity with the very nature of the human subject and of expressing these orientations in normative fashion in the form of precepts or commandments. (9)

In sum, the term "orientation" (and "orient") is employed in a variety of ways in this document. At times it is used as a stylistic alternative to "inclination." At other times it has a more active sense than the document's use of "inclination." Sometimes that active sense is due to context, as when the orientation (like an inclination) is regarded as a "given" but one that is actively engaged by a person, as in the document's description of how a person can "assume the orientations given by his nature" in freedom (68). Sometimes the active sense is provided by the document describing how people "orient [their given natural dynamisms] towards their own complete realization" (63), or express "these orientations in a normative fashion in the form of precepts or commandments" (9).

Conclusions on the Document's Usage of These Terms

What does this survey of the ITC document's uses of the terms "inclination" and "orientation" reveal about how the document presents the role of natural inclinations in a person living according to the natural law? A careful look at where and how both terms are employed reveals that whereas "orientation" is at times synonymous with "inclination," there are also occasions where the term "orientation" is used in a manner in which the document rarely uses "inclination." The conclusion offered here is that though the document in no way repudiates the term "inclination," it at least implicitly recognizes a common, overly circumscribed meaning of that term as referring solely to what is given to or discerned by practical reasoning, and therefore employs the term "orientation" (as well as "dynamism" and "tendency") to avoid limiting the function of orientations to that "passive" (10) role.

This conclusion is evident in that the term "inclination" is used predominantly to refer to what is given, that is, the natural law as something discerned in practical reasoning. At times the term is used to refer to a rejected version of natural law, mainly physicalism, where "absolutized" and "juxtaposed" natural inclinations fail to be "integrated into the unity of the overall, personal plan of the subject," clearly a task of prudential reasoning (79). At other times the document uses "inclination" positively to refer to what is "given" and discerned by practical reasoning, affirming such a role for the inclinations as long as they are not "absolutized" as in physicalism. In sum, "inclinations" is clearly associated with natural law as "discerned by" practical reasoning. Though there are inadequate versions of natural law that employ "inclinations" in this way, the document does not repudiate some such important role for the inclinations in natural law.

This is also evident in that the document uses the term "orientation" (as well as "dynamism" and "tendency") in a manner that includes, but is broader than, the way it uses "inclination." The overlap is important. The usage of "orientation" is not meant to be an alternative to replace "inclination," but a way to include the connotation of "inclination" while also expanding it beyond that meaning.

How is the use of "orientation" "broader"? First, as noted above it has a more active meaning at times. This point was made in more detail above, but it might be summarized again with a quotation from the document:

> Creatures are animated by a dynamism that carries them to fulfill themselves, each in its own way, in the union with God. . . . [Spiritual creatures] interiorize the dynamisms that define them and freely orient them towards their own complete realization. They formulate them to themselves, as fundamental norms of their moral action — this is the natural law properly stated — and they strive to realize them freely. The natural law is therefore defined as a participation in the eternal law. (63)[20]

Here the "orienting" is not just given, but also an active process of the person. It is natural law as "constituted by" practical reasoning. Second, the term "orientation" is used in the document in a more obviously teleological sense, suggesting movement toward a person's fulfillment. There is of course no reason that the term "inclination" could not be used in this broader teleological manner. The very word suggests an inclination *toward* something just as "orientation" (or "dynamism" or "tendency") suggests a *telos* toward which it is pointed. Yet the

---

20. See also paragraph 70: "Man, since he is defined by reason or *logos*, participates in it in an eminent manner. In fact, by his reason, he is capable of freely interiorizing the divine intentions manifested in the nature of things. He formulates them for himself under the form of a moral law that inspires and orients his own action. In this perspective, man is not 'the other' in relation to nature."

term "inclination" is not used, as the term "orientation" is, with reference to the broader goal of the whole person's "benefit" (10), "fulfillment" (64), "full realization" (43, 69), "complete realization" (63), "full development of his humanity" (112), or even "last end" (79).[21] The document employs the term "orientation" to explain the natural, teleological activity of the person toward fulfillment.

Having identified the "broader" sense in which "orientation" is used, it is important to emphasize once more that the document affirms the role of the inclinations in natural law understood *both* as discerned by and constituted by practical reasoning. To continue the quotation from the previous paragraph, the document cites both the classic Thomistic and *Veritatis splendor* descriptions of natural law (respectively):

> The natural law is therefore defined as a participation in the eternal law (n. 63). It is mediated, on the one hand, by the inclinations of nature, expressions of the creative wisdom, and, on the other hand, by the light of human reason which interprets them and is itself a created participation in the light of the divine intelligence. Ethics is thus presented as a "participated theonomy" (n. 64). (63)[22]

In sum, the conclusion of this essay is that the document's use of "inclination" and "orientation" is a helpful lens into its treatment of the issue of how the natural inclinations function in human practical reasoning. The document affirms that the natural law is both discerned by and constituted by human practical reasoning, and its use of these two terms reveals this dual affirmation. The document's use of "orientation" (as well as "tendency" and "dynamism") in a manner that includes yet is broader than its use of "inclination" is best viewed as an attempt to ultimately rehabilitate the term "inclination" beyond an overly circumscribed meaning. It is an attempt to present the natural law not only as something "out there" to be discerned, but also as something active and teleological, constituted by human practical reasoning.

21. There is one exception, namely, the Pope John Paul II quotation in paragraph 79 offering a rehabilitated sense of inclination as distinct from the inadequate physicalist usage of that term: "John Paul II explains, 'natural inclinations take on moral relevance only insofar as they refer to the human person and to his authentic fulfillment.'"

22. See also paragraph 79: "The doctrine of the natural moral law must, therefore, maintain at the same time both the central role of reason in the actualization of a properly human plan of life, and the consistency and the proper meaning of pre-rational natural dynamisms." It should be noted, however, that inclinations understood as "given" or discerned by practical reasoning need not be solely "pre-rational, as indicated by the document's affirmation of St. Thomas's third level of inclinations, those distinctive to the rational human person (50).

Pragmatic and Christological Foundations of Natural Law

Livio Melina

"I am afraid we are not getting rid of God because we still believe in grammar."[1] So it was that Friedrich Nietzsche sanctioned and radicalized the separation between the dynamics of a freedom that is conceived of as an absolute arbitrary power and the possibility of a rule of language founded on the reality of things and so on their givenness prior to thought itself. The question with which we should concern ourselves here deals precisely with the existence of such a grammar of action and its possible theological foundation. The assertion of the German philosopher provokes us because it affirms the intimate connection between the two questions and because it sees in the negation of every rule of language the outcome, and perhaps also the practical condition, of a completed atheism, understood as the guarantee of human liberty.

Inspired by the International Theological Commission's (ITC) document *In Search of a Universal Ethic: A New Look at Natural Law,* this essay begins by positing an analogy between action and language, and intends to study the possibility of a grammar of action that guarantees the truth of the communication among persons. We will look at the experience of the body, in which action is rooted, and the experience of interpersonal relations in the network of which action is inserted, proposing a "pragmatics" of love, which avoids the extrinsicism of both naturalism and rationalism. In this way we will arrive at a renewed interpretation of the natural law, according to which the fundamen-

---

1. F. Nietzsche, *Götzendämmerung,* in Werke: *Kritische Gesamtausgabe,* ed. G. Colli and M. Montanari, vol. VI/3 (Berlin: De Gruyter, 1969), 72. English translation: F. Nietzsche, *Twilight of Idols,* trans. Duncan Large (Oxford: Oxford University Press, 1998), 19.

tal human goods, which give orientation to the spontaneous inclinations of human nature, acquire an original moral meaning — the dynamic and personalistic horizon of love. In the third part of this essay we will take a theological perspective. The theology of creation can grasp in the theology of the image of God in humankind the foundation of a participation in the wisdom of the Creator. In the "pragmatics" of Jesus the vocation to love shines forth. From the very beginning the natural law is oriented toward this vocation.

The Grammar of Action, Starting from Its Pragmatics

Nietzsche holds that the time is mature for liberating oneself from even that last of theological residues that is represented by the idea of a universal rule of reason based on immutable meanings inscribed in human nature. But we must ask ourselves whether it is possible to live and think without grammar. Or, even when we pretend to deny grammar, can we prescind from its rules in the very same discourse that we are formulating, at least if we wish that it have some meaning that is communicable to others? And also, is it possible that such rules are merely conventional and formal, or must they in some way be based on being?[2]

The analogy between action and language, intimated from the introduction of the theme of grammar, asks to be adequately formed, be it in its elements of equivalence or in the difference that it carries.[3] This parallel, introduced by Ludwig Wittgenstein, has the advantage of highlighting how action is always a mediator of meaning and cannot be thematized separately from language. His understanding falls, therefore, in the context of interpersonal relationships: with respect to an intentional content that the agent expresses and in reference to the possibility of communication that this allows.[4] The natural law, from this point of view, could perhaps be defined — as a first approximation — as the set of the most basic grammatical rules that guarantee the possibility of a universal communication between human subjects who interact with one another.

2. This is J. Habermas's statement of the problem, *Erläuterungen zur Diskursethik* (Suhrkamp: Frankfurt am Main, 1991).

3. A good review of the philosophical reflections on this issue is offered by R. Bubner, *Handlung, Sprache und Vernunft: Grundbegriffe praktischer Philosophie. Neuausgabe mit einem Anhang* (Suhrkamp: Frankfurt am Main, 1982). Concerning the analogy between words and action and their difference, see *La sémantique de l'action. Ière partie: Le discours de l'action* (Paris: Éditions du Centre National de la Recherche Scientifique, 1977), 101-21.

4. Cf. G. E. M. Anscombe, *Intention* (Oxford: Basil Blackwell, 1957).

On the other hand, action implies a dimension that exceeds mere linguistic communication. In the first place, it refers, as Maurice Blondel well understood, to a meaning that always surpasses the intentions that are thematically willed by the subject and that become accessible in their transcendence only through the effective passage into action. Consciousness does not dominate action in advance, but rather, it is precisely through acting that it can finally accede to itself, at least in the perception of the incessant disproportion between the desire that moves it and every concrete goal that becomes the object of determined intention. Second, it should be considered that action introduces a novelty to a reality inasmuch as it implies a transformation of the subject himself, who not only expresses himself through action, but also determines his identity such that he may gradually acquire a greater personal perfection.

How, then, ought one think of the relationship between the person and his free action? A certain foundation for action in the very being of the person must be recognized, precisely so as to avoid the arbitrariness of freedom. The traditional formula *agere sequitur esse,* often repeated so as to exorcise the risk of subjectivism, asks, however, to be clarified so as to avoid falling into naturalism, which disregards the contribution of personal freedom in the moral domain.[5] The grammar of action cannot simply be deduced from the observation of the dynamics of man's natural faculties and of his objectives, which are shaped by spontaneous inclination.[6]

This was well understood by St. Thomas Aquinas, who recognized the original epistemological character of ethics as a "practical science" as compared with other purely "speculative" forms of knowing. The issue that we are addressing concerns that order which reason institutes in the operations of the will, inasmuch as these are mutually connected and oriented toward an end.[7] In its practical dimension, then, reason does not merely reflect an already

---

5. Cf. J.-J. Pérez-Soba, "Operari sequitur esse?" in *Verità e libertà nella teologia morale,* ed. L. Melina and J. Larrù (Rome: PUL, 2001), 109-21.

6. The document of the International Theological Commission, *The Search for a Universal Ethic: A New Look at Natural Law,* avers that "the doctrine of the natural law must, therefore, maintain at the same time both the central role of reason in the actualization of a properly human plan of life, and the proper meaning of pre-rational natural dynamisms" (79).

7. Cf. St. Thomas Aquinas, *Sententia libri ethicorum* I, 1, 1-43. In this regard, cf. L. Melina, *La conoscenza morale: Linee di riflessione sul Commento di san Tommaso all'Etica Nicomachea* (Rome: Città nuova, 1987; 2nd ed., Milan: ISU, 2005), 24-25. See also the foundational study by W. Kluxen, *Philosophische Ethik bei Thomas von Aquin,* 2nd ed. (Hamburg: Felix Meiner Verlag, 1980).

existing order, but itself creates an order of the voluntary act. And here, the decisive questions come once again to the fore: With which order does one deal? Which grammar does the reason obey since it seems to function "creatively"?

There comes into play here a new and decisive element: the fact that the moral good that belongs to the person, since it is realized through a person's acting, does not *sequitur* simply from *esse*. Father Joseph De Finance has shown the specific character of *esse morale* as a second act and proper perfection of the person, entrusted to his liberty and irreducible to the dynamics of nature.[8] The experience of absoluteness typical of the moral dimension is related to the person as such and to the vocation that one perceives in action since it is here that one's identity is at play.

At this point, it would be opportune to make a critical observation about the metaphor of "grammar," which makes clear the function of the natural law in the dynamics of action when interpreted as a language. In the logic of what we have been developing so far, it seems more appropriate to speak of a "pragmatics" of action than to speak of a "grammar," provided that this term is not confused with a pragmatism that rejects the truth.[9] In fact, what we are speaking about concerns a light that illuminates from within the end of action and in this way makes normative the relations between the acting subject and the language of his act.

This light of reason, far from being an autonomous and arbitrary power, is a participation in divine wisdom.[10] This participation comes about from within the experience of moral responsibility for one's own action, which itself stems from the encounter with the person of the other. Thus one can say that the natural law *in actu exercito* is the pragmatics of action, while *in actu signato*, which is in the moment of critical reflection, can be defined as its grammar.

8. Cf. J. De Finance, *Être et agir dans la philosophie de saint Thomas*, 3rd ed. (Rome: Presses de l'Université Grégorienne, 1965).

9. By "pragmatics" is intended that part of semiotics that studies the relationship between language and the one who uses it, including the significance given by narrative and practical contexts. An interesting interpretation of the natural law according to St. Thomas conducted in a narrative key, and interesting in the sense just indicated, is that proposed by P. Hall, *Narrative and the Natural Law: An Interpretation of Thomistic Ethics* (Notre Dame, Ind.: University of Notre Dame Press, 1994).

10. Cf. M. Rhonheimer, *Natural Law and Practical Reason: A Thomistic View of Moral Autonomy* (New York: Fordham University Press, 2000).

Experience, the Body, and Love

Experience seems to recommend itself as a point of departure in the discussion concerning the pragmatics and so also the grammar of action. One does not understand which things are moral by means of a law that is given *a priori* to acting. The reflection that began some thirty years ago by Alasdair MacIntyre in his famous work *After Virtue*[11] has shown the inadequacy of rationalistic hermeneutics that conceive of the natural law as a series of rational principles that are known beforehand and that would impose themselves extrinsically on action, determining its course in a univocal way. It is in the exercise of one's own freedom and in the perspective of the acting subject that one captures the specific dimension of the moral good as the good of the person, realized through his own acts.

Now, if it is true that, in acting, human freedom is not an absolute that arises without preconditions but rather is rooted in the body and finds, instead, its starting point in the motivational space determined by its desires,[12] then it is precisely in the juncture between the body and the dynamics of free action that one should search for the basis of the grammar of action. Subjectivity implies an awareness and a freedom in the ordering of one's own actions toward an end. Now, according to the encyclical *Veritatis splendor,* this unique dimension of human action is rooted precisely in the unity of soul and body.

The denial of the subjectivity of the body and its reduction to a mere object involves the deconstruction of its original grammar, starting with the aspect defined by sexual difference. In this regard, the non-recognition of the identifying character of the man-woman difference, typical of an ideology of gender, carries with it a narcissism in which there is truly no longer any space for the other, nor for the Other (with a capital "O"). The lived body is the threshold of the world, the place of encounter with reality and, in particular, the encounter with the other.[13] This is accomplished in two directions, which reveal the two basic meanings of the body.

The body itself refers back to the constitutive relationship with our origin, with our own mother and with our own father from whom we derive. The body is, therefore, always a received body, a filial body. After the moment of

---

11. A. MacIntyre, *After Virtue: A Study in Moral Theory,* 2nd ed. (London: Duckworth, 1985).

12. Cf. P. Ricoeur, *La sémantique de l'action* (Paris: Editions du Centre national de la recherche scientifique, 1977), 169-73.

13. Cf. F. Botturi, "Il corpo degli affetti," in *La generazione del bene: Gratuità ed esperienza morale* (Milan: Vita e pensiero, 2009), 195-244.

parting in our birth, the connection with one's Origin is to be rediscovered in a communion of persons.

The originality implied by this relational nature consists in the fact that all of this comes about precisely by means of the body, including its essential receptivity, because the body is vulnerable to the other and is sensitive to the goods shared. This renders possible the affective presence of the other person in the subject himself, that "intercorporeity"[14] that is capable of conforming the desires of the body in a new way. This opens from within unto a common good that is now understood in a new dimension of reciprocity, precisely because of the experience of being inhabited by the intentionality of another person.

The common good becomes the fascinating novelty of a fullness in reciprocal communion that can be realized in practice through a variety of actions that now appear as authentic goods for the persons and that are to be attained together in friendship and social life.[15] In effect, because of this affection, the inclinations of the body become relevant in the pursuit of happiness, which is itself the fundamental orientation of human action.

It is in the body, marked by sexual difference, that this unique encounter between a man and a woman takes place, "unique for the promise of happiness that it opens up," because in it the body and the soul are inseparably joined.[16] A characteristic relation in this second opening up of the body shows itself here, namely, that which orients one to the nuptial gift. The body is also a spousal body, open to something greater than itself: encounter and communion.

This sexual connotation is an evidence that any erotic perception acquires a specific meaning that refers to the person. Pope John Paul II in his *Catechesis on Human Love in the Divine Plan* (1979-84) calls this the "nuptial meaning,"[17] thus indicating the call to express in the body and through the body one's love for another person, that is, the call to the gift of self. This meaning is rooted in the receptivity of the body and therefore requires as its foundation an ontological opening to the other that is given by the Creator and that can be called original communion.[18]

14. M. Merleau-Ponty, *Phénoménologie de la perception* (Paris: Gallimard, 1945).

15. Cf. A. MacIntyre, *Dependent Rational Animals: Why Human Beings Need the Virtues* (Chicago: Open Court, 1999), chapter 9.

16. Pope Benedict XVI, *Deus caritas est*, 2.

17. Pope John Paul II, *Uomo e donna li creò: Catechesi sull'amore umano* (Rome: Città nuova — Libreria Editrice Vaticana, 1985), xiv-xviii, 74-89; for the theology of the body, see the recent treatment by C. Anderson and J. Granados, *Called to Love: Approaching John Paul II's Theology of the Body* (New York: Doubleday, 2009).

18. Cf. Pope John Paul II's apostolic letter *Mulieris dignitatem*, 7; M. Nédoncelle, *La ré-*

This original communion, given freely in the encounter between persons, gives rise at the same time to an expectation of a more complete unity in the flesh that is to be built through action.

This action, which is rooted in the body, is always already oriented to the meaning that is inscribed in human nature by the Creator. It finds its beginning in passion, which is precisely that reaction which reveals to man the possibility of a new and greater fullness that freedom is called on to acknowledge and embrace in the light of reason.[19] The spontaneous inclinations of human nature and the affective orientations involved in such an experience indicate some of the "goods of the person," which in the practical perspective of reason and in the light of love for the person assume a meaning proper to moral goods (natural law). It is this horizon of love that offers the definitive hermeneutic for the meanings of the body, its emotions, and its affections.[20]

A decisive role is taken on by the moral virtues in achieving the personal subjectivity of the body and in integrating bodily dynamics in the light of the truth of the person and in the perspective of love. The moral virtues are the creative energy of a freedom that reaches out to the good; they shape one's natural inclinations in the light of reason and love.[21]

From this perspective of love on which they depend *(virtus dependet aliqualiter ab amore)*,[22] the virtues represent the hermeneutical criterion for living the pragmatics of action in light of the authentic good of the person and, therefore, for adequately interpreting, at the reflective level, the primordial grammar. These virtues show how human goods can be occasions to answer the fundamental vocation of love. They present the possibility for growth in those essential dimensions in which one realizes oneself: in fraternity with others, as a child, as a spouse, as a father or a mother.

---

ciprocité des consciences. *Essai sur la nature de la personne* (Paris: Aubier-Montaigne, 1942), 10-47.

19. Cf. J. Noriega, *Il destino dell'eros: Prospettive di morale sessuale* (Bologna: EDB, 2006), 99-110.

20. Allow me to suggest L. Melina, "Esperienza, amore e legge," in *Azione: epifania dell'amore. La morale cristiana oltre il moralismo e l'antimoralismo* (Siena: Cantagalli, 2008), 141-55.

21. Cf. S. Pinckaers, *Le renouveau de la morale. Études pour une morale fidale à ses sources et à sa mission présente*, 2nd ed. (Téqui: Tourneau, 1978), 144-64.

22. St. Thomas Aquinas, *ST* I-II, q. 56, a. 3, ad Ium.

The *Logos:* The Grammar of Creation and the Pragmatics of Jesus

It is in the light of revelation that even the natural law finds its full meaning. The Word, present in creation and fully expressed in the redemptive incarnation, confirms and brings to completion that grammar of action which reason itself can discover and can recognize as the logic of love in the experience of the dynamics of the body and in the encounter with others. At this point, therefore, the subject of our inquiry becomes the theological significance of the natural law and its proper placement in the horizon of the law of Christ.

I develop, first of all, a brief and foundational reflection. Revelation helps us to receive reality not only as a fact *(datum),* but also as a gift that is the result of an ongoing divine action.[23] At the root of creation is an act of love that tends toward completion. All of being can, therefore, be seen in the dynamism of this first divine communication that is deeply rooted in the Trinity. If man is created in Christ, then the natural law, which belongs to his original state, expresses already an orientation toward the covenant.[24] This reveals not only the rationality inherent in our condition as creatures, but also the call to live in friendship with God, who first loved us.

The first covenant, sealed in the Ten Commandments of Sinai, while confirming the main elements of the original covenant with the creative Wisdom, reveals the ultimate horizon of an invitation to imitate God in the path of freedom and friendship.[25]

The natural law is the mark imprinted in the human spirit, in our very being, which is made in the image of God. Returning to the patristic tradition, which distinguished between "image" and "likeness" and which ascribed to the first an ontological aspect and to the second a dynamic ethical character,[26] St. Bonaventure of Bagnoregio thinks of the moral life as the task of freely bringing to fruition the *expressio* of that creaturely image, the *impressio* of which we received in our origin.[27]

However, this characterization of the natural law as simply a creaturely endowment moves one, in the context of a contraposition between natural and

---

23. Cf. K. L. Schmitz, *The Gift: Creation* (Milwaukee: Marquette University Press, 1982), 34-42.

24. Cf. A. Chapelle, "Legge di natura e teologia," *Communio* 34 (1977): 35-45.

25. Cf. P. Beauchamp, *D'une montagne à l'autre: La Loi de Dieu* (Paris: Seuil, 1999).

26. Cf. St. Irenaeus, *Adversus haereses* V.6.1; V.8.1. See on this issue, H. U. von Balthasar, *Le persone del dramma: l'uomo in Dio,* vol. 2 of *Teo-Drammatica,* trans. G. Sommavilla (Milan: Jaca Book, 1982), 298-316.

27. San Bonaventura da Bagnoregio, *Collationes in hexaemeron* XI.16.

supernatural and of a theology of a double final end, to an extrinsicism and even to a separation from and opposition to the New Law of Christ.[28] In the neoscholastic conception, natural law was attributed to an autonomous reason, based on the ontological structures of creation, while the law of Christ was juxtaposed as a super-added additional element.

If, however, we consider the natural law not as a hypostatization of a pure nature, but as a dimension that runs through the order of history, then it cannot be simply identified with the "beginning."[29] The predestination of Christ stands at the beginning, and the "co-predestination" of man is contained within this, since from eternity he is called to be a "son in the Son." Christ Jesus, on account of the Son's perfect humanity, is the original form and archetype of man. He is the image of the Father, in relation to whom we are called to be *ad imaginem,* both in a fundamental ontological sense and in the dynamics of the moral life. The eternal law of God is, therefore, to be understood theologically in relation to the original predestination of Christ: it has a Christological form.

In this sense, natural law is an "ingredient" of the integral truth of man's origin since he is always already thought of in the Son and is created in view of him. In this way, the foundation of those characteristics that are proper to the natural law (intrinsic meaning, immutability, and universality) are theologically traced back to its roots in the eternal law, understood Christologically. The universality of nature is founded on the universality of predestination and salvation in Christ. One can, therefore, understand Christ as both the principal and, at the same time, the end point of the law, even the natural law.

From this foundational theological reflection one recovers also the original point of view of the practical perspective in which moral truth is given. Here, Christ is not understood first of all as the ontological foundation of the natural law, that is, as the eternal Word in which the *rationes* of creation have their place, but rather he is understood as he is seen in his historical unveiling and action. These came about precisely because Christ is the Son who sees the Father and who, allowing us through faith to participate in that vision, offers us the possibility of orienting ourselves to him in love.

The Word is, therefore, the ultimate hermeneutic for the meaning of action: in the pragmatics of the mysteries of his earthly life he reveals that the

---

28. Cf. especially H. de Lubac, *Il mistero del soprannaturale,* Opera Omnia 11 (Milan: Jaca Book, 1978; orig.: Paris, 1965).

29. Cf. I. Biffi, "Integralità cristiana e fondazione morale," *Scuola Cattolica* 115 (1987): 570-90.

original grammar of our being is love and invites us to participate therein. And Jesus, the Word made flesh, does so not only by his teaching, which gathers together the entire law of God in that double and indivisible commandment of love (cf. Matt. 22:34-40), but most especially in his personal life. From the events and gestures of Jesus' life, the fullness of light shines on this vocation to love, which, as we have seen, constitutes the fundamental orientation written in the very nature of the person and in the substance of our bodily existence.

The body of Christ is, in itself and at the same time, a body that is filial, fraternal, and spousal: the relation of filial obedience with the Father and the gift of love for the salvation of men have a corporeal dimension and so also a dimension that is Eucharistic and ecclesial.

The recognition of this filial character becomes also the foundation of brotherhood and of spousal fecundity. He, in his life, passion, and death on the cross, offers the perfect gift of self that completes human freedom in love. He is the Bridegroom of the Church, to whom he gives the Eucharist. The gift that the Son makes of his body and his blood is fruitful because it creates the Church as a communion of persons who are each, in turn, capable of self-gift. The Eucharistic body of Christ is the nexus between the body of Christ, given once and for all on the cross, and the body of the Church, which lives in history. It is also the place where the moral action of Christians finds its criterion and its nourishment.

The filial, fraternal, and spousal body of Christ is thus the foundation of the obedience, fraternal love, and self-giving that are at the heart of the Christian moral life. The horizon of love, which is revealed in the Eucharist, is the definitive hermeneutic for those meanings that are always already anticipated by man's natural inclinations and which are inscribed by the Creator in the human body.

*   *   *

Thus we can conclude our discussion by returning to the Nietzschean challenge with which we started. The analogy between action and language, inspired by a rereading of the ITC's document on natural law, allowed us to face the challenge of nihilism and at the same time to honor the aspiration for freedom. The denial of a grammar of being and of action was born from an exasperated, but not unfounded, claim of freedom. This challenge considers any rule that might impose itself from without on freedom's desire for infinite expansion as a limit to be crossed over, and it rejects as a mortal threat even a truth that might attach itself extrinsically to the energy of life.

The light of love that — as anticipated in experience — is fully revealed in the incarnate Word manifests that the truth that can guide the action of the person is not an external imposition but the intimate appeal for self-fulfillment that comes about in the encounter and communion with God and with others: a truth that is born from the heart of life itself, that is, from the relationships which form us as moral subjects and which, taken on responsibly in practice, establish us in our identity.

Reasonable Faith and Natural Law

Sherif Girgis and Robert P. George

Focused on the objectivity of moral norms and on how we can know them, *In Search of a Universal Ethic: A New Look at the Natural Law* revisits a familiar theme in Catholic thought — the harmony of faith and reason — as it relates to morality. That theme appears as early as St. Paul's insistence that the Gentiles, by the operations of their consciences, "show that the requirements of the law are written on their hearts" (Rom. 2:15). It finds painstaking and sophisticated elaboration in St. Augustine, St. Anselm, and St. Aquinas; its most definitive statement in Vatican I's *Dogmatic Constitution on the Catholic Faith;* its most prominent papal analysis in Pope John Paul II's *Fides et ratio;* and illuminating treatment in the writings of Pope Benedict XVI, among many other pastors, theologians, and philosophers.

The harmony of faith and reason implies a negative thesis: that the doctrines of the faith, and the deliverances of properly functioning natural reason, never conflict. Within ethics, this can be defended by showing that any apparent conflict involves a misunderstanding of definitive Christian moral teaching, faulty natural-ethical reasoning, or both. But in its latest document, the International Theological Commission (ITC) also echoes the Catholic tradition's *positive* claim on behalf of faith and (moral) reason: that, more than consistent, they are *complementary;* that they overlap without redundancy, each perfecting rather than obviating the other.

Thus, *In Search of a Universal Ethic* points out, "discursive reason" is often required to unpack general moral principles (including, presumably, revealed ones) and to apply them intelligently to concrete circumstances. Conversely, while denying that Christianity could "have the monopoly on the natural law

... founded on reason, common to all men" (9), *In Search of a Universal Ethic* affirms that Christian faith has something distinctive to contribute to our natural ethical reasoning: "the Christian community, guided by the Spirit of Jesus Christ ... has assumed, purified and developed this teaching on the natural law as a fundamental ethical norm" (9). The same question is revisited at the end of the document, if less precisely:

> Grace does not destroy nature but heals, strengthens, and leads it to its full realization. As a consequence, while the natural law is an expression of the reason common to all human beings and can be presented in a coherent and true manner on the philosophical level, it is not foreign to the order of grace. (101)

But *In Search of a Universal Ethic* fails to address crucial questions. What exactly is it for Christianity to assume, purify, and develop natural law claims? If the moral law can be ascertained philosophically, apart from revelation, in what sense is it yet "not foreign to the order of grace"? Granted that the faithful have more ascetical and supernatural means of adhering to the natural moral law even against powerful temptations, what *theoretical* contribution does revelation make to our *understanding* of the moral law?

St. Thomas Aquinas begins his *Summa theologiae* with one answer: some truths had to be revealed despite being naturally accessible because philosophy could make them known only to a few, after long effort, and amid many errors — too little, too late when it comes to saving truths. Given the complexity of many moral questions, and the centrality of repentance to the gospel, it is no surprise that God would so reinforce our natural understanding of moral norms. But does the faith serve a Christian ethicist only as a calculator serves a math student — by allowing him to check his answers, and supplying the ones that he cannot find on his own? Are there not *other* ways in which the faith illuminates our natural moral reasoning? Might these connections help explain away the charge that natural law theory is merely Catholic theology in secular disguise, by showing *why* these two disciplines are, despite their independence, so consistent?

Perhaps some would consider the answers interesting but not significant, much less crucial to an overview of natural law. On the contrary, we think that in leaving these aspects of the relationship of faith and reason ambiguous, the ITC misses an opportunity to block common misunderstandings that can have adverse moral, theological, and pastoral consequences. To contribute to this task, though hardly exhaustively, we wish to propose one way in which the faith could *not* supplement a natural understanding of the moral law and one way in which it can. Our goal is to begin to *explain* what the ITC *asserts:* the consistency as well as genuine (if limited) autonomy of these two God-given sources of moral knowledge.

I

What we consider impossible is that faith should generate or reveal *entirely new* moral norms — ones that do not just specify or apply norms accessible apart from revelation. We can show why by sketching our view of what grounds moral norms and of how they can be known.[1]

Moral norms are the requirements of properly orienting one's will toward (respecting and advancing) the human good: human flourishing. And the human good is variegated. It consists of *various* irreducible and inherently valuable (basic) human goods: conditions and activities worth pursuing for their own sake as constitutive aspects of human fulfillment. Unlike money and other merely instrumental goods, basic human goods provide reasons for actions even when one expects no benefit beyond that of participating in them.

How do we identify basic goods? Reflecting on our inclinations and experiences can give us the direct insight (non-inferential act of understanding) that certain things are worth pursuing for their own sake. Indeed, all intentional human actions are taken ultimately for the sake of some such benefit (real or apparent). So we can tease out the basic goods presupposed by our deliberations and acts by asking the point of our choices until we reach a rational stopping point — an answer to "Why did (or would) I do that?" at which it would be reasonable (though not necessary) to stop, or to answer simply, "For its own sake."

By such practical insights we can grasp — or by such means-end chains of reasoning show — that the basic human goods include knowledge, life and health, aesthetic experience and skillful performance, and various forms of harmony: among one's emotions, judgments, intentional choices, body, and inner self and behavior (inner peace or personal integration); between or among persons (friendship); between oneself and whatever supernatural source of meaning there might be (religion); and between oneself and some-

---

1. For more on the contemporary natural law theory on which we rely, see Germain Grisez, Joseph Boyle, and John Finnis, "Practical Principles, Moral Truth, and Ultimate Ends," *American Journal of Jurisprudence* 32 (1987): 99-151.

one to whom one commits in the one-flesh union inherently oriented to family life (marriage). Each of these goods provides basic reasons for action by promising an inherent benefit.

And again, every moral norm can be traced back ultimately to these goods — to some specification of the requirement that in promoting such goods, we act compatibly with a will toward *integral human fulfillment:* the fulfillment of all persons and communities in all these respects. This forbids intending damage to any of the goods as realized in anyone (e.g., by destroying life as a means to medical knowledge; or as an end, out of hatred) or allowing our pursuit of them to be deflected by emotions not integrated with reasons (e.g., sloth or partiality).

In Search of a Universal Ethic affirms this general connection between moral norms and the human good when it asserts that "the moral good corresponds to the profound desire of the human person who . . . tends spontaneously, naturally, towards realizing himself fully" and that a choice is immoral if and only if it cannot be integrated with "the authentic realization of the person" (41). But later, in what some might read as a qualification of this claim, the ITC states that the Decalogue "perfects the fundamental principles of the natural law" (n. 64).

However this ambiguous claim was meant, we do not think that the Ten Commandments *add to* the set of fundamental principles of natural law. Like any set of sound moral norms, the Decalogue just embodies the implications of serving basic human goods (including marriage, life, friendship, and personal integration) in a fully reasonable way. Even the norms against idolatry and blasphemy, and for keeping holy the Sabbath, are grounded in the basic goodness of harmony with the higher-than-human source of meaning and value (i.e., religion). Yes, they also depend on certain historical, social, or revealed facts that imply, for example, that it is Sunday that should be set aside, and this or that utterance that should be revered as referring to God. But the need for these "extra facts" does not make revelation a source of entirely new moral norms any more than the need for biology to determine whether an entity is a human embryo makes biology a source of the norm against embryo-killing. Like biology and other sources of knowledge, revelation provides certain facts in light of which the antecedently knowable, most general requirements of morality (of proper respect for the human good) are made concrete and specific.

Some have held — and might read the ITC document to claim — that theology is different because moral norms can wholly originate in God's *commands.* But even God's commands cannot give us reason to obey them unless such obedience is a requirement of respecting religion (harmony with the divine), which is in turn a constituent of human well-being. There are familiar philosophical and theological reasons for thinking so, and they converge. To risk simplistic summary: if moral norms hold only because God commands them, in the sense that there are no *reasons* for his doing so, then they could vary independently of our nature. In that case, they are arbitrary limits on our freedom, as *In Search of a Universal Ethic* points out:

> when [the natural law is] presented as an objective datum that would impose itself from the outside on personal conscience, independently of the work of reason and subjectivity, it is suspected of introducing a form of heteronomy intolerable for the dignity of the free human person. (10)

And this result is untenable both philosophically and theologically: if God's laws were ungrounded in our good and so could have been otherwise even holding our nature constant, then the God issuing them would be a capricious despot — but he is revealed to be a provident lover. Love is distinguished from whimsy in being the active willing of the *good* of the beloved for the beloved's sake. So a loving God's commandments must be guides to respecting and advancing — to cooperating with him in serving — the human *good*. Moreover, all creatures participate in God's goodness insofar as they have being; so God, loving the good that he is, also loves creatures and desires their full participation in his good — their full-being, or fulfillment. So he does not create us and "separately" decide which moral norms to establish. Rather, he creates us with a certain nature and then reminds us of the intrinsic requirements of its good.[2] He is not so much a lawmaker as a lawgiver. Thus, *In Search of a Universal Ethic* argues:

> The moral obligation that the subject recognizes does not come . . . from a law that would be exterior to him (pure heteronomy), but arises from within the subject itself . . . [and] indicates to the moral subject what kind of action is in accord with the basic and necessary dynamism of his being that tends to its full realization. . . . It is not therefore a matter of subjecting oneself to the law of another, but of accepting the law of one's own being. (43)

While most modern Christians do not expressly endorse divine command ethics, in subtle forms it may still infect Christian thought and enhance the

---

2. See Gen. 1:26-30; 2:18-24; Wis. 7:21–8:1; *ST* I-II, q. 71, a. 2; q. 91, a. 2; q. 93, aa. 1-2; q. 100, a. 8.

relative appeal of secular humanism. For some Christians seem to believe that moral norms are *both* divine commands that could have been otherwise even keeping our nature constant, *and* guides to the human good, but only *extrinsically* so. On this view, morality is a sort of divinely administered test. The reward for passing is the human happiness of heaven; the punishment for failing, human misery in hell. So morality is connected to the human good, but only in that God would throw us into hell (though he could do otherwise) for disobeying his commandments (which could have been otherwise). The implication is that a change in the commandments would free us up to do with "impunity" what was once "outlawed." Hence, for example, calls for the Church to "relax" its teachings on direct abortion and euthanasia, embryo-destructive research, contraception and sterilization, non-marital sexual conduct, and divorce and remarriage — norms that it cannot alter any more than it can alter human nature to make life or marriage no longer basic human goods.

Such calls flow from a legalism fostered by voluntarism, which focuses on norms as *posited* — rather than as inherently required by the human good. For on this view, the *fact* of their having been posited is what gives moral principles their normativity, much as the legislature's positing traffic laws is *all* that makes turning left at red lights illegal. It is this mentality that fueled hopes in the 1960s, for example, that the Church would sanction oral contraceptives since its condemnations had focused (for contingent historical reasons) on preventing conception using barriers and non-coital acts. It was as if a certain (expressly "outlawed") physical performance or technique made contraception immoral, rather than the orientation of the spouses' wills against the specific perfection of their marriage and the transmission of life.[3]

But there are other reasons that *In Search of a Universal Ethic* should have been clearer about how the faith *cannot* supplement reason: Besides breeding legalism (with its twin tendencies to moral liberalism and pharisaism), voluntarism *instrumentalizes* this life to the next — much as totalitarianism would instrumentalize individuals to the collectivity, or the current generation to a future one. It also licenses — in theory if not also in practice — fanaticism: if everything in this life is a mere means to a happy reward in the next, what should not be sacrificed to that end, if only God demanded it?

---

3. For a sounder understanding of the justifications of the norm against contraception, see Elizabeth Anscombe, "Contraception and Chastity," *Orthodoxy Today,* http://www .orthodoxytoday.org/articles/AnscombeChastity.shtml; Germain Grisez, Joseph Boyle, John Finnis, and William E. May, "'Every Marital Act Ought to Be Open to New Life': Toward a Clearer Understanding," *The Thomist* 52 (1988): 365-426.

II

One general way that we think the faith *can* contribute to, or purify, our natural understanding of the moral law is by revealing truths that reduce our motivation to *distort* that understanding by rationalization. Here we focus on the doctrine that God's providence directs all of created reality to a radical ultimate transformation: the kingdom in which suffering and evil are eliminated and the blessed enjoy complete fulfillment and communion with God and each other forever.[4] Obscuring or denying this truth heightens our temptations to the *theoretical* errors of utilitarianism or other forms of consequentialism and a redrawing of the boundaries of certain basic goods. Yet in expounding on fundamental human goods and the principles by which we should serve them, the ITC mentions the kingdom only twice (24, 95). Here, then, we aim to draw out some of the implications of the doctrine of the kingdom.

(a)

Note first that consequentialism in any form and belief in divine providence are incompatible. According to the former, one ought to do whatever leads to the greatest good (or net best proportion of benefit to harm) overall and in the long run. According to the latter, God brings good and more good out of all the evil that he allows — including out of our immoral choices. Together, then, consequentialism and the doctrine of divine providence lead to the conclusion that we may do whatever we please, for God will bring good out of *any* choice. But of course, consequentialism is proposed as an *ethics*, aiming to distinguish some choices as *immoral*, to be foresworn. So it is incompatible with the truth of divine providence.[5]

Rather, if God will achieve his good purposes — including the kingdom — no matter what, then our *true* lot as free and intelligent parts of the creation to be transformed is to choose whether to *cooperate* with him (by grace) in building up the kingdom. We do this principally by making our selves — the character constituted by our free choices — fit for life within it: we promote as we can, and do not oppose, the human good in ourselves and others — and

---

4. See *Gaudium et spes*, 38, 39.

5. John Finnis, "On the Practical Meaning of Secularism," *Notre Dame Law Review* 73 (1998): 513; Germain Grisez, "Catholic Faith and Intrinsically Evil Acts," *Proceedings of the First Convention of the Fellowship of Catholic Scholars* (1978): 27-38.

thereby promote and preserve our communion with others and with the ultimate source of their and our good, who also wills and is thus glorified by its promotion (1). In other words, we fulfill our vocations for love of neighbor, self, and God, and avoid or repent of any choice incompatible with a will toward the integral fulfillment to be realized in the kingdom. For the rest, we trust that providence will secure the realization of even those goods that now seem unattainable except by sin. For any such good cannot be pursued in a way that *truly* serves the kingdom (fulfillment of, and communion with, everyone in God) or our fitness for it. On the other hand, our eternal fitness of character is something that not even God can achieve *for us* — that is, without our cooperation here — since our free choices partly constitute it. Hence this life's staggering *intrinsic* significance as the only arena in which great goods of eternal consequence can be secured — or not — by our free cooperation with grace, but nowhere and nowise else.

In this way, a sound understanding of providence and the kingdom perfects what reason apart from revelation can show: namely, that some choices are intrinsically immoral, impossible to justify as means to unqualifiedly greater good. For the various realizations of the human goods available in options for choice (e.g., this human life, that friendship, this part of someone's knowledge, those aesthetic or religious experiences) cannot be objectively aggregated or netted (and thus substituted) in such a way as to render the idea of "the greatest good" coherent and workable. The reason is that they are not reducible to each other or to some other, objective common factor of value. The basic human goods do not share a common substance, merely manifesting it differently. They are distinct and irreducible realities. (The feature common to them all that justifies the general designation "good" is that each is capable of providing a basic reason for action.) So in each choice, at least some good will be forgone whose value is not included (much less included and surpassed) in the selected option. Otherwise, the option offering the putatively lesser good would not have been a live option at all, for the greater option would have offered everything of value in it, and then some.[6] But if acting against a good in general cannot be justified as serving some greater good, then it is unjustifiable.[7]

Without a belief in providence and the kingdom, however, it is tempting

6. Germain Grisez, "Against Consequentialism," *American Journal of Jurisprudence* 23 (1978): 21-72.

7. John Finnis, *Moral Absolutes: Tradition, Revision, and Truth* (Washington, D.C.: Catholic University of America Press, 1991), chapters 2 and 3.

to think that the highest intelligence and will concerned with human affairs are *human* intelligence and will, and that the only age in which integral human fulfillment could be even approximated is this one. On these grounds, it is tempting to conclude that human beings should, to the extent possible, aspire to a sort of omniscience, omnipotence, and providence of all things toward the good by whatever means necessary — including means judged immoral by an ethics focused on upright willing (and cooperation thereby with providence) rather than hedonistic[8] or messianic efficiency.

The twentieth-century totalitarianisms show the political implications of these moral errors — the grim futility of any five- or thousand-year plan to achieve integral human fulfillment in this age. But even today, there are other and subtler manifestations of how a denial of providence and the kingdom leads to rationalizations of evil and distorted understandings of the human good.

(b)

Consider an example: because of disability, disease, or deterioration, many human beings are prevented from enjoying — at least any more, or appreciably — such goods as knowledge, friendship, aesthetic experience, and skillful performance. Now we will feel compelled to reduce the proportion of persons thus impeded, *by any "humane" means,* the more we feel compelled to guarantee the fulfillment of all in *this* world, having no hope in a celestial kingdom. So where we cannot do so by removing the *impediment* from the *person,* we may be tempted to do so by deeming the one impeded not a *person* at all. Thus, the destruction of pre-implantation human embryos deemed "defective," abortion of the severely retarded, euthanasia for the demented and comatose, and other injustices against human life may be abetted by a rationalization that gains appeal when we reject the doctrines of divine providence and a kingdom hereafter.

And this, again, even though the facts so obscured are naturally accessible: that human lives are irreducibly valuable; that the body-self dualism that would identify persons with minds merely inhabiting (nonpersonal) human bodies is metaphysically untenable; and that predicating moral worth on the accidental property of the *degree of intellectual development* rather than on being a rational substance vitiates the principle of equality and unjustly

---

8. Thus, St. Paul attributed unprincipled hedonisms to a disbelief in bodily resurrection (1 Cor. 15:32).

grounds a difference in kinds of treatment on a difference in degree of development.[9]

Something similar may be true of motivations for the debate about marriage. On the one hand, natural human reason can appreciate that the kind of comprehensive union that is inherently fulfilled by family life is intrinsically valuable; that it is completed (consummated) and renewed by acts that can unite only a man and a woman as one flesh; and that its inherent orientation to childbearing and childrearing contributes to its distinctive structure (including its norms of monogamy, permanence, and fidelity) and its distinctive value for human fulfillment.[10]

But some are impeded from entering into a certain marriage by physical disabilities that make consummation impossible, by ongoing "failed" marriages, or by same-sex or other non-marital inclinations so dominant that *marriage* (permanent, exclusive, monogamous, and opposite-sex) is psychologically difficult, imprudent, or impossible. Now insofar as we see the great value of marriage but deny the possibility of integral human fulfillment hereafter, we feel compelled to reduce the proportion of persons so impeded from happy marriages, *by any means.* So where we despair of shaping the persons to fit the good, we will be tempted to stretch the good to fit the persons (i.e., the most marriage-like arrangements that they *can* form). Hence, perhaps, the temptation to rationalize our distortions of marriage into a fundamentally *emotional* union, which requires no real bodily union, or any basic orientation to children,[11] or any norm of permanence (or, increasingly, of monogamy[12] or exclusivity[13]). In this way,

---

9. Patrick Lee and Robert P. George, *Body-Self Dualism in Contemporary Ethics and Politics* (Cambridge: Cambridge University Press, 2008).

10. Sherif Girgis, Ryan T. Anderson, and Robert P. George, *What Is Marriage? Man and Woman: A Defense* (New York: Encounter Books, 2012).

11. E. J. Graff celebrates the fact that recognizing same-sex unions would make marriage "ever after stand for sexual choice, for cutting the link between sex and diapers." "Tying the Knot," in *Same-Sex Marriage Pro and Con: A Reader,* ed. Andrew Sullivan (New York: Vintage Books 1997), 134.

12. "Beyond Same-Sex Marriage: A New Strategic Vision For All Our Families and Relationships," signed by hundreds of scholars and activists, http://beyondmarriage.org.

13. "Same-sex unions often incorporate the virtues of friendship more effectively than traditional marriages; and at times, among gay male relationships, the openness of the contract makes it more likely to survive than many heterosexual bonds. . . . There is more likely to be a greater understanding of the need for extramarital outlets between two men than between a man and a woman. . . . Something of the gay relationship's necessary honesty, its flexibility, and its equality could undoubtedly help strengthen and inform many heterosexual bonds." Andrew Sullivan, "What Are Homosexuals For?" in *Virtually Normal* (New York: Random House, 1996), 202.

the push to redefine marriage in our law and culture may also be partly motivated by rationalizations that seem necessary to realize as much fulfillment as possible in this world, our only chance.

*   *   *

Thus, natural reason enables us to grasp the most basic practical principles — those directing action toward human fulfillments and away from their privations — that every moral norm somehow specifies. There are good philosophical and theological reasons for thinking that revelation cannot generate or reveal entirely new moral norms, and negative pastoral, ethical, and political consequences to denying this. Even so, faith reveals certain truths without which the temptation is much stronger to rationalize intrinsically evil choices and even to obscure the structure of certain basic human goods. This may be one way to understand the ITC's claim, so prevalent among Catholic pastors and scholars, that faith and reason do not just neatly overlap, but purify and perfect one another.

Contributors

John Berkman, Regis College, University of Toronto

Serge-Thomas Bonino, O.P., General Secretary of the ITC , Dean of the Faculty of Philosophy of the Pontifical University of Saint-Thomas (Rome).

David Burrell, C.S.C., University of Notre Dame

Lisa Sowle Cahill, Department of Theology, Boston College

Joseph E. Capizzi, School of Theology and Religious Studies, The Catholic University of America

David Cloutier, Mount St. Mary's University

Anver M. Emon, Faculty of Law, University of Toronto

Robert P. George, McCormick Professor of Jurisprudence, Princeton University

Sherif Girgis, Ph.D. candidate, Princeton University; J.D. candidate, Yale Law School

Jennifer A. Herdt, Yale University Divinity School

Russell Hittinger, University of Tulsa

M. Cathleen Kaveny, Boston College

Anthony J. Kelly, C.Ss.R., Faculty of Theology and Philosophy, Australian Catholic University

Fergus Kerr, O.P., School of Divinity, University of Edinburgh

Steven A. Long, Department of Theology, Ave Maria University

William C. Mattison III, School of Theology and Religious Studies, The Catholic University of America

Gilbert Meilaender, Valparaiso University

Livio Melina, John Paul II Institute for Marriage and Family

Michael S. Northcott, New College, University of Edinburgh

David Novak, University of Toronto

Jean Porter, Department of Theology, University of Notre Dame

Martin Rhonheimer, Faculty of Philosophy, Pontifical University of the Holy Cross

Tracey Rowland, John Paul II Institute for Marriage and Family, and University of Notre Dame, Australia

Index

Abolition of Man (C. S. Lewis), 117, 224
abortion, 79, 112, 137, 151, 160, 194, 216,
    309, 312
Adam, 85-86, 167
    Jesus Christ as new, 85-86, 243
adultery, 23, 40n21, 58, 118, 224
aesthetics, 107, 197-98, 306, 311-12
analytic philosophy, 5, 18, 167-78, 231, 267
anthropological constants, 64, 118-19,
    240-41, 262
anthropological dualism, 71, 72-74, 100,
    185, 187-89, 202, 223, 279-80, 286, 291,
    297, 299, 312-13
anthropology, 111-13, 117-19, 121-22
    and natural law, 31, 78, 106, 159-62,
        222, 224, 227, 278-79
    negative anthropology, 113, 115
    philosophical anthropology, 177
    theological anthropology, 31, 43, 113,
        164, 222-24, 235, 237, 273
Aristotelianism, 82, 158, 179, 210n8
    and metaphysics, 139-40, 142
    and virtue ethics, 61, 169, 176
ascetic theology, asceticism, 113, 196, 305
Ash'arites, Ash'arism, 37, 126
atheism, 157, 196, 293
Augustinianism, 179, 183, 247, 265n4
autonomy, 147, 176

of human beings, of the moral subject,
    47, 54-55, 61, 67-68, 72, 89, 95-96,
    115, 186, 214, 261, 265-68, 271
of law, political order, 45, 81, 143, 150,
    154, 192
of natural inclinations, 73, 286
of nature, 206
of reason, 45, 163, 186-87, 270, 296, 301,
    306

Beatitudes, 88, 113
beauty, 26, 85, 170, 194-95, 197, 265
bias, 105, 240, 247, 249
Bible, Sacred Scripture, 40-41, 43, 211
    God in, 140-42
    and natural law, 8n9, 40-41, 83, 212
    and nature and grace, 81, 85
    and political authority, 81
    and wisdom literature, 41, 193
biodiversity, 180-81
bioethics, biomedical ethics, 111, 168, 240
Buddhism, 35, 51

Calvinism. See Reformed theology
capitalism, 185-86, 221, 239
Caritas in Veritate, 12, 219n36, 253n7, 254,
    256

Printed in Great Britain
by Amazon

82014355R00195